# STRATEGIES
## A Rhetoric and Reader

# STRATEGIES
## A Rhetoric and Reader

### Fourth Edition

**Charlene Tibbetts**
**A. M. Tibbetts**
*University of Illinois at Urbana-Champaign*

HarperCollins*Publishers*

Executive Editor: Constance A. Rajala
Development Editor: Hope Rajala
Project Editor: Bob Ginsberg
Design Supervisor: Mary Archondes
Text Design Adaptation: North 7 Atelier, Ltd.
Cover Design: Kay Cannizzaro
Production Assistant: Linda Murray
Compositor: Better Graphics, Inc.
Printer and Binder: R. R. Donnelley & Sons Company
Cover Printer: Lehigh Press Lithographers

**Strategies: A Rhetoric and Reader,** Fourth Edition
Copyright © 1992 by HarperCollins Publishers Inc.

**Library of Congress Cataloging-in-Publication Data**
Tibbetts, Charlene.
   Strategies, a rhetoric and reader / Charlene Tibbetts, A.M.
Tibbetts.—4th ed.
     p.  cm.
   Includes index.
   ISBN 0-673-46268-4 (student ed.).—ISBN 0-673-46673-6
(instructor manual)
    1. English language—Rhetoric.  2. College readers.  I. Tibbetts,
A. M.
PE1408.T494  1992
808'.042—dc20                         91-12300
                                          CIP

95 96 97 98 99 9 8 7 6 5 4 3

# CONTENTS

# PREFACE

This fourth edition of *Strategies: A Rhetoric and Reader* is divided into two sections—the Rhetoric and the Reader.

## The Rhetoric

In the Rhetoric, we have touched up certain exercises and added materials that instructors suggested would help their students: a section on Avoiding the *You* Stance in Chapter 2; a unit on using support diagrams in Chapter 4. In Chapter 5, we have added an explanation of *creative repetition* to show how paragraphs can be tied together with the repetition of key words or phrases. In Chapter 18 we have added a discussion of the Toulmin approach to argumentation.

## The Reader

In the Reader, we have thirteen new readings on a variety of subjects, ranging from a defense of the horror movie *Night of the Living Dead,* to a discussion of why our forebears built their strangely "blind" shelters on the open plains, to an explanation of the aerodynamics of that weird creature the housefly.

The authors we have kept are modern classics: Martin Luther King, Jr., Virginia Woolf, E. B. White, Mark Twain. Our new authors come from many walks of life—they are a blue-collar worker, a professor, a free-lance writer, a historian, a journalist, a social philosopher. Women writers are well represented: Carol Treasure tells us what working the swing shift does to her psyche; Penny Ward Moser makes fun of football TV commercials; Barbara Lyles says, Just call us human; Christine Davidson tells her readers, I'VE HAD IT!

Altogether, the readings—new and old—range among many ideas, temperaments, and attitudes: from the comic to the serious, from the subjective to the coolly scientific.

## The Organization of the Text

The Reader is organized according to ten strategies of development: description, narration, process, cause and effect, classification, illustration, definition, comparison and contrast, analogy, and argumentation. In addition to these strategies, we include an introductory section on mixed strategies, with two student-written models and two professional models. Each strategy has its own chapter—along with instruction on techniques of development, as well as representative models, discussion topics, and writing assignments.

Each chapter in the Reader includes readings chosen for the interest and appropriateness of the model being studied. For each of the first nine strategies, we include one short, one medium-length, and one long model —each with its own set of discussion questions, vocabulary list, and writing assignments. These provide some flexibility for the instructor. The chapter on argumentation contains five readings; in addition, it discusses ethical proof, authority, use of evidence, fallacies, and the Toulmin approach. The three important patterns of argumentative organization (fact, action, and refutation) are discussed and analyzed.

Throughout the text, we emphasize both reading and writing, interrelating these skills in a variety of ways. At least a third of the book contains instruction on organizing and developing compositions. We discuss the writer's stance, the promise pattern, and creative repetition—all effective ways of dealing with the writer's approach to subject and audience. In the Rhetoric, we provide a variety of representative models of writing from both professional and student writers. We have made extensive use of annotated models; consequently, students need not depend wholly on the Reader's selections for their examples. Finally, every chapter in the book includes at least one set of exercises, called Practices, that provide topics for discussion and writing assignments.

Designed for use in the freshman composition course, this edition arose from and includes those sections of *Strategies of Rhetoric with Handbook,* Sixth Edition (HarperCollins, 1991), that we believed would be most useful for a course using a reader. If you wish to cover sentence construction, diction, and the research paper, perhaps you'd like to supplement the text with a handbook.

The separate Instructor's Edition provides an answer key and commentary for all of the Practices. As always, we depend most on the advice of you teachers who use the book. Please write to our publisher or—better yet—to us directly.

## Acknowledgments

We want to thank the many professionals who helped us with this edition of *Strategies: A Rhetoric and Reader.* Our reviewers on this edition were Anne C. Armstrong, Walters State Community College; Sally Bishop-Shigley, Oklahoma State University; Linda Corbin, San Diego Mesa College; Kent Cowgill, Winona State University; Genevieve Gulan, Illinois Valley Community College; and Linda Rollins, Motlow State Community College. To our project editor, Robert Ginsberg, who expeditiously moved the manuscript along, and to Hope Rajala, our developmental editor, whose contributions are an integral part of this book, we owe our gratitude.

*Charlene and Arn Tibbetts*
*1902 G. Huff*
*Urbana, IL 61801*

# STRATEGIES
## A Rhetoric and Reader

# Rhetoric

# CHAPTER 1

# FINDING SUBJECTS—
# AN INTRODUCTION

"Growl!" the student said. At least that is what she wrote (and under-lined) at the top of the page. Here is the rest of what she wrote:

> I'm working on a new paper, one which is causing me a good deal of trouble. I hope it's worth the trouble. Topics and subjects for papers don't come easily to me, and when they do come, they aren't docile. I beat on them until they submit. Stop! they cry. I'll cooperate if you will just let me alone. For this new paper I have developed new techniques of harassment to get the subject tamed.
>
> Today I feel like a hunter. I go tiptoeing around, hoping the subject won't suspect I'm coming, making sure to stay downwind; then I slowly sneak up on it, watching out for all the pitfalls of the past, when I have scared it off—I'm very superstitious. When I finally get close I pounce. The subject remains very cool through this. It pretends to ignore me. I grapple and bite. The subject must enjoy being pursued a little; it has to like my grip, I suppose.
>
> Finally, I get it pinned down on paper, get it all written out in several pages (by now I am really sick of the thing). I hand it to someone, and they read it and say: "That's very good!" Then the subject hisses in my ear, "I told you so." I yell back, "What do you mean, Told you so? I did all the work!"

This is a chapter about finding subjects—finding, trapping, caging them; and then keeping them under control once you've got them in mind. We subtitle this chapter "an introduction" because it is just that—the beginning of a program in writing which continues through the rest of the book. At almost any stage in writing, you can "find" an idea. Ten years after you write something, you can read it over and have an idea pop into your head about the subject. Indeed, as long as you are alive, your brain never stops its process of discovering ideas. What it needs is encouragement. In that last sentence is a major theme of this chapter—and also of the following three chapters in Part 1: *Preparing to Write.*

Psychologically speaking, our "needs" as writers are somewhat different. A device for finding ideas for papers may be useful to you but not to your friend, sister, or roommate. A method of organizing may satisfy your roommate but drive you to distraction. Every human being has a creative engine, but not all engines run at the same rate or on the same fuel. Accordingly, the strategies for finding ideas for subjects given here are meant to be suggestions rather than hard-and-fast rules.

Textbooks used to say that the parts of a typical writing process could be sharply outlined, one stage neatly following another:

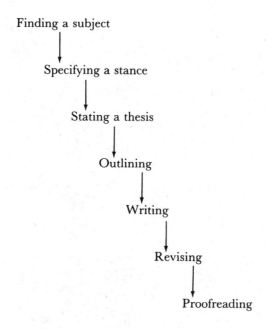

Finding a subject

Specifying a stance

Stating a thesis

Outlining

Writing

Revising

Proofreading

Recent research has shown that the writing process is rather different. If it could be diagrammed at all, it would look something like the drawing on the next page. In other words, writing is less a linear process than a complex set of processes, verbal tactics, and rhetorical strategies. All of these tend to occur both singly and together. The subject-finding stage, for example, often seems a part of everything else. It's as if writers move forward and backward, even sideways, at the same time they inch toward the goal—a finished paper.

## Writing Is . . .

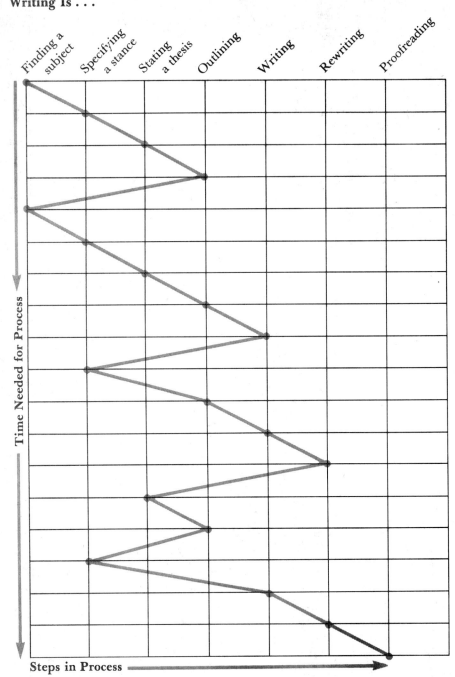

# FINDING SUBJECTS

## Brainstorming

Originally, *brainstorming* was a term used to describe a "conference method" for solving problems. The method has been used for many years in business. You get a group of people around a table, and they try to solve a problem—for example, to find new uses for a *resealable plastic bag*. The people around the table simply start talking and reacting to each other:

*Joan:* "Use it for wet bathing suits."
*Chairman:* "How about album covers for phonograph records."
*Joan:* "Toothbrushes . . . Soap."
*Sally:* "How about the fisherman."
*Chairman:* "How about for bait. Live bait, you could put that in this."
*Jim:* "How about taking something down when you go skin diving."
*Joan:* "How about for vegetables or cheeses."
*Chairman:* "How about using it to contain paint or coloring material."
*Bill:* "Put the fish in it after you catch it."
*Sam:* "Use it as a rain shoe."
*Albert:* "How about the invalids who have to take a certain type of prescribed
    pill so many times a day . . . a very small package in place of a box which is
    cumbersome."
*Chairman:* "Maybe it could even have little packages inside the major package."
*Joan:* "Artists could use that for carrying pastels and oils."
*Chairman:* "Or for their wet brushes."
*Mary:* "Women could carry their makeup."
*Joan:* "Yes."
*Paul:* "Packaging food for restaurants."
*Bill:* "Use it to take the bones home to feed the dog."
                              —Charles Whiting, *Creative Thinking*

Brainstorming is particularly valuable to the writer because it offers a technique for getting *suggestions* and *leads* for a subject. You can do it with roommates or friends. But most of us brainstorm alone, using sheets of scratch paper. Done alone, brainstorming becomes an association game on paper. You start with something—anything—and with a pencil and paper you talk to yourself (see p. 6).

Here you see an example of *controlled brainstorming,* in which at first you let your thoughts freely associate, writing down whatever comes to mind. But after a few phrases appear, you gently apply pressure and *shape* some of the material as it emerges. But not too much pressure at first. Only when the ideas tend to get specific should you come to a conclusion that may provide a subject. Then, as in the example, you try to shape the conclusion into a sentence: *Prevent thefts in college lots by adding lights and regular police patrols.* This may not be your final subject (it may not even be close to the final one), but at least it is a beginning.

```
Here comes Mickey up the stairs wearing his Walkman

Walkman -- radio

radio what?  Lost. No, stolen

Cherie's car, they stole radio & stereo, broke into car

(in college lot)

parking lot

why steal?

why not keep from stealing?

cars broken into often in college lots

stop it!!!

how to stop them from stealing (breaking into?)

add lights

regular patrols -- use 'em

_____

Prevent thefts in college lots by adding lights and

regular police patrols.
```

You will note that we suggest ending a brainstorming session—whether you are doing it alone or with other people—with a sentence that is written down. Writing the sentence is not meant to be a final act in your search for a subject. Rather it is merely a "closure" on the brainstorming session, one that enables you to pick up easily where you left off if you think more work is necessary.

In the pages that follow, we will give more suggestions for finding and shaping subjects. As you read them, keep in the back of your mind what we have said about *brainstorming*—a technique which is useful in combination with other subject-hunting devices.

## Freewriting

*Freewriting* is a form of brainstorming, the difference being that in freewriting you tend to use "running prose"—sentences and parts of sentences that run from margin to margin of the page. Most brainstorming, as we use the term, consists of words and phrases in list form. Most freewriting looks like ordinary writing on the page, although it is somewhat choppier and often rather disconnected.

The advantage of freewriting is that it loosens you up psychologically and allows your brain and hand to coordinate and warm up together (many writers have cold engines). The point of it is to start and keep going: write from the left margin to the right margin and don't stop until you feel like a baseball pitcher after a good warm-up—loose and ready for action. Here's an example of freewriting:

> Here I am, sitting under this tree, half dozing in the sun. Shouting and bellowing; it started almost without warning. One minute, silence on the quad. Long curves of flights of frisbees and oofs of pleasure when the frisbee is caught. Whirl and turn and throw again. "HAVE YOU THOUGHT ABOUT GOD TODAY?" No, and I didn't yesterday, nor the day before nor the day before—tomorrow and tomorrow creeps in . . . what's the rest of that and what's it from? "GOD IS WITH YOU, HE WANTS TO KNOW. . . ." I want to know why I can't sit here in the sun without somebody bellowing in my ear. 100 ft. away and he's the noisiest thing in 6 acres of quadrangle. What do preachers want to come here and bother us for anyway? Do they ever get converts? I don't need them—I'm *already* a believer. They are raucous, noisy, tiresome, irrelevant, and a plain bore. UNDERLINE THAT!

The idea that the student told himself to underline suggested a subject for writing. He eventually wrote a paper that described how he felt about the event he freewrote into his notebook. He called his paper: *Godspelling the Quad: One Form of Noise Pollution.*

## Keep a Journal

A *journal* is a set of scribbled notes and personal remarks that you put down when something intriguing happens, or when you hear about an idea that you want to remember. A journal is useful because it is full of information, and also of little observations that can trigger the imagination. The entries can consist of a sentence, a phrase, a conversation, a quotation from a magazine article, a line from a movie or story. It can be your reaction to an event. It is also a good warm-up device; write for awhile, and then find an idea.

*A JOURNAL ENTRY:*

> Went to lunch with Lillian, who said that she found the concert last night "sickening." The movie two nights before she said was "sickening." The lunch was "sickening." Lillian is becoming, well, repetitive.
>
> Worked on the report due in Psych until 5:00. Then played a little touch football for a while. Knee still hurts.

Lillian called and said she got a job at the bookstore and would I come over and talk about it with her. She seemed subdued, and didn't say that the thought of 20 hours of work a week would make her sick. As it turned out, she *was* subdued. I can't decide whether she is 12 years old or 22. She can run the range of 10 years in a few seconds. She's not as bad as Duane [his roommate] tho, who acts like he's 12 all the time.

Lillian proofread my psych paper and found six errors that I had missed. "Sickening," she said.

I went home and went to bed.

NEXT DAY: I found an idea! *Discuss the current slang on the campus.*


## *Look Around You*

In a lecture, a professional writer told her audience: "If it's ideas you're after, get out of your chair *and go look*. Walk around; listen." After the great flood in Corning, N.Y., in 1972, R. N. Hoye wondered: What is a flooded house like after the water is gone? What do people face when they return to their homes? He went to look:

[1] The first problem is just to get in. If the front door has swollen, is blocked by mud, or has something jammed against it, it may be necessary to break a window to gain entry. Inside, the first thing observed is a waterline four or six or ten feet high all around the walls. The floors themselves are warped into unbelievable waves of wood six to ten inches high, very easy to stumble over. Everything in every room is coated with mud between two and four inches deep, and the mud not only is still wet, but has an unforgettable odor. Rugs, sofas, pillows, tables, and chairs are all soaked, not just sodden or damp. Books have swollen and burst their bindings. Any ashtray or vase you pick up is full of brown, cold water. Everything drips.

[2] Go into the kitchen. The doors on some cabinets are so swollen that it takes a few hard pulls to get them open. When you do open the cabinets, water runs out. The washing machine is filled with water; there is an ugly waterline on the refrigerator. Now go upstairs. In the bedrooms, the mattresses are soaked and covered with mud. The mattresses are so heavy that two people can barely drag one, and then only a few feet at a time. Everything folded in drawers and hanging in closets is soaked, too. Even the shoes on the floors of the closets have water in them.

[3] Of course, if you have a basement, it's still full of water; you may be able to see the top of the furnace. There's nothing to do here until the pumpers start making their rounds. In your garage, bikes, sleds, lawnmowers, and tools already have begun to rust.

—R. N. Hoye, "The Flood and the Community"

Nearly every sentence of Hoye's represents an observation—a going-to-look at something which could provide ideas for several papers: (a) A flood causes irreparable damage to a house, clothing, and equipment. (b) A flood leaves a mark on a family's possessions that can never be paid for. (c) Some flood-damaged goods can never be used again.

## Surprise Yourself

One problem with looking for material is that you may find more of it than you know what to do with; life is full of surprises. But if surprising ideas won't come easily to you, go to them. Surprise yourself.

A student remarked in class one day: "It seems that every good idea I have about writing is just an ordinary one, seen from a new angle."

"Meaning what?"

"Well, if you take an ordinary idea and look at it from a different angle, it may come out unordinary—surprising. When I was in high school I read that statement of Admiral Oliver Hazard Perry's: 'We have met the enemy, and they are ours.' When my brother took the SAT test to get into college, he and thousands of others the same year had to write an essay for the SAT based on a statement from the comic strip *Pogo:* 'We have met the enemy, and he is us.' The change in the quote is surprising, and helps to suggest ideas."

Surprise yourself (and your reader) with a *description* one might not normally expect. The scholar Elaine Partnow writes: "Through all this sleuthing I have come to feel that the public regards women in past and current history very much like fine character actors—we recognize them but do not know their names; we need them but do not pay them homage; we make demands on them but do not document their contributions." Women as character actors: the surprise inherent in the description is itself a "found idea," one which helps find and shape other ideas.

## Other Options for Finding Subjects

Another student writes home regularly. Before mailing her letters, she copies them on the photocopier in the library. Into the letters she puts everything she can think of, making her parents happy and also supplying ideas for papers and essays to come. A third student is an annotator of books and magazines. Never lend him a book unless you want it back full of underlinings and remarks in the margin like *This is not true!!* He also keeps a notebook of observations and quoted material from his reading. We would hesitate to use his notebook method by itself. Think of having to read all the way through a notebook to find a remark you were sure you remembered putting down—somewhere. But his notebook works for him.

And that, of course, is the point. If brainstorming, freewriting in books, or keeping a diary, notebook, or journal works for you, do it. Indeed, don't be afraid to try anything that may produce or trap an idea. *Skim* a magazine or book; *watch* a TV channel you seldom watch; *read* a newspaper as if you were from a foreign country; *chat* with a stranger at the laundromat or supermarket. Interview a professor who teaches a course you never heard of: "How did the course come to be taught? What do your students learn in it?"

## ◆ *P R A C T I C E*

Read the student paper below. Work backwards from the paper, and make guesses on the strategies the student used in choosing and shaping the subject. How might she have used *brainstorming, freewriting,* a *journal, "looking around,"* and *surprise*?

### *ONE DOZEN WAYS TO PICK UP A CAT*

1 My brother, when he was little, picked up a cat (a small cat, to be sure—no more than a kitten) by both its ears. The kitten hung in the air, looking rather surprised, but without fear or noticeable resentment. Perhaps it understood that the little boy holding its ears was without experience or understanding and was more to be pitied than scratched. If one of us adults had tried this, that kitten would probably have located a few of our finger bones with its claws.

2 You can pick up a cat by any one of four legs, or by all four legs at once. Or by its head—or, as we all know, by that favorite handle, the tail. Marjorie, a tough old woman on the farm south of us, had a couple of cats on her property to keep down the mouse population. They were never allowed in her house. But they always tried to get in. Whenever Marjorie opened the screen door, it was a signal for at least one cat to make a dash for the warm kitchen inside.

3 Usually the cat never got more than a few inches inside the kitchen. As it whipped through the half-open door, tail at full mast, Marjorie would lean gracefully down like a ballet dancer, close her hand on ten full inches of tail, and smoothly swing the cat through the air and out of doors, where it would land on the porch with a light thump and look around with a great pretense of disinterest and fall to licking one paw. If the cat got safely into the kitchen, which seldom happened, it was allowed to stay for a while, and perhaps even to dip its nose into a saucer of milk.

4 On the farm, we had a cat named Furde which got into the basement furnace when Dad was working on the machinery. Furde—a fine, intelligent, if overly curious calico cat—climbed into the open furnace and then into the cold-air ducting system. Dad closed up the furnace and departed. Not being able to get out of the furnace, Furde climbed up the cold-air duct to the second floor until she found a cold-air entrance (with tiny holes in it) from the duct into a bedroom. There she uttered horrible noises which, amplified by the metal ducting system, frightened my two-year-old sister so badly she ran into the bathroom and refused to come out.

5 We took off the cover to the duct and discovered Furde barely visible and wedged sidewise in the hole. Taking a pair of tongs from the fireplace, we gently pulled at what we could see of her, and finally picked her up out of her predicament.

6 Including the use of fireplace tongs, one can think of about a dozen ways to pick up a cat, some of them more appropriate than others. The cat itself has natural handles on both ends. Oddly enough, a full-grown cat does not like to be picked up by the scruff of the neck, the way a mother cat picks up her young. In fact, most cats don't like to be picked up by any method, as

the barely healed scratches on my arms remind me. As of last week, I have finally determined that the thirteenth and best way to pick up a cat is not at all.

## Hooking an Idea

One cold winter day we were talking to a student who had too many ideas. His father was a high school principal, and he was planning to write about the joys and sorrows of being a school principal in a small town.

The student showed us a dozen pages of false starts. We read them and asked, "How many subjects have you got here?"

"That's the trouble," he said. "I've got so many ideas about being a principal and so much to say that I don't know where to begin. If I could just get started . . ." We pointed to the back of the classroom. Along the wall was a line of coat hooks, and his coat was hanging on one of them. "Look at your coat," we said. "When you came in, you didn't throw your coat at the wall and hope it would miraculously stay up there off the floor. You hung it high and dry on a hook. You are trying to throw your next piece of writing at a rhetorical wall, hoping it will stay there. But your writing keeps falling down in a heap. Try some hooks. For example:

*Why* school principals *fail.*

The hooks are provided in the words *why* and *fail.* As you plan your paper, keep hanging your ideas on those two words."

We told the student about other possible word-hooks for this paper:

The *successful* principal *listens.*
How a *good* principal *prepares.*
A principal who keeps his job is *lucky.*
A principal and town *politics.*
Should you be a principal? Yes, if you have *patience* and physical *stamina.*

For two reasons, we recommend the hook strongly to writers. First, it dramatizes clearly and simply one of the natural ways the human brain works, and so helps us find and clarify ideas. It is natural for us to characterize and capsulize our experiences in single words (and, sometimes, phrases):

—That course is *boring.*
—For some American citizens, President Reagan was a *teflon* president.
—But I'm not *ready* to get married!
—All he wanted in life was *to act.*
—The Civil War was a *bloody disaster,* the first *modern war.*
—To me, God is a woman, and every thing about Her reminds me of the *female.*

—A partial solution to the apartheid in South Africa is [is not] *disinvestment.*
—The war on poverty *can be won.*

Each italicized word or phrase represents an idea-hook on which you can hang a paper or theme. Note, by the way, that the hook can be more than one device of grammar. In the examples above:

*Boring, teflon,* and *ready* are adjectives.
*Female* and *disinvestment* are nouns.
*To act* is an infinitive.
*Bloody disaster* and *modern war* are noun phrases.
*Can* is an auxiliary verb (consider the difference between "*can* be won" and "*may* be won").

A second reason why we recommend the hook is that it supplies control throughout the writing process, as shown in the drawing on p. 4. No matter where you are in the process—whether in finding ideas, outlining, rewriting—the hook provides a check on what you are doing. If, for instance, you are writing on why principals *fail,* throughout the writing process keep checking the *fail* hook to see that your paper is still hanging on it. For example: You will *fail* as a principal if you are not a good listener, an adept politician, and an organized planner. A student writing about a successful principal might use different hook(s): A principal's job is not an easy one but if you have *patience* and *physical stamina,* you will be successful.

Here, at the stage of finding ideas, we suggest only that you consider hanging your paper on something—or on something*s.* (Some ideas need two, even three, hooks.) Also, in this early stage, it is not important whether your hooks are expressed in a title, a sentence fragment, or a full sentence. The main thing is to get those hooks on scratch paper so you can think about them and get started writing.

## MARTIN AND THE NERD: A CASE HISTORY

To demonstrate some ways of finding ideas, we taped an interview with Martin, one of our students. As background, you need to know that students in our community start studying computers in about the seventh grade, and that our university, one of the centers of computer training in the world, has many computers available for practice and study. The italicized questions in the interview are ours. Martin begins:

Walking home from class, I was thinking about an idea for my paper. As you know, my major interest is in computers, and so it was natural to think about computers as a general subject. I'd recently heard the argument that Computer

Science—like many technical-training majors—does not prepare students well for life. This seemed like a line of thought to follow. Should I hang the paper on "preparation for life"?

Later I talked this over with my roommate, and he reminded me of my complaint about "computer nerds"—you know, computer addicts—and that some of them smell bad—they don't wash often enough, and live in squalor.

So what, I thought, has that got to do with anything? I wandered around the subject some more, and scratched on some paper with a pencil. Here's the paper with my scratches:

> The computer did it.
> Computers can't...
> Contains a lot of numbers...
> Nerds smell bad.
> Addresses like houses.
> How often do we consider the human cost...
> <u>nerds are human</u>
> Should they be allowed to use computers at all?
> They ruined him — all he ever did was sit in front of a computer and play games.
> There are two main species of computer needs.

I don't know what some of these entries mean now.

*It looks as though you were wandering all over the map at this stage.*

Well, yes, I'd started with that business about computer training—no, with *technical* training not preparing people well for life. Until my roommate reminded me of what I had said about nerds, I hadn't thought about them at all. (I believe in *talking* to people about papers and paper topics. People should talk more about their ideas anyway, bounce them off somebody else.)

At this point, I started a typical journal entry. I keep these in a spiral notebook—there's not much order or sense in them usually. Here is the way the entry looked, with my own comments on it:

> We all know about the benefits of computers, but how often do we consider the casualties — those who use the machines? I refer to that subspecies of mankind known to those in the computer trade as "computer nerds." Who are these people, and how did they become computer nerds?
>
> In this exposition I will discuss methods of detecting computer nerds, and examine their relations with computers (the role of computers in their lives?)

As you can see, this did have some direction. I was focusing on the idea of the computer nerd; the technical training subject was too big and unmanageable. But after letting this sit for a while, I read it and was bothered by the number of little ideas in the big subject; *benefits of computers, casualties, nerds, how they got to be nerds, detecting them and examining them* . . . all too much, too much.

*Where did the term* nerd *come from? Is it yours?*

Oh, no, it's the standard term. That's what people call them.

*What did you do next?*

I tried typing a paragraph. This one had a title.

```
                    Computer Addiction

    We are often told of the benefits of computers.

But how often do we hear of the casualties among those

who use the machines?  I refer to those who become

addicted to computers.  In the trade, we call them

"computer nerds."
```

Now here I was trying to do something about all those little ideas I'd had earlier. You know, now I was focusing on the paper, getting some control of it. This paper was going to have as hooks *computer nerds* and how they have become *addicted*. In fact, it was the *addiction* hook that made the paper grow—go, I should say. I was moving toward a thesis: *Computer programming is addictive.* [A *thesis* is the main point of a paper.] But then I realized that a better and more manageable thesis would deal with the *computer nerd* and *his addiction.* Therefore, my thesis became: *A computer nerd is a person who has become addicted to computer programming.*

Here is Martin's paper, the result of his search for ideas and a subject.

### COMPUTER NERDS

[1] We are often told of the benefits of computers, but how often do we hear of the casualties among those who use the machines? I refer to those who become addicted to computers, known to the trade as "computer nerds."

[2] There are two main varieties of these people—the day nerd and the night nerd. By choice, most of them choose to be day nerds, but at many computer installations supervisors or teachers allow them to work only at night, thus converting them into night nerds. A less common variety live with a 25- or 26-hour clock, being fixed as neither day nor night nerd.

[3] How do you distinguish computer nerds from the general public? Beginning nerds are recognized by the (programmable) calculator worn on the belt, ready for a quick draw in a financial emergency—such as a restaurant bill that must be split, or a tax return. As nerds gain experience, the calculator is replaced by a punch-card, which is carried in the left front shirt pocket. The punch-card phase is short, however, because considerable status is attached to the acquisition of the ultimate distinguishing sign: "terminal eyes," named after the computer terminal at which the computer nerds spend most of their waking hours.

[4] During development of the fully fledged computer nerd, several behavioral traits are evident. He (*he,* since female nerds at this time do not appear to exist) becomes more withdrawn; he is unwilling to communicate with people,

preferring instead communion with the computer; and his health deteriorates as he spends more and more time out of natural light. In the final phases, the nerd develops characteristics common to hunted animals. He knows that his days at the computer are numbered, yet he cannot stop. He prefers developing better and better game programs to doing school work. Eventually, lack of sleep or inadequate course grades bring his downfall.

5 There is no doubt that computer programming is addictive, particularly for the nerd. Programs are never free of errors, but the challenge always is to find the final perfect one. Just as that one error is "fixed," another appears. And so on. The principle is the same as those underlying alcoholism and gambling: "One more, and then I'll give up." Aggravating the problem are supervisors or teachers who don't try to distinguish between someone working on a computer assignment and one working on a game program. By the time the problem becomes evident, much time has been lost and another addict has been created.

## ◆ *PRACTICE*

### *Discussion*

1. Consider again Martin's paper, above. How effective is it? Can you suggest improvements?

   Suppose that you believe Martin should begin again on his general subject. How might he formulate his ideas or get new ones? Can you suggest a *surprise* in his topic? Different *hooks*?

2. Let us assume that you want something changed. This change may involve better service for your car, different scheduling of classes, more money from home, the highway in front of your house repaired, or improved funding for women's sports at your college, etc.

   Look back at the strategies for finding ideas that we have examined. Prepare for class discussion a few specific answers to these questions:
   a. What change do you want?
   b. How did you decide on the change?

3. Andy Rooney called an essay "Can We Find the Hiding Places We've Lost?" Here are the first three paragraphs from his essay:

   1 It seems to me it's getting harder and harder to find a place to hide things. Some people are better at hiding things than others, but even the good hiders are having trouble these days. Traditionally, Americans have done their hiding under mattresses, in cookie jars, under the front door mats, behind pictures, on top of shelves, and under underwear. These hiding places are no longer secure and the time may fast be approaching when we will run out of hiding places.

   2 The United States government can't even find a satisfactory place to hide the missiles from the Russians and there's been a big squabble about it in Congress. One of the ideas has been to build a lot of missile sites in

Nevada but only put actual missiles in a few of them. The Russians wouldn't know which sites had them and which were dummies. This is a very clever idea but not actual hiding.

³ One of the biggest hiding problems on a homeowner's level is where to put the silver so burglars won't steal it. In many cities you can't rent a safe deposit vault at the bank because they've all been taken by people who thought of that before you did. All across the country Americans with silver knives, forks, and spoons have hidden them away in the bank and are now eating off dime-store utensils. This way they can leave their silverware to their children, who won't dare leave it around the house to eat off either.

Work backwards from these paragraphs. Make a scratch list of the ideas that might have occurred to Rooney as he prepared to write. What were his surprises? His hooks?

Here is Rooney's eighth paragraph. How do you suppose he got the idea for this paragraph on the garage and other areas in the house?

⁸ Hiding places like our garage, our attic or our cellar are fast disappearing. Houses are being built without attics or cellars, and architects are designing houses with less of what they call "waste space." What all of us want is more "waste space," not less. That's the best kind of space and it's the kind of space you hide things in. The architecture that provides a place for everything imposes an order on our lives that precludes the haphazard arrangement of the things we own that permits us to hide them so well.

4. Titles are often a good way to create (and express) a *hook* for writing. Suppose you are writing a paper about the number of still-useful appliances that homeowners throw away. You want to emphasize that something else can be done with them, so you title your paper, "Repair, Don't Buy." The hook is in that word *repair* and your point is going to be: Don't buy a new toaster or lawnmower—repair the old one.

Another example: A friend of yours pays a professional résumé company to write and print his job application for summer work. You look at the application and say to him, "You could have done that yourself on your own computer." You write a paper using a similar argument, titling it: "Student Résumés—Self-Design Is the Best Design." Your hook is in the words *self-design* and *best design*.

Make up five titles for papers. Try to build in the *hook* for each title. Prepare to defend two of your titles in class.

*Writing*

1. Write a paper based on Practice **2**, under Discussion questions.

2. Take a blank sheet of paper and start writing. Don't stop to think—simply begin. If nothing else gets you moving, write "One, two, three, four, get up and bar the door . . ." Write anything that crosses your mind until you get to the bottom of the page.

Pick up a second sheet. From the first sheet, make a few lists of words and phrases that strike your fancy, like: "I can hear the faucet dripping. I remember Lee left the cap off the toothpaste again. Sloppy roommate." Make a judgment: "He is sloppy but easy to live with." Generalize: "Sloppy roommates are tolerable if they are easy to live with."

Spend a few minutes working back and forth between your first sheet of paper and your second. Listen for the meanings. On your second sheet, write a column heading: *Hooks*. How many hooks can you find from the first sheet? From the second? Can you find or create any surprises?

# T*HE WRITER'S STANCE*

## A*N EXAMPLE*

Glen Bantz waved the engineer's report in the air, then dropped it on his desk. Bantz is the executive vice-president of his company. We were interviewing him for an article on college graduates and what they should know about writing.

"If you want to know what to teach engineers about writing, I'll tell you," Bantz said. "It's the same thing I'd tell you to teach accountants, lawyers, technical editors, MBA's, anybody who works for this company—or any other outfit, for that matter."

Bantz picked up several folders from his desk.

"In each of these folders is a report from one of our field offices. In my in-basket, there's a bunch of letters and memos from these same offices. I'm going to tell my secretary to buy a great big rubber stamp. Without reading any of these letters and memos, I'm going to rubber-stamp each one on the first page and send it back to the author for rewriting. Here's what the stamp will look like."

We peered at the piece of paper he handed us. It had three questions on it:

Who am *I*??
Who are *YOU*??
What is my *POINT*??

Ninety percent of the company's problems in communication, Bantz told us, come from writers not answering those questions before they write something . . .

*Who am I?*—this question reminds the writer to identify the *role* he is assuming for that particular message. (As you will see later in this chapter, every writer can have many different roles.)

*Who are YOU?*—this question reminds the writer to identify the *reader* (or group of readers) she is writing to. One particular idea can have different "readerships," each of which may require a somewhat different strategy of writing.

*What is my POINT?*—this question reminds the writer to give the reason for her message. *Why is she writing it, and why should anybody be persuaded to read it?*

## APPLYING THE PRINCIPLES OF STANCE

So far, we have been discussing *stance* in fairly general terms. Now let's be specific, and apply the principle to some writing problems you may have. Our examples will come from two student writers, Michael and Nancy. Michael's example is brief; Nancy's is longer, and we will follow it from conception to finished paper.

Michael drives a cab part-time. He has an interesting idea for a paper: that cab driving is an unglamorous job. Here is one of the paragraphs in his first draft:

> Traffic can destroy patience faster than threading heavy thread through a needle. City driving sneaks up on your nerves. It doesn't blast you; it just gnaws at your stomach. Cars are death traps. It takes so little to be behind a wheel—almost anyone can get a license. And there's not much money in it. Driving all day I saw them all, wild drivers, incompetent drivers, angry drivers. I made mistakes too and put lives in jeopardy; I came to respect the power of the automobile.

When he talked to us, Michael said that he did not feel comfortable with what he had written. Something, he wasn't sure what, had gone wrong; he was stuck and could not continue with any confidence.

The problem was that he had not yet found an appropriate stance for the essay. What was he trying to say about cab driving? His paragraph rambles, making three or four points without developing any one of them adequately. To improve his work, he needed to specify the three elements of stance:

| | |
|---|---|
| *Role:* | I am a student working part-time as a driver for a local cab company. I am nineteen years old. |
| *Thesis:* | Driving a cab part-time is a poor way for a college student to make money. |
| *Reader:* | The "general reader," who might be curious about what it's like to drive a cab. |

About the general reader we will have more to say later. Michael began to rewrite his paper, getting this result for two paragraphs:

> On an average twelve-hour workday on Saturday or Sunday, I make twenty-five to thirty dollars after paying for half of the gas I use—a company requirement. I start at six o'clock in the morning, and finish at seven in the evening. But since the supper hour is the busiest time of the day, I often have to stay an hour late. The cabs eat gas like luxury cars. Twenty-five percent of my profits are lost in paying for gas. In the winter, between calls, I either turn off the engine or burn up all my profits. Cold, cold.
>
> I receive tips from perhaps one-fifth of the fares. If a person gives me a quarter he smiles benevolently as if he has finally proved to himself that he really has a philanthropic heart. "Well, how much do you get as a tip?" some will ask. Or: "What's the right amount to tip?" A common comment, after a toothy smile: "Well, you got me here safely, didn't you? I think you deserve a tip." An extra dime falls into my hand, and after my word of thanks, I hear a chuckle or two, and a pleasant, "You're welcome, you're quite welcome."

These paragraphs are not perfect, but they're better than Michael's first effort—more interesting, readable, and informative. We know who the writer is, why he wishes to communicate to us, what the point of his communication is.

As a part of a new assignment, Michael tried shifting his stance:

> Your cabs are in terrible condition; some are actually unsafe. The horn did not work on mine all last weekend. The brakes on No. 37 are so badly worn that they will not respond without pumping. Since most of us have to drive fast to get from one place to another to pick up a new fare, we are endangering our lives and other people's—just to do our jobs.

The writer's role here stays the same, but Michael has changed his thesis and his reader, who is now the owner of the cab company.

Let's consider another writer. Nancy was working on a paper for her composition class. But the paper—on her experiences backpacking in Europe last summer—refused to get written. She made several false starts, tried an outline that got nowhere, and filled parts of three pages with neat handwriting that turned into scrawls as she realized that the paper just was not coming out right.

What to do? She remembered her instructor's suggestion: "If you get into trouble on a paper, don't keep fighting it—come see me right away!"

So, bundling up her material (false starts, scrawls, and the outline that went nowhere), off Nancy went to her instructor's office. He looked at what she had written so far and said to her: "Surely we can do something with this. But before we go on, tell me—just how do you feel about your subject?"

"Traveling in Europe? A perfect subject for me," said Nancy. "I just spent over two months living it. I'm following your advice: 'Write about what you know.' I have a lot of concrete materials, so the paper ought to write itself. I don't usually have much trouble writing, but right now each word comes harder than the last one. I feel as if I should tear it all up and start over. But *how* do I get a better start? Talk about frustration!"

The basic solution to Nancy's problem, her instructor told her, may lie in improving her stance. She had forgotten that a successful paper is always written by somebody, to somebody, and for a purpose. Using her material as an example, let's examine the elements of stance—*role, thesis* (point), and *reader.*

## The Role

You do not use a role to cover up your true self or to give a false impression to a reader. Nor do you use it to play out a fictional part, as you might if you were acting on stage or in film. Your role as writer is a legitimate part of you and your existence. Who are you and what do you do? How many roles do you adopt as a matter of course in your daily life?

Nancy is eighteen years old. She graduated from high school last spring. She lives in a dormitory and has a part-time job. She is taking a general science course, and hopes eventually to be a hospital technician. She saved her job money during her last year in high school in order to backpack through Europe in the summer with a friend. Here are some of her roles that she mentioned to her instructor:

| | |
|---|---|
| —babysitter | —owner of a bicycle |
| —consumer | —stenographer-typist |
| —taxpayer | —cook |
| (five cents on every dollar) | —daughter |
| —sister | —amateur pottery maker |
| —U.S. citizen | —environmentalist |
| —college student | —member of Sierra Club |

Her instructor had told her that he could not find Nancy in the first drafts of her paper—that, in effect, he could not see one of her clear roles as a writer in them. "Before you start writing again," he told her, "pick a role and stick to it. What do you want to be?"

"An American traveling in Europe."

"Pretty vague," he said. "Politicians, movie actors, tourists, soldiers, business executives—they can all be 'Americans traveling in Europe.' Can you be more specific?"

"OK, I am a woman; I'm eighteen; I know a little French, but no other foreign languages. I took 2,500 hard-earned dollars out of my bank account—that was all there was in it—and flew off to another part of the world, not knowing any more what I was getting into than if I were flying to the moon. But I was going to see everything!"

"Good enough," he said. "There's a genuine role for you: a young American woman on the loose over there without much money who's going to see every castle and museum on the continent. Now—what is your thesis?"

## The Thesis

Her instructor talked to Nancy about several possibilities for a *thesis*—the point of the paper, *its main idea stated in one specifically written sentence.* She could discuss the language problems she encountered, the difficulties of travel for someone without much money, the sights to see, the problem of communicating with parents and friends thousands of miles away.

But Nancy kept coming back to one idea that she considered important. Too many young Americans, like herself, went off merrily to Europe without being properly prepared for what they would encounter. Her thesis suggested itself. Why not try to warn travelers about three or four problems they might encounter, and suggest how they could go about solving them? At this stage, then, her hooks for the paper were *traveling in Europe* and *problems.* (For a discussion of *hooks,* see Chapter 1, pp. 11–12.)

Her instructor agreed that this idea could lead to a sensible thesis. (The final version of her thesis is given below.)

## The Reader

Now Nancy needed to specify a reader.

"You already know," said her instructor, "that you seldom (if ever) write anything that is directed to every person who reads English. Most pieces of writing are directed to a special reader or group of readers. Your own composition textbook is directed to one group of readers; an article in *TV Guide* is directed to another; a set of directions on repairing a motorboat engine to yet another. While these groups of readers may overlap somewhat, they usually do have a certain distinctness. Write for a specific reader, Nancy; aim for a particular target."

Nancy commented that her thoughts about her role and thesis also seemed to suggest a certain group of readers—those young American backpackers with little money who intended to see Europe but wouldn't always know what to expect.

## A Completed Stance

Nancy's completed stance now looked like this:

> *My role:*　I am a young American who traveled through Europe this summer. I would like to show how other backpackers can do the same thing, but do it more easily than I did.

*My thesis:*   In order to make traveling easier and more pleasant in Europe, buy three informative books, learn about Youth Hostels, and be prepared for the "male problem."

*My reader:*   Young Americans who might want to travel as I did. My essay will be slanted somewhat to women, but men should definitely be interested too.

Here is Nancy's completed paper.

### WHAT YOU ALWAYS WANTED TO KNOW
### ABOUT BACKPACKING IN EUROPE
### (BUT DIDN'T KNOW ENOUGH TO ASK)

1 So you're going to hike around Europe! You have saved some money; you have your backpack all ready to go (complete with a box of bandages for the very sore feet you're going to get); and you have pored over your collection of travel folders, looking again at those glamorous canals and castles and mountains that will shortly be in front of your camera.

2 But have you talked to other young people who have recently been there? Do you know what to look for and what to expect? I thought I was well prepared in every way, but some problems came up I did not expect. I could have dealt with them much more easily if I had had the information I am giving you here. I'll omit a lot of little things in order to concentrate on three larger ones: certain useful books to buy, the nature of Youth Hostels, and the problem of men in southern Europe. (I assume that, like myself and most of the other young travelers I met, you are traveling light and on a small budget— I got home with twenty-five cents.)*

3 Before you begin your trip, there are two or three books I would recommend you buy and read. One is a budget guide, Arthur Frommer's *Europe on Thirty Dollars a Day.* This book tells you a great deal about all the major cities in Europe. It has descriptions of the fascinating places to go and often how to get there. It also includes names of inexpensive restaurants and hotels. The book is a reassuring thing to have when you arrive in a big city with no place to sleep. Also, by reading about what is in a city before you go, you can decide in advance if you want to visit it.

4 Another important book to get is a *Rail Schedule.* It includes train schedules for all of western Europe. If you have a Eurailpass, which is probably the cheapest and fastest way to travel in the free countries on the continent, this book will be a great help. Having a complete *Schedule* allows you to stop in little out-of-the-way places because you know when and where you can get connections *out* of them. It's usually not wise to jump on a train going to a tiny town if you have no idea when you can catch another train to leave. Also, having the *Rail Schedule* will inevitably save you long hours of waiting in train stations. Since many of the southern countries do not post schedules, it is extremely time-consuming to stand (sometimes for hours) in information lines trying to find out when you can leave.

---

*In order to make your sentences flow smoothly in your introduction, you may have to paraphrase your thesis rather than state it word for word. Note that Nancy's original thesis (above) is paraphrased in paragraph 2.

[5] A third book I recommend is the *Youth Hostel Guide*. This book tells you where the hostels are and how far they are located from the train stations. It gives hostel facilities, hours, and (sometimes) prices. I tried to get along without a hostel book some of the time by using the information offices at railway stations. The information clerk could usually tell me if there was a hostel and how to find it. But if you are planning to do any traveling in rural areas, like Normandy in France, as I did, you will definitely need a *Hostel Guide*. The townspeople in such areas often don't even know their hostel exists.

[6] Staying in Youth Hostels can make your living expenses much lower, but sometimes the problems and restrictions of staying in a hostel may make other accommodations more desirable. Hostels are dormitory-type hotels that rent a place to sleep for between $2.75 and $6.50 a night. Their quality varies greatly. Some of them are very clean and have all the comforts of home. Others are incredibly dirty and primitive. Before you plan to make a habit of staying in hostels you should know that they have two large drawbacks.

[7] First, hostels are usually located far away from the center of the city, sometimes too far to make staying in one economical. Be prepared either to walk a long way into town or to spend money on subways and buses. Second, the early curfews in most hostels makes staying in them a problem if you want to go out on the town. Most of them have a curfew as early as 10:00 P.M. Although there are a few hostels that will charge a small fine for being late, most of them simply lock the doors at 10:00 so no one can get in *or* out. If you are in a city like Munich or London where you want to stay out late, I would advise staying in a cheap hotel rather than in a hostel.

[8] Hostels are closed during the day between 9:00 and 5:00. This causes some difficulty if you arrive in a new town early in the afternoon and go straight to the hostel. You will end up wasting a lot of time just waiting for it to open. And you will have plenty of waiting ahead of you in the check-in line. Because hostels are closed all day and because many of them require that you reregister every night, you could end up in some very long lines, especially during the summer months. The fact that the hostels are closed from 9:00 to 5:00 means that you may have to keep walking around all day. In the southern countries like Italy and Spain, where an entire town closes up during the afternoon, you can end up with nothing to do and no place to go.

[9] If you women are planning to spend any time at all in Italy, Greece, or Spain, you should be forewarned about the male population. (This section should be read by you men too because you will undoubtedly be approached by an American girl looking for someone to protect her or just to sit with her until her harassers leave.) The first thing you have to realize when traveling in these countries is that a local woman does not ordinarily walk out on the street without a sister or an older woman with her. So when you go out on the street alone you are automatically taken to be a tourist—and available. Also, the men have some kind of Early Detection device for American girls. It doesn't matter what you look like or what you are wearing. In Italy particularly you will be leered at, jeered at, whispered to, pinched, and generally driven crazy by the men. Don't think you can go unnoticed; the mere fact that you are an American on the street draws attention to you. Being with a man helps sometimes, but not always. My girl friend and I were with eight British and American boys in Rome, and it made absolutely no difference. You can be wearing a potato sack and the men will still bother you—I wouldn't recommend wearing a dress or shorts and halter tops anywhere. Wearing jeans instead will save you a lot of

trouble. All of this may sound exaggerated to you, but it isn't. And it's better to expect the worst. If you are bothered less than you expected to be, it's better than entering a country like Italy unprepared for the hassles.

[10] A final point. Don't be discouraged by any of the things I have warned you about. Just know what to expect, and prepare carefully for your trip. Europe is a wonderful place, and I had a wonderful time. I have no regrets, and I would go again. Have a great time—and hang on to your Eurailpass!

## AVOIDING THE YOU STANCE

You have just read a paper in which the author, Nancy, addressed her reader directly as *you,* or implied *you* in making suggestions or commands—as in ["*You*] be prepared to walk. . . ." Nancy did this because her stance (see p. 24) called for a reader to whom she was speaking directly. This situation is fairly common, as the following examples show.

*SITUATION*

1. You are telling readers how to understand a satirical cartoon

2. You are explaining a process

*SAMPLE SENTENCE from the paper*

If *you* look in the bottom left corner, *you* will see the tiny comment by the cartoonist's "stand-in," a comic mouse.

Before setting the margins, check the manual on the printer. (*You* is understood in [You] check the manual. . . .)

If, for any reason, you wish to avoid using the informal *you,* change your stance so that *you,* explicit or implied, can be smoothly avoided. Employing the two examples above, we can change the stance of each so that the *sample sentences* contain no *you:*

> [1] In the bottom of the left-hand corner, the cartoonist put his tiny comment in the mouth of his "stand-in," a comic mouse.
> [2] Before setting the margins, the operator checks the printer.

In both these examples, after adjusting the stance, the writer employs the objective third-person viewpoint, thus allowing *you* to disappear painlessly.

It is unwise to say that good writing either uses *or* does not use *you* as a matter of good taste or propriety. *You* appears in writing more as a consequence of stance than anything else. And like anything else in writing, *you* can be overworked—even tiresomely so.

In her paper on traveling in Europe, Nancy employed *you* throughout. She could have used the same material but changed her stance to avoid *you,* as this version of paragraph 3 shows (compare the same paragraph, p. 24):

> Before students begin their trip, there are two or three books I would recommend they buy and read. One is a budget guide, Arthur Frommer's

*Europe on Thirty Dollars a Day.* This book tells the student a great deal about all the major cities in Europe. It has descriptions of the fascinating places to go and often how to get there. It also includes names of inexpensive restaurants and hotels. The book is a reassuring thing to have when students arrive in a big city with no place to sleep. Also, by reading about what is in a city before they go, they can decide in advance if they want to visit it.

## ◆ PRACTICE

### Discussion

Before discussing the following questions, review the summary of Nancy's *writer's stance* (pp. 23–24).

a. In her first two paragraphs, how does Nancy show a concern for her reader? How does she *involve* her reader in her topic?
b. The thesis of the essay is stated, in paraphrased form, at the end of paragraph 2. Given the nature of Nancy's topic, is this a natural place for the thesis? Are there other places where the thesis might comfortably be placed? Why must the reader's reactions be closely considered when you decide on a location for your thesis?
c. Why will the reader appreciate the expression "*Another important book* to get . . ." at the beginning of paragraph 4?
d. Toward the end of paragraph 5, Nancy writes: "But if you are planning to do any traveling in rural areas, like Normandy in France, as I did, you will definitely need a *Hostel Guide*." How, if at all, does this sentence reinforce Nancy's adopted role in her writer's stance? Do you find other sentences in other paragraphs that remind the reader of her role?
e. What other readers could this paper be directed to? What changes would be necessary in Nancy's role for other readers?
f. What kinds of readers (other than those we have already mentioned) would not find this paper very useful? Explain.
g. In paragraphs 6 and 7, how does Nancy make sure that her reader can follow the organization of her ideas?
h. A well-made paragraph can often be considered as a small "essay." Discuss the effectiveness of paragraph 9 as a little essay. Does it have a stance any different from that of the whole essay?
i. How does Nancy's conclusion fit her stance? Is there any contradiction in her conclusion?
j. The purpose of writing, of course, is to communicate ideas, attitudes, facts, and values. When a reader finishes a piece of writing, he should know more than he did when he started. Using brief phrases, make a list of "new knowledge" you have gained from Nancy's writing. What does this list tell you about a successful paper?

k. As a typical reader, write a note to Nancy making comments or suggestions about her writer's stance and her material. What, for instance, would you wish she had covered in her paper that she did not?

# THE WRITER'S STANCE AND *YOU*

Are you wondering whether Nancy's writing problem is typical of most of the problems you will face? It *is* pretty typical. She had started out simply to write a paper on her European experiences, and she specified her stance using that idea as a broad base on which to build. For most assignments (whether you choose a topic or it is given to you by your instructor), you can follow a procedure roughly similar to Nancy's when you specify your own stance.

To help you with your various stances in preparing to write your papers, we suggest that you ask (and answer) certain questions about role, thesis, and reader:

> *Role:* In this paper, who am I? What role can I most reasonably adopt? Will I feel comfortable in this role? What are my purposes in adopting it? Can I maintain it consistently throughout the paper?
>
> *Thesis:* What main point do I want to explain or prove to my reader? Can I state this point specifically in a single sentence?
>
> *Reader:* What reader, or group of readers, do I want to inform or convince? Have I identified the most appropriate reader?
>
> *Overview:* How does my writer's stance look as a whole? Are its three parts logically related?

## Your Role and Your Reader

Of course you are limited to some extent by the roles and readers that, in a practical way, are available to you. A readership of middle-aged bankers or Los Angeles cabdrivers would not have been practical for Nancy's essay on traveling in Europe. And if she were given the topic "Defend or Attack Offshore Drilling for Oil," her writer's role would probably be limited because, as she mentioned in her list of possible roles, she is an environmentalist and a member of the Sierra Club, an organization pledged to preserve the coastline against offshore drilling. As to what this specific limitation would amount to, she would have to decide for herself. Each of you will have your own limitations in roles—limitations governed by age, philosophy, political and religious beliefs (or lack of them), experience, knowledge of the subject, and so on. But on most topics, even within the framework of such limitations, there should be several writer's roles you can choose for your papers.

For most topics, there are also several possible audiences. On the offshore drilling topic just mentioned, your readership might be one of these:

—legislators considering an offshore drilling proposal
—drivers of cars who buy gasoline
—other college students of your "type"
—any persons interested in the topic
—any persons uninterested in the topic (a challenge to the writer)
—a writer who has written an argument for or against offshore drilling

Some of these audiences are more general than others. On many topics you may find that it is practical to address these *general readers*, a class of people who vary somewhat in age, occupation, and interests. But you should always specify and describe even your general audience because it will usually have certain characteristics that set if off from the "whole world" of readers. A letter written to your local newspaper on rezoning prime farmland for industrial use should not be directed to all readers of the newspaper because all of them are not equally interested in the subject or able to do anything about it.

To take another example, a critical essay on a novel should not be written for "everybody" but only for those interested in serious fiction generally and in your novel specifically—usually someone who has read the novel. If your group of readers has not read the novel, then that fact affects your thesis and your essay, which in this instance is likely to take the form of a review ("For the following reasons, this book is good—read it").

Too many students believe that their audience consists of one person, the instructor. In some cases, he may be your only reader. But in reality, he is quite often your *teacher-editor*, a trained professional who stands between you and your readers, pointing out where you have gone wrong in your essay, what you have done well, how you can make your work more convincing.

## Guidelines for Identifying "The Reader"

Most papers are written for reader*s*, in the plural. To see how we can identify them, let's look in on a brainstorming session (for *brainstorming,* see pp. 5–6). The students in the session are brainstorming the audience for a short paper discussing requirements for the film study major at the college. The paper will argue that the requirements should be *increased.*

*Arthur:* Audience is all students here.
*Scott:* Not all are interested.

*Catherine:* Just majors.
*Wilda.* No, majors and minors.
*Francisca:* They are not the ones who make the requirements.
*Wilda:* Decide on one group.
*Scott:* Who has the most power? To make changes?
*Instructor:* Faculty committee on Majors and Minors.
*Scott:* Tenured professors on the committee, then.
*Catherine:* Are all professors on the committee tenured?
*Wilda:* What's the membership like?
*Instructor* (reading): Two full profs., one in 18th century lit, one in film study; two assistant professors, one in film study, one in composition; one student—five people total. Student's name is Gary Nelson.
*Wilda:* Anyone know the student?
*Francisca:* I think that's the Nelson who writes movie reviews for the paper.
*Shannon:* Three people, then, who care about film; two unknown. Shall we write for the three we are sure of, and guess about the others?
*Don:* They wouldn't be on the committee unless they were reasonably sympathetic to film study.
*Shannon:* Assumption: The committee wants the film study courses to succeed. Would not mind increasing hours for the major.
*Scott:* But another assumption: At least two people on this committee might think doing that would decrease the majors in either rhetoric or "straight" literature. Watch out for *them.*
*Catherine:* You mean they might be hostile to the proposal in the paper?
*Francisca:* OK, assume two hostiles in the audience.

We'll break off our account of the brainstorming session here. The group has clearly moved toward a good sense of their audience for an argument that requirements should be increased for the major in film. In essence, their conclusion was that the audience should be taken as mixed in several ways—student and professorial; possibly hostile to the argument, and non-hostile; knowledgeable about film study and not knowledgeable. The paper should be written to "spread" to this audience. In other words, no part of the audience should be ignored in certain parts of the argument. If, for example, the writer assumes that all members of the audience know the history of the major in film and why certain requirements have been put in, he or she may miss the student member and possibly the two professors who do not teach in the film program.

We can set up flexible guidelines for considering readership or audience:

1. If possible, list the people in the audience—or, at least, the *types* of people. Know who and what they are.

2. Consider their knowledge; how much do they *know* about your subject and its various parts? (Are they very familiar with one part but not another?)

3. What are their prejudices—or prejudgments? What kind of automatic acceptance or rejection of your ideas are you likely to encounter? Familiar (and controversial) subjects like abortion, capital punishment, and "big" government touch many nerves in people. But sometimes subjects that are less familiar and controversial can bring strong reactions you never expected. That can be awkward! A few years ago there was a worldwide firestorm of negative reaction caused by former president Reagan's decision to lay a wreath in a German military cemetery where SS troops are buried—a case of an audience that was seriously misread.

4. What parts of your argument—or of your material—are they likely to accept? For whatever reason, what parts are they not likely to accept? Shape your paper accordingly.

5. As you write, keep in mind the typical faces of your readers. Imagine, as you write, that you are speaking to them and that they are reacting to your ideas as listeners would. Doing this gives you an immediate imaginative feedback on your ideas as you write them.

## Your Thesis

Much of what we have said on the practical limitations of role and reader also applies to the thesis. The thesis, discussed at length in the next chapter, is dependent on role and reader. If you change either of these latter two, your thesis will probably change as well. A thesis is also dependent on what you know about your subject. Nancy said that so far as foreign languages are concerned, she knows only "a little French." Given this fact, it is doubtful that any thesis of hers could easily deal with the Italian language, classical French literature, or modern Greek grammar. But given the knowledge about Europe gained in her travels, she might construct a number of interesting theses, as follows (for the purposes of illustration, we will ignore here the problems of role and reader):

—The average Englishman seems friendlier to the backpacker than the average Frenchman.
—If you want to stay healthy in Europe, stick to simple foods and carry plenty of stomach medicine.
—For an American traveling in Europe, French is the most useful foreign language to know.
—Although France has the reputation of being anti-American, France seems more Americanized than England, Germany, Greece, Italy, or Spain.
—The American Youth Hostel Association needs tighter control from its top administration.
—The beauty of Greece is undeniable, but its beauty is unvarying and, after a while, rather boring.

## ◆ PRACTICE

### Discussion

1. Here is a brief essay that tries to influence the thinking of the reader. Answer the questions following the essay.

> [1] A traveler enters Maine at the very spot where John Paul Jones's *Ranger* slid from the ways in 1777. A flawless thoroughfare of cement has replaced the winding, rutted trail of olden days. . . .
>
> [2] It was a road, not long since, of small white farms nestling in the shadow of brooding barns and sheltering elms; of old square homes built by shipbuilders and shipmasters; of lilac-scented Junes, and meadows rich in the odors of mallow and sweet-grass; of irregular stone walls; ancient taverns; solid, mellow little towns happy in the possession of architecture and tradition and family pride; of long stretches of pine woods, cool and fresh in the heat of summer; of birch-clad hill slopes, forests of oaks and sugar maples, swelling fields and flat salt marshes shimmering mistily in the warm summer sun; of life-giving breezes from the strip of deep blue sea at the far edge of all these things.
>
> [3] It was a beautiful road: a road for health and rest and peace of mind; a priceless possession, to be cherished and forever held in trust for the descendants of those who laid it out and made it possible. It was the essence of Maine; the gateway to the great and beautiful Maine wilderness to the north and east.
>
> [4] Today it is a road of big signs and little signs and medium-sized signs; of cardboard signs tacked to pine trees and wooden fences and dilapidated barns; of homemade signs tilting drunkenly in ragged fields and peering insolently from the yards and walls of furtive-looking houses; of towering signs thrusting garish, mottled faces before forests, fields, and streams, like fat, white-faced streetwalkers posing obscenely in a country lane; of little indecent litters of overnight camps, crawling at the edges of cliffs and in trampled meadows as though the countryside had erupted with some distressing disease: of windrows of luncheon boxes, beer bottles, paper bags, wrapping paper, discarded newspapers, and the miscellaneous filth of countless thoughtless tourists; of doggeries, crab-meateries, doughnutteries, clammeries; of booths that dispense home cooking on oilcloth and inch-thick china in an aura of kerosene stoves, smothered onions, and stale grease; of roadside stands resembling the results of a *mésalliance* between an overnight camp and an early American outhouse; of forests of telephone and electric light poles entangled in a plexus of wires.
>
> [5] It was a road rich in the effluvia of clams in batter, frying doughnuts, sizzling lard; in tawdriness, cheapness, and bad taste, but in little else.
>
> —Kenneth Roberts, "Roads of Remembrance"

   a. What is Roberts' thesis? Has he supported it adequately?
   b. Why should Roberts care about a road in Maine? What is his role?
   c. For whom is Roberts writing? Do you consider yourself a member of his audience? How are you affected by his essay?

2. One of us received this letter, quoted in its entirety. How do you think the writer viewed the reader? The subject of the letter? The writer himself? Is the letter effective?

> Dear Professor Tibbetts:
> This letter is to inform you of the death of Mr. _____, who is currently enrolled in your English 302, Sec. B. The student's registration will be officially cancelled by the appropriate college office in the near future.
>
> Sincerely,
>
> _____, Associate Dean

3. Read this extract from a student's research paper. Describe and justify the student's use of *stance*.

> [1] Most authorities agree that *handedness* is the tendency to use a certain hand to perform most tasks. Modern authorities agree that handedness is related neurologically to the brain. One popular theory is that of "cerebral dominance," which means that one side of the brain dominates the other, this dominance being translated into the preference of one hand over the other.
>
> [2] The researcher encounters difficulty finding good authorities on the subject of handedness. First, the subject itself has no common name. One may have to look in his sources under *left-handedness, right-handedness, laterality,* and *handedness* before he can find information. Many good reference works (for example, the *Collier's Encyclopedia*) have no material on the subject. Those authorities which are available fall roughly into two groups: (1) the medical and (2) the psychological and educational. Since these two groups of authorities often do not agree with each other, one must decide whether to use certain information or to throw it out as being unscientific or unreasonable. In the latter category may be put the theory of Professor _____ in Educational Psychology 280. He told his class that handedness was the result of accident, depending upon which hand a child used in his crib or ate with. If the professor were correct, the laws of probability should require that about half the population be right-handed and half be left-handed.

4. The four paragraphs following represent the introduction to a longer article by Nancy Hunt. From these paragraphs, you should be able to describe the author's use of stance in the rest of the article. What is Hunt's role? Who is her audience? Identify her thesis.

> [1] When I landed in Utica, N.Y., one recent weekend, I had been flying 7½ hours with just one fuel stop at Youngstown, Ohio, to break the journey and wash my hands. Tired, dirty, and hungry, I wanted only to tie down my Piper Tomahawk, find a motel room, and get a drink.
>
> [2] I spotted the only vacant parking spot on the ramp and was heading for it when a Cherokee taxied past, whipped around directly in front of me, and

grabbed my space. I jammed on my brakes and sat there in stupefied indignation. I've seen some pushy people on the ramp at Midway Airport [in Chicago], but not *that* pushy.

3 Welcome to the surly East, home of bad manners!

4 Because I was born in New York City and reared in Connecticut, I consider myself an expert on Eastern manners. Chicagoans often laugh derisively when I say that Midwesterners are kinder and more courteous, but a trip back East confirms my view. . . .

## *Writing*

1. As a writer, some of your first questions are: Who are my readers? How do I want to affect them? That is,

   —What do I want them to believe?
   —Do I want them to take action? Of what kind? Why?
   —How and where should I tell them the point of my paper?
   —How can I tell them who *I* am? (I'm not a ghost, after all, but a human being—*writing*.)

   Write two versions of the same essay. For your major you are required to take a course for which you believe there is no practical use.
   a. Write an essay directed to the dean of your college, explaining why you and your fellow majors should not be required to take the course. Be cool and objective.
   b. Write to other students in your major field. Try to get them to support you in your efforts to have the requirement abolished. In this version, your stance and approach to the subject will be more personal.

2. There is a bill before the state legislature that will impose a severe punishment for hitchhiking in your state. (We will assume that the laws now covering hitchhiking are often not enforced and the punishments, if any, are mild.) Consider these roles, along with the suggested readers. You are:
   a. A state trooper writing to your state representative.
   b. A student living 50 miles from campus; you are writing to your campus newspaper.
   c. A trucker writing to the Opinion column of your union's monthly magazine.
   d. A woman student writing to your worried mother who lives in another state.

   Write a paragraph for each of these situations, filling out your stance with a clear thesis. Let your paragraph be the *introduction* to your letter or article.

Given the general problem, what other stances are citizens in your state likely to take?

3. Write a paper in which you disagree (a little, a lot, or entirely) with Nancy Hunt's thesis that Easterners have worse manners than Midwesterners. Write for a different reader or group of readers. Be sure to use facts to support your thesis. (Check *facts* on pp. 366–368.)

# CHAPTER 3

# MAKING A POINT— YOUR THESIS

After you have worked for a while with the idea of the writer's stance and practiced creating your own stances, you will probably discover that only the thesis gives you any continuing trouble. So let's consider a few practical strategies for arriving at a thesis and making it more useful in planning your essays.

Every written communication must make a point. A letter to your newspaper, a note to the postman, an article on Democrats in the state legislature, a memo to your boss at work, a textbook on the American colonial period, one of your papers—each makes a point about something. The sharper the point, the more successful the communication. In written form, your paper's point is its thesis—*the main idea stated in one specific sentence*. The thesis that you use to guide your early planning does not always appear word for word in the essay itself. Sometimes, in order to fit a thesis into the flow of your writing, you may have to reword it slightly or take two or three sentences to state it. But for the purposes of planning, practice putting each thesis in a single sentence.

Why is a thesis useful? First, it helps you respond to the essay assignment and shape your ideas before you write. Second, the thesis helps you organize your material as you write; it keeps you from wandering away from your topic. Third, after you have completed your essay, you can use your thesis to judge whether you have done what you set out to do. Fourth, in conferences both you and your instructor will refer to your thesis when you discuss your essay's effectiveness—for example, its organization and the relevance of supporting material. And, of course, the thesis as expressed in your essay is a great help to your reader.

## ◆ PRACTICE

### Discussion

1. Read the following essay for class discussion. The student stopped writing toward the end of paragraph 4. Can you guess why? What seems to be the *thesis* of her essay? Can you give her any advice for rewriting and improving it? Center your comments on the problem of the essay's point.

> ¹ I first got interested in horses when our family went to my uncle's farm and he let me ride an old plow horse. He was an old horse and was never used for anything, and he would not go faster than a walk. But I was fascinated by his personality, if that is what you want to call it. He seemed very wise and responsive, as if he were listening to you talk to him. I used to ride him two or three times a day and talk to him and he would act as if he understood me.
>
> ² That same year I started taking riding lessons at a stable near home (there is only one in the area). Since we are not particularly well off, I had to work for my lessons. Every Saturday, I would ride my bike—along with several girl friends—to the stable and work out the horses, clean the stall, and do general handyman work. For this I would get a half-hour's lesson which consisted mainly of yells and shouts of "Donna, GET YOUR FEET TURNED IN!!!" and "You got TERRIBLE hands, Donna!"
>
> ³ My grandmother in Nebraska heard about my working in the stable and wrote me a worried letter saying that the stables were no place for a girl and that I should stay away from them except when taking lessons. She apparently remembers the stable life from her girlhood in Texas, which was probably very different from today's.
>
> ⁴ I got to ride in a few shows, and won a ribbon or two, and then I was really hooked. I wanted my own horse, but we could not afford one. The situation got worse at the stables—the instructor yelling at me and telling lies about me to my mother, who insisted that I keep riding no matter what. I wanted to ride but I hated the instructor, and my mother kept getting in the situation, until finally I didn't know what to do. So I quit for a while. . . . [end of draft]

2. Read the following brief essay by Isaac Asimov and prepare to discuss it in class. What is Asimov's *thesis*? How does he organize his essay around that thesis?

> ¹ What is intelligence, anyway? When I was in the army I received a kind of aptitude test that all soldiers took and, against a normal of 100, scored 160. No one at the base had ever seen a figure like that, and for two hours they made a big fuss over me. (It didn't mean anything. The next day I was still a buck private with KP as my highest duty.)
>
> ² All my life I've been registering scores like that, so that I have the complacent feeling that I'm highly intelligent, and I expect other people to

think so, too. Actually, though, don't such scores simply mean that I am very good at answering the type of academic questions that are considered worthy of answers by the people who make up the intelligence tests—people with intellectual bents similar to mine?

3 For instance, I had an auto-repair man once, who, on these intelligence tests, could not possibly have scored more than 80, by my estimate. I always took it for granted that I was far more intelligent than he was. Yet, when anything went wrong with my car I hastened to him with it, watched him anxiously as he explored its vitals, and listened to his pronouncements as though they were divine oracles—and he always fixed my car.

4 Well, then, suppose my auto-repair man devised questions for an intelligence test. Or suppose a carpenter did, or a farmer, or, indeed, almost anyone but an academician. By every one of those tests, I'd prove myself a moron. And I'd *be* a moron, too. In a world where I could not use my academic training and my verbal talents but had to do something intricate or hard, working with my hands, I would do poorly. My intelligence, then, is not absolute but is a function of the society I live in and of the fact that a small subsection of that society has managed to foist itself on the rest as an arbiter of such matters.

5 Consider my auto-repair man, again. He had a habit of telling me jokes whenever he saw me. One time he raised his head from under the automobile hood to say: "Doc, a deaf-and-dumb guy went into a hardware store to ask for some nails. He put two fingers together on the counter and made hammering motions with the other hand. The clerk brought him a hammer. He shook his head and pointed to the two fingers he was hammering. The clerk brought him nails. He picked out the sizes he wanted, and left. Well, doc, the next guy who came in was a blind man. He wanted scissors. How do you suppose he asked for them?"

6 Indulgently, I lifted my right hand and made scissoring motions with my first two fingers. Whereupon my auto-repair man laughed raucously and said, "Why, you dumb jerk, he used his *voice* and asked for them." Then he said, smugly, "I've been trying that on all my customers today." "Did you catch many?" I asked. "Quite a few," he said, "but I knew for sure I'd catch *you*." "Why is that?" I asked "Because you're so goddamned educated, doc, I *knew* you couldn't be very smart."

7 And I have an uneasy feeling he had something there.

—Isaac Asimov, "Intelligence"

## THE ASSIGNMENT AND THE THESIS

You write because you need to, whether the "need" is imposed from within or without. Ordinarily, in your composition class, you write in response to an instructor's assignment. So let's now turn to the problem of the typical writing assignment and consider how it can lead to a thesis.

There are, roughly, three kinds of assignments. Here are examples, ranging from the general to the specific:

1. A brief general request for written work:
   "Write a paper for next Friday."

2. A request for a type of essay or for a particular essay topic:
   a. "Write an essay convincing someone to take up your hobby."
   b. "Write an essay explaining a cause or effect."
   c. "In your essay, discuss the characterization of Willy Loman in *Death of a Salesman.*"

3. A more specific request that tends to control your response as you write:
   a. "Write a paper that supports an idea that some people ordinarily do not agree with—for example, that organized athletic programs do not foster team spirit or group loyalty in the players; that strongly religious persons can be evil; that going to college may be a serious mistake for certain young people."
   b. "If you were to call for a change in any university (or college) policy or practice, what would that change be? Write a letter to someone in authority outlining the policy or practice and stating your reasons for suggesting the change."
   c. "Some persons believe that Willy Loman is not a tragic character. Define the term *tragic character,* and argue that Willy either is or is not tragic. (You may take the position that he is partially tragic.)"

While assignments **1** and **2** give you more freedom than **3** does, they may be harder to prepare. You have to specify most of the elements of the topic yourself, and you may spend as much time finding and limiting a topic as you spend actually writing the paper. But instructors continue to use assignments like **1** and **2** because with them you can choose your own material and create your own stance. You can write essays that you might not otherwise get a chance to write with the more limited assignments.

## The Thesis Journal

Journal entries can help you to develop an appropriate thesis in response to an assignment. After Jack's instructor spent two class periods discussing these, he gave assignment **3a** above. Jack thinks about the assignment in his dorm room, wondering what he will write about, when he hears a sharp blast on a car horn. This blast is followed by a howl of locked brakes, a yell from somebody, and then the familiar crashing sound of metal meeting metal. By the time he gets his eyes focused on the street, the accident is over. The two cars are locked together there on the street, one of them at right angles to the other.

Jack watches from his window as the police come, and then he gets a glimmer of an idea for a paper. He writes in his journal:

---

Auto accidents are something that I know about. For two years I've worked as an assistant to the ambulance drivers for the Pemberton Funeral Home on weekends and during the summer. As a part of the ambulance team, I've seen thirty or forty accidents, a few of them fatal. Let me jot down a thesis or two for this assignment:

Auto accidents should be prevented.

(Objection: Of course they should be prevented; who would argue that they shouldn't be?)

There are fewer auto accidents in Tennessee than in Illinois.

(Wait: I don't really know very much about auto accidents in Tennessee.)

Maybe I'd better take my instructor's advice and make a list:

| | |
|---|---|
| autos | casket? |
| accidents | relatives worried |
| injury | cost -- expensive! |
| mothers | cost of blood - how much? |
| fathers | cost of surgery? |
| worry for them because they're hurt | doctors' fees |
| auto accidents expensive | nurses |
| new engine -- cost? | ambulance costs |
| burial | ambulance driving |

Look at all those items that have to do with the financial cost of the accident! If somebody pays money for accidents, someone earns it--doctors, nurses, hospitals, morticians, garages, mechanics. Everybody always talks about the cost of accidents but never about the profit in them.

I've found my hook! There's good money in accidents.

---

THE ASSIGNMENT AND THE THESIS ◆ 41

This is something that I know about because I had made good
money as part of the ambulance team.

Here is my thesis:  <u>Contrary to what many people think there is
a lot of money to be made from automobile accidents.</u>

Now I need to establish my authority:  I know the costs and also
the money to be made from ambulance calls, and I know from being
around Pemberton Funeral Home how much caskets and funerals cost.
Other fees--those charged by garages and hospitals--I'm not so sure
about.  I guess I'd better check on that tomorrow.

Entries for the following day:

I just called two local hospitals and two garages and obtained a
page of typical charges for typical injuries and damages, from broken
legs to smashed fenders.  I believe that I can write with reasonable
authority on the subject.  Or can I?  I'd better check out my thesis
again:

" . . . a lot of money to be made from auto accidents."
Where?  New York State?  Am I implying that auto accidents "cost" the
same everywhere?  I don't have any authority for making a judgment.

Maybe I'd better limit my thesis.  How about this?  <u>Contrary to
what many people think, there is a lot of money to be made from
auto accidents in the Phillipsburg area.</u>

Jack's essay now has a focus. In addition he feels comfortable with the
subject because he has available material, most of it taken from memory.

## *The Thesis as Answer to a Question*

Finding a workable thesis often seems to involve "thinking out loud," as Jack did, picking your way through ideas as they occur to you, selecting and discarding as you go along. Look for key words in an assignment and underline them. If other key words or hooks occur to you, put them down on scratch paper before they get away. As you think out loud, ask yourself the questions in the following list. (The word *something* stands for your subject or an important idea about it.)

—What was the effect of *something*? Its cause?
—Can I break *something* down or analyze its main parts in order to understand it better?
—Can I compare *something* to another thing?
—Can I define *something*?
—Is *something* typical for some persons and not for others?
—Is *something* good or bad, or partly good and partly bad?
—Who knows about *something*? Who would I see or what would I read to find out?
—What class or category of ideas or objects is *something* in?
—What are the facts about *something*? What things aren't known?
—Can I tell a story about *something*?
—Does *something* do any job that is necessary for a group, large or small?
—How is *something* made or created? Destroyed?
—How can one do or perform *something*?
—Can I recommend *something* to other people? Not recommend?
—Should I suggest changes in *something*?

*Note:* We discuss the development of answers to many of these questions in Part 2.

Here are two examples of how a thesis can be an answer to a question:

> Question: How can one do *something*?
> Thesis: *Anyone can put up a standard house wall if he buys good-quality, straight studs, can use a level accurately, and makes all measurements carefully.*

> Question: What is a *word processor*?
> Thesis: *A word processor is a piece of computer software that is designed to help someone design, write, and revise a document.*

# IMPROVING YOUR THESIS

As you work on your thesis, consider these suggestions for making it useful and effective:

1. *Make Your Thesis Authoritative.*

In other words, "Write about what you know"—one of the soundest pieces of advice on student writing. Even though you may not picture yourself as such, you are an authority on a variety of subjects. So write about them: your family; your friends; your hometown; the politicians, doctors, mechanics, plumbers, carpenters, or lawyers you know; the crabgrass on your front lawn; your parents' divorce; your stereo set; your friend's broken arm; your first vote; your failure to pass trigonometry; your *A* in Spanish.

But do not try to write about the United Nations, poverty in America, racial problems in our cities, Lincoln's first administration, the creation of the American Constitution, the writings of Norman Mailer, the movies of Humphrey Bogart, *unless* (1) in the past you have done considerable research on one of these subjects, and have made yourself an amateur "authority" in the field; or (2) you are willing to commit yourself to hours of research in the library or elsewhere to make yourself reasonably authoritative on the subject.

This advice is necessarily somewhat general. Check with your instructor when you have doubts about your subject and your "authority."

2. *Narrow Your Thesis.*

Because most essays are relatively short, you can't adequately support a very broad thesis in 500 words or so. Narrow your thesis to fit your essay's length by testing your tentative theses, as Jack did (see pp. 40–41). You will find certain questions helpful, especially questions beginning with *why, what,* and *who.*

| | |
|---|---|
| *Tentative thesis:* | People in my hometown are selfish. |
| *Questions:* | Why do you call them *selfish*? What do they *do*? Who are the *people* you refer to? *All* of them? |
| *Revised thesis:* | Some people in my hometown will not give to the United Fund because they do not wish to support some of the agencies that receive money from the Fund. |

| | |
|---|---|
| *Tentative thesis:* | Computers are a popular form of mass communication. |
| *Questions:* | *All* computers? What *kind* of communication do you mean? *Who* uses the computer for communication? |
| *Revised thesis:* | Among some of my friends, notes on the *Plato* computer terminals are so popular that they have replaced the telephone as the chief method of talking to one another. |

3. *Unify Your Thesis.*

In your essay, discuss one thing or group of things. You might ask yourself questions like *How many terms do I have in this thesis? Are they separate topics to be dealt with in different papers? Are some of my terms subtopics of the larger topic?*

| | |
|---|---|
| *Tentative thesis:* | A blind child is often treated badly by other children because he is different from them; consequently they are embarrassed, because they don't realize how talented a blind child can be. |
| *Questions:* | If blind children are *talented,* does that still make them *different*? Are other children embarrassed by the blind child's "differences"? |
| *Revised thesis:* | A blind child is sometimes treated badly by other children on the playground because they do not know how to deal with his "differences." |

| | |
|---|---|
| *Tentative thesis:* | Motorcycles are fun, providing fast, inexpensive, and dangerous transportation. |
| *Questions:* | Is riding a motorcycle *fun* because it is *dangerous*? Is it *dangerous* because it is *fast*? What is the relationship between *inexpensive* and *dangerous*? |
| *Revised thesis:* | Motorcycles provide inexpensive but dangerous transportation. |

The last tentative thesis would require the writer to juggle four somewhat illogically associated points about motorcycles. The improved thesis reduces these to two easily associated points by saying, in effect: the machine may not cost much but it can kill you.

4. *Specify Your Thesis.*

As you have probably guessed by now, the whole business of improving a thesis is a continuous process. When you make your thesis authoritative, and when you narrow and unify it, you are simply sharpening your essay's point. And the best single way to make that point even sharper is to avoid general words and to use specific ones instead.

You might ask questions like: Can I tie my point to a more specific word than the one I have used here? What evidence do I have? How can that evidence be translated into specific terms?

| | |
|---|---|
| *Tentative thesis:* | Sororities are getting better. |
| *Questions:* | What do I mean by "better"? If they are better, what *difference* does that make? |
| *Revised thesis:* | Because they offer better housing, better food, and better facilities for study than the dorms, sororities at this college are getting more pledges. |

| | |
|---|---|
| *Tentative thesis:* | America should have more freedom of speech. |
| *Questions:* | What do I mean by *freedom of speech? Where* in America should this happen? What do I propose to *do* in order to get more freedom of speech? |

Revised thesis: The Library Board in Paxton should have a strict procedure to follow whenever a citizen objects to one of
the books in the library's collection. (Notice the hook in
the phrase *strict procedure.*)

# ✦ PRACTICE

## Discussion

1. For class discussion read the following essay. What is its thesis? Where
is the thesis stated? Discuss its unity and specificity. In what way has the
writer "narrowed" her coverage of the topic?

### HUSSIES AND HOLES IN YOUR EARS

[1] In the old neighborhood, piercing ears of young girls was an exotic
ritual.

[2] All the neighborhood noseys would gather around in a kitchen like
eager interns as someone's shaky and half-blind grandmother would miraculously become a surgeon, eagle-eyed and steady of hand. The girl's ear-
lobes were anesthetized with an ice cube, and the largest needle in the
sewing box would be heated on the stove and dipped in alcohol for the
procedure. The patient would wear a loop of thread, then a piece of straw
from a broom before getting her first ladylike pair of earrings.

[3] But some of us were never initiated. "Only gypsies and hussies have
pierced ears," Mother maintained. A few girlfriends proved Mother right,
becoming bona fide hussies by the sixth grade, even wearing lipstick and
stockings and unloosening their braids. There were no gypsies on the block,
but Mother knew best.

[4] Away from Mother's overprotectiveness, I finally had my ears pierced
in my mid-20s. Not by anyone's grandmother, but in a sanitized doctor's
office with no spectators. I should have listened to Mother.

[5] One hole was pierced on an angle and began to stretch, nearly splitting
the earlobe in two. A fortune in pierced earrings sat idle as I went back to
clip-ons. I began to notice other casualties of ear piercing who had split lobes
and infections, even some who had gone through the grandmother method.
I pondered a malpractice suit, but too much time had passed. I consulted a
plastic surgeon, but it was too costly to have the lobe sutured and the ears
repierced.

[6] Other friends, of course, had the fashionable two and three holes in
their ears with no complications. My childhood desire never waned.

[7] I'd look for free ear-piercing offers in department stores, even stood in
line at one, but chickened out. Finally last month I relented on a lunch hour
impulse and had both ears repierced above the original holes. No grandmothers, no doctor, just your basic sales clerk.

[8] I wore the training studs for the requisite 24 days, religiously and
liberally applied the antiseptic twice a day, twirled the posts to keep the scar
tissue from mending around the holes and polished my pierced earrings.

⁹ For not listening to Mother, not once but twice, I now have an infection. But I have no regrets. Fortunately, I still have the same two ears. I have four pierced earring holes, three of which are serviceable. And above all—look, Ma, I never became a hussy.—Leanita McClain

2. Discuss and evaluate each of the following tentative theses. How can they be improved?
   a. Traffic destroys superhighways.
   b. Biking and hitchhiking through Maine are safe.
   c. The Berlin Wall was necessary to the Soviet Union.
   d. Adopting the metric system is a mistake.
   e. Working and eating in a pizza parlor is boring, hard work, and gives me indigestion, plus the boss is a jerk.
   f. The earth is getting hotter.
   g. Intercollegiate sports cost the university too much money.
   h. Nuclear power plants should be shut down.
   i. Welfare takes too much of the tax dollar.

*Writing*

1. You can learn much about writing useful theses by imitating those used in successful essays. Here are six such theses with certain key words and phrases in italics. Imitate them using your own ideas and material. For example, an imitation of **a** might be: "Unlike my sister, who went out for the swimming team because she thought swimming was a challenging sport, I tried out only because I badly needed the exercise." Are any particular writers' stances suggested by the theses?
   a. *Unlike* my uncle, *who* was a compulsive *alcoholic,* my father *drank* too much simply because he *liked* the *comradeship* of other drinkers.
   b. *Racial problems* in Penant High School *existed* for two years *before busing started.*
   c. For good *apples* in September, *spray* the *trees* with dormant oil just before the *buds* open in the spring.
   d. We *lost* eight basketball *games* that year because we didn't *practice* our basic *plays* enough.
   e. To get a natural color on fresh hardwood, use *first* a light *stain* and *then* a quick-drying standard *varnish.*
   f. Since the independents did not *campaign* in all campus areas, *they failed* to reach many students and *lost* the *election.*

2. Here are some typical assignments you may encounter early in the term. For each assignment, (a) underline the important words or phrases; (b) write a narrowed, unified, and specific thesis.
   a. Tell your reader about the most important event in your life. Do not merely relate the event; describe it and explain in detail why you

believe it is "important." (Do you need to define *important*? What might your hook be here?)

b. In the past two or three years, several things probably have happened in your hometown, or area where you have been living, that you do not approve of. Write an essay explaining one of these events—a decision by an authority, a change in local government, and so on. State specifically why you do not approve. *Hint:* Don't spend so much time in description that you are unable to be specific concerning your disapproval.

c. Write an essay about a clash of personalities that you have experienced or closely observed. What effect on friends or relations did this clash have? Explain by giving details and examples.

d. Write a paper about a person—you or someone you know—who has been successful or unsuccessful doing something. Describe the person's success, or lack of it, and explain in detail why he was (or was not) successful.

3. Write a paper, using one of the theses you developed for **2** above.

4. Review the section "The Thesis as Answer to a Question" (p. 42). Ask questions about *two* of the following topics. (Obviously, not all of the questions will be appropriate for all of the topics.) Based on your answers to the questions, develop a thesis on each topic. Be sure that your theses are reasonably authoritative, narrowed, unified, and specific.

a. seat belts in cars
b. fishing
c. intramural sports programs
d. house plants
e. movies
f. hobbies
g. video games
h. reading

Choose one of the theses and write an essay.

# SHAPING AND OUTLINING IDEAS

In this chapter, we will discuss a number of devices for planning a piece of writing. And that is what they are—plans. None of them is a fixed structure that you must follow blindly. Generally speaking, successful writers, whether amateur or professional, use whatever planning devices they need—and use them flexibly. They may go through all the steps of a *shape, support diagram,* or *outline* (all of which will be discussed in this chapter). But writers may also work forward and backward through the process, refining, changing, switching main ideas or moving them about, inserting and deleting details. A writer may often consider, or actually follow, all the steps in the essay-writing process. But no successful writer allows the process to overrule his or her good judgment concerning any part of the final essay and its plan.

For instance, if you can't make your plan fit your thesis exactly, it may be wise not to force a perfect fit. Theses and plans are *tools* for shaping materials, and sometimes materials refuse to be perfectly shaped. If you think it is necessary, try changing the thesis to fit the plan or changing both to fit each other. But don't change them so much that you distort the truths in your subject.

Sometimes you may have trouble following your plan as you write the essay. This may mean that the plan is poorly made—try inspecting it for logic and order. But this may also mean that a "logic of writing" is (legitimately) taking over. A piece of writing often seems to develop an order and a coherence all its own that are determined partly by the subject, by your supporting materials, and by the way you choose to organize it. If you like the way your paper is going, and its new direction appears to be appealing and honest, consider changing the plan to fit fresh developments. Plans are helpful and good, but they are not written on tablets of stone.

Let's see how John Jackson Chase, a successful writer of TV plays, used a plan in the form of a drawing. When he planned a new play (he worked on as many as two or three at a time), he worked in a large room at the end of which was a big blackboard. On the blackboard was this drawing in white chalk (Figure 1):

**Figure 1**

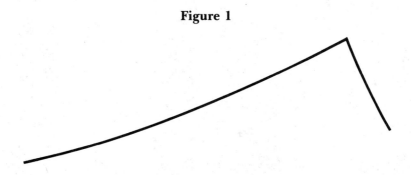

As Chase worked on his play, he scribbled on this white-chalk drawing; the scribblings were in red chalk (Figure 2). What did the drawing mean? (It looks a little like a mountain peak with one steep side.) What were the scribblings in red about? If you questioned Chase, he would gladly tell you what all this meant.

**Figure 2**

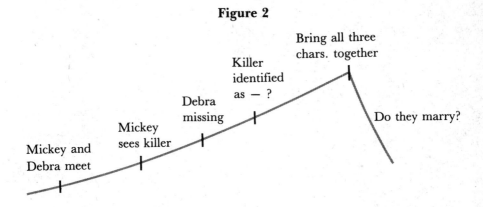

"I start every play with a *shape*," he said. "There on the blackboard in white chalk is my permanent shape for a story. Then I introduce (in red chalk) my characters at the left, give them some conflict to solve as the line moves upward to the right, and finally get to the peak of the shape with the climax of the story, where everything is brought together. The little drop-off after the climax is something almost every story has: a relaxing of tension—like somebody saying, 'They lived happily ever after.'

"Sometimes," Chase continued, "I start with the high point, the climax, and write that. Then I move backward to fill in parts of the story."

But why the blackboard with the "shape" on it?

"Oh, it reminds me to fill out the structure of the story. It gives me a feeling of where I'm going and where I've been. Besides, I'm a visual person. I like to see the skeleton of a play, the big bony pieces of it."

## GIVE YOUR PAPER A SHAPE (OF ITS OWN)

Chase's idea about the shape of a piece of writing is not new, although perhaps his application of it is. Most of us—at one time or another—have visualized a paper as starting at the top of a page and continuing downwards, the result being the rough geometry of a composition (see Figure 3).

**Figure 3**

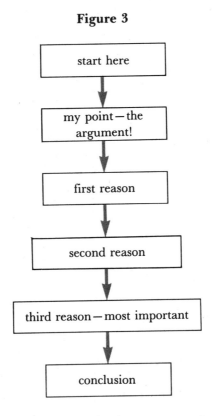

The total *shape* here is that of the classic argument, the thesis stated first, with the proofs or reasons coming after. The reasons are given in the order of importance, from least to most. The increasing size of the balloons symbolizes this order.

Indeed, the shape of a paper is a symbolic outline of your material. Using only the main ideas in your paper, you doodle a shape on a piece of scratch paper until you are satisfied that these main ideas are in the proper order and are given the proper emphasis, which is represented visually. For instance, in the argument we have been discussing you would *not* want a shape like that in Figure 4.

**Figure 4**

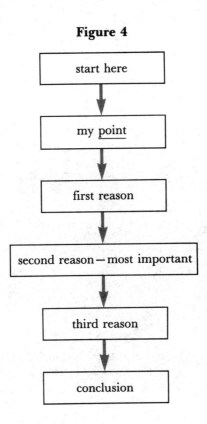

Here the third reason would just be an anticlimax. Nor would you want a shape like that in Figure 5, which shows a fat conclusion that is as long as the rest of the paper—out of proportion.

**Figure 5**

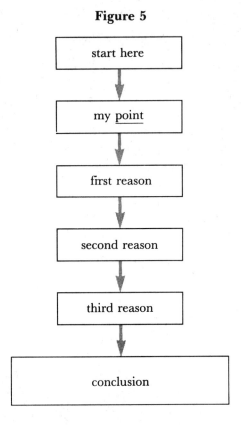

## *SHAPING A SAMPLE PAPER*

In Chapter 2, we saw several students brainstorming an audience for a paper arguing that the requirements for the film major be increased. When one student (named Arthur) planned this paper, he first started with a list of ideas that he would put in it:

—Need more courses in film major
—Students don't know much about modern techniques of acting
—Students don't know much about modern films
—Students don't know much about modern directing
—Many things are right with the major

To deal with these logically, Arthur considered several shapes that the paper might take, using sheets of paper to draw on. He finally settled on the basic shape in Figure 6—question and answer. Why? Arthur said he thought that starting with a question would intrigue his readers and make them want to read on.

**Figure 6**

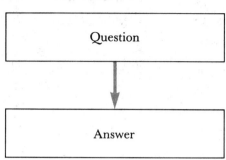

To fill in the shape of his paper, Arthur made the drawing in Figure 7. In this drawing, he tried to illustrate to himself the parts of the argument, especially in the section where he notes that the film major is already being well managed. Arthur does not want to attack the major; he only wants to make it better. The three basic subpoints he wanted to stress equally, so he makes them all the same size in the drawing.

**Figure 7**

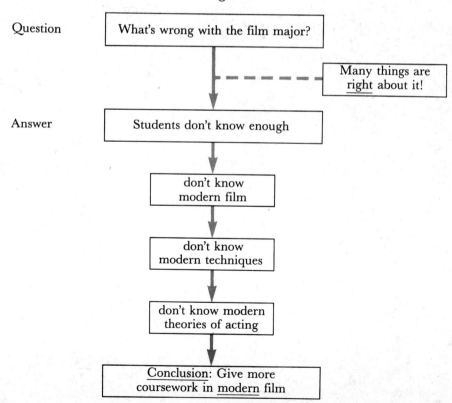

## Advantages and Disadvantages of the Paper "Shape"

The *shape* is a quick way of getting an overall pattern of your paper quickly in mind—and in your eye. It is essentially a big doodle on a large piece of scratch paper, taking only a few minutes to draw. In fact, on many subjects you can draw half a dozen shapes in a short time, each one supplying a different pattern or structure to your paper.

A disadvantage is that the shape gives only the big pieces of the pattern, and if you don't have the smaller ones already in mind you have to search for them.

# SUPPORT DIAGRAMS

The *support diagram* is another version of the planning *shape* (see pp. 50–53). Both are "visuals." But there are two basic differences between these types of planning device. First, the *shape* is linear; it represents the one-dimensional progress of your paper as it "develops" *down* the page. The support diagram works in two dimensions: up and down, and left and right. Second, the support diagram shows logical relations rather more clearly than the shape does.

Support diagrams typically connect pieces of evidence to your statement or generalization. That is, they show how examples, details, and facts *support* or explain a main point or idea in the paper. For example, see Figure 8, which illustrates how a basic support diagram can be drawn.

**Figure 8**

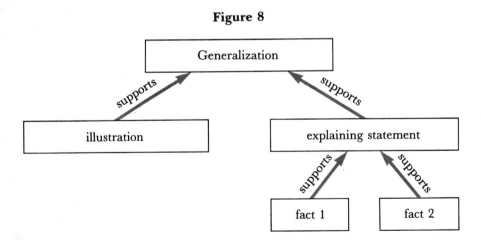

In Figure 9, we put material into the diagram.

**Figure 9**

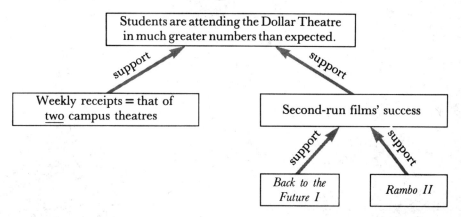

As you add more evidence and specific facts to your main point, the more detailed your support diagram becomes. Consider now the diagram in Figure 10.

**Figure 10**

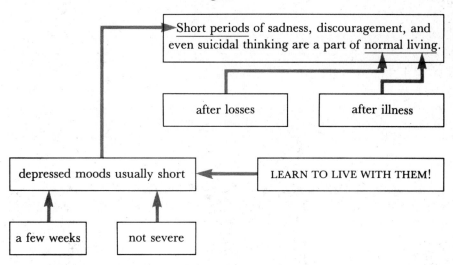

The support diagram *connects* and *explains* relationships. All of the arrows you use should tie ideas logically together, as in Figure 11 (p. 56), which is merely Figure 10 without the writing.

Following Figure 11 is the paragraph we can write from the support diagram on "periods of sadness."

**Figure 11**

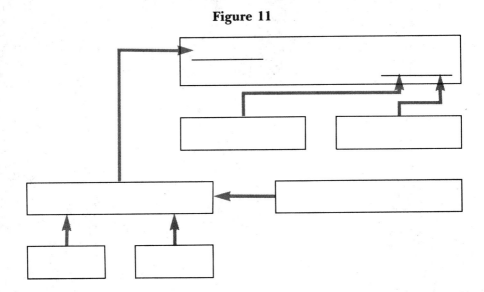

Short periods of sadness, discouragement and even suicidal thinking are a part of normal living, particularly after losses and physical illness. These depressed moods usually last a few days, perhaps a few weeks at the most. They are not severe enough to interrupt the business of everyday life. Most of us learn to live with them.—Anne H. Rosenfeld

## THE FORMAL OUTLINE

The question of whether to make a formal outline or not depends upon the needs and the requirements of the course. Even professional writers disagree about outlining. To suggest that writers are either out-liners or anti-outliners is an oversimplification. One reason is that *outline* is an ambiguous term. It can mean a few jottings on scrap paper, or a detailed piece of formal architecture covering several pages and with every roman numeral, arabic number, and upper- and lowercase letter reverently placed in its assigned niche. So the important thing to remember is that an individual has many options for showing the plan of a paper.

Some writers and teachers have found that a formal outline clearly shows how pieces of evidence (A, B, and C) support the generalizations or main points (I, II, III) of a paper. Even if a writer has used another kind of planning, it is easy to convert such a plan into a *formal outline*. Note how the *support diagram* in Figure 10 on p. 55 can be converted into a formal outline, mainly because the writer has a clear notion of how her evidence supports her main idea.

*Thesis:* Recognizing that short periods of sadness are natural, psychologists are more concerned about long periods of depression.

I. Short periods of sadness, discouragement, and even suicidal thinking are a part of normal living.
   A. They often occur after losses.
   B. They may occur after physical illness.
   C. These depressed moods usually last a few days.
      1. They may last a few weeks at most.
      2. They are not severe enough to interrupt the business of every-day life.
   D. Most of us learn to live with these short periods of depression.
II. . . . (rest of outline omitted)

## The Relationship Between "Shapes" and Outline

If a writer chooses one of the *shapes* for organizing a paper, it is possible to translate that shape into an outline. Here is how one girl, named Cathy, came up with some ideas about junk mail (p. 32), and how she translated those ideas into a shape and later into two kinds of formal outlines.

*LIST OF IDEAS ABOUT JUNK MAIL*

Every day I come home to a mail box full of mail.
Mail box won't hold it all. Stuck in door. ⟩← INTRO

Father is woodworker, so gets related catalogs. ⟩← why?

I talked to the mailman about the problem. He'd like to stop junk mail.

I go through the mail by throwing out half of it.

I don't know how we get on some lists.

Mother invited to "make a million."

Our hobbies and interests are result of our junk mail. ⟩← why?

Some junk mail elegant.

Some of it looks like there's a check inside.

I threw away an airline ticket because it looked like junk mail. ⟩← Description

Junk mail is garbage—throw it out.

L. L. Bean stopped sending me a catalog because I didn't order anything else. Only one I can remember. They all keep coming.

Some junk mail comes in plastic covers. ⟩← Description

We ordered clothes once. That was a mistake. ⟩← why?

Companies must sell their lists.

what ʋe do with it

After grouping her main ideas, Cathy could see that she had a shape for her paper.

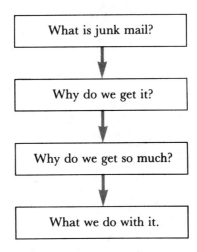

# TOPIC OUTLINE

Next, Cathy developed a thesis and a topic outline—an outline that lists topic ideas in the form of phrases or single words in the headings.

> *Thesis:* Because our family has a variety of hobbies and interests, we get a lot of junk mail that we treat like junk.

  I. Definition of *junk mail*
     A. Bulk rate postage
     B. Advertising
 II. Hobbies and interests of the family
     A. Woodworking
     B. Investing
     C. Gardening and camping
III. Lists sold by companies
     A. Farm, fleet, work clothes catalogs
     B. Financial brochures
     C. Camping, clothing, and gardening catalogs
 IV. Junk mail as *junk*
     A. Clutter
     B. Garbage

Cathy decides that the topic outline isn't adequate for her needs because she wants better control of her paragraphing. She makes a sentence outline where she can see every idea in its complete form. She has found that a formal outline is useful when she wants to organize a paragraph deductively, going from the general (topic sentence) to the specific examples and details as she eventually does in her paper on junk mail.

> *Thesis:* Because our family has a variety of hobbies and interests, we get a lot of junk mail that we treat like junk.

I. Junk mail is a particular kind of mail. *(paragraph)*
   A. Junk mail goes for "bulk rate."
   B. Junk mail consists of advertising or soliciting brochures.
II. The hobbies and interests of our family reflect the kind of junk mail we receive. *(paragraph)*
   A. My father is a woodworker, so he gets everything connected with carpentry.
   B. My mother is an investor in stocks and bonds, so she gets investment brochures.
   C. I once had a garden, so I get garden catalogs.
   D. I ordered something from L. L. Bean, so now I get sporting goods catalogs from all over.
III. The companies we order from have sold their lists of customers. *(paragraph)*
   A. My father gets farm and fleet catalogs as well as work clothes catalogs.
   B. My mother gets invitations to "make a million."
   C. I get every conceivable kind of catalog related to clothing, camping, and gardening.
IV. We treat the catalogs like junk. *(paragraph)*
   A. We seldom look at them.
   B. We throw them in the garbage.

> *Conclusion:* As a result of all our junk mail, our family has reduced the number of things that they order by mail and have taken to buying from the local stores.

## The Form of Outlines

Since Cathy has been well trained in the conventions of formal outlining, she knows that it is customary to employ numerals and letters in this order, according to the rank of ideas or to the *levels of subordination*.

I. First level (main heading)
   A. Second level
      1. Third level
      2. Third level

        a. Fourth level
        b. Fourth level
   B. Second level
II. First level (main heading)

Headings on the same level of subordination should be roughly parallel—that is, equal in importance and grammatical form. The following example violates this principle in four ways:

 I. Definition
   A. Bulk rate
   B. Junk mail is a good way for advertisers to sell their merchandise.
II. The hobbies and interests of our family reflect the kind of junk mail we receive.
   A. Father woodworker

A and B are improperly subordinated to Part I. A and B are not parallel in importance or grammar. Part II is put in sentence form, which violates the form established in Part I. (The rule is this: When for the first time you use a particular form for a heading—a full sentence, a phrase, or a single word, for example—*use the same form in subsequent entries for that level of heading.*) Furthermore, you should avoid single headings like II-A above. When you break a heading into subordinate headings, you must get at least two of these lower-level headings. Often when a single heading hangs out in space, you will find that it really belongs with the previous major heading.

## *FOUR TYPICAL QUESTIONS ABOUT OUTLINES*

1. *What type of outline should I use?*
    The answer to this depends on many factors—the length of your paper and the complexity of your material, to name only two. When preparing to write a long paper which presents a lot of material and complex issues, you might like to make a complete sentence outline that maps out every detail of your argument and its evidence. If you are going to do a short, relatively uncomplicated paper, perhaps a brief topic outline would be sufficient.
    Not the least important factor in your choice of outline is your own preference. What type of outline do you feel most comfortable with? For most assignments, which type seems to work best for you?

2. *How specific should an outline be?*
    Specific enough to do the job. It should suggest what your paper is going to do—what its thesis is and what its main supporting points

are. It should also supply some examples of evidence or detail that you will use in developing your ideas. But the outline is, as we said earlier, just a skeleton; and it can suggest only the bare bones of your completed paper.

If you have any doubts about a particular outline, show it to your instructor.

3. *What can I do if I start an outline, get a point or two down, and then can't continue?*

When this happens, you may be trying to build a house before acquiring concrete, bricks, lumber, and shingles. Before you can build a paper, you need materials for it. Here is where the *shapes* or *support diagrams* can be useful. These forms may help to show you where you need more material.

Some writers find the card system useful: Get some 3 x 5 or 4 x 6 file cards, or small pieces of stiff paper cut to size. Next, write down your thesis on a sheet of paper and place it where you can see it. Start writing your ideas down on your cards, one idea to a card. Note that—*one idea to a card*; preferably, one complete sentence to a card. The point is to separate your ideas so that you can later classify and organize them.

4. *I know I shouldn't do it, but I always make an outline after I write the paper. How can I train myself to make one before writing?*

Writers often check their organization *after* they have written a paper. It is usually a good practice, however, to plan before you write. Consider your outline as a figurative road map—refer to it before you start on your trip so that you won't end up at the seashore when you wanted to go to the mountains.

## How a Thesis Suggests an Outline

The phrasing of the thesis often suggests a pattern in the outline. A typical thesis:

I

Since St. James Catholic Church has recently been remodeled, it is a

II                                        III

more pleasant place to worship, and thus may draw members from other churches in the area.

In creating your stance, you direct your ideas to someone who is not directly familiar with the Catholic churches in your area. After considering the phrasing of the thesis, you can construct an outline like this:

  I. Description of the remodeling
 II. Description of the effect of the remodeling
III. Why this may bring new members to the church

# THE HOOK AND THE OUTLINE

As you recall, we recommended the hook as a useful device in finding ideas (see pp. 11–12). Like the thesis and the outline, hooks are often valuable throughout the writing process. They provide control, a simple reminder of where you want to go and how effectively you are getting there. Here's an example of their value as related to the outline.

A student wrote a paper that, in its first draft, did not satisfy her. Something was wrong with the fit between the material and her organization. She thought of throwing the paper away, but then decided to make one last attempt to salvage the large amount of work she had put into it. So she wrote her title, hooks, and paragraph topic sentences on an "outline page":

| | |
|---|---|
| *Title:* | Power to Both Parents |
| *Hooks:* | *power, both parents* |
| *Topic sentences:* | 1. Introduction (thesis): Neither the husband nor the wife should be the dominant figure in the family. |
| | 2. Both the husband and wife should share major financial decisions. |
| | 3. Both parents are responsible for the discipline of the children, and they should share this responsibility equally. |
| | 4. Both should share in the maintenance of the house. |
| | 5. The children also have a responsibility to the family unit. |
| *Conclusion:* | 6. Cooperation is important between parents if a family is to be successfully maintained. |

After inspecting this "outline page," the student saw her own problem immediately. Paragraph 5 was hooked to an idea outside her topic, so she cut it.

# HOW TO CHECK AN OUTLINE

If you choose to write from an outline, the following suggestions may be helpful to you.

1. See that all the *parts* of the outline are there—thesis, main headings, and subordinate headings.

2. Use the proper outline *form* (see pp. 59–60). Make particularly sure that your headings are reasonably parallel. There are minor exceptions to this rule. Sometimes you can't quite get your headings parallel; the idiom of the language won't allow it. But you should get as close to complete parallelism as you can.

3. Make your outline reasonably *specific,* particularly in your thesis and the main headings (I, II, III, etc.).

4. Check the outline for *logic*. Do all the parts fit together? Does every supporting point firmly fit your thesis? If necessary, try the subject-predicate test. To make the test, write the major parts of your outline in full-sentence form, using subject-predicate patterns:

I   MY CAR MECHANIC *was very thorough.*
   A.  HE *checked the distributor twice.*
   B.  HE *cleaned the carburetor, even though it did not appear to need cleaning.*
II.  But THE MANAGER *did not appreciate the mechanic's work.*
   A.  THE MANAGER *said that the mechanic spent too much time on routine jobs.*
   B.  HE *refused to give the mechanic overtime to complete important repairs.*

If your outline is logical, and all its parts fit together, you can draw connecting arrows (as shown above) from SUBJECT to SUBJECT and from *predicate* to *predicate*. You may also develop a *support diagram* of your ideas to check them for logic (see pp. 54–56).

5. Check the outline for the proper *order*—that is, for a sensible sequence or organization of ideas. Check each level separately—first I, II, III, etc.; and then A, B, C, etc.; and so on. Except for the general rule that important ideas are often placed last, there is no special rule about order. The arrangement of your points should make sense and should not be incongruous. The order of points below, for example, would not be very sensible:

  I. The manager did not appreciate the mechanic's work.
  II. The mechanic was very thorough.

This order would force you to describe the manager's attitude toward the mechanic's work before you had described that work. It's hard to write a paper backwards.

## ◆ *PRACTICE*

### *Writing*

1. We borrowed the outline from an essay on moving furniture and scrambled its main and subordinate points. We also took the thesis and combined it into the list of points. Copy each item from the list below onto a separate card. You may rewrite for the sake of clarity or consistency. Identify the thesis. Arrange the cards into a logical order. Draw a shape that fits the material. Make a sentence outline.

A mover's workday can vary from 10 to 18 hours.

A mover has to work in temperatures that vary greatly.

Some days it is 95 degrees with 95% humidity.

Going in and out of air conditioning is hard on the body.

Moving furniture demands speed because movers must keep to a schedule.

A mover is expected to lift at least 100 pounds alone.

When customers live in second- or third-floor apartments, moving furniture is difficult.

Sometimes a crew moves 2 or 3 households in a day.

Apartment buildings often have narrow stairs and landings.

Heavy furniture and appliances sometimes must be lifted over the head to get upstairs or downstairs.

Some furniture has sharp edges which cut into the hands.

Moving furniture, particularly on stairways, demands agility and strength.

A mover must hold onto the furniture to prevent accidents.

The boss-driver, not the furniture mover, sets the pace.

The mover has to please the driver, customer, and management.

Moving furniture in the summer requires stamina to work long hours in hot weather.

2. Outline the following student-written paper. Pick out the thesis, and write out the main and subordinate points in outline form. What kind of an outline—topic, sentence, or mixed—would be most satisfactory for a paper of this length? What kind of a *shape* would you develop at the planning stage of this paper?

[1] I am writing this in reference to some letters that I have sent to you which were never answered. These letters concerned the possibility of my working full-time at your restaurant during my month-long vacation from college. The fact that you didn't answer any of my many inquiries regarding employment shows much inconsideration in your attitude toward me.

[2] When I left my job at your restaurant at the end of August, you promised me a job any time that I would be home from school—Labor Day, Thanksgiving vacation, weekends, etc. I was also told that the Christmas season is one of the busiest times of the year at the restaurant. Many people travel by car during this period, and the restaurant is located near the intersection of several main interstate roads. More workers are needed if the restaurant is to be smoothly and efficiently run. Why didn't you keep your promise to me?

[3] During the time that I worked for you, I worked hard—I did everything that I was told to do, and I did it quickly and efficiently. Besides keeping fifty tables in the cafeteria dining room cleaned off and ready for the customers, I was expected to unload dirty dishes from a cart and stack them on the dishwasher's counter. I was also told to vacuum the dining room carpet every day, clean and dust the booths and furniture, and fill condiment containers on every table. I was expected to do all of this alone, even when busloads of people would stop at the restaurant. I managed to

always get all of my work done on time, and you complimented me frequently on the good job I had done.

⁴ When you had some other job for me to do, I always did it willingly. Several times I did dishes when other workers had too many other things to do or if they didn't come to work. Also, during the Fourth of July holiday period, I worked on the foodline serving customers. Several times, also, I gave up my day off to go in and work for other bus girls who got sick. I was never paid any extra wages for the extra jobs I did.

⁵ I am sure that you were satisfied with my work. I realize that I didn't have any experience working in a restaurant when you hired me, but you did give me a raise after I had only worked three days. As I said before, you complimented me often on the job I had done. The customers must have been satisfied with the appearance of the dining room, because many people left tips for me, which is not a common practice in a cafeteria-style restaurant.

⁶ I feel that I treated you fairly as my boss. I was never late to work, and I never stopped working early. I took my breaks only when you told me that I could, and I never took any "extra" breaks when a manager wasn't around (like many of the other workers did). Busing tables isn't a very interesting job, but I never complained. I worked every day that I was scheduled to, and never asked for any extra days off.

⁷ I hope that you realize, after reading this, how inconsiderate you were by not answering my inquiries. I treated you with fairness and respect, but in this case, you didn't treat me in the same way. If I had been lazy and done a sloppy job while I worked for you, I probably would have expected my letters to be ignored. Because I waited weeks for a reply from you, I was unable to find any other type of work over vacation. I hope that in the future you will be more considerate and fair to the college students who work for you.

*CHAPTER 5*

# THE PARAGRAPH—
# THE BUILDING BLOCK
# OF THE ESSAY

## THE PROMISE PATTERN

There are many ways to organize a piece of writing. The most frequently used—and for many purposes, probably the best—employs what we call the *promise pattern*. You "promise" your readers at the beginning of your paper that you will tell them certain things, and as you write you fulfill your promise. The promise pattern is most easily seen in a typical paragraph. (This kind of paragraph is often called *deductive* because it begins with a general statement supported by particular details and examples.)

Near the beginning of the following paragraph about surviving in the desert, the author makes a promise (note italics) to his reader:

> These few examples make one thing clear: for anyone who has to survive in the desert, the heat of the day, both cause-and-effect of the lack of water, is the chief danger. *Temperatures reach an amazing height.* In Baghdad the thermometer in the hot summer months often climbs to 150°F., occasionally even to 180° and over (in the sun). In the Sahara near Azizia (Libya) temperatures of 134° in the shade have been recorded, and in July 1913 that was also the temperature in the Great Salt Lake Desert (also in the shade). But if the thermometer is put in the sand there at noon during the summer, the mercury goes up to 176°. On the side of Highway 91, which goes through the Mohave Desert, it has sometimes been 140° in the shade at noon; in the evenings the thermometer sinks to a "low" of 90°. In Libya, Montgomery's and Rommel's soldiers sometimes fried eggs on the armor plate of their tanks.
> —Cord-Christian Troebst, *The Art of Survival*

In the rest of the paragraph after the italicized sentence, Troebst keeps his promise—to discuss and illustrate amazingly high desert temperatures.

Much of what we say here concerning the organization of paragraphs applies generally to complete papers. For example:

A paper's promise = the paper's *thesis*
A paragraph promise = the paragraph's *topic idea*

The *topic idea* of a paragraph is its main, controlling statement, which is often expressed in a *topic sentence*. The topic idea of Troebst's paragraph is expressed in the italicized topic sentence, *Temperatures reach an amazing height*. Some paragraphs need two or three sentences to express their topic ideas (or promises), while a few paragraphs have no topic ideas at all. A paragraph that contains no topic ideas may fulfill the promise made in a preceding paragraph, or it may provide a transition between paragraphs.

It is important to understand that when you make a promise to your readers you set up an expectation. Suppose you make this statement near the beginning of an essay: *The problem of recreation at Windsor College is not as great as the administration believes.* Immediately your readers expect you to show them in some detail why the problem is not as great as some might think. If you wander off into another subject (like academic achievement, for instance), or do not give details concerning your thesis/promise, you will fail to satisfy the expectations of the readers. They will then say you haven't done your job of communication—and they will be right.

Idealized, the promise pattern for a typical paper looks like this:

**Promise Pattern**

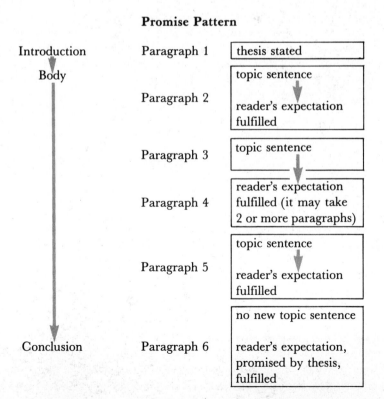

## Developing Paragraphs That Support Your Paper's Promise

A paragraph is a collection of sentences that helps you support your thesis. Itself a small "essay," a paragraph should be clearly written and specific; and it should not wander or make irrelevant remarks. Each paragraph should be related in some way to the thesis or the paper's "promise." Since a paragraph is usually part of a larger piece of writing (essay, research paper, report, etc.), use your *shape, plan,* or *outline* to help you construct paragraphs that support the thesis.

*Keep your topic sentence in mind.* After you have decided on your paragraph topic sentence, jot down all the facts and details that you have previously collected by brainstorming, freewriting, or thinking about your subject. Arrange these ideas in a logical form and sequence, with your details and *specific* examples fulfilling the paragraph promise.

Consider this ex-smoker's support of his topic sentence:

| | |
|---|---|
| *Topic sentence (promise)* | *My body was sicker than I thought it could be.* The joints in my arms and shoulders and the muscles in my chest and my calves hurt so badly the first night I hid in the dark and cried. The |
| *Joints, muscles, and calves hurt* *General aching* | pain lasted only one day, but for at least a week I was always aching somewhere. My mouth, nose, throat, stomach, and each tooth were deprived of smoke and nicotine, and their reactions lasted much longer. I kept arching my mouth wide |
| *Results of deprivation in mouth, throat, nose* | open as if adjusting cheap store-bought teeth. My throat was sore as if I had smoked too much, perhaps from inhaling too hard on an absent cigarette. I blew my nose needlessly. It is staggering how many parts of me—phalange, organ, membrane, and hair—wanted a smoke, each in its own sore way. |
| *Nausea* | For two full weeks I was nauseated. Peanuts and Irish whiskey are as good a way as I found to calm this sick desire of the body for tobacco. The cure, however, is expensive. |

—Budd Whitebook, "Confessions of an Ex-Smoker"

*Get to the point.* Don't waste time or words in stating your topic sentence. Here is a paragraph where the beginning sentences are so vague the paragraph never gets going. The writer can't fulfill a promise because he hasn't made one.

The first step involves part of the golf club head. The club head has removable parts, some of which are metal. You must consider these parts when deciding how to repair the club.

Specify the beginning of this paragraph and get to the point quicker:

Your first step in repairing the club head is to remove the metal plate held on by Phillips screws.

This solid, specific paragraph beginning gives your reader a clear promise which you can fulfill easily without wasting words. (Observe, by the way, that establishing a writer's stance can help you write clearer paragraph beginnings.)

*Avoid fragmentary paragraphs.* A fragmentary paragraph does not develop its topic or fulfill its promise. A series of fragmentary paragraphs jumps from idea to idea in a jerky and unconvincing fashion.

[1] My freshman rhetoric class is similar in some ways to my senior English class in high school, but it is also very different.

[2] In my English class we usually had daily homework assignments that were discussed during the class period. If we were studying grammar, the assignments were to correct grammatical errors in the text. If we were studying literature, we were supposed to read the material and understand its ideas.

[3] In rhetoric class, we do basically the same things, except that in the readings we are assigned, we look much deeper into the purpose of the author.

[4] In my English class . . .

Fragmentary paragraphs are often the result of a weak stance. In this case, the writer has no clear idea of his role or audience, and so needs to revise his stance.

*Keep your thoughts related.* Don't allow any paragraph to be a collection of unrelated statements that looks like freewriting or brainstorming. Notice that the following paragraph contains at least six paragraph promises, none of them properly supported.

Paul Schrader's remake of the *Cat People* (1942) has come to the screen as a chilling horror film. The story revolves around a young woman named Irene who believes that making love will cause her to change into a leopard. Irene switches back and forth between cat and human. The actors—Nastassia Kinsky, Malcolm McDowell, and Annette O'Toole—are caught up in this dilemma with anthropological overtones. Nastassia Kinsky, a Russian, is well-known for the Avedon photograph of her with a snake. She is considered one of the most beautiful women in film today. Malcolm McDowell, playing her incestuous brother, is British and married to Mary Steenbergen, who played Marjorie Kinnan Rawlings in *Crosscreek*. In fact, McDowell played the famous editor Maxwell Perkins in the same film.

*Avoid irrelevancies in your paragraphs.* As with the fragmentary paragraph, the problem of irrelevancies in a paragraph is often the result of a vague *stance.* Notice how the italicized sentence does not fit the development of this paragraph, probably because it does not seem to be written for any particular reader:

We need a better working atmosphere at Restik Tool Company. The workers must feel that they are a working team instead of just individuals. If the men felt they were part of a team, they would not misuse the special machine tools, which now need to be resharpened twice as often as they used to be. *Management's attitude toward the union could be improved too.* The team effort is also being damaged by introduction of new products before their bugs have been worked out. Just when the men are getting used to one routine, a new one is installed, and their carefully created team effort is seriously damaged.

## Try Different Organizational Patterns

Experiment with variations on the promise pattern. Read this student's paper in which she uses *time* and *space* as a means of organizing her paragraphs.

### A TRIAL

**Introduction**
*(promise)*

1 About two years ago, my brother was charged with armed robbery, and I attended all the sessions of the trial. Three days stand out in my memory as being the most difficult of my life—the first day, the day the jury brought in the verdict, and the day my brother was sentenced.

*Space and Time*

2 The first day I became acquainted with the unfamiliar surroundings of the courtroom. When our family entered, it was full of spectators sitting in rows at the back of the court. We sat on two benches near the front. My brother and his lawyer sat on the left side of the room, facing the judge. The prosecuting attorney sat at the right front. The jury sat in a box along the wall on my right. As I sat there, I could feel all the eyes in the courtroom moving back and forth along the row where we were sitting. Whenever I glanced up I saw people smiling at us, but I knew what they thought. If someone laughed, I felt ashamed, and when someone whispered, I was offended.

*Time*

3 On that first day, a young man told the jury that he recognized my brother. He pointed to him and said, "That's the man. That's him!" The girls who worked at the place he supposedly robbed were the next witnesses, and they said they were unsure of his identity. That first day I had to get used to the humiliation of the prosecuting attorney and the witnesses talking about my brother and the robbery.

*Time*

4 The day the jury returned and announced the verdict of guilty, I felt a lump in my throat. I did not want to cry in front of all those people. Instead, I cried inside. I could see a tear on my father's face, and that made my agony worse. My mother was shaking her head and tears trickled down her cheeks.

5 A few days later, my brother was sentenced to a term in the state penitentiary. This time I could not hold back the tears. It seemed that the pool of tears I had cried inside were now rushing up at once. They kept flowing. I tried to wipe

them away with my hands, but I couldn't. Crying uncontrolla-
bly, I rushed past the people sitting behind us to the restroom
to clean my face, but all I could find were rough paper towels
that wouldn't absorb the tears. I stayed in the restroom, crying,
until they took my brother, handcuffed, downstairs to the jail.

Use the *suspense paragraph*—a class of paragraph that writers organize
differently from the promise pattern. We call them *suspense paragraphs*
because the writer does not put the topic idea near the beginning, but
places it later, near the middle or even the end. This technique allows the
writer to concentrate on details and keep the reader in suspense as to what
they add up to. The point is held back in order to make the paragraph
more dramatic, interesting, or emphatic. This kind of paragraph is often
called *inductive,* because it develops from the particular to the general. (It is
the reverse of the promise paragraph.) Here is an example.

*Details and*
*observations*

My generation of actors were trained to entice our prey. We
kept an eye open, a claw sharpened, even when we professed
to slumber. However deep the tragedy or shallow the farce, we
never forgot to face front. Nowadays, the relation between
player and public tends to be more sophisticated. Together
they share a mutual experience of pain and sorrow. Sometimes
the actor seems able to dispense with his audience—to no
longer need them. He may choose or chance to perfect his
performance on a wet afternoon in Shrewsbury, with hardly
anyone watching, and thereafter the repetition for him may
stale. For me this never happens. I never perfect a performance, though obviously I am sometimes better or worse, but I
have learned that without a perfect audience, my struggle to
the summit is impossible. I am aware as the curtain rises of the
texture of the house. Some nights they will appear eager and
willing; on others, listless and reluctant to follow the play.
Once or twice during the evening they will change course,
become willing and cooperative or grow sullen and bored.
Suddenly the laughter is stilled, the coughing commences. Is it

*Topic idea (point)*

our fault or theirs? I have long ceased to wonder. An audience
is like the sea, ever changing, never to be taken for granted.
—Robert Morley, "The Play's Still the Thing"

## Use the Strategies of Development

In Part 2 (the *Reader*) we provide models of other organizational
patterns available for paragraph development: *description, narration, process,
cause and effect, classification, illustration, definition, comparison-contrast,* and
*analogy.* As you study these rhetorical patterns, use them for organizing
your paragraphs.

## ◆ *PRACTICE*

### *Writing*

1. Assume that you must get rid of every appliance in your home in order to save electricity. Using *time* organization, write a paragraph in which you describe your decision about which appliances must go first—down to the very last one.

2. Write a paragraph, organized by *space,* on:
   a. The stage as it appeared to you the first time you were in a play.
   b. The college registration procedure the first time you registered.
   c. Your first visit to your dormitory room or apartment.
   d. Your mouth after your dentist applied braces.
   e. Your car after it was wrecked.
   f. Your _____ before/during/after _____.

3. Write a *suspense* (inductively organized) paragraph on one of the following topics:
   a. A description of a problem, with your solution at the end.
   b. A series of details reporting an event in college life, with a generalizing explanation at the end.
   c. A series of statements or descriptions building up to a prediction.

4. Do a complete rewrite of an old paper, concentrating on paragraph organization.

## USING PARAGRAPHS TO LEAD YOUR READER BY THE HAND

It is likely that you know more about your subject than your readers do. Much of your material may be unfamiliar to them. A capable writer is often much like a professional guide in a jungle who leads his group of travelers toward an objective by avoiding wild animals, pitfalls, and quicksand traps. It is easier to lose a reader on the page than a fellow-traveler in a jungle. Here are a few suggestions that can help you become a more experienced guide through such dangers using particular paragraph organization.

### *Start with a Simple or Familiar Idea*

If your subject warrants such treatment, you can plan the paper to *lead* the readers from a simple (or familiar) idea to a more complex (or unfamiliar) one. Be sure that they understand each idea before the next is introduced. In the following example, the writer uses this strategy.

Familiar detail:
beach ball

[1] To help us get a better picture of this solar system let us imagine a model of it reduced some five billion times. In this model, the sun is a beach ball about twelve inches across. Now, how far away would you imagine the planets to be from the sun on this scale? . . .

Familiar details:
dust specks
and pinhead

[2] Mercury, the closest planet to the sun and as small as a speck of dust in this scale, would be forty-two feet away. Venus, the second speck, about twice as big as Mercury, would be seventy-eight feet away. Earth, about the size of a pinhead next to the twelve-inch beach-ball sun, would be one hundred eight feet away; Mars, fifty-four yards; Jupiter, one hundred eighty yards; Saturn, three hundred forty yards; Neptune, one thousand eighty yards; and more than a mile away, tiny Pluto would move along its slow orbital path around the sun.

Application of
familiar detail to
scale of solar system

[3] Beyond this model of the solar system, the nearest star, on this same beach-ball scale, would be four thousand miles away. And farther still, the nearest galaxy would be almost four million miles out.

—John Rublowsky, *Life and Death of the Sun*

In this series of paragraphs, Rublowsky uses the promise pattern to give his readers a relevant familiar detail (the beach ball) and works from it in order to lead us to a partial understanding of the vast distances in the solar system. His three paragraphs work as a unit in this instance.

## Use a Graded Order of Ideas

In a piece of writing you may deal with ideas or actions that vary in interest, importance, usefulness, practicality, or value. For example, there are five ways to leave our college town when vacation starts and one could "grade" them according to:

—How expensive they are
—How fast they are
—How dangerous they are
—How practical they are
—How interesting they are
—How reliable they are

Here is an example of a student's graded order using the organizing principle of *reliability* in a paragraph:

For you new students who have not yet fought the battle of the student exodus, let me suggest the best way to get out of town before Christmas. Hitchhiking is illegal and dangerous—not very reliable. Planes are fast, but they don't go to enough hometowns, and airports get snowed in this time of year. Somewhat more reliable is the train, but the locals recently have had a nasty habit of running six or seven hours late. A car is better than the train, if you have one or know someone who does—and he happens to be going your way. The most reliable transportation for the average student is the bus. Buses aren't crowded and they are inexpensive. Also they are surprisingly fast, since if you plan ahead you can get an express bus that does not stop at small towns.

It is customary when employing any graded order to go from the "least" to the "most"—for example, from the *least reliable* to the *most reliable,* as in the paragraph above. You should follow this pattern partly because you want to get the less important ideas out of the way quickly so that you can get on with the more important ones. Also, you build up interest if you leave your best point until last. If you give readers your best idea first they may quit reading in the middle of your paper.

Here is another example of graded order:

*Lowest class of the poor*

The *idea* of poverty is simple enough—it means that one does not have very much money. Beyond this simplicity, poverty in our real American world is surprisingly complex. It is the worst poverty we continually talk about in Congress and the media, the grinding poverty of the ghetto where at the bottom of the life-chain of the poor we find our standard example: the single illiterate parent with hungry children who don't attend school. They all live (on welfare) in a wretched household where there is no food, and drug use leaches away money, life, and hope.

*Middle class of the poor*

But let's look at two other examples of the poor in the same ghetto, indeed in the same apartment building. On the fourth floor of the building lives a two-parent family with three children. Nobody is on drugs, and the children go to school. The mother works as a maid, and the husband is often sick; the children barely get enough to eat. What they do eat is bad for teeth and growing bones. But here in this second example there is some decent life, and perhaps even a little hope.

*Highest class of the poor*

Now consider another step up in the life chain of the poor. In this same building lives Mrs. X, a widow, aged 70. She is fairly healthy, eats pretty well, has a working television that she watches all day long. She lives on social security and a small pension. True, she is afraid to go out, and has been mugged two times in the past four years. (She has learned never to carry money or valuables in a purse.) But she is not as bad off—as "poor"—as my first two examples.

All three of these examples have one thing in common: they have almost the same amount of money coming in every month. But as examples of the wretchedness of poverty, they are significantly different, representing three classes of the ghetto poor: low-, middle- and upper-class. The seventy-year-old widow actually has more creature comforts than millionaire Queen Victoria of the nineteenth century. And, paradoxically, since she lives in perfect anonymity, the widow is usually safer than was Queen Victoria, who lived permanently in the public eye. The queen was shot at several times and once smashed on the head with a heavy cane.—Lewis Hornick

## Use Signposts

*Use Single-Word or Phrase Transitions.* Transitions point forward and backward. They are the reader's signposts; without them he or she might easily get lost. The simplest and most obvious transitions are those that count in order: "This is my *first* idea. . . . Now for the *second* idea. . . . *Third,* I think . . ." Less obvious are those transitions that do not so much lead readers by the hand as smooth their way: "*It is certain* that the reactor could not have been shut down so easily if . . . *Nevertheless,* the men in the black suits were blowing up the bridge. . . . *Moreover,* the two physicists could not agree on what to do."

Here are some typical transitional words and phrases:

—To explain or introduce ideas: *for instance, for example, such as, specifically, in particular, to illustrate, thus*
—To count or separate ideas: *first, second, third* (but not *firstly, secondly, thirdly*), *moreover, in addition, another, furthermore, also, again, finally*
—To compare ideas: *likewise, similarly, in the same way*
—To contrast or qualify ideas: *however, on the other hand, on the contrary, but*
—To show cause or effect: *as a result, consequently, therefore, thus*

Such a listing could continue indefinitely, for under special circumstances hundreds of words and phrases that are not ordinarily thought of as being transitional (like pronouns and certain key words) can be used to link words, ideas, sentences, or paragraphs.

*Use Transitional Paragraphs.* The transitional paragraph, which usually acts as a bridge between two other paragraphs, is often found in a fairly long piece of writing. As the short italicized paragraph below illustrates, it can prepare the reader for a plunge into a new topic.

There was, however, a darker and more sinister side to the Irish character. They are, said a land agent on the eve of the famine, "a very desperate people, with all this degree of courtesy, hospitality, and cleverness amongst them."

*To understand the Irish of the nineteenth century and their blend of courage and evasiveness, tenacity and inertia, loyalty and double-dealing, it is necessary to go back to the Penal Laws.*

The Penal Laws, dating from 1695, and not repealed in their entirety until Catholic emancipation in 1829, aimed at the destruction of Catholicism in Ireland by a series of ferocious enactments. . . .

—Cecil Woodham-Smith, *The Great Hunger: Ireland, 1845–1849*

## Use "Creative Repetition"

Repetition, we are told, is an evil in writing; and it seems that we are told this practically from the time we begin to write. Yet the skillful writer instinctively recognizes that carefully repeating certain key words and phrases can help tie ideas together. The mathematician Norbert Wiener begins his discussion of Brownian motion in this way: "To understand the Brownian motion, let us imagine a *push-ball* in a field in which a *crowd* is milling around. Various people in the *crowd* will run into the *push-ball* and will move it about. Some will *push* in one direction and some in another."

To use repetition creatively, you repeat certain words or phrases in order to keep the reader's mind firmly on the subject. Sometimes you change the grammatical form slightly in order to prevent the repetition from becoming a bore. Here is how one writer employs creative repetition in examining the positive side of aging.

### *GROWING* OLD: AGING *IS A POSITIVE THING*

[1] My granddaughter said to me the other day, "Gram, don't you just hate growing *old*?" My answer—and it surprised even me a little—was No, I love growing *old*. I like the process; I like the reality; I enjoy *aging*. Now before you decide to back up the funny truck and have me hauled away, consider what is good about *age* setting in.

[2] First, everybody else I know in my own circle is in the same boat. *Age* hits all of us. It gives us something to talk about, to be a part of. For example, my right knee won't let me jog anymore, so I swim three times a week. Janice's back is sore enough that she is unable to tend her garden as she used to. So she merely moved her garden inside the house, or at least that part which could be moved, and hung plants at eye level. When we two *aged* ladies get together we can babble happily together about plants and knee joints. Much more entertaining than gossiping about the young widow down the street.

[3] Second, like most of my friends, I have *aged* right past my problems, whether they are of this earth or otherwise. I woke up one morning to discover that I had only one pay slip left in my mortgage book. With the next payment, the house was paid for! Looking back, it seems I didn't do anything, really, to own this 35-year-*old* split-level dream—just got *older* every year until the place paid itself off. My *age-old* debt disappeared one day, rather like my tendency to have serious headaches which, by my 70th birthday, had apparently decided to go torment somebody else.

[4] But the best thing about growing *old,* to me at least, is that I don't have to worry any more—about so many things. About what my fellow workers think about me (I am retired). About who should replace the failing minister down at church (is it really important? the sermons will still be ferociously dull). About whether my children are going to make it in life (it's their problem now).

[5] What being *elderly* has done for me is to create space for my own happiness. I have become as confidently unimpressed about this tired world's problems as a petrified dinosaur's egg. Maybe that's what is implied in the biblical three score and ten: when you reach it, you have calmly become one with the *ages*.—Elsa Sterbi

# INTRODUCTIONS AND CONCLUSIONS

An effective introduction ordinarily does two things: (1) it catches the readers' interest and makes them want to read on; (2) it tells them what the essay is about, perhaps by stating the thesis or suggesting the main points.

An effective conclusion rounds off the paper. As you will see in the following examples, a conclusion often "matches" its introduction by referring to or restating the writer's early material. If the rest of the paper has been planned carefully, conclusions often seem to write themselves.

Here is an example of an effective introduction and conclusion.

*Introduction*

Very few people would sit at the TV for hours to watch a cargo of potatoes take off from planet earth in a spaceship. Yet a single potato orbiting the sun could hold infinitely greater significance for the future of humanity than would the landing of a man on the moon. For a man on the moon can tell us nothing new about injecting happiness into life on earth. *But a* *Thesis* *potato in solar orbit might lead to the secret of how all growth—hence life itself—is regulated.*

*Conclusion*

*References to* The last of the comments above concern Professor Brown's *material in the* experiments principally. They convey some sense of the values *article* inherent in orbiting a potato around the sun. NASA has not yet set a date for this expedition, but a "Spudnik" has been *Allusion to thesis* designed and if the conventional scientific opposition to innovation can be overcome, the chosen potato may take off next year.—John Lear, "The Orbiting Potato"

There are as many ways to write introductions and conclusions as ways to write papers. A short, blunt beginning may make an effective promise: "The amateur productions in the University Playhouse are poorly directed this year." One-sentence conclusions are occasionally worth trying, although you should be wary of using conclusions that are too brief, for they may leave the reader with a feeling of having been let down.

Here are some ideas for writing introductions. You might start with:

—An apt quotation
—A literary allusion
—A story or an incident relating to your subject
—A statement that shows how interesting your subject is
—A question that limits your subject; the answer to the question is your paper
—A statement of a problem that readers should know about
—A simple statement of thesis that limits your subject
—A definition of an important word or phrase relating to your subject
—The historical background of your subject (be brief)

—A statement that popular ideas about your subject are wrong and that you intend to refute them in a specific way
—A statement that your subject needs new examination; your paper is the examination
—Pertinent facts about your subject
—Combinations of some of these methods

For a conclusion, you might end your paper with:

—An allusion to the hook of your introduction
—A reference to the question, definition, statement of thesis, historical background, etc., that you started the paper with
—A restatement of your thesis
—A brief answer to the question you raised in the introduction
—A brief statement of the solution to the problem you raised in your introduction
—A new question that relates to your paper, a question that gives the reader something to think about (but be careful not to introduce an undeveloped idea)
—A summary of the main points in your paper (this is often useful if materials are complex, but beware—a summary can be dull and redundant)
—A punchy, single sentence—don't punch too hard
—A new story or incident that relates to your subject

Avoid these errors in writing introductions:

—Writing a vague or ambiguous introduction, leaving the thesis of the paper unclear
—Failing to define terms that the reader is not familiar with; terms should be defined if you are using them in a special sense
—Writing an introduction that is too long; for most short papers, it is a mistake to write more than a one-paragraph (or, at most, a two-paragraph) introduction

And these errors in writing conclusions:

—Failing to fill out a conclusion, leaving the reader hanging
—Adding irrelevant or unnecessary details
—Adding an undeveloped idea; a conclusion is not the place to develop or introduce ideas

## ✦ PRACTICE

### Discussion

For class discussion, review suggestions for writing introductions and conclusions. Then read the pairings below and evaluate how well they fulfill the requirements for introductions and conclusions.

## 1. Introduction

Many geologic features of the Midwest define the terrain of that area and indicate to scientists that glaciers once covered this portion of the continent. The effect of glacial activity is evident throughout the Midwest—in moraines, eskers, kettles, and erratics. If a traveller knows about these features and can identify them, driving through the flat agricultural area known as the "bread basket of the world" can be more meaningful and less dull.

## Conclusion

The flat but rich and productive topsoil of the Midwest region known as Illinois is not the only result of the former presence of the glaciers. Such features as moraines, eskers, kettles, and erratics are all remnants of a bygone age which help to define the Midwest, at least geologically.

## 2. Introduction

Last summer my friend Debbie cut her foot on broken glass while playing in a lake. Because the water was murky, she failed to see the glass and accidentally pushed it into her foot when she stepped in the area. This incident illustrates how senseless littering really is. Littering is not only harmful to people (and animals), it causes needless destruction of the environment, destruction which is very hard to undo.

## Conclusion

A clean environment is less likely to harm someone than a polluted one. A landscape is much more breathtaking if there aren't any beer bottles to mar it. More important, it is much harder to clean up our environment than it is to contaminate it. And just how hard is it to find a garbage can, anyway?

## *Writing*

1. Write three paragraphs in which you use a *graded order* to explain an unfamiliar process, device, or activity. Where you can, help your reader by moving from simple or familiar ideas to more difficult ones.

2. Choose a subject that you know something about (or pick one of the suggestions following). Brainstorm everything you know about the subject, keeping a record of your thoughts. Identify clusters of ideas, and develop at least three *promises* that will operate as topic ideas for your paragraphs. From these promises, identify some key words and phrases that you can use for "creative repetition." Then identify some signposts or transitions that will help your reader make connections between your paragraphs. Write a paper, using your paragraph promises, creative repetition, and signposts.
   a. stress

    b. junk food
    c. aerobics
    d. hard rock music

3. Choose one of your papers written for this class or another one. Rewrite the introduction and conclusion.

# CHAPTER 6

# THE PRACTICE OF REVISION

## IMPROVING AND SHARPENING YOUR WORK

If you look at the drawing again on p. 4, you will notice how often as a writer you back up to reconsider (revise) something. For instance, from **Outlining,** you may back up to **Getting a Subject;** from **Writing,** you may back up to **Specifying a Stance;** and so on. Also note that each "backing up" affects other elements in the paper. If you go back to reconsider and revise your stance, this often changes something in the *Outlining stage,* which in turn has its effect on *Writing.*

In this book we talk about revision in two ways. First, in this chapter, we will discuss it as a matter of improving and sharpening your work until you achieve a *working draft.* Second, in Chapter 7, we continue this discussion, but in this chapter we emphasize *sentence structure.*

### Two Questions About Revising

*When do I start revising?*

Answer: from the very beginning. A *revision* is any change in planning or writing.

*When is the best time for revising?*

Let's answer that by pointing out there are *worst times.* For example, if ten minutes before you hand the paper in, you decide to revise it for *audience* you are probably in difficulty. Decisions about audience are usually a part of decisions about *stance,* and in most circumstances they all govern your design of the whole paper so completely you can't revise them late without distorting the paper dramatically. There are exceptions to this, of course. But we wish to emphasize that a piece of writing tends to set like wet concrete. You can work both prose and concrete only up to the point where they begin to harden.

Usually the best time to revise the "preparation parts" of your paper is when you decide on them. If possible, revise these early:

Choice of subject
*Hook* or angle of attack
Stance: writer's role
        audience
        point of thesis
Shape or outline of paper

So much depends on these areas of preparation that if you don't get them firmly in mind, you may find yourself doing more revising than original writing.

## An Example of Revision

Brian has an assignment to write a paper using *process*. His instructor encourages the class to write a lighthearted process paper, one that might entertain by supplying some *description* or *narration*.

[Process, description, and narration are covered in Part 2 of this text.]

As we relate the story of Brian's paper, note where and why he stops to *revise*.

"I didn't really have to hunt for a process subject," Brian said. "When Ms. Carlisle said *entertain*, I thought only one word—'funny.' And the funniest process I ever saw was . . ."

"Wait a minute," we said. "Let our readers see some of your first draft."

"OK," Brian said. "I just started writing, with no plan. You'll see what happened."

### THE DAY GRANDPA LOST HIS TEETH

Grandpa takes care of his cars. He has had a manual for every one of them, going back to a 1940 Plymouth. He buys the manual from the manufacturer, who supplies real mechanics' manuals, each one about a thousand pages long. But he never uses the manuals. They are stacked on top of the *World Book*— which he never uses either—and get dusted regularly by Grandma, who always complains that they are in the way and are only good for door stops.

"Where is this headed?" we said.

"Not much of anywhere," said Brian. "The assignment said *process* and *entertain*, and I was not processing or entertaining. I only wanted to write about 2–3 pages, and at the rate I was getting to the point I'd be telling it to the reader on page 14.

"I stopped and considered my audience. Easy—the general reader, no special difficulty there. But I needed a hook to hang the paper on—my process I already had in mind, and you will see it in a minute. I thought of another title:

*HOW GRANDPA GOT HIS TEETH AWAY FROM THE AIR CONDITIONER IN A 1971 PONTIAC*

Catchy, huh? But not *process:* steps leading to an end point. I had to tell the reader how to do something or how something worked."

"Who would care?" we asked.

"I thought of that right away. Then I thought of starting the first paragraph differently, appealing directly to the reader, and making the process angle clear. I decided to hang the whole theme on this hook: the difficulty of what should be a simple procedure, getting an object out of a hole it has fallen into."

From this point on, Brian will tell you himself how he wrote and revised, and revised yet again. We will number his paragraphs, and show the development of the paper. Following each revision, Brian's comments on it will appear in italics.

*Note:* The revisions were not always made paragraph by paragraph or at the same time.

## FIRST VERSION OF TITLE AND PARAGRAPH 1

Title:              How to Get an Object Out of Your Car's Air Conditioner

Paragraph 1.    If you are typical, it has happened to you. You are sitting in your car. You put an object in front of you, on top of the dashboard. And then it's gone, dropped down through the vents in the dashboard. This happened to my grandfather's teeth. Down they went into the bowels of the car, and it took him two days to get them out. If they had been smooth or not drawable by a magnet, he would have never gotten them out. Here's how to do it if it happens to you.

## REVISION OF TITLE AND PARAGRAPH 1

Title:         *Grandpa's Teeth:* How to Get an Object Out of Your Car's Defrosting Vents

Paragraph 1.      "Oops," Grandpa said. *Tinkle, tank, tinkle.* Silence.
"What do you mean, *oops?*" Grandma said. And then she knew.
"They went down the $"%$# vent," Grandpa said.
"How many times have I told you, keep them in your mouth." She had him. "She'll never let me forget this one," Grandpa said later. "I had to get 'em out, and quick, right after we got home."

*Brian's Comments on the Revision*

     *1. I needed a more accurate title.*

     *2. The first version wasn't bad, but the narrative seemed more interesting. I thought I could put some of the first version later in the essay, once I caught the reader's interest.*

     *3. I rewrote paragraph 1 before going on to paragraph 2.*

## FIRST VERSION OF PARAGRAPH 2

Paragraph 2.  If my informal sampling is representative, two out five Americans loose stuff down the vents in the top of a dashboard. Coins, hairpins, five-dollar bills, pills, aspirins, car keys, marbles, short pencils—and Grandpa's teeth. Anything small can fall down there and be gone forever! How to get it back? You can't see it, and you don't know where it's gone. (If you start the engine, will it be ground up in there?)

## REVISION OF PARAGRAPH 2

Paragraph 2.     If my informal sampling is representative, two out *of* five
Americans *lose* stuff down the air vents in the top of *their
car* dashboard. *Car keys,* coins, hairpins, *Lifesavers,* five-
dollar bills, aspirins and other pills—and Grandpa's teeth
*(actually a two-tooth bridge).* Anything small can fall down
there and be gone forever! *If it's something important you
want to get it back.* But how to get it back? You can't see it,
and you don't know where it's gone. (If you start the
engine, will it be ground up in there?)

*Comments on the Revision*

*I had different kinds of revisions here.*

   *1. Some simple errors: I left out the word* **of** *in line 1 and misspelled* **lose** *in
line 2.*

   *2. I put in* **their car** *for specificity in lines 2–3.*

   *3. Readers know only what you tell them, and I was afraid that they would
visualize* **false teeth** *in line 4, and they would immediately think I was just making
the whole thing up; false teeth are way too big to go down one of these vents.*

   *4. Also for the readers' sake, I added a sentence in lines 6–7, just to take care of
the objection that most stuff that goes down the vent you don't care if you ever see
again.*

   *5. For the sake of emphasis in line 3, I put* **car keys** *first. Obviously, they are
the worst thing you can lose. In the next line, I added* **Lifesavers** *because Joanie
Riggs says she keeps a roll on her dash, and once the package is open the little candies
are always rolling out and disappearing into the vents.*

---

*FIRST VERSION OF PARAGRAPH 3*

---

Paragraph 3.   Here is how to get the object out of the hole. First, determine what the object is. There are only two methods of removal, depending on what you lost. If the object has no hole in it, or if it won't respond to a magnet—say goodbye to it. If it's either one of the above . . .

There was no revised version of paragraph 3 (at this point). Brian got stuck in his first draft and stopped writing. He explains what happened below.

*Brian's Comments*

*All right, now I have to admit that I didn't write an outline for this paper—or make a* **shape** *for it (see pp. 50–54). I am basically lazy. I am also basically lost in this paper. Paragraph 3 is out of sync somehow, and I had lost Grandpa and his teeth as a theme in my story. So I made this scratch outline:*

> Thesis: *Getting an object out of your car's vent is easy if you have the right equipment and know how to use it.*
> Hooks or *Grandpa's teeth*
> "themes": *Equipment (and knowledge of it)*

> I. *Introd.—his teeth lost*
> II. *The kind of stuff lost in a typical car vent*
> III. *How to get it out*
>   A. *Two methods*
>   B. *Go to hardware store*
>     1. *Buy wire*
>     2. *Buy fishing magnet*
>   C. *Techniques of fishing*
> IV. *Conclusion—How to avoid the entire problem*
>   A. *Grandpa loses teeth again*
>   B. *Grandma's reaction*

*There's no use chewing me out for not making an outline earlier. I didn't, and that's that.*

*First I wrote a new* **Paragraph 3;** *then I wrote the rest of the paper about as fast as I could type. This gave me a working first draft (see next page).*

---
## CONTINUATION OF BRIAN'S PAPER
---

3. When Grandpa got home, he retrieved his teeth in a matter of five minutes. Five minutes later, he also retrieved two screws, a metal loop that held his car together, pieces of a three-year-old shopping list, and an unidentified piece of metal. In addition to these, he now has a windshield vent that works much better, once the junk is out of its system. Here is how he did it—and how you can do it.

4. First recognize the fact that to get an object out of the vent, you have only two methods available. These depend on the nature of what you have lost. If it doesn't have holes in it or if it cannot be attracted by a magnet, forget it. (Grandpa's teeth bridge has several holes for lightness.)

5. Next, go to the hardware store and buy two feet of soft brass wire about the thickness of the lead in a wooden pencil. Also buy a "fishing" magnet, which is about the size and shape of a wood pencil. The magnet has a head which rotates.

6. Now you are ready to fish for the object in your vent. Grandpa's teeth are made of a metal that magnets do not attract. So he took his piece of brass wire and made a hook in one end. He stuck this end down the vent and wiggled the wire, pushing it gently along until about a foot of it was inside the hole. He wiggled the wire some more until he could hear his teeth bouncing against metal. He then fished for the teeth until he could hear them scraping against the sides of the hole, which meant that he had hooked them. He pulled them out with the wire.

7. After finding his teeth, he drilled a hole in the end of the fishing magnet and looped one end of the brass wire through, twisting it tight. Then he went fishing for metal. After a few minutes of this, he went back to fishing with just the wire, ending with the result already mentioned.

8. The best way to get objects out of your dashboard vents is not to let them in there in the first place. Much to Grandma's satisfaction, Grandpa no longer puts his teeth on the dashboard. He puts them in his pocket. They fell out of his pocket when he put his pants over a chair while undressing for bed. He stepped on them, cutting a hole in his foot—the ends of the hardened metal (which curve over the teeth and hold the bridge in place) are very sharp.

9. Grandma's remarks have not been preserved for posterity.

Brian waited two days and then revised his working draft. As before, we will show you what he did to the paper. His comments are italicized.

### Grandpa's Teeth: How to Get an Object
### Out of Your Car's Defrosting Vents

1. |←"Oops," Grandpa said. *Tinkle, tank, tinkle.* Silence ~~in the car.~~

   |← — *They sat there in the gas station, just outside Indianapolis.* ✗

   "What do you mean, oops?" Grandma said. And then she knew.

   "They went down the $%&(*)% vent," Grandpa said.

   "How many times have I told you, keep them in your mouth!"

   She had him. "She'll never let me forget this one," Grandpa said

   later. "I had to get 'em out, and quick, right after we got home."

2.     If my informal sampling is representative, two out of five Amer-

   icans lose stuff down the ~~air~~ *defrosting* vents in the top of their car dashboard.

   *wedding rings*
   Car keys, coins, hairpins, Lifesavers, five-dollar bills, aspirins and

   other pills—and Grandpa's teeth (actually a two-tooth bridge). Any-

   thing small can fall into the vent and be gone forever! If it's some-

   thing important you want to get it back. But how to get it back? You

   can't see it, and you don't know where it's gone. (If you start the

   engine, will it be ground up in there?)

*The attendant was wiping the windshield.*

*Brian's Comments*

   *In paragraph 1, I added a little explanation to "place" the event. It had to be happening somewhere! And it really happened in a gas station.*

   *In paragraph 2, I wanted the reader to understand what these "vents" were—so added* **defrosting.**

   *While talking about my paper with friends, someone said his mother dropped her wedding ring down a vent when the family went to the beach. Seemed like a good detail.*

3.  When Grandpa got home, he retrieved his teeth in a matter of five minutes, *after he got some equipment,* A half-hour later, he *had* also retrieved two screws, a metal loop that *had once* held his car *keys* together, pieces of a three-year-old shopping list, and an unidentified piece of metal. In addition to these, he now has a windshield vent that works much better, once the junk is out of ~~its~~ *the venting* system. Here is how he did it—and how you can do it, *too.*

4.  First, recognize the fact that to get an object out of the a vent, you have only two methods available. These depend on the nature of what you have lost. If it doesn't have holes in it or if it cannot be attracted by a magnet, forget it. (Grandpa's teeth bridge has several holes for lightness.)

5.  Next, go to the hardware store and buy two feet of soft brass wire about the thickness of the lead in a wooden pencil. Also buy a "fishing" magnet, which is about the size and shape of a wood pencil. The magnet has a head which rotates.

6.  Now you are ready to fish for the object in your vent. Grandpa's teeth are made of a metal that magnets do not attract. So he took his piece of brass wire and made a hook in one end. He stuck this end down the vent and wiggled the wire, pushing it gently along until about a foot of it was inside the hole. He wiggled the wire some more until he could hear his teeth bouncing against metal. He then fished for his teeth until he could hear them scraping against the sides of the hole, which meant that he had hooked them. He pulled them out with the wire.

*Brian's Comments*

*The revisions here are mainly for clarity and "tightening" loose ends.*

7.    After finding his teeth, he drilled a hole in the *non-magnetic* end of the fishing magnet and looped one end of the brass wire through, twisting it tight. Then he went fishing for metal. After a few minutes of this, he went back to fishing with just the wire, ending with the result already mentioned.

8.    The best way to get objects out of your dashboard vents is not to let them in there in the first place. Much to Grandma's satisfaction, Grandpa *no* longer puts his teeth on the dashboard. He puts them in *his* pocket. They fell out of his pocket when he put his pants over a chair while undressing for bed. He stepped on them, cutting a hole in his foot—the ends of the hardened metal (which curve over the teeth and hold the bridge in place) are very sharp.

9.    Grandma's remarks have not been preserved for posterity.

*Brian's Comments*

*Paragraph 7—I was afraid the reader would visualize this wrong. You can't drill into a magnet without ruining it, and I wanted to explain what the process really required.*

*Paragraph 8—Fixing typical typing errors.*

# REVISION: AN OVERVIEW

We have seen Brian work his way through the typical strategies of revision, moving backward and forward in the process as he made changes to improve a particular essay. There are no mysteries about what he did, nor are his techniques unusual with him. Every writer revises—although some writers tend to revise more heavily at certain stages than at others.

It is generally true that experienced writers like to revise early, to get a good "foundation" for their papers before starting on a first draft. This foundation can be an outline or "shape" plus a title and first paragraph. These give a sense of *direction* to a paper that even the experienced writer needs. You will recall that once Brian got a scratch outline, title, and first paragraph he thought might work, he was able to move rapidly through to the end of a satisfactory first draft.

Once you have completed such a draft, you have (broadly speaking) two choices. You can continue to look it over, rewriting and revising. Or you can set it aside for a while. We recommend setting it aside.

Why? Because most of us will tend to half-memorize the paper, mistakes and all. By *mistakes,* we mean anything that might be wrong with it—from lapses in logic, to clumsy sentences, to out-of-order paragraphs. If you put it away out of sight, it will in time become a fresh paper, one whose failures (if any) may become evident. How long should you set it aside? As long as you can, without making it difficult to do a final draft and proofread *it.* For most writers, this schedule is reasonable:

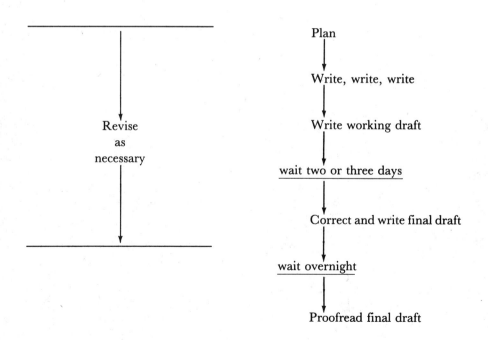

Revise
as
necessary

Plan

↓

Write, write, write

↓

Write working draft

↓

wait two or three days

↓

Correct and write final draft

↓

wait overnight

↓

Proofread final draft

# FINAL PROOFREADING

Material on final proofreading is included in Chapter 7.

## ♦ PRACTICE

### Discussion

Study the following paragraph from a longer essay. Discuss the changes in the revision. In particular, identify the changes that were made because of a shift in role or audience. In what ways does the paragraph set the scene for the thesis? How have the changes limited the original point of view?

Original

> *Thesis:* People who are not directly involved in motor accidents seem to be drawn to them.

About a year ago, there was a motorcycle accident near my house. I was on the phone, talking to a friend about an assignment due in school the next day, when I heard a noise like a loud hedge-trimmer on the loose. My mother, who was in the living room with my father and me, ran to the front window. She gave a gasp, gesticulated down the street, and turned around to us and said, "There's a man! There's a man!" and took off out the front door. My father and I, thinking that the strain of her work (she is a teacher) had finally snapped her mind, stayed put, until she came running back in to tell us "Call the ambulance! Call the Police!" My father got up and ambled out the door to see what the excitement was. My curiosity got the best of me, too, and I told my friend that I would call her back later, hung up, and went to the scene of the accident, for indeed it was an accident although I didn't realize what it was until I got nearer. A motorcyclist, zipping through a stop sign, had hit the back of a car and was, at the time I first saw him, lying on the street pavement.

Revision

About a year ago, there was a motorcycle accident near my house, making a noise like a hedge-trimmer on the loose. My mother, who was in the living room, ran to the front window. She gasped, gesticulated down the street and said, "There's a man! There's a man!" and took off out the front door. My father, thinking that the strain of her work had finally snapped her mind, stayed put, until she came running back to tell him to "Call the ambulance! Call the police! My father called the police and ambled out the door to see what the excitement was. Neither of my parents realized what kind of an accident it was until they got closer. A motorcyclist, zipping through a stop sign, had hit the back of a car and was lying on the street pavement.

## Writing

1. Select a paper you have written for this course. Following Brian's techniques, go through the paper analyzing what you could do better if you were to revise it.

2. Revise the paper analyzed.

# CHAPTER 7

# REVISING SENTENCES, EDITING, AND PROOFREADING

Only the genius gets a sentence right the first time. Most of us write . . . rewrite . . . and then write again—trying to get the proper match between meaning and structure. Revision usually improves this match; but with revision, as with other techniques in composition, you need a plan—or a set of suggestions—in order to make it more purposeful. After writing a "bad" sentence, how do you fix it? In this chapter we will offer a number of suggestions for revision, all of them based on the following premise: As you inspect your own sentences, imagine that you are a cool, objective, and slightly negative editor who does not mind telling himself to rearrange, cut, and reword.

## SUGGESTIONS FOR REVISING AND EDITING*

1. *Think about what you've said.*
   Many bad sentences are a result of the writer's failure to think about and visualize what he has written. Leo Rosten found a sentence in the *New York Times* that shows how such a failure can result in unintentional comedy:

   > There is Mr. Burton growling and grousing and endlessly chewing the lips, ears, and neck of Elizabeth Taylor as the faithless wife of a dull ambassador with whom he is having a clandestine affair.

---

*Editors and instructors often hear this complaint from writers after they have rewritten a sentence: "But you changed my meaning!" The objection has some validity, but the response to it has more: "One cannot usually make a significant improvement in a weak sentence without changing the meaning." In fact, when writers revise or edit a sentence, they try to make *meaning* more exact at the same time that they improve *structure* and *word choice*. In the sentence, everything works (or does not work) together.

Rosten commented: "I am glad, in a way, that Mr. Burton was endlessly chewing the neck of Miss Taylor as the faithless wife of a dull ambassador, because it probably wouldn't be fun to chew her neck as anyone else; but who is the ambassador with whom Burton, it says here, is having a clandestine affair?" Rosten quoted another sentence from the *Times*:

> Among her biggest gambles was during their tempestuous court-ship.

Said Rosten: "I hate to be a spoilsport, gentlemen, but you just can't 'was' during anything."

2. *Check your stance.*
Is a weak writer's stance hurting your sentence? A student wrote about a class project:

> The availability of time is an important factor in the project choice.

The stance is vague here—no writer, reader, or clear point. Clarify the stance and rewrite completely:

> In choosing a problem for our project, we must remember that we have only three weeks' time.

3. *Make your subject-verb relationship as clear and specific as possible.*
A vague relationship helped make a mess of this sentence:

> Parental *endeavors* (subject) in regard to education *suggest* (verb) that. . . .

How can an endeavor *suggest?* Specify the subject and verb; then clarify the rest of the sentence:

> *Parents* at Elm School now *insist* that their children be taught to read.

Here is another example of vague subject and verb:

> *One* of the most important reasons for supporting the union *is* stable employment.

Edit this by changing both the stance and the subject-verb relationship:

*Workers* who want stable employment *should join* the union.

Or:

>Do you want stable employment? Then [*you should*] *join* the union.

4. *Read your sentences aloud.*

>Pedalling hard, she reached top of the hill.

That is a sentence one of us wrote several years ago. It went through our hands and the hands of an editor before the omission was found—by a proofreader reading the sentence aloud:

>Pedalling hard, she reached *the* top of the hill.

Since people read hundreds of words a minute, it is easy to miss all kinds of errors—dangling modifiers, misspellings, illogicalities, vague usage, careless punctuation, omissions. *The ear will catch what the eye will not.* Human beings spoke and heard language a million years before they wrote it, which is why the best editing often combines the talents of ear and eye and voice.

5. *Make sure your sentence openers logically fit the clauses that follow.*

>*Faulty:* Like many specialties in engineering, you must learn. . . .
>(*dangling modifier*)
>*Improved:* Like many kinds of engineers, you must learn. . . .
>
>*Faulty:* To be considered for the debate team, the voice must be trained.
>*Improved:* To be considered for the debate team, you must first train your voice.

6. *Avoid "nouniness" and "preposition piling."*
Good sentences use no more nouns than are absolutely necessary. Abstract nouns are particularly troublesome. This sentence is "nouny":

>*Personality analysis* is the *determination* of *function defects* and *utilization* of their *cures.*

The sentence contains seven nouns—two of them used as clumsy modifiers: "*personality* analysis" and "*function* defects." This sentence is so bad it can't be edited; who knows what it means?

In a sentence, prepositions can multiply like rabbits. Such "preposition piling" occurs with nouniness and is a sign of it:

> English teachers agree that personal ownership and use *of* a good dictionary is a prime necessity *for* every student *in* obtaining the maximum results *from* the study *of* English.

Rewrite, cutting some of the nouns and altering others; for example, make *ownership* and *use* into verbs. Then the prepositions can be reduced from five to zero, the nouns from ten to three:

> English teachers agree that students should own and use a good desk dictionary.

Here is a portion of a satiric essay on nouniness in modern prose:

> [1] Have you noticed the new look in the English language? Everybody's using nouns as adjectives. Or to put that in the current argot, there's a modifier noun proliferation. More exactly, since the matter is getting out of hand, a modifier noun proliferation increase. In fact, every time I open a magazine these days or listen to the radio, I am struck by the modifier noun proliferation increase phenomenon. So, I decided to write—you guessed it—a modifier noun proliferation increase article. . . .
>
> [2] Abstraction is the enemy both of clear expression and easy understanding. And abstract is what these strings of nouns become. And very quickly the reader or listener doesn't know what the actual relationship is. Take "Reality Therapy," the name of a new book. Do you gather that the author uses reality as a means of therapy or that the goal of his treatment is facing reality or that he has worked out some sort of therapy which he applies to reality? Take a phrase puzzled over in *Newsweek:* "antenna television systems operation." Manufacture? broadcasting? consulting? The article said that somebody was going into that field and I still don't know where he's going. I suspect that the people who turn out these phrases might insist that they are seeking greater precision, as though each new noun pinned down the matter a bit more. Wrong. Another article like this one and we'll have a modifier noun proliferation increase phenomenon article protest campaign, but will you know what you've got?
>
> —Bruce Price, "An Inquiry into Modifier Noun Proliferation"

7. *Cut out deadwood—words and phrases that are not doing enough work in the sentence.*
   The sample sentence in 6, on using the dictionary, illustrates how to cut out deadwood. Here are more examples:

> *Poor:* A woman who was present there saw the break-in.
> *Improved:* A woman there saw the break-in.

| | |
|---|---|
| *Poor:* | We are in receipt of your memo of August 14 making reference to football tickets sold by some of the players. |
| *Improved:* | We received your letter of August 14 about football tickets sold by some of the players. |

| | |
|---|---|
| *Poor:* | In relation to his idea, it does not seem to me to be a workable one. |
| *Improved:* | I doubt that his idea will work. |

| | |
|---|---|
| *Poor:* | A second area in which Jane should have a better knowledge involves rules of attendance. |
| *Improved:* | Second, Jane should know more about rules of attendance. |

8. *Rewrite to avoid monotony or lack of emphasis.*

| | |
|---|---|
| *Poor:* | Many favorable comments are beginning to be made about fantasy movies by the critics. These comments are long overdue and welcome to students of film. |
| *Improved:* | Recently many critics have made favorable comments about fantasy movies. To students of film, these comments are welcome—and long overdue. |

| | |
|---|---|
| *Poor:* | I took the job happily when the head of the company offered me more money because of my long experience and also technical school training in the field. |
| *Improved:* | When he found out that I had both technical training and experience, the head of the company offered me the job with a higher salary. I accepted his offer happily. |

9. *Change a vague or clumsy passive.*
   The easiest way to understand the *passive* construction is to contrast it with the *active,* which follows the formula "Something does [something]":

| **Something** | **does** | **[something]** |
|---|---|---|
| The wolf | howls at | the moon. |
| The wolf | bit | my ear. |

The passive construction reverses the formula—"Something is done [by something]":

| **Something** | **is done** | **[by something]** |
|---|---|---|
| The moon | was howled at | by the wolf. |
| My ear | was bitten | by the wolf. |

The typical relationship between active and passive statements looks like this (the *agent* does the acting):

| Active | Passive |
|---|---|
| [agent] | [agent] |
| The *wind* blew the flowers. | The flowers were blown by the *wind*. |
| [agent] | [agent] |
| *Explorers* found the cave. | The cave was found by the *explorers*. |
| [agent] | [agent] |
| The *saw* cut my arm. | My arm was cut by the *saw*. |

These examples show the *complete* form of the passive, and every complete form will have all the parts, including the agent. The shortened form of the *passive* (what we will here call the *short passive*) omits the *by* and the *agent:*

> The gift will be delivered.
> The police have been notified.
> The job was completed.
> The worker should be fired from his job.

Each of these four short passives can be made into a complete passive—if you know the agents. The complete passive of the last sentence, for example, might read:

> [agent]
> The worker should be fired from his job by the *supervisor*.

The passive is a minor sentence form. Skillful writers use certain other forms—particularly the active—much more often. The reasons are not hard to find. One is that the passive can be very awkward, as in "The moon was howled at by the wolf." A second is that the passive encourages vagueness, even dishonesty, because in its short form—without the agent expressed—the writer can fail to assign responsibility for an action: "The highway was blocked." But who or what blocked it? "The vice-president was discouraged from inspecting the firm's books." Who discouraged him?

A third reason why the skillful writer often avoids the passive is that in modern times it has become associated with jargon and gobbledygook:

> Currently utilized population estimates leave much *to be desired* in future planning.
> The experimental rationale *was explained* in the Foreword and *was* more fully *detailed* in Chapter 3.
> Psychological characterization *will be considered* as a major factor in the present analysis of Huck Finn.

Whenever a passive is wordy, awkward, unemphatic, or so gob-bledygooky that a reader cannot understand it, there is a simple strategy for improving it. Make the statement active:

| | |
|---|---|
| *Poor:* | A picnic table was located by Jim. (7 words) |
| *Improved:* | Jim located a picnic table. (5 words) |

| | |
|---|---|
| *Poor:* | The banquet was held during which speeches were made and songs were sung. (13 words) |
| *Improved:* | During the banquet, we heard speeches and sang songs. (9 words) |

The solution to the gobbledygook passive is *never* to write a sentence like this in the first place:

> It has been decided that to maintain optimum learning conditions in the library, evening hours will be extended to 2:00 A.M.

But if a sentence like this sneaks up on you in a first draft, identify the agent(s) in the situation, and put the idea into one or more specific active statements:

> The library has announced that its evening hours will be extended to 2:00 A.M. Mr. Harlan Smith, Director of the Library, has announced that . . .
>
> Mr. Smith announced today that, starting Sunday, the library will close at 2:00 A.M. Smith claimed that closing the library later will allow more students to use it.
>
> So that more students can use the library, it will close at 2:00 A.M. from now on.

10. *Change an unnecessary or clumsy expletive.*
    The expletive sentence starts with *it* or *there:*

> *It is* a beautiful day in San Francisco.
> *There's* no fool like an old fool.

As these sentences demonstrate, the expletive is both normal and pleasant when properly used. But when it occurs in wordy or awkward constructions like the following, you should revise the sentence:

| | |
|---|---|
| *Poor:* | For those who wish more heat, *there is* a heater switch on the dashboard. |
| *Improved:* | If you want more heat, turn the switch on the dashboard. |

> *Poor:* At the feet of the corpse *it was* found that *there were* five empty jewel cases from three different robberies. (*Two* expletives!)
>
> *Improved:* At the feet of the corpse, the police found five empty jewel cases from three different robberies.

In both these examples, we edited and improved the weak sentences by shifting to active constructions. A lot of sentence editing works exactly like this: You look at the sick sentence; ask "What is happening here?"; and answer the question with an active construction.

*Note:* In order to balance our discussion of passive constructions and expletives, we need to point out that both have their place. The passive is useful for variety and is appropriate for statements in which the agent is either unknown ("My books were stolen in the library,") or understood ("The embezzler was paroled after serving five years."). The expletive is useful in beginnings: "There are a thousand ways to write an introduction"; or "Once upon a time, there was a fair princess who loved a frog." Expletives are also useful in writing short, informal sentences: "It's a long way to Tipperary."

Yet all authorities recognize that the expletive and the passive have their dangers. So we say: Don't avoid the constructions entirely, but be wary of them—and edit them when necessary.

## A FINAL NOTE ON EDITING

Recently, a student came in to see one of us about his writing problems, particularly about his weak sentences. We talked over several of them, bringing out ideas and possibilities hidden inside (or behind) them. In effect, we were "co-editors," identifying, analyzing, rethinking, and rewriting some of the troublesome constructions. You can do the same job by "talking" over your own sentences with yourself. Here are two of the student's sentences, with comments about their weaknesses:

> *Poor sentence:* The students were accused of plagiarism, and they were told in terms of their careers in academia that they should not be too hopeful.
>
> *Comments:* Stance and viewpoint are weak—*who* told the students? The two passive constructions are vague. Deadwood: *in terms of, Their careers* and *in academia* are not doing much work in the sentence either. Vague: *They should not be too hopeful.*
>
> *Edited sentence:* After she accused the students of plagiarism, the Assistant Dean told them that they might be expelled.

Together, we created a clearer stance, cut out the deadwood, employed an opener, changed the vague passives to active constructions, and made the whole sentence more specific.

> *Poor sentence:* The misuse of the environment must be improved in regard to the liquor industry.
>
> *Comments:* Read the sentence aloud—we must *improve* our *misuse?* This says exactly the opposite of what the writer intended. He was probably thrown off the track by several weaknesses: the poor stance, vagueness and deadwood *in regard to the liquor industry,* the passive *misuse . . . must be improved.*
>
> *Edited sentence:* Let's pass a law in this state abolishing throwaway beer bottles.

We changed the stance. Now the writer is addressing a more specific group of readers. We cut unnecessary words, changed the bad passive to an active verb, and substituted the more specific phrase *beer bottles* for the vague phrase *liquor industry.*

## ◆ PRACTICE

Edit and rewrite these sentences. Don't be afraid to change them when necessary. The point is to write a *better* sentence.

a. The assassination of Lincoln had much speculation to it.
b. The fact that the new trainees at first do not get to do much work on the actual engines should not give them a feeling of demotion.
c. It must be considered a possibility that the student nurse must be able to face physical damage, broken bones, cranial disorders, pregnancy, or even death.
d. It happened at the hour of three when there is much relaxing during the coffee break.
e. The nerve center of the oboe lies in its reed, and in its bore is its soul; the need of a good reed is the bane of the player's life.
f. Mr. Coleman announced his resignation this morning. He would have liked to have stayed a while longer.
g. "Don't expire before your license do."—from the Illinois State License Bureau.
h. He only dislikes action pictures and neither does his brother.
i. The next point to make about idiom differences is one of the most difficult problems for many foreigners.
j. It is not believed that the critics show complete rationality in their judgments when they criticize the Fall Frolic.
k. After explaining my job to me, there was a car sent by the Head Ranger to take me to the office.
l. Our family has been really having huge difficulties with hard-core

> resentment on the girls' part, who have been claiming that we play favorites for the one boy.
>
> m. Thus the continual success, interest, and the test of endurance are reasons why marathon bicycle racing is an important topic.
>
> n. Although these statistics may look suspicious, it is because there is not a more specific breakdown of them.
>
> o. In response to the attack on my report on Adventure Playgrounds, I will prove to you, the newspapers, radio, and TV its validity.
>
> p. Perched prettily on the branches, we watched the first robin of spring.
>
> q. Invariably the problem of the car breaking down will sometimes arise.
>
> r. The exploration of student differences in response to the instructor's stimulus questions cause the students to return to the textbook seeking justification for their opinions and ultimately encourage the articulation of their personal views.
>
> s. The loss of professors' credibility represents an indispensable foundation upon which authority structures are undermined.
>
> t. The nation's domestic ills may keep, although there is a risk in deferring them.
>
> u. Last year the campus had a great increase in narcotics arrests, most of them on a marijuana possession charge or for smoking marijuana.

# POLISHING AND PROOFREADING

Writers create in different ways. Some work hard on their thesis statements; others concentrate on outlines; a few scribble draft after draft, searching for ideas they sense are inside them somewhere. It has been argued that it matters little where you begin in the writing process—as long as at the end of your first satisfactory draft everything ties together. A *satisfactory* draft is not usually a final draft; it is not perfect in grammar, punctuation, and other compositional matters. It is one that has a firm thesis and outline and that specifically satisfies the main details of the assignment.

## Polishing

After you have finished a satisfactory first draft, a good deal of polishing will probably have to be done on the manuscript. You can insert sentences and phrases, delete words here and there, repunctuate, correct misspellings, and generally improve the entire essay. It's a good idea to leave wide margins and plenty of line space on the first-draft manuscript for corrections. If you handwrite on lined paper, skip every other line; if

```
                          or                              My father, mother, and I
          I was four,∧about that age, when our farmhouse burned. We were
                               cannot remember
     in the barn doing something--I have no idea what--when I happened to
                          clouds of yellowish   billowing away from the house.
     look out the big front door and saw a great deal of smoke∧ It seemed

     to come from every‿where, even from the sides of the house and the
                          y
     basement windows. I ⅄elled to my father, who came to the barn door.
                               quietly as if in surprise
     He looked at the house∧ and said quitely and surprisedly:  "Well, I∧'ll

     be damned, the house is burning down."
                                                   My parents
          We all ran for the house, to save what we could.  They ordered me
                                        they could,
     to stay out, while they dashed in to save what little we had. ∧ainly
                                              and some bedclothes.
     this was clothing and sheets, and a few pieces of furniture∧ I carried
     bedclothes
     what I could away from the flying sparks, crying and blubbering and
                               ∧
     tripping over the ⅄eets and quilts.  I said over and over to myself
                    my
     through∧tears:  "I'll be damned, the house is burning down."
```

you type, triple space. Above you will see part of a satisfactory first draft, with the writer's corrections.

The writer's polishing of these paragraphs is of several kinds. He inserts words he omitted, corrects punctuation and spelling, and makes the sentencing smoother. More importantly, he tries to explain matters more clearly and precisely. *We* becomes *My mother, father, and I,* and *a great deal of smoke* becomes *clouds of yellowish smoke billowing away from the house.* The reader will probably be grateful for the writer's changes, since they improve the original considerably.

## *Proofreading*

After you have polished your draft, let it cool off for a while—overnight, longer if possible. You want it to look unfamiliar, so that problems or errors will stand out as you read it. (Don't read the essay over and over; you'll just unconsciously memorize it, flaws and all.) Make whatever changes are necessary and copy your work into the final draft.

Let the final draft cool for another period. Now proofread the essay before handing it in. Proofreading is a small but important art. It consists mainly of trying to fool your brain into picking up errors it either hasn't caught before or has inadvertently memorized. Persons who read proof in publishers' houses usually do the job in pairs. One reads the original manuscript to the other, who has the freshly printed version before him. In this way, each word and punctuation mark are orally checked by two persons. (Despite this system, errors still appear in a great deal of published material.)

A variation on the oral method works quite well for the student writer. Take your cooled-off final draft to a secluded spot and read it aloud *slowly* to yourself, pronouncing each word exactly as you wrote it. Read each paragraph *out of its normal order*. For example, if you have a seven-paragraph essay, read the paragraphs in a sequence like this: 3, 2, 7, 4, 1, 6, 5. In doing this, you can make the whole essay appear odd and unfamiliar, and your ear will pick up errors of several kinds—in logic, for example, as well as in spelling. A faulty generalization may well stand out as you read it aloud, and you can then insert a word or phrase to qualify it. ("Fraternities are dens of iniquity" becomes "Most fraternities at People's College are dens of iniquity.") Such words misspelled sound so odd when pronounced as written that you may catch the mistake (*eariler,* for example, instead of *earlier*).

Even if you take all of these precautions, prepare yourself to accept the fact that errors are going to slip through. But accurate proofreading will cut down their number considerably.

# READER: TEN STRATEGIES

# CHAPTER 8

# MIXED STRATEGIES

## INTRODUCTION—STRATEGIES OF DEVELOPMENT

As we have indicated in previous chapters, writing situations are not all alike. Each of them tends to present its own problems. For this reason you need to investigate every situation carefully and create a special *stance* that will work best for it.

But while stances and writing situations may often vary greatly, your choices of methods for developing papers are somewhat more limited. These methods include a variety of techniques and rhetorical devices that we call *strategies*.

The *strategies* are actually thinking techniques that you have employed in a variety of ways in and out of school since you were very young. For example, when you had a choice between two flavors of ice cream, you made a *comparison-contrast*. If you made a list of homework assignments, you *classified*. In changing your bicycle tire, you were engaged in a *process*. In history classes you studied the *causes and effects* of the Civil War. In science you *defined* the elements, and in English you identified *analogies* in literature. Whenever you were asked to give an example to prove your point, you used *illustration*. *Narration* and *description* you use every day when you talk about your *personal experiences*. So you can see that the strategies are not elements related only to composition. They are natural ways of dealing with information so that we can think and communicate more effectively.

To see how the strategies can be used to organize a paper, we will follow Greg, a pre-med student, as he thinks about a very real problem: The college Board of Trustees has voted to increase tuition at his school by 30% in the next academic year. Then the trustees plan to increase tuition the following year by 10%. Since he is one of five college-age children in a family, he cannot depend on his parents for much financial help. The federal government is cutting its funding for Guaranteed Student Loans (GSL's), so he isn't sure if he will be able to borrow enough to pay his tuition. He is a pre-med major; consequently he cannot transfer to a "cheaper" college because pre-med programs aren't offered in the other state schools. He works summers as a lifeguard, and he works 20 hours a week in the college cafeteria during the school year. That income, combined with his GSL, barely covers expenses.

Greg considers the effect that a 40% hike in tuition will have on him. He gets increasingly angry about the prospect of having to go in debt, and this anger is reflected in his comments jotted down quickly on scratch paper:

> Not fair. The debt is going to be impossible to pay back.
> Mom doesn't work.
> Parents proud of me wanting to be a doctor.
> Dad is a self-made man who works hard in his own business. Never took anything from anyone.
> Never any money left over, after paying debts and mortgage.
> Pre-med expensive.
> University charges more tuition for pre-med courses.
> Chose a public university because cheaper.
> Job at cafeteria barely covers room and board—no tuition or books.
> If I leave school to get some money for school, can I pick up my studies again?
> John and Susie barely managing to stay in school, even with loans.
> Takes a lot of persistence to apply for work.
> The total cost for college is increasing twice as fast as the inflation index. Does this make sense?
> The government is decreasing funds for loans. Harder to get in future.
> What could I do if I left school?

Certain observations that Greg has just jotted down can be translated into *the strategies of development* mentioned earlier. Applied to Greg's situation as a pre-med student, the strategies could be used as follows:

1. *Description*—A description of the financial situation of Greg's family: number of children, amount of mortgage, and other debts.

2. *Narration*—A true story narrating his finding and keeping jobs in order to supplement his student loan.

3. *Personal Experience*—A historical account of Greg's single-mindedness in wanting to be a doctor and how it has been a consistent thread influencing his life.

4. *Process*—An accounting of the steps in applying for a student loan.

5. *Cause-effect*—An analysis of the effect of his having to leave school since he may not be able to qualify for a student loan to pay the increased tuition.

6. *Classification*—A breakdown of the kinds of loans available, most of which he is not eligible for.

7. *Illustration*—An account of three friends who will have a difficult time staying in school with increased tuition and reduced student loans.

8. *Definition*—An extended definition of *student loans.*

9. *Comparison-contrast*—An explanation of the kind of program Greg is enrolled in, compared with the program he could get in other colleges.

10. *Analogy*—An extended comparison in which he shows that the rate of tuition increases over a period of years in the college is higher than the rate of inflation. Nationally, college tuitions are increasing at double the rate of inflation, and experts believe that this will be the pattern for years to come.

After thinking about the subject of increased tuition, and after studying his jottings, Greg decides that the best argument he can make is to write to the Board of Trustees and his state legislator, objecting to the tuition increase. He knows that all the points in his jottings won't be relevant because he can't deal with all the possible topics on the subject. Nevertheless, he chooses those points that he believes would be most convincing and those that would perhaps be applicable to other students in his predicament. For instance, using *cause and effect* as a strategy to show that he—and others—might have to leave school (as a result of an increase in tuition) should convince his readers that the increase will cause unnecessary hardship.

After choosing this strategy, Greg outlines his stance.

> *Role:* College sophomore (pre-med) who has relied on part-time jobs and student loans to pay college expenses.
>
> *Audience:* The Board of Trustees and a state legislator.
>
> *Thesis:* The proposal to increase tuition over 40% by the school year 199—should be reconsidered because restrictions on federally subsidized Guaranteed Student Loans (GSL's), and the inability of most students to get high-paying jobs, will result in many students having to drop out of school.

As the thesis just shown implies, Greg's thesis is one of *cause and effect,* and the developmental strategy of his paper will reflect that fact.

Whether your choice of strategy is appropriate often depends on the nature of your subject. Some subjects seem to encourage a writer to employ certain methods of development; for example:

1.    *Subject:* A relative
   *Thesis:* *My grandmother is not typical of the stereotype of grandmother; she is young, independent, and athletic.*
   *Strategy:* **Description**

2.    *Subject:* Vacations
   *Thesis:* *A trip to Russia last summer taught me that the Russian educated class is often discriminated against.*
   *Strategy:* **Narration**

3.    *Subject:* Feminism
   *Thesis:* *Over the years I have had to resist the temptation to retreat from conflict and be a docile person, something I don't want to be.*
   *Strategy:* **Personal experience**

4.    *Subject:* Running for student office
   *Thesis:* *There are three important steps in running for student office: applying, campaigning, and developing a constituency.*
   *Strategy:* **Process**

5.    *Subject:* Nervous headaches
   *Thesis:* *My headaches are caused by the pressures of having to meet strict course deadlines.*
   *Strategy:* **Cause and effect**

6.    *Subject:* Nonflowering house plants
   *Thesis:* *Of the foliage house plants, succulents and cacti are the easiest to grow in a dry climate.*
   *Strategy:* **Classification**

7.    *Subject:* Camping
   *Thesis:* *Campers who travel in recreational vehicles are typically congenial people who bring their television sets and motor bikes and the like to camp in commercial or park campsites.*
   *Strategy:* **Illustration**

8.    *Subject:* "Pass/fail" courses
   *Thesis:* *"Pass/fail" courses are an educational opportunity to study a subject without having to face the pressure of a conventional grading system.*
   *Strategy:* **Definition** (of the term *"pass/fail"* course)

9.    *Subject:* Two science-fiction movies
   *Thesis:* The Empire Strikes Back *is a movie with a thin plot, unconvincing characters, and bizarre situations;* Close Encounters of the Third Kind *is a film with a strong plot, realistic characters, and situations based on actual happenings.*
   *Strategy:* **Comparison-contrast**

10.    *Subject:* Hand guns
    *Thesis:* *Like automobiles, hand guns are dangerous but controllable mechanisms.*
    *Strategy:* **Analogy**

# MIXED STRATEGIES

Proper use of the ten strategies can help you express your ideas precisely and efficiently, and after you have learned to employ them you will find that writing most essays and papers is much easier. But you may—and you should—use the strategies in combination. In dealing with the subject of running for student office, for example, it is likely that you could use the personal experience of others along with process. In managing the subject of hand guns, you might need to employ the strategies of definition, analogy, and comparison-contrast. While you will probably use one of the strategies as the main unifying principle behind your paper, you will often employ some of the others in creating your supporting material.

To give you an example of mixing the strategies, we will describe one student's method for handling a topic.

Jane is frustrated with the lack of transportation between her hometown and her college town, Collegeview—no train or plane, only buses. She believes that, since the bus transportation in and out of Collegeview is undependable, the College should charter buses for weekends and holiday traffic so that students can go home more efficiently and cheaply than they presently do. In supporting her thesis she could use combinations of certain strategies.

As we pointed out earlier, the strategies involve thinking skills, so in the prewriting stage Jane thinks through her topic, considering how the strategies can be used. The most obvious connection she sees between her topic and the strategies is that she has had *personal experience* with the buses and her experience has not been happy. She decides that narrating her experience would be a good way to get the attention of the reader. As she works through her facts and ideas, thinking about the strategies, she develops a scratch outline. Here is her outline showing how she will use combinations of strategies to write her argument.

## INTRODUCTION

*Thesis:*     *The University should charter buses so that students can leave and return to Collegeview efficiently and cheaply.*

*Strategy:*     Personal experience—Jane will recount her experiences of being forced to stay alone in her dorm because no transportation was available when she wanted to go home. Intertwined with her personal experience, she will use *narration* and *description*—narration to tell her story, description to illuminate her feelings.

*Strategy:*     Definition—The reader must understand what Jane means by *charter*. She will support her definition with *illustration* by giving examples of the variety of ways the school may charter buses.

*BODY*

I. The college needs better transportation out of Collegeview on weekends and holidays.

A. Not enough buses come into Collegeview for the number of students who want to leave on weekends and holidays.

*Strategy:* Description—Jane will describe the bus station on a Friday afternoon when all the students are clamoring to get seats on too few buses. She will support her *description* with *illustration.*

B. Alternate forms of transportation are too expensive—or dangerous (hitchhiking, for example).

*Strategy:* Comparison and contrast—Show how bus transportation is cheaper than owning a car or hiring a taxi, the only good alternatives to buses.

*Strategy:* Cause and effect—Because Jane wanted to get home in a hurry, she tried to hitchhike—a harrowing experience. *Narration* of her experience mixed with *cause and effect.*

C. Fighting for bus tickets and waiting to get a seat on the bus is a waste of student time and resources.

*Strategy:* Process—Jane will identify the steps of getting a ticket and a seat on the bus. She will supplement process with *cause and effect,* showing how wasted time limits educational productivity. Wasted time also creates frustration and anger.

II. Chartered buses are practical and will benefit the school.

A. Bus companies are willing to make a contract with the school.

*Strategy:* Classification—Jane has made inquiries and has classified the rates and companies who are willing to make a contract to provide bus service.

B. Students will be happier, and enrollment may increase if transportation is easier.

*Strategy:* Cause and effect—The college has had trouble keeping students after the freshman year, so Jane shows that this new system may help solve the problem.

*CONCLUSION*

*Strategy:* Analogy—An *analogy* is useful for concluding remarks. Perhaps Jane could draw an analogy between being stuck on the weekends and being a prisoner.

Before studying each of the strategies in more detail, we will look at four selections—two student-written models and two professional ones.

These writers have combined some of the strategies in their essays. The first of each group of essays will be annotated. The second essay in each group will not be annoted, but certain sections will be bracketed to help you identify the strategy used. At this point you may think that you do not know enough to identify all of the strategies. If so, do not hesitate to review the list of strategies on pp. 111–112. You may look ahead to later chapters if you feel you need additional information.

But remember, the purpose of this analysis is not to test you, but to help you see how writers—both student and professional—use the strategies to support a *point* or *thesis*.

## STUDENT ESSAY 1

The student-written paper below uses seven of the ten strategies to prove her thesis: *The bumper sticker is basically an argument.* The writer has taken a position about bumper stickers that is debatable, so she herself has written an argument. It is important to define terms early in an argument, a point the writer seems to understand, because her *definition* of *bumper sticker* comes close on the heels of the thesis. Since there is a wide variety of bumper stickers, the writer classifies them in order to give some kind of logic to her paper. (Listing all the bumper stickers without any kind of order would create an indigestible mass.) Another important reason for classifying is to support a particular point in the paper: *Bumper stickers aren't always serious. Illustration* is intertwined with *classification* because the reader needs to understand exactly what the writer means by the categories of *serious* and *unserious*.

The other strategies—*narration, process, comparison,* and *cause and effect*—the writer uses with some degree of success to help her build an argument in support of her thesis.

### STICKING TO BUMPERS

¹ Four children in the back of a car can drive vacationing parents crazy. At least our parents told us this often enough. "Shut up, and quit fighting! Look at the scenery!" (The scenery was hot dog stands and Taco Bells.)

² Suddenly, right in the middle of Flagstaff, Arizona, my father said: "God bless America—and please hurry." A minute later he said: "Become a doctor—and support a lawyer." And then: "You touch-a my car, I break-a you face."

*Introduction*
**Narration**
³ He was, of course, reading bumper stickers in busy traffic. My mother is smart; she knew that if you can keep four hot, unhappy young people—ranging in age from nine to eighteen—from killing each other for only a short time, you are ahead of the game. The other kids were appointed look-outs, and I was made secretary for the Great Sticker Hunt. I was also appointed Drawer of Conclusions—father is a lawyer.

⁴ For the next few days, we saw enough bumper stickers to

fill a small notebook, and I outlined my conclusions. First, the bumper sticker appears everywhere. It is glued on old rusty VWs and new Cadillacs—more on the former than the latter, however. Drivers of very expensive cars—foreign or domestic—do not, we think, buy bumper stickers.

*Thesis and Definition*

5 *The bumper sticker is basically an argument.* It may or may not be serious; but it has to be short. It tends to be epigrammatic. It can state a "fact"—SOFT JUDGES MAKE HARDENED CRIMINALS—or a call for action—FIGHT ORGANIZED CRIME: ABOLISH THE IRS. The subject of the argument is seldom much older than last month's newspaper.

*Elaboration of thesis*
*Classification—first large category: unserious*
*Illustration—two subcategories of unserious*

6 Bumper stickers seem to fall into seven broad groups. Four groups are relatively unserious, or even represent overt attempts at humor. The first of these is personal. Examples:
I'M A TENNIS BUM.
I TRAVEL THE FIFTH ST. BRIDGE. PRAY FOR ME.
In a second group are the determinedly wacky:
GET STONED—DRINK WET CEMENT
SURF NAKED
CLEAN AIR SMELLS FUNNY
FIGHT SMOG—RIDE A HORSE
DON'T STARE; I'M DANGEROUSLY ATTRACTIVE

*Illustration—third category of unserious*

7 In a third group of the relatively unserious stickers are derivations of other messages: HAVE YOU HUGGED YOUR KID TODAY? becomes HAVE YOU HUGGED YOUR HARLEY TODAY? and KEEP ON TRUCKIN' becomes KEEP ON TOLKIEN. Such derivations—or "echoes"—are important to the determined collector. On a dull day of vacationing you can trace eight or ten themes that undergo relatively unsubtle variations. On different bumpers you can be asked whether "today" you have hugged your wife, husband, grandparents, kids, motorcycle, and the defensive line of the Pittsburgh Steelers.

*Illustration—fourth subcategory of unserious*

8 A fourth group of the unserious stickers makes little sense—at least to me. Examples:
FLOWERS DO IT!
JOHANN'S BACH (printed in gothic script)
CUSTER HAD IT COMING
I FOUND IT!
WOULDN'T YOU RATHER BE RIDING A MULE ON MOLOKAI?
I BRAKE FOR UNICORNS AND HOBBITS
SUPPORT ONOMATOPOEIA

*Classification—second large category: serious*
*Illustration—first subcategory of serious*

9 The next three groups are relatively more serious. In the first of these, the driver of the car makes a clear pitch for his or her profession:
FIREMEN STILL MAKE HOUSE CALLS
LOVE A NURSE
IF YOU CAN READ THIS THANK A TEACHER
ENGINEERS DO IT WITH PRECISION
IF YOU DON'T LIKE HOW WE TAKE CARE OF YOUR GARBAGE, WE'LL RETURN IT. (seen on the bumper of a garbage truck)

*Illustration—*
*second*
*subcategory of*
*serious*

[10] In the second group of serious stickers, we find arguments that are related to marriage, sex, and the family:

ANOTHER FAMILY FOR ERA

CELEBRATE FAMILY VALUES. THIS IS FAMILY YEAR!

WE BELIEVE IN MARRIAGE

A WOMAN WITHOUT A MAN IS LIKE A FISH WITHOUT A BICYCLE

SOULS OF GREAT LIFE ARE WAITING TO BE BORN: HAVE ONE!

ABORTION NOW!!

*Illustration—*
*third subcategory*
*of serious*

[11] The last group of serious stickers argues a political point, sometimes with an unpleasant edge of meanness or satire:

TAKE A WOLF TO LUNCH. FEED HIM AN ENVIRONMENTALIST.

SPLIT WOOD, NOT ATOMS

NUCLEAR POWER PLANTS ARE BUILT BETTER THAN JANE FONDA

A BUSHEL OF GRAIN FOR A BARREL OF OIL

CLEAN UP AMERICA—SHOOT A REDNECK

*Process*

[12] In furthering our attempts to understand the bumper sticker syndrome, we tried writing a few, and in doing so learned a little about how to produce them. What you try for is a short statement that is both pointed and relevant to a recent event which most people are aware of. So first pick such an event. Next, associate it with another thing, idea, or person that is well known. Then, try to use a play on words or a pun. The readers should have "instant recognition" when they read the message, and perhaps be persuaded by the argument, serious or not. You can see the elements of the process work-

*End point*

ing in this sticker: KEEP AIR CLEAN AND SEX DIRTY. (I won't reproduce any of the stickers we made up—they are too awful.)

*Cause-effect*

[13] Why do thousands of American drivers go to the trouble to buy bumper stickers? They seem like such trivial messages to display to the world. One answer may be that they reflect the triviality of modern "media journalism." News stories on television, for example, are typically short and abbreviated, as are bumper stickers. Only one point is highlighted in both types of messages, so that the viewer gets a dramatic, but distorted idea of the complexities involved. When the President spoke in Chicago, the evening TV news account of his long speech showed him speaking only two sentences, both taken out of context. One of them was not even the full sentence as he spoke it.

*Comparison*
*(with other short*
*communications)*

[14] We live in an age of bumper-sticker journalism. The Letters columns in magazines and newspapers often use letters of one sentence. These deliver no more than an opinion without evidence or reasons given. Like the chopped-up TV interview and the one-sentence letter in a national magazine the bumper sticker gives us a message lacking background, con-

text, or development. These are messages without authority or anybody standing behind them; and they are as forgettable as today's comic page. They are meant to last only a few seconds in one's consciousness and then disappear.

[15] Given the way we live today, the bumper sticker probably satisfies an American need to make a point quickly, painlessly, and—most of all—anonymously. The car involved may be identified clearly as a Ford, Chevrolet, Plymouth, etc. But when was the last time you saw a signed bumper sticker?

## ◆ PRACTICE

1. A definition should clarify, limit, and specify. Taking these requirements into account, how satisfactory and complete is the writer's definition of *bumper stickers*?

2. It was necessary for the writer to *divide* bumper stickers into two groups and then sub-classify. Do you agree with the writer's classifications, considering the thesis she wished to prove? How would another classification be more or less useful in proving her thesis?

3. How is the narrative in the introduction important to the writer's *role*? Is the narrative important for an understanding of the writer's *thesis*? What revision would you suggest for the introduction in relation to the thesis and the paper?

4. Except for the intertwining of illustration with classification, the other strategies used in this paper are discrete paragraph units (paragraphs 12–14). How is the thesis supported by these three strategies? For example, is it important to know *how* to write a bumper sticker if you are being persuaded that they are short arguments?

5. If you were to make suggestions to this writer about revising her paper, what would you recommend? Can you think of other strategies she might have used to support her thesis?

## STUDENT ESSAY 2

The student writer of this next essay has used a variety of strategies to support his point that how one sings the national anthem has nothing to do with patriotism. The writer has found at least five of the strategies useful. Read the essay and evaluate the effectiveness of the strategies in supporting the thesis. You may find more than one strategy employed in one paragraph, which was not always the case in "Bumper Stickers."

## POP SINGERS AND THE NATIONAL ANTHEM

A {

Thesis implied

[1] When I was a little kid, my Dad would take me to baseball and football games in the sports stadiums around the country—Busch in St. Louis, Tiger's in Detroit, and Soldier's Field in Chicago. I remember distinctly my first reaction to the singing of "The Star Spangled Banner." When the woman's voice came over the public address system, the men around us put down their beers and took off their hats. The children stopped jumping up and down and stood quietly. The players, all standing in a row, hats off, bright and shining in their colorful uniforms, filled me with awe. As my father put his hand over his heart, I asked, "What the heck is going on?" He shushed me and told me to stand still. It was obvious to me from the very beginning that the singing of the national anthem at a sporting event was a serious affair and had something to do with patriotism and respect.

B {

[2] Up until the time I got to high school, the singers who opened the game at sporting events were usually concert musicians like Beverly Sills and Robert Merrill. The national anthem is a difficult song to sing because its range is over an octave and a fifth, spanning the range of twenty notes on the scale. It takes a concert musician to sing it right—a singer who performs opera or presents recitals in places like Carnegie Hall or the Lincoln Center for the Performing Arts. Such singers go through a long, intensive training in order to sing the range of two or more octaves—or twenty-five notes. They do not usually depend upon sound systems when they perform because they are trained to sing for long periods of time, using their own volume to fill an auditorium. As a result, they can reach all the notes—top and bottom—of "The Star Spangled Banner," and with a microphone their voices can fill a stadium seating thousands of people.

C {

[3] After I got in college, I noticed a big change in the musicians who sang at athletic events. The trained concert singer was replaced in many instances with popular recording stars. Apparently, the managers of athletic events wanted to boost their television ratings, thinking that popular names and faces would draw better than trained opera singers.

D {

[4] José Feliciano was one of the first of the pop singers to sing the national anthem at an athletic event. His rendition of the song was controversial because it was different from the accurate and precise performances of concert singers. Called undignified and unpatriotic by some, José used a swinging style, pausing in unusual places, and cutting out the high and low notes. Ray Charles, the blind jazz singer and pianist, was also criticized because his rendition was different from those who had customarily sung the song. But perhaps the most controversial rendition was by the soul singer Marvin Gaye,

who sang at the NBA All-Star game in 1983. He used a gospel-rock syncopation and vocal inflection. His interpretation was called "creative" and "soulful" by those who approved and "unpatriotic" and "disrespectful" by those who disapproved.

*E* {

5 But does patriotism, respect, or devotion to country have anything to do with the way a singer interprets the national anthem? Pop musicians like Marvin Gaye change the notes and give the song a different beat because they are not trained singers. They have a limited range, so they can't hit the top or low notes of the song as it was written. They depend upon sound systems in the recording studios to provide volume and range. In an athletic stadium, they do not have that kind of back-up to make them sound better than they are. So they aren't necessarily "soulful" in their rendition—they just can't sing it. Since they have a limited musical talent, the only way they can sing the song is to change it according to their "style." Their interpretations have nothing to do with patriotism, loyalty, or respect.

*Thesis*

6 So people who criticize a pop singer for interpreting the national anthem in an original way shouldn't assume that he loves his country less than the trained singer or give him too much credit for being creative. *He isn't less patriotic or devoted to his country because he can't sing the song. He is doing all that he knows how to do*—making the national anthem a pop song or gospel hymn so that he can reach the notes.

## ◆ PRACTICE

1. The writer of "Pop Singers and the National Anthem" uses the three *hooks (national anthem, patriotism,* and *respect* or *devoted)* in three different places in the paper: *implied thesis* (paragraph 1), rhetorical question (paragraph 5), and *thesis* (paragraph 6). How are these *hooks* related to the strategies employed in specific paragraphs and in the paper as a whole?

2. The writer introduces Beverly Sills, Robert Merrill, and the difficulty of singing the national anthem before the strategy in bracket B. Why does the reader need that information?

3. You will notice that many student-written papers begin the same way this one does. Why do students find this strategy useful in introductions? Discuss the writer's *stance*, and his *role* in particular. How is the writer's role established in the introduction?

4. Discuss the amount of detail and illustration in bracket C (paragraph 3). How well does the paragraph use the strategy? What advice for revision would you offer the writer about this paragraph?

5. Where in the paper is most of the proof for the thesis? What strategies have been used to present the proof? Is it adequate? If you wrote this paper, what causation would you attribute to the different renditions of the national anthem?

# *PROFESSIONAL ESSAY 1*

Next we will examine two professional essays that use a variety of strategies within each essay. We'll use the same format as before—the first essay will be annotated; in the second you will find the strategy within the bracketed material.

"My Fat Problem and Theirs" is a *cause and effect* essay which uses a variety of other strategies to answer the writer's question: *"Why had I equated being thin with happiness?"* The strategy of *process* is also important in this selection because the writer wants the reader to understand *how* her fat problem affected her parents' treatment of her and also her own behavior.

### MY FAT PROBLEM AND THEIRS

***Subject introduced:*** *Growing up overweight*

¹ I think I'm the appropriate age to write about growing up as an overweight child. While I have enough perspective to look at the fat child who endured my first 18 years, I haven't lost the ability to reexperience the painful emotions she felt. At any moment I could be stripped of the new confidence that two years of college have brought and could plunge backward into the sea of insecurities that almost drowned my younger self.

***Contrast:*** *Differences between fantasy and reality*

² The difference between us, me then and me now, is that I used to think: "if I were thin I'd be perfect." And being perfect of course meant getting male approval. I used to fantasize about being thin on a seasonal basis. Every April I'd dream of a thin me by the first day of camp. I'd create elaborate and detailed scenarios of a summer full of romance—I knew what color Lacoste shirt I'd be wearing when the boy of my dreams would confess his deeply felt love for me. But when the fateful June day arrived and the still fat me boarded the bus for camp, I moved my dreams one season ahead. I began to imagine the thin me on the first day of school. September came; nothing had changed. So I dreamed of Thanksgiving. Then of Christmas. Then spring vacation. By then I was back at camp again.

***Transition:*** Thesis Implied *Thin is not necessarily happy*

³ It was only after nine summers at camp and nine first days at school that I became bored with this obsessive daydreaming and recognized its drain on me. That's when I set out to try and understand why I had equated being thin with being happy.

*Contrast:*
*Differences*
*between ideal*
*weight in 1940*
*and now*

⁴ Had I been born years ago, when America worshiped a different beauty ideal, I might have been not only happy as is, but a sex object. In 1940, according to the company, the nude woman pictured on the label of the White Rock soda bottle was five feet four and weighed 140 pounds (my proportions exactly). Today's White Rock "girl" is five feet eight and weighs 118 pounds. Imagine! Forty years ago I could have appeared naked on a soft-drink bottle, while today I cannot leave my house in anything less than long wide-legged pants and a roomy, long-sleeved shirt.

*Refutation of*
***cause-effect:***
*Teasing is not*
*a cause of*
*unhappiness*

⁵ Many people blame the unhappiness of overweight people on the teasing of other children. Of course I encountered my share of jests from my classmates—such as altering my last name to "Pork-Noy." But attributing all my misery to kids' bullying just didn't explain it. Most children find ways to chide their playmates whether they are called "braceface," "foureyes," "metalmouth," or "pizzaface." The difference is that no one tells pizzaface or foureyes to do *something* to get rid of those pimples or glasses. And bracefaces can eat anything they want for dinner—and know someday their braces will be gone.

***Effect*** *of fatness*
*on other*
*children's parents*

⁶ Others who were overweight as children have told me that it was their parents' reaction that made them feel the worst. Some parents refused to acknowledge the existence of excess weight: one woman remembers her mother yelling at a saleswoman for suggesting that she buy the "chubby" styles for her daughter. Other parents overreacted: panicked that the weight gain would increase geometrically for the rest of the child's life—and had to be stopped NOW! Looking back on my family's response, I simply wonder why everyone made such a *fuss* over my weight.

***Effect*** *of fatness*
*on her parents:*
*(1) character flaw*
*(2) diet work shop*

⁷ I had my share of talents, I took lessons, I was busy with a lot of activities, and yet the importance of my weight overshadowed those virtues. My fat was treated as a behavioral trait, a *character flaw*. So, along with art classes, piano lessons, Little League, and Hebrew school, came diet workshops. I started going in the fifth grade. More precisely, my mom, dad, and I went together—a team effort.

***Process*** *of diet*
*workshop*

⁸ Every Tuesday night I was taken behind a royal-blue curtain where one of the formerly fat group leaders subjected me to a battery of questions and my weekly weigh-in. I had to tell the woman if I'd cheated (and I always had). "Yes, I had an extra piece of fruit on Tuesday," I admitted, which really meant that I'd had Oreos and milk, or I ate the hamburger I was allowed on Friday and Saturday as well. (On Fridays I was allowed four ounces of broiled hamburger meat on half a bun. That was supposed to be a *treat*). This confession would explain my one-and-a-quarter-pound gain. Outside the blue cur-

tain I was met by my parents. "How'dja do?" they'd chime brightly and in unison. I had three choices: gained, lost, or stayed the same. All I ever answered was lost or stayed the same, even if I'd gained.

*Process continued*

⁹ After the weigh-in came the lecture. One I distinctly remember is the lecture on ridding oneself of the unsightly flab that forms beneath the chin when one loses weight. We were instructed to look up at the ceiling and pretend to kiss it while slowly oscillating our heads—now left, now right. There I was, 11 years old, doing exercises to renew the elasticity of the skin on my neck.

*Effect of diet workshop: cheating and feeling cheated*

¹⁰ Since I started that diet in the fifth grade I have been a habitual cheat. "You're really only cheating yourself," my mother would say. Maybe so, but it always felt as if I was the one being cheated. Every day my lunch box contained a sandwich on thin bread and a piece of fruit. Who wouldn't feel deprived when Cindy Goldman unpacked her bulging brown bag full of peanut butter and jelly sandwiches, Fritos, Yodels, miniature Hershey bars, and Hawaiian Punch. And on visitor's day at camp, when other kids got obscenely delightful armloads of Doritos, Oreos, and Twinkies, I got a grocery bag of plums, peaches, and sugarless bubble gum.

*Cause-effect: Effect of mother's reprimand **causes** cheating*

¹¹ I perceived my mother's choice of foods for me as a reprimand. I fought back by eating whenever no one was looking. Train rides were a great opportunity to eat M & Ms among strangers. I also loved the afternoons when I would get home earlier than my mom and eat whatever was in the fridge—cheese and crackers, cold cereal, leftover Chinese food. Nor was I above sneaking down to the kitchen while my parents were asleep and stuffing Oreos into the pockets of my pajamas. Or holding a handful of Mallomars behind my back while peeking my head in to say an innocent good-night.

*Effect of cheating: secret food*

¹² I had perfected my indispensable trick of soundlessly opening and closing the refrigerator doors. What you do is first slide your fingers inside the rubber gasket around the door edge so that you break the suction seal and it doesn't make that telltale smack. Then pull the door open very, very slowly so that the horseradish and mustard jars on the inside of the door don't rattle. Then grab your Mallomars and close the door in the same fashion. This cheating habit has been hard to break. I still have ice cream for breakfast when I wake up earlier than everyone else. Food can be a secret pleasure.

*Effect of weight on father: rage (cause) for effect of rage on her: never be thin*

¹³ As much as I resented my mother's constant hinting, at least she tried to tiptoe around my feelings. My father, on the other hand, approached my weight problem with the sensitivity and tact of a sledgehammer. Once he told me I looked like a horse. I could see the rage rising in him. It was weird, actually. Of all the times I'd been scolded—for being stubborn or selfish or fresh—I'd never seen that rage before. After that I vowed never to give him the satisfaction of my being thin.

*Effect of*
*overweight*
*on father:*
*blow to his ego*

14 How could a few extra pounds have provoked such uncharacteristic behavior from an otherwise generous and gentle man? Why did *my* being overweight mean so much to *him*? He had never been overweight. Is it really so important? Yes, he was telling me by the intensity of his reaction. No, I would now argue back: I think my being overweight was a blow to his ego, a blight on his otherwise aesthetically correct family.

*Refutation of*
**cause and effect:**
*thinness does not*
*solve all your*
*problems*

15 The myth that "thin is in" and that "in" is happy is used as an incentive to keep you in these diet programs. But after all that hype, thinness is anti-climactic. Your problems don't disappear with the pounds. And a better brain and love life do not suddenly appear with the new silhouette. I know this because I did go through my thin phases. But I never felt any different. I didn't feel "in."

**Effect** *of thinness*
*on others*

16 I look at myself among my friends. We're women of all shapes and sizes. Are the thinner ones happier than I? My friend Sara recently traded in 30 pounds for a five-feet-one, 105-pound frame. I asked her if she liked her new body. She said it was nice, but she'd had more bouts of depression in the year she'd been petite than ever before. Sara says thinness isn't all it's cracked up to be, and by believing her, I shed a burden much heavier than 30 pounds. I felt relieved, but also angry— at my parents, the media, and society for having misled me, and at myself for having been duped.

**Narrative Thesis**
*stated*

17 A few nights after my talk with Sara I shared this realization with my parents. Their voices quavered in congratulations and approval. Their words said, "We're glad you're happy," but the quaver betrayed their fear that I'll give up trying to control my weight and blow up like a balloon. I told them that thin doesn't mean happy and I'm happy as I am right now. I'm not certain that they believed me, but soon they will have to accept my attempt to accept my body.

*Narrative*
*continued*
**Conclusion**

18 I bombarded my parents with all my old resentments, angers, and fears. I reminded them of the summer before I went to college when they put me on an expensive diet. "You can go to college as a new person," my mother beamed. It didn't occur to either of us at the time that this "supportive" statement concealed a very damaging opinion. Why did I need to go as a new person? What was wrong with the *old* me? I told them that from now on my weight problem is my own and the sooner they stop worrying about it, the sooner I'd stop resenting them. My mom said that she was shocked that she had transmitted so many negative unspoken messages. I said I was shocked that she was shocked: a sensitive child feels whatever you're feeling without hearing a single word. My dad said he was sorry. So did my mom. I said it was okay. And it is okay. Things happen, so it's okay now. Okay. —Sharon Portnoy

## ◆ *PRACTICE*

1. At what point in the essay does the author introduce the theme of insecurity/unhappiness? Cite the examples by paragraph number where she supports that theme.

2. What strategy does Portnoy use in paragraph 5 to refute the idea that teasing causes unhappiness in fat children?

3. Discuss the use of the implied thesis in paragraph 3. In what way would the paper have been different if she had stated her thesis in this paragraph, rather than in paragraph 17? What is the effect of her saying that she had "set out to try and understand why I had equated being thin with being happy"? Evaluate how effectively she learned what she set out to do.

4. What strategy does the writer use to describe her method of opening a refrigerator door? How well could you imitate her method?

5. Why does Portnoy use questions in paragraphs 14, 16, and 18? Are the questions in all three paragraphs used for the same reason?

## *PROFESSIONAL ESSAY 2*

In the second of the professional models, the writer, a psychologist, argues against the tendency of modern man to make excuses for his failings (thesis, paragraph 8). The primary strategy used is cause and effect; however, you will find a number of other strategies embedded in the essay.

Note, in particular, the series of contrasting statements: the assertion with an excuse following. Note also the use of rhetorical questions: the question, then the answer in the form of an excuse, all based on cause-effect reasoning.

Study the bracketed material and identify the strategies used. Evaluate the effectiveness of the strategies in supporting the thesis.

*STRESS—AND OTHER SCAPEGOATS*

*Introduction*

*A*

¹ Once upon a time we lived in a simple world controlled by understandable forces. Life then consisted of the unrelenting struggle of talent, will and luck against nature, evil and misfortune. Sometimes we won, sometimes we lost. Sometimes fortitude and talent produced victory and pride, sometimes bad luck and weakness resulted in loss and shame. Sometimes we hated ourselves. Sometimes we hated our enemies. Sometimes we even hated God. But always the object and righteousness of our anger were clear and just a little bit uplifting.

2 Then, ever so slowly, came the specter of science, casting its shadow over all human problems. One by one, all the evils of the world fell prey to the most powerful of scientific weapons—explanation. Storms became weather fronts, crop growth became agricultural science and death became the product of microorganisms and a myriad of biochemical events. The grand struggle is no longer that of man against nature, but science against nature. The force of evil has disappeared from nature; sinfulness is no longer man's fate. The new "sciences" of sociology, psychology and psychiatry have cast aside such concepts as will, willpower, badness and laziness and replaced them with political and psychological repression, poor conditioning, diseased family interaction and bad genes. One by one, human failings have been redesignated as diseases.

3 If a drunk driver kills my wife, how dare I hate him? We all know alcoholism is a disease and that no one gets a disease on purpose. But if I do hate him, if I'm out of my mind with rage and kill the driver, you can't be angry with me. After all, wasn't I suffering from temporary insanity? (That's a brief disease, like the flu.)

4 Now don't worry if you find yourself angry with your spouse or boss. You just have an emotional problem. Eating too much? That's OK, you're simply suffering from obesity. Certainly you needn't concern yourself with any lack of willpower. As we have all learned, your food problem is really just repressed sexuality, or maybe you don't have enough pineapple in your diet. Well, maybe the problem isn't perfectly clear, but some book with a new theory, and certainly a new word for the problem, will explain it all shortly. The one thing that is clear is that the problem isn't your fault and the solution could never be as simple as "Just stop eating so much."

5 Do you find yourself lacking energy? Are you accomplishing less than others think you should? Could you be suffering from that 19th-century imperfection called laziness? Not a chance; you've got hypoglycemia, the most deadly epidemic since the plague. Are you bored with work? You probably suffer from burnout, one of the newest pet diseases of the middle class. Remember the old days when you thought they called it work because it was difficult, unpleasant and boring? Remember when you believed the reason you were being paid was to do your job, whether you liked it or not? Those days are over. Remember when drug or alcohol abuse was a product of some combination of hedonism and foolishness? That era has ended, too. Now you're an addict. You have no will, so you are not to blame; the disease got you.

6 No list of these new diseases would be complete without that vile cancer which, experts say, is slowly killing us all: stress. How remarkable it is that this illness was unknown several

hundred years ago. During the 18th-century, when disease and war wiped out hordes, when people toiled long hours under poor conditions, when there was no modern medicine, no unemployment insurance, stress somehow slipped the minds of medical thinkers. Now, when people merely need to worry about the few hardships that have survived progress, we are suddenly dying of stress.

C ⎨ 7 This diseasing of America has spawned a new growth industry—caretakers and experts. The fusion of capitalism and science has resulted in thousands of new experts setting up treatment programs certifying each other, publishing books and flitting from talk show to talk show. If you have pain, sorrow or the slightest discomfort, there are only two questions you need answer. First, "What's my disorder?" Second, "Whom can I talk into paying for the treatment?" In such an atmosphere only a very sick person would even attempt to figure out his own problems.

*Thesis* 8 The American lust for scientific-sounding explanations is completely out of control. *It is time to rehabilitate the concept of will and restore it to its proper place in our lives.* To fight the notion that we are flimsy lumps of protoplasm that will crumble under the next bit of stress. To reduce the percentage of our population that gives or takes advice, as well as the number of media reports about the latest fad in diseasism. Ultimately, we must assume responsibility for our actions, and stop the promotion and exploitation of human frailties and imperfections.

*Conclusion*

D ⎨ 9 What would life be like if we were stripped of our 20th-century maladies? Certainly there would be many problems—including massive unemployment among the "helpers." But the most visible effect would be on the English language. Suddenly there would be a resurgence of such phrases as "I've decided to . . . ," "I will . . . ," "I won't . . . ." A quick death would befall terms like "I am thinking about it" or "I'm working on it." Every psychologist knows that when a client says he's "working" on a problem, he means he's working out some great excuse for not doing it. Most important, life would become a little simpler, for we could explain behavior in terms of inner directives, desires and decisions rather than the cryptic psychobabble that dominates current pop psychology.

10 Finally, men and women would become declarative, non-deterministic and, as a result, dignified human beings. Science and medicine would still be left plenty of real diseases to conquer. And although pain and outrageous fortune would still be a part of life, at least it would be the individual who fought against them rather than some army of self-declared experts. —Rex Julian Beaber

## ◆ PRACTICE

1. In his introduction, the writer uses "once upon a time." What strategy do you usually associate with these words? How many paragraphs follow the "once-upon-a-time" strategy? How effective is this introduction in setting up the *past* versus the *future*?

2. In the bracketed material B (paragraphs 3–6), the writer gives several examples of his point that "human failings have been redesignated as diseases" (paragraph 2). Even though cause and effect is the basic strategy, the four paragraphs work to support his thesis by the use of which strategy? Discuss the effectiveness of mixing the strategies in this way. We noted, in the introduction to Beaber's essay, his use of rhetorical questions with answers (bracket B). Discuss the effectiveness of this device in a cause-and-effect paper.

3. What class(es) of people is the writer criticizing? Note that the author is a psychologist. Does he admit that he might be part of the problem? Is his failure to mention his training related to his *stance?*

4. Beaber argues for a change in human behavior. Therefore, he is obligated to prove that the change will be beneficial. Where in the essay does he provide "benefits"? How successful is he in proving the effect will be beneficial? Is this essay a discussion of the importance of language on behavior?

5. Discuss the convincingness of the strategies in supporting the thesis. What recommendation, if any, would you make for revision?

# CHAPTER 9

# DESCRIPTION

## DESCRIPTION

When you describe a thing, you give its qualities, nature, or appearance. The word *describe* comes from the Latin *describere* ("to copy" or "to sketch"), which implies that the thing described has a material existence. Customarily, the words *describe* and *description* have been used to refer to material things, although of course one may describe abstractions such as states of mind or moral attributes.

You will find description useful in either single paragraphs or full papers. It is often necessary when you want to talk about a person or place; but description can be used to support your point in any kind of writing.

### Sensory Images

Good descriptions often appeal to one or more of the five senses. The writer tries to make the reader see, hear, feel, smell, or taste the experience being described. These word pictures or sensory images help the reader experience vicariously what the writer has felt. They also help to create the mood that the writer wishes to achieve.

Descriptions usually support a larger purpose. Not only must you be an astute and careful observer, but you also need to relate your observations to a point or a descriptive purpose. Notice how Anaïs Nin, through her description of sights and smells in Fez, Morocco, makes the point about the importance of women's eyes.

> SIGHT    Colors seep into your conciousness as never before: a sky-blue jellaba with a black face veil, a pearl-grey jellaba with a yellow veil, a black jellaba with a red veil, a shocking-pink

jellaba with a purple veil. The clothes conceal the wearers' figures so that they remain elusive, with all the intensity and expression concentrated in the eyes. The eyes speak for the body, the self, for the age, conveying innumerable messages from their deep and rich existence.

*POINT:*
*Importance*
*of eyes*

After color and the graceful sway of robes, the flares, the stance, the swing of loose clothes, come the odors. One stand is devoted to sandalwood from Indonesia and the Philippines. It lies in huge round baskets and is sold by weight, for it is a precious luxury wood for burning as incense. The walls of the cubicle are lined with small bottles containing the essence of flowers—jasmine, rose, honeysuckle, and the rose water that is used to perfume guests. In the same baskets lie the henna leaves that the women distill and use on their hands and feet. For the affluent, the henna comes in liquid form. And there is, too, the famous *kohl*, the dust from antimony that gives the women such a soft, iridescent, smoky radiance around their eyes.

*SMELL*

*Importance*
*of eyes*

Behind every good description there is a point being made: the sunset is *beautiful*, the earthquake was *frightening*, the birth of a baby is *miraculous*, the political ideas of Theodore Roosevelt were *pragmatic*. Consider the point in the passage below, which describes the break-up of Ernest Shackleton's ship during his expedition to the Antarctic in 1915:

*Sounds of the ice*

[1] There were the sounds of the pack in movement—the basic noises, the grunting and whining of the floes, along with an occasional thud as a heavy block collapsed. But in addition, the pack under compression seemed to have an almost limitless repertoire of other sounds, many of which seemed strangely unrelated to the noise of ice undergoing pressure. Sometimes there was a sound like a gigantic train with squeaky axles being shunted roughly about with a great deal of bumping and clattering. At the same time a huge ship's whistle blew, mingling with the crowing of roosters, the roar of a distant surf, the soft throb of an engine far away, and the moaning cries of an old woman. In the rare periods of calm, when the movement of the pack subsided for a moment, the muffled rolling of drums drifted across the air.

*Details*

*Pressure of the ice*

[2] In this universe of ice, nowhere was the movement greater or the pressure more intense than in the floes that were attacking the ship. Nor could her position have been worse. One floe was jammed solidly against her starboard bow, and another held her on the same side aft. A third floe drove squarely in on her port beam opposite. Thus the ice was working to break her in half, directly amidships. On several occasions she bowed to starboard along her entire length.

*Details*

*Accumulation of*
*ice on bows*

[3] Forward, where the worst of the onslaught was concentrated, the ice was inundating her. It piled higher and higher

*Details* against her bows as she repelled each new wave, until gradually it mounted to her bulwarks, then crashed across the deck, overwhelming her with a crushing load that pushed her head down even deeper. Thus held, she was even more at the mercy of the floes driving against her flanks.

*Ship's reaction to pressure of ice* ⁴ The ship reacted to each fresh wave of pressure in a different way. Sometimes she simply quivered briefly as a human being might wince if seized by a single, stabbing pain. Other times she retched in a series of convulsive jerks accompanied by anguished outcries. On these occasions her three *Details* masts whipped violently back and forth as the rigging tightened like harpstrings. But most agonizing for the men were the times when she seemed a huge creature suffocating and gasping for breath, her sides heaving against the strangling pressure.

*Comparison: ship like a dying "giant beast"* ⁵ More than any other single impression in those final hours, all the men were struck, almost to the point of horror, by the way the ship behaved like a giant beast in its death agonies.—Alfred Lansing, *Endurance*

The point behind the description is that the destruction of the ship was terrifying, and the descriptive details contribute to this point.

## Point of View

Lansing wrote his description over fifty years after the expedition, a fact which partly controls his point of view. *Point of view* is the angle—psychological or physical (or both)—from which the writer views his subject. Lansing's point of view is that of the researcher, poring over old diaries and accounts of Shackleton's voyage and listening to the stories of the few survivors still alive. To recreate the incident, Lansing blends his point of view with that of the men inside the ship. You—the reader—hear, see, and feel what the trapped sailors heard, saw, and felt. Lansing's ruling principle is the terrifying physical effect of the ice on the ship and the terrifying psychological effect on the crew members. He presents his paragraphs in deductive fashion, following topic sentences with brilliant descriptive detail; we hear the weird sounds ("gigantic train with squeaky axles," "the moaning cries of an old woman"), and we feel the pressure of the ice ("she retched in a series of convulsive jerks," "her three masts whipped violently back and forth as the rigging tightened like harpstrings"). The climax of the passage occurs in paragraph 4, where the ship is described as a huge, dying animal fighting for life. All of these details give the reader an idea of the terror the sailors must have felt.

When writing description, do not lose control of point of view, your physical and psychological "angle." Here is a student's paragraph in which the point of view is fuzzy:

| | |
|---|---|
| *Point of view implied in* we | As we strode through the alleyways between the houses, we met a few shy, ragged children who were gleefully playing with an equally ragged dog. From the stoop of his front door, a |
| *Details* | wrinkled old man with a red bandana wrapped around his head meditatively surveyed the distances beyond the mesa. In |
| *Shift from* we *to impersonal* one | the distance, one could discern the dim shapes of the farmers in their sparse corn patches. The rhythm of a woman grinding corn could be heard along the yellow street from within one of |
| *Who is "hearing"?* | the small apartments. |

Although the student uses clear details, his shift in point of view blurs their effect. The reader may wonder how the writer saw "dim shapes in the distance," and heard sounds "along the yellow street," and knew at the same time that the dim shapes were farmers and that the sound came from a "woman grinding corn." This is not just a pedantic objection. Both description and narration demand a sense of reality in handling point of view. The reader should be made to feel that he is observing the scene in a natural way, the way he might observe it if he were there. The writer of this passage would have treated the scene more naturally and convincingly had he first described a dim shape in the distance, and *later* described it as a farmer. Also, the description would have been strengthened had the writer not recognized the noise from the apartment until he asked someone what it was, or until he went into the apartment to find out for himself.

The shifts in point of view in this student's paragraph are not particularly bad. Violent shifts, however, may cause the reader to feel that instead of being led into a scene he is being yanked into it. The following paragraph demonstrates the problem.

> I was driving around that night, not thinking about anything particularly. I was completely unaware that before the evening was over I was going to witness the most horrible experience of my life. It was when I reached the top of the hill overlooking the valley where the accident occurred that I got an empty feeling in the pit of my stomach. It is strange what mixed thoughts run through your head when you see a bad accident.

Besides "telling" his reader too much and not allowing the details of the accident to speak for themselves, the writer shifts from the experience as it unfolded to his later reactions to the experience.

In the following passage from the same paper, the writer uses point of view accurately:

> I stepped out of the car and walked toward the ditch. Suddenly I heard a man's voice clearly over the muffled sounds of the crowd. The voice said: "Bring a flashlight over here!" A highway patrolman who was standing next to me turned the beam of his big flashlight down between the rows of corn. The voice kept speaking, and I could see by the patrolman's flash that it belonged to the county sheriff.

When the writer walked toward the ditch, he heard a voice. He accurately reports here the series of events as he saw and heard them: an unidentified voice spoke, the patrolman turned his flashlight toward the voice, the speaker turned out to be the sheriff.

## ◆ *PRACTICE*

### *Discussion*

Discuss the point of view, use of details, and sensory images in the following description of a boy's father:

> ¹ My father's world was monstrous. He knew places like Corsicana, Waxahachie, Nacogdoches, Wichita Falls, Monahans. His world was more than half the size of Texas. He would come home and tell us about it and expand our boundaries. He knew what the road looked like between Sonora and Eldorado, between Borger and Pampa. He loved roads and the way they looked. We would be driving to Grandma Hale's farm and come to a place that wasn't characteristic of our immediate world and he would say, "This looks like the road between Cuero and Yoakum."
>
> ² He brought home the very best kind of gifts. A puppy in a shoe box. A chicken with a bad leg. A 25-pound sack of peanut brittle. Once he brought two milk goats. He had traded the old Ford for a smoking Chevy with the door wired shut on the driver's side. I can see him turning in off the road, grinning behind the cracked windshield, those two goats riding on the back seat with their heads poked out the windows.
>
> ³ Another time he brought an entire stalk of bananas. I wrote a theme about it for school. He brought home the first loaf of sliced bread our neighborhood ever saw. Bread, cooked in a bakery 150 miles away and sliced on a machine, and every slice just perfect. People came from two streets over, to see and taste. It was sure fine having a hero for a father.
>
> ⁴ The sweetest times of my growing up came when he'd take me with him on the road, beyond my world, to the edges of his own. We'd go smoking along at 35 miles an hour. He'd push the brim of his hat up in front, and he'd brace the wheel between his thin old knees and steer that way. He'd take out his harmonica and play "Red River Valley" and "Coming Around the Mountain," and "Springtime in the Rockies." I am so grateful now for those days, inside my father's world.—Leon Hale, "My Father's World"

### *Writing*

1. Observe someone (on a bus, train, elevator, or in a classroom) engaged in some activity, unaware of being watched. Make eye contact and keep it for as long as possible. Write a short description of the person's reaction. For example, here is a description of a child:

One day, as my bus swerved around a corner, and I was clinging tightly to the edge of my seat to keep from sliding onto the floor, I noticed across from me a young black girl, no more than ten years old. She was singing. Her white hat, perched on her braided hair, bobbed up and down, and her scuffed brown boots tapped on the floor, keeping time to her song. She had a soft, high voice, but she didn't stay in tune. My eyes met hers, and I smiled. Her mouth snapped shut and she quit singing. Her brown eyes turned icy cold, then she slowly and deliberately turned her head to look out the window, her mouth clamped tightly shut for the rest of the ride home.

2. Visit one of the following places. Spend some time there observing the people and taking notes. Try to record the way the place smells and feels; brainstorm for a possible hook. Then, using your notes, write a description. Before you begin to write, decide on the particular point you intend to make.
   a. A college cafeteria at lunchtime
   b. A clothing store that caters to the well-to-do
   c. A warehouse clothing outlet or an army surplus store
   d. A boutique
   e. A beauty salon

## SUGGESTIONS FOR WRITING DESCRIPTION

1. Limit the focus of your description in order to make a single point.

2. Keep a consistent *point of view.*

3. Use sensory images when relevant and suitable.

4. *Show* with vivid language and specific details.

## WRITING AND REVISING DESCRIPTION (AN EXAMPLE)

When Jan set out to describe her grandmother, she had a point that she wanted to make: *Even though my grandmother was stiff, formal, and countrified, I respect her for giving me a sense of pride in my heritage.* However, in her first jottings taken from notes in her journal, Jan has only the bare bones of a paper.

### GRANDMA

[1] I remember Grandma all right—but not really as a preferred member of the family. She was Polish and a very rigid person, always preferring the harsh idea or the harsh saying to the warm grandmotherly one.

[2] Actually, I didn't know her very well, although I can remember that she always seemed the same: rather stiff, formal, countrified. It seems odd that she was both countrified and formal, but that is the way she appeared to me. She only understood me if I talked loud to her, which meant that I always talked slowly, pronouncing each word carefully in a formal way.

[3] The only time I can remember when she seemed human and warm was the time when she came down to her basement with a jug full of alcoholic beverage. We had been hauling firewood and stacking it in the basement, and she said that since we had been working as hard as men we could drink like men. The four of us (my cousins and my sister, and I) drank down the foul stuff and really enjoyed it, just because Grandma had finally noticed us.

[4] When Grandma died, I did not feel anything. I stood by her grave and tried to cry. But the tears would not come. I have never understood why. I respected her but could not grieve for her.

As Jan rereads her journal, she is struck by her use of particular terms to describe her Grandma: *rigid, countrified, formal,* and *stiff.* She also notes that she has given no examples to support those descriptive terms. She searches her memory to find specifics in the form of anecdotes, sensory details, and examples. She remembers:

How Grandma made chicken soup
How she looked in her wedding picture
How she accepted gifts
How her house smelled
How she gave us liquor
How her funeral left us feeling, etc.

With these and other details, Jan fleshes out her paper. After several drafts, the paper supports her main point.

### GRANDMA (Revised)

[1] Some people remember deathdays as naturally as others remember birthdays. Without hesitation my father can recall the exact month, day, and year she died—but I can't. It was June, I think, about six or seven years ago and I was at work with my dad. I didn't cry because I didn't really know her. I had to tell my father that she died. "She" was his mother, but he didn't cry either.

[2] I referred to her as "Grandma," not using more affectionate names like "Gram," "Granny," or "Grams." Grandma was a rigid, aloof elf of a woman who was foreign by birth and by nature. She spoke Polish to my dad. She called my mom Re VeRand for undeterminable reasons. She preferred the outhouse to the upstairs bathroom. And when she made chicken soup she left both chicken feet adrift in the pot—claws and all. She rarely baked bread; she never baked cookies. Her house wasn't full of the sweet, warm smells that accompany such activities. It smelled of coal dust and time. Much to my dismay our

biannual family vacations inevitably led to backwoods Pennsylvania and that idiosyncratic immigrant.

[3] I didn't really know her as a person, much less as a grandmother. In my entire sixteen years of life she had never taken me on a picnic, or told me a bedtime story, or even tucked me into bed. She never initiated conversation and, on the rare occasions I addressed her, I had to shout. To this day I don't know if she was deaf, or if I just thought she understood shouted English better than spoken English.

[4] Looking back, I can remember her wedding picture on top of the china cabinet in her dining room. She wasn't smiling—her arms were akimbo and her fists were clenched. A look of grim determination overpowered any bridely radiance she might have possessed. Surprisingly, she never changed. I have always envisioned grandmothers as being silver-haired ladies with gentle voices, adoring eyes, and eager smiles. My grandmother didn't possess any of those qualities—in her pictures or in person.

[5] It isn't hard to recall the many incidents that helped me formulate and later strengthen my opinion of Grandma. When I was seven my family spent Christmas with her. I was just learning to crochet, and my first project was a present for her. I remember spending months working on that ugly aquamarine potholder—crocheting, unraveling, starting over, until I was satisfied that it was perfect. I was bursting with pride when I finally finished it. I somehow thought she would appreciate all the work that went into that gift and love me for it, as a grandma should. I don't remember being hugged or thanked. I don't even remember seeing it around the kitchen, ever. I never gave her another gift, and my father never dragged our family back to Pennsylvania for Christmas again.

[6] Several years later, when I was fourteen, my two cousins, my sister, and I spent an entire afternoon hauling firewood and stacking it in Grandma's basement. We had wanted to go shopping in Johnstown, but Grandma hadn't, so no one went anywhere. Grudgingly we stayed home to work instead. That evening Grandma appeared with a dusty old jar filled with a powerful-looking concoction. She declared that if we could work like men we could drink like men too. I think that was a peace offering, because Grandma catered to her sons and grandsons while virtually ignoring her daughters and granddaughters.

[7] Now, at twenty-three, I can remember standing under the canopy at her funeral and honestly trying to cry, to feel some sort of loss. I am one of the few grandchildren that bear the family name and I thought that should have made us closer. I didn't feel anything. Time, experience, and knowledge have made me realize that she had reasons for being different and aloof. She had a hard life: thirteen children, an alcoholic husband, the depression, and war— she had proven that she was a survivor, and that she wasn't obligated to live up to my standards or anyone else's. She may not have fit my definition of what a grandmother should be, but I had no right to place demands on her. She didn't owe me anything. No matter, when I think of her now I'm proud of my heritage. I gladly carry her name. Most importantly, I'm grateful for the priceless gifts she left me . . . a stubborn Polish pride in the family name and the will to be a survivor too.

## ✦ PRACTICE

### Discussion

Read the final version of "Grandma", and answer these discussion questions:
a. Why does the writer spend so much time describing the negative or bad qualities of her grandmother?
b. Discuss the effectiveness of using the past to discuss the present.
c. Discuss the writer's use of sensory images.
d. What is the writer's point of view?

MARK TWAIN

## THE CAT

*Samuel Langhorne Clemens (1835–1910) took his pen name, Mark Twain, from the term for "safe water" used on Mississippi riverboats. Born in Hannibal, Missouri, along the Mississippi River, Twain traveled around the country and, later, the world as a journalist and lecturer. Among his many famous novels and stories are* Tom Sawyer *(1876) and the classic American novel* Huckleberry Finn *(1885). Twain is considered the master American humorist, and he used his humor for the purpose of social criticism that good-naturedly prodded Americans from their parochialism, pettiness, and greed. Humor, a keen eye for detail, and a touch of irony are apparent in his description of a cat, taken from* The Mysterious Stranger *(1906). While* The Mysterious Stranger *as a whole reflects the gloomy bitterness of Twain's later years, his perspective on the cat shows that he had not entirely lost his famous sense of humor, at least not where an honest, straightforward cat with incredible aplomb was concerned.*

¹ The cat sat down. Still looking at us in that disconcerting way, she tilted her head first to one side and then the other, inquiringly and cogitatively, the way a cat does when she has struck the unexpected and can't quite make out what she had better do about it. Next she washed one side of her face, making such an awkward and unscientific job of it that almost anybody would have seen that she was either out of practice or didn't know how. She stopped with the one side, and looked bored, and as if she had only been doing it to put in the time, and wished she could think of something else to do to put in some more time. She sat a while, blinking drowsily, then she hit an idea, and looked as if she wondered she hadn't thought of it earlier. She got up and went visiting around among the furniture and belongings, sniffing at each and every article, and elaborately examining it. If it was a chair, she examined it all around, then jumped up in it and sniffed all over its seat and its back; if it was any other thing she could examine all around, she examined it all around; if it was a chest and there was room for her between it and the wall, she crowded herself in behind there and gave it a thorough overhauling; if it was a tall thing, like a washstand, she would stand on her hind toes and stretch up as high as she could, and reach across and paw at the toilet things and try to rake them to where she could smell them; if it was the cupboard, she stood on her toes and reached up and pawed the knob; if it was the table she would squat, and measure the distance, and make a leap, and land in the wrong place, owing to newness to the business; and, part of her going too far and sliding over the edge, she would scramble, and claw at things desperately, and save herself and make good; then she would smell everything on the table, and archly and daintily paw everything around that was

movable, and finally paw something off, and skip cheerfully down and paw it some more, throwing herself into the prettiest attitudes, rising on her hind feet and curving her front paws and flirting her head this way and that and glancing down cunningly at the object, then pouncing on it and spatting it half the length of the room, and chasing it up and spatting it again, and again, and racing after it and fetching it another smack—and so on and so on; and suddenly she would tire of it and try to find some way to get to the top of the cupboard or the wardrobe, and if she couldn't she would look troubled and disappointed; and toward the last, when you could see she was getting her bearings well lodged in her head and was satisfied with the place and the arrangements, she relaxed her intensities, and got to purring a little to herself, and praisefully waving her tail between inspections—and at last she was done—done, and everything satisfactory and to her taste.

   [2] Being fond of cats, and acquainted with their ways, if I had been a stranger and a person had told me that this cat had spent half an hour in that room before, but hadn't happened to think to examine it until now, I should have been able to say with conviction, "Keep an eye on her, that's no orthodox cat, she's an imitation, there's a flaw in her make-up, you'll find she's born out of wedlock or some other arrested-development accident has happened, she's no true Christian cat, if *I* know the signs."

   [3] She couldn't think of anything further to do, now, so she thought she would wash the other side of her face, but she couldn't remember which one it was, so she gave it up, and sat down and went to nodding and blinking.

## ✦ *PRACTICE*

### *Discussion*

1. Has the cat in the description ever been in the room before? How can you tell?

2. What senses does the cat use to get her bearings? What senses does the narrator use to observe her observations?

3. What is the purpose of the second-to-last paragraph? Would you have considered cutting it from a final draft?

4. What frame does Twain place around his picture, that is, what scene both opens and closes his piece?

5. List the verbs that Twain uses to describe the cat's actions. What does the length and variety of the list tell you about Twain's effort? How does he use adverbs? participles?

6. Study the sentence that begins, "If it was a chair . . ." Is it outrageous or effective? Explain.

7. How does the word "if" appear and function in the piece?

8. Mark Twain was once a riverboat pilot, and the vocabulary of the trade stuck with him for useful assignments to later writings. Where can you find "river talk" in his description of the cat? Why is it especially appropriate to her?

*Vocabulary*

| | | |
|---|---|---|
| disconcerting | overhauling | spatting |
| cogitatively | archly | orthodox |
| elaborately | cunningly | arrested-development |

*Writing*

1. This is an obvious suggestion. Observe a cat in action for about fifteen minutes and describe in careful detail its movements. Like Twain, try to figure out what the cat may be thinking.

2. Describe the same scene that Twain describes but from the point of view of the cat.

3. Find a room where something is happening. Close your eyes and listen carefully for the sounds of that activity. By describing the progression of sounds, try to create for your reader a picture of the room.

CAROLE TREASURE

# THE MIDNIGHT SHIFT DOES MURDER SLEEP

*In a letter dated October 17, 1990, Carole Treasure wrote us: "I was born 48 years ago today, in Cumberland, Maryland. I have been variously, public health sanitarian, insurance salesperson, and power plant operator. On the side, I run a farm, raise horses and cattle, read a lot, and write a little. I have one son, who has turned out to be my most successful project so far. I write a column for the local Mensa publication, and am trying to figure out how to become gainfully employed as a writer. So far, I'm still working at the coal-fired power station, Fort Martin, on the Monongahela River, near Morgantown, West Virginia. Still working swing shift." And the swing shift, as Ms. Treasure tells us in her essay, causes some problems for human beings.*

¹ Imagine you are an owl: a nice, middle-class barn owl. You raise 3.2 owlets, commute to the meadow, and have mousie-o's for breakfast.

² One day, one of the farmer's kids, mistaking you for a football, grabs you off your perch, heads out to the yard, and makes a long forward pass.

³ You are stunned. Your beak is wide in soundless terror, and you are too shocked even to spread your wings. You plummet into the waiting hands of the receiver, who is immediately tackled by every sibling in sight, and you are on the bottom.

⁴ Welcome to the world of overnight shift. That's about what it feels like.

⁵ On the midnight shift, you are forever picking your metabolism up by the scruff of its neck, giving it a good shake and letting it down on a new track. It shudders groggily, and staggers off. Who on earth would want to do that, one wonders? Hardly anyone. But those who must include hospital care-givers, police, firefighters, utilities operators, anyone whose services are round-the-clock.

⁶ One out of four workers is enmeshed in this schedule, and its effects are all-pervasive.

⁷ Would you like to attend academic courses? Count on missing at least one out of three meetings. It will probably affect your grade. Join an organization? Don't expect to participate much. You'll either be at work or sleeping to get ready to go to work. The odds of getting child care that meets your schedule approximate those of walking to the moon. You may very likely have to trade shifts or take vacation to see your kid off to a prom, or play important games, or participate in other functions.

⁸ Would you like to sit on a school board, run for local office, run a small business on the side? Remotely possible, if you're very motivated and have good help. Don't buy season tickets to anything unless you have

someone who wants to attend a free game or symphony. Get an answering machine. Even if you hate them, you will learn a grudging affection for it, not unlike the smiling regard of a medieval castle dweller for his moat.

[9] Would you like to guess what we talk about on the midnight shift? We discuss sleep, with the intensity the starving reserve for food. We talk of sleep, its length and qualities, the way gourmets discuss wine. There is Shakespearean sleep, knitting up its raveled sleeve of care; Montaignesque sleep, sleeping wake and waking sleep; but mostly it is Frostian sleep, deferred to miles and promises.

[10] There are good days for sleeping and bad days. A good day is cold and rainy, slate-gray and dull. A bad day is sparkling and clear, a first warm day of spring, a multicolored day in fall, enticing and seductive to activity. Misery is lying there, desperate to sleep, exhausted and blank, summoning an elusive wraith. Mantras, prayers, multiplication tables, envisioning lower curtains, encroaching numbness, sinking . . . 10 past, half-past, quarter 'til . . . writhing like a lovesick cat, seeking a more comfortable position, the position that with luck will grant sleep. Always there is the haunting knowledge that, if the day was bad, the night will be worse.

[11] And it is. A blink erases a corner of white flirting peripherally in my sight. Is this a ghost, a phantom? No, just a sheet, a 200-count percale, sleek and silky, beckoning me to enter. My mind sighs with desire and begins to conjure up a pillow to cradle my head. My spine protests the vertical, each vertebra urging recline. I think of you out there, mindlessly snug under your electric blanket, coolly inert behind your air conditioner.

[12] You take us so for granted, you blessed with a nine-to-five, Monday-to-Friday job. Of course, if you are rushed to the hospital at four in the morning, staff will care for you. If you hear a prowler, the police will come. Have the urge for a late-night snack? Somewhere there's an all-nighter.

[13] We get paid a few cents more on the hour for the midnight shift. We pay, in turn, with higher rates of divorce, strokes and heart attacks, short-ened life spans. Our spouses pay, our children pay.

[14] Perhaps companies could declare a shorter work-week the norm for overnight workers or concede some more vacation. Society as a whole, benefits from our discomfort. Remember Three Mile Island? Happened on the midnight shift. And Chernobyl? Also on the midnight shift.

[15] It's called burning out the midnight owl—after a while, you don't give a hoot about anything.

## ◆ PRACTICE

*Discussion*

1. Treasure's title does two things for the reader. What are they?

2. The author's use of *point of view* is very important. Explain.

3. Explain the *technique* and *content* of the introduction and conclusion

(paragraphs 1–4, 15). Do you find any weakness in the introduction and conclusion?

4. How do you suppose Treasure would justify the "wildness" of some of her metaphors? Do the metaphors have anything in common?

5. Many good descriptions strive for a single overriding effect. Discuss Treasure's description in light of this statement.

6. Where is the argument of action in the author's description? Why didn't the author build it up more?

7. How does the author use repetition to build her description?

*Vocabulary*

| | | |
|---|---|---|
| mousie-o | enmeshed | wraith |
| sibling | medieval | mantra |
| metabolism | Montaignesque | |

*Writing*

1. Write a description of one of your activities (past or present). Use Treasure's technique of exaggeration and hallucinatory metaphor.

2. Pick a comic strip that uses some or all of Treasure's technique of description in telling a story. Explain how the creator of the strip creates his or her effects.

3. Consider this thesis: "Life's too short to dance with ugly men [women]." Write a description of why this is true.

## THE NEW YORKER

# MY FATHER

*Every week* The New Yorker *magazine opens with "The Talk of the Town," a collection of short essays on a variety of topics and in a variety of modes and moods. These essays are written by current* New Yorker *staff writers and occasionally by staff writers* emeriti, *all of whom possess the qualities of writing upheld by the magazine's editors for over fifty years: clarity, accuracy, discipline, and style. No individual credit is given these writers, although veteran* New Yorker *readers can easily identify essays penned by Anthony Hiss, Roger Angell, or others of their favorites. The essay printed here from the first issue in 1983 was written, according to a brief editorial note, by "a young woman." That it is loaded with specific details is soon obvious, but note also the implied but important generalities which dictate these details.*

¹ The carpenter is at my house replacing the frames and glass panes of some windows. She (it is a woman, a round, fair woman who looks more like a cook than like a carpenter, but she is a good carpenter, as I soon see) has around her strips of wood, panes of glass, a glass cutter, a large portable electric saw, nails, hammers, and something called a caulk gun. She measures, she saws, she cuts, she sighs: it is a much more complicated job than she at first thought, the house being a very old and crooked house. The work is taking place in a bedroom, and I sit on the edge of a bed all the time, watching her. There are many things for me to do around the house; I should also go out and run some errands. But I cannot leave the carpenter's presence. Perhaps I will be able to assist in some way; perhaps she will say something to me.

² My father was a carpenter, and a cabinetmaker, too. In the world (and it was a small world: a hundred and eight square miles, a population of sixty thousand, no deep-water harbor, so large ships had to anchor way offshore), my father was the second-best carpenter and cabinetmaker. The best carpenter was Mr. Walters, to whom my father had been apprenticed as a boy and for whom he had worked when he was a young man. Mr. Walters had been dead for a long time, even before I was born, but he was still the best carpenter and cabinet maker. My father was so devoted to this man that he did everything just the way Mr. Walters would have done it. If, for instance, in 1955 you asked my father to build you a house and make you some simple chair to sit on in it, he would build you a house and make you a chair exactly like the house and the chair Mr. Walters would have built in 1915.

<sup>3</sup> My father left our house for work every weekday morning at seven o'clock, by the striking of the Anglican church bell. If it was his first day on a new job, one of his apprentices would come by a little before seven o'clock to pick up my father's toolbox. If it was one of the older apprentices, he could walk along with my father, and they might talk. If it was one of the younger boys, he would have to walk a few steps behind. At around four o'clock in the afternoon, my father returned home. If he saw me then, he would say, "Well, we got everything in place today." And I would say, in reply, "Oh, sir, that's very good." After that, he would disappear into his shop, where he made furniture.

<sup>4</sup> In my father's shop, everything was some shade of brown. First, there was the color of his skin; and he wore khaki trousers and khaki shirts, brown shoes, and a brown felt hat. He smoked cigarettes (Lucky Strikes) one after another, and he smoked so much that the thumb and the index and middle fingers of his right hand were stained brown. His hands were stained another shade of brown from handling stained wood, wood oils, and glues. Everything was brown, that is, except the red, flat carpenter's pencil (such an unusual, distinctive shape for a pencil, I thought, and I was sadly disappointed when I discovered that it was not a good writing pencil) that he carried perched always behind his right ear. Sometimes when I went to watch him work, he would tell me little things about himself when he was a young man. He would talk about himself as if he were someone he used to know very well, someone he thought really an admirable person, someone he would like very much. Mostly, they were stories about himself as a cricketer. He never told me that he was good at playing cricket; I already knew that.

<sup>5</sup> My father made very beautiful furniture. Everybody said so—especially my mother, who would then point out that unfortunately none of this furniture was in our own house. I think almost every time she saw my father make something she would say to him that it would be nice to have one like that, and he would then promise to make another one, for her specially. But he never did. Finally, one day, he told her that the reason he was reluctant to make us up lots of furniture was that the furniture in Mrs. Walters' house (the widow of the man to whom he had been apprenticed) was really his: that he had made it up for himself when he was a very young man; that he had lent it to Mrs. Walters after her husband died and she had moved into a smaller house, the house she still lived in; that he would ask for it back one day; and that he would ask her for it soon. He never, of course, asked for the furniture—I don't think he could bring himself to. My mother could not believe that we were never to have that beautiful furniture; that at Christmastime, when our friends stopped by to have a glass of rum, if too many of them came by at once some of them would always have to sit on the floor. My father would visit Mrs. Walters quite often, and every once in a while my mother would go along with him. Afterward, she would always be furious that she had had to leave what she began calling "my furniture" behind, and she would have a big row with

herself, for my father never quarrelled with anyone—not even his wife. Once, my father took me with him on one of the visits. I got a good look at the furniture, and I began to understand my mother's point of view. There was a dining table with six matching cane-bottomed chairs (my father did all his own caning); there was a little round table the edge of which was scalloped; there was a table with fancy decorative carvings on its sides and, above it, a mirror in a frame with decorative carvings that matched the ones on the table; and there was a sofa, a cabinet with delicate woodworking on the glass front, and two Morris chairs. (At the time, I did not know—nor, for that matter, do I think anyone else knew—that there was someone named Morris who had made chairs of which these two were replicas.) We had nothing like any of this in our house.

⁶ Once, my father got sick, and the doctor said that it was his heart, and gave him some medicine and told him to stay home and rest. My mother, looking up heart diseases in one of her numerous medical books, said that the sickness was from all the cigarettes he smoked. At the same time, I took sick with a case of hookworm, and my mother, looking up hookworm in one of her numerous medical books, said that it was because I had walked around barefoot behind her back, and it was true that I did that. (I was disappointed when it was discovered that I had hookworm, and not beriberi. I would have liked to say to my friends when they asked why I wasn't in school, "Oh I have beriberi.") Since my father couldn't go to work and I couldn't go to school, we spent all day together. In the mornings, I would go and lie with him in my parents' bed. We would lie on our backs, our hands clasped behind our necks (me imitating him), and our feet up on the windowsill in the sun. We would lie there without saying a word to each other, the only sound being *pttt, pttt* from my father as he forced small pieces of tobacco from his mouth. He continued to smoke, though not as much as before. At midmorning, my mother would come in to look at us. As soon as she came into the room, she would always ask us to take our feet off the windowsill, and we would do it right away, but as soon as she left we would put them back. When she came, she would bring with her little things to eat. Sometimes it was barley water and a special porridge, made from seaweed; sometimes it was a beaten egg-yolks-and-milk drink, sweetened with powdered sugar; sometimes it was a custard of some kind. Whatever it was, she would say that it would help to build us up. Before she left, she would kiss us on our foreheads and say that we were her two invalids, the big one and the little one. In the afternoons, after our lunch, my father and I would go off to look for a wild elderberry bush and pick elderberries. He was sure that a draught prepared from the elderberries would make his heart get better faster than the medicine the doctor had prescribed. In fact, I think he took the medicine the doctor gave him only because he thought my mother might perhaps die herself if he didn't. After we had picked the elderberries, we would go and sit in the Botanical Gardens under a rubber tree. Then he would tell me stories about his own father. He had not known his father very well at all, since his father was

always going off somewhere—usually somewhere in South America—to work, but he never said anything that showed he found his father at fault. Once, he said, his father had taken a boat to Panama to build the Panama Canal. The boat got caught in a storm and sank. His father was in the sea for eleven days, just barely hanging on to a raft. He was rescued by a passing ship, which took him on to Panama, where he built the Panama Canal. For a long time, I thought that my father's father had built the Panama Canal single-handed except perhaps with the help of one or two people, the way my father himself built things single-handed except with the help of one or two people.

## ◆ *PRACTICE*

### *Discussion*

1. What is the point of the opening paragraph? Why is it significant that the carpenter is female? What is significant in the narrator's staying to help or listen?

2. The narrator obviously admires her father. How would you characterize her feelings for her mother? How would you characterize her parents' feelings for each other?

3. Describe the community in which the narrator grew up. What values are apparent among the people of the community?

4. Draw up a list of the father's characteristics. Opposite that list make two columns, one for direct statements and another for indirect statements, then note in the appropriate columns the direct statements or indirect details that communicate the characteristics. What does your completed chart tell you about the author's descriptive method?

5. How does the author appeal to different senses? Which senses are neglected? What details can you suggest for appealing to those senses?

6. If you were the editor of this essay, would you suggest cutting the opening paragraph and/or the final part about the grandfather? Defend your editorial suggestion.

7. Is the author wise in using so many parenthetical remarks? Try your hand at cutting the more unrelated ones and rewriting without parentheses the more necessary ones. Are you pleased with the result? Explain.

8. One usually thinks of description as relying on straightforward facts, but this descriptive essay uses many symbols effectively. What larger ideas are represented by the carpenter's pencil, Mrs. Walter's furniture, the elderberries, and the Panama Canal? What other symbols can you find in the essay? What ideas do they represent?

## Vocabulary

| | | |
|---|---|---|
| caulk | cricket | Morris chairs |
| Anglican | row | beriberi |
| khaki | caning | botanical |

## Writing

1. Write an essay describing your father or mother. Try to show that parent's connection to you and, if possible, to his (or her) father or mother.

2. Describe someone you know at rest; then describe that person in action; finally, describe that person interacting with someone else. Now try combining all three descriptions into a single essay.

3. Choose a concept that you value (for example, *honesty*) and a person who represents that concept to you. Write an essay about the concept without once referring to it. Rely entirely on the description of the person to communicate what you value.

# NARRATION

## NARRATION

A *narrative* is an account of an incident, or series of closely related incidents, that makes or illustrates a specific point. Since a narrative is a story, a writer can use narration when it is important for the reader to know "what happened." When writing a narrative, you need to ask yourself two questions: (1) Is the narrative relevant to my purpose? (2) Assuming that it is relevant, how can I tell it effectively? The first question you have to answer for yourself, as circumstances arise. To the second question we can suggest some partial answers.

In order to be effective, a narrative must get smoothly and quickly to its point and make that point dramatically. A narrative that dawdles along, introducing unnecessary people and irrelevant detail, is usually a failure. The reader will skip over it to get to something else. In writing vivid and convincing narratives, you should know how to compress certain details and expand others in order to give shape and emphasis to the incident you are relating. Here is how one writer uses narrative to emphasize the general ideas he is conveying:

*Compressed description and historical account*

From birth, the Fijians are in and out of the jungle. They understand the tangled greenery that covers the South Pacific Islands the way a New Yorker understands Times Square. Their senses are sharper than the white man's and their strength and endurance are greater. There is very little left for them to learn about the jungle. Certainly the news, a year or so ago, that they were to be "trained for jungle fighting" by the Allies must have struck them as comical, though none of them ever said so. In fact, I was recently told by a New Zealand captain stationed at the Fiji camp on Bougainville that the men there had been unfailingly deferential and kind to their white tutors. They are a people with an extraordinary sense of

*Story*

humor, but they have an almost pathological aversion to hurting the feelings of a friend. However, at the end of their training, which took place in the Fijis, they allowed their sense of humor a fairly free hand. The company of white soldiers who had trained them arranged to fight a mock battle with them in the bush. After dark, each side was to try to penetrate as far as possible into the other's lines. The main idea was to see how well the new Fiji scouts had learned their lessons. It *Climax* turned out that they had learned them pretty well. During the night some of the white scouts worked thirty or forty feet into the Fiji lines, and figured they had the battle won, since they hadn't caught any Fijians behind *their* lines. When they came to check up at daylight, it developed that most of the Fijians had apparently spent the night in the white headquarters. They had chalked huge crosses on the tents and the furniture and had left one of the most distinct crosses on the seat of the commanding officer's trousers, which he had thrown over a chair around 4:00 a.m.

—Robert Lewis Taylor, "The Nicest Fellows You Ever Met"*

The climax of the story nicely points up the ideas presented in the first part of the passage: that Fijians are at home in the jungle and that they have a sense of humor.

Sometimes, for reasons of space or economy of effect, you may wish to compress many details. Edward Iwata compresses years of life into just a few paragraphs, but the narrative he calls "Barbed-Wire Memories" is hard to forget.

1 My parents rarely spoke about it, and I rarely asked them to.

2 Manzanar has emerged in recent years as a symbol of racial oppression for many Asian Americans, but it remained a painful subject in my family home. For my parents, the very word "Manzanar" calls up shameful memories of a four-year period of their lives when their citizenship and patriotism, their simple belief in the unalienable goodness of America, meant nothing amid the flood of wartime racism. I never asked them about it in any detail because a fearful part of me had refused to believe that my parents had been imprisoned by their own country. Their only crime was their color of skin and slant of eye.

3 It was as if too long a glimpse into their tragic past would shatter the rules of our relationship, a relationship peculiar to Japanese people that relies heavily on unspoken but deeply understood values, emotions, and expectations. My knowledge of their stay in Manzanar was scant, a hazy mix of childhood tales and harmless anecdotes they told with a smile whenever their curious kids asked about "that camp in the desert."

4 Until recently, I did not know that my mother and father had met and fallen in love while behind barbed wire at Manzanar. I did not know that my grandmother cried daily the first two weeks in camp, hoping somehow that the

tears would wash away the injustice of it all. I did not know that my mother's youngest brother, who later died in the Korean War, dreamed of fighting for the United States while he grew up as a little boy in Manzanar.

5 I learned all of this in what seems the most absurd, impersonal manner: while interviewing my parents for a newspaper story. In my role as reporter, I was able for the first time to ask them about their concentration camp experience. In their roles as interview subjects, they spoke about Manzanar for the first time in an unashamed manner to their son.

6 Japanese Americans learn the stark facts early: On February 19, 1942, President Roosevelt issued Executive Order 9066, sanctioning the evacuation of our people. One hundred ten thousand, most of them citizens, were evacuated to ten camps throughout the United States, where they would remain for four years. Most of the evacuees were given two to seven days to sell a lifetime of belongings, although some ministers and language instructors were arrested immediately with not even that much notice.

7 The sudden evacuation order shocked the Issei, the industrious first generation in this country, and the Nisei, their children. One Pismo Beach man shot himself in the head to spare his family from his shame. He was found clasping an honorary citizenship certificate from Monterey County, which thanked him for his "loyal and splendid service to the country in the Great World War."

8 In my own family, my uncle, a minister, was not given the customary notice to evacuate. He was visited at his San Fernando home by two FBI agents at nine o'clock one evening. Within the hour, he was carted off, without his wife, for an undisclosed location.

9 Ironically, the evacuations came despite the fact that the only pre-war government study found a high degree of loyalty among Japanese Americans and concluded, "There is no Japanese 'problem' on the (West) Coast."

—Edward Iwata, "Barbed-Wire Memories"

## Dialogue in Narration

*Dialogue,* the written representation of conversation, is often useful when you wish to relate an incident or describe something—a state of mind, an attitude, a belief, etc. In most nonfiction works, writers use dialogue sparingly, compressing or reporting it indirectly when they can. In employing dialogue, you may find these suggestions useful:

1. Where it is possible, avoid unnecessary repetition of the speakers' names or unnecessary description of the way they speak. It is old-fashioned and tiresome to write:

   "I see you in the corner," whispered Baker softly.
   "How did you find me?" inquired Charles curiously.
   "I smelled the pipe you've been smoking," purred Baker evilly.
   "Oh!" exclaimed Charles alarmedly.

2. Present dialogue simply:

I'll not forget my first—and last—meeting with that old Texan. He came striding down the line I had just surveyed on his property, pulling up my line stakes and tossing them over his shoulder as he came. When he got up to my surveying truck, he wasn't even out of breath:

"Get off my land."

"O.K., I will—in just a minute. If you'll just—"

"Get off *now*."

"Yes sir, right now, just like you say."

And I did leave, as fast as possible.

3. Above all, remember to compress and shorten your dialogue whenever you can. Harry Crews reports a "conversation" he had as a farm boy in Georgia with his dog Sam:

[1] The moment I sat down in the shade, I was already wondering how long it would be before they quit to go to the house for dinner because I was already beginning to wish I'd taken two biscuits instead of one and maybe another piece of meat, or else that I hadn't shared with Sam.

[2] Bored, I looked down at Sam and said: "Sam, if you don't quit eatin' my biscuit and meat, I'm gone have to cut you like a shoat hog."

[3] A black cloud of gnats swarmed around his heavy muzzle, but I clearly heard him say that he didn't think I was man enough to do it. Sam and I talked a lot together, had long involved conversations, mostly about which one of us had done the other one wrong and, if not about that, about which one of us was the better man. It would be a good long time before I started thinking of Sam as a dog instead of a person. But I always came out on top when we talked because Sam could only say what I said he said, think what I thought he thought.

[4] "If you was any kind of man atall, you wouldn't snap at them gnats and eat them flies the way you do," I said.

[5] "It ain't a thing in the world the matter with eating gnats and flies," he said.

[6] "It's how come people treat you like a dog," I said.

## ◆ PRACTICE

*Discussion*

1. Discuss the effectiveness of the narrative and dialogue in the following passage. How does Roberts achieve the sound of real people talking? Identify his introductions to dialogue. What is Roberts' thesis? What is his point of view?

[1] I rounded a bend (on my recumbent bicycle), and suddenly, through an opening in the trees, saw a great splash of spilt truck on the landscape. Two semis had recently collided, and one was strewn in dramatic disarray down the hill, its cargo a giant splat on the countryside.

[2] As I paused to gaze at the scene, I heard a rustling in the leaves behind me. Turning to look, I saw five of the biggest, meanest-looking characters I

have ever seen heading toward me from the nearby Potomac. I nodded in friendly but uneasy greeting.

3 "What's this?" asked a mountainous black man.

4 "It's a recumbent bicycle," I replied, "with solar panels to power the electronic equipment. I'm traveling cross-country."

5 "Where you coming from, buddy?" asked a burly redhead.

6 "Columbus, Ohio. I'm doing a 14,000-mile loop around the United States that should take about a year," I said, mouthing my standard response.

7 "Yeah? You crazy, or what?"

8 "Sorta." I grinned. "What are you guys doing here?"

9 A white guy with long black hair in a ponytail answered. "We're convicts, man, from the Maryland Correctional Facility over in Hagerstown."

10 "Hey, is that right?" I chuckled nervously. "Well whaddya know. You escaping?"

11 "Naw, man," spoke the giant black. "You kiddin' me? We workin', man. We out here to clean up that truck." He gestured over his shoulder.

12 "Ah, I see," I answered with some relief.

13 After a bit more banter, I prepared to leave. "Well, I better hit the road," I said, "I'm shootin' for Shepherdstown . . ."

14 "Whoa!" interrupted the redhead. "We gotta fix you up, man!" He turned on his heel and motioned for me to follow. The others set off in the same direction—toward the truck—laughing.

15 I apprehensively followed them through the woods, arriving at a couple of yellow state trucks and a few armed guards. Other inmates milled about. We took a turn into another part of the woods and came upon a large bundle under a tarp set back in the bushes. "Our stash, man," explained the huge black guy.

16 He pulled back the tarp, exposing their private stock of the truck's cargo. Beneath the cover . . . what else but a giant mound of Sara Lee pastry!

17 He grabbed a box and shoved it into my hands. "Have some walnut cake, my man."

18 Another spoke up. "Oh, man, you don't want no walnut cake. Cheese danish, man. Cheese danish. *That's* where it's at!" Another box was placed on the first.

19 The redhead handed over another. "You want some of these apple things, buddy?"

20 Before long I was standing there in the beautiful Maryland woods amid a jovial crowd of murderers and bank robbers, laughing helplessly as my armload of Sara Lee pastries grew to an absurd height. "I'm on a bicycle," I finally managed to blurt out. "I can't carry all this!"

21 "C'mon," suggested the giant. We returned to the bike, still sitting in the middle of the towpath with a crowd of decidedly rough characters standing around it. Nothing appeared to be missing.

22 I started struggling with a box of apple danish, at least securing it under a bungee cord. The giant grabbed the walnut cake. "Gimme that." He stuffed it between the fairing and the electronics package on the front of the machine. "Don't worry, it'll stay." I managed to hang a bit more here and there, then diplomatically declined the rest.

²³ We said our goodbyes and I set off again down the quiet trail, festooned with pastry, laughing for miles. You just never know in an enterprise like this. You just never know. —Steve Roberts, *An Encounter in the Woods*

2. Following is a narrative describing an experience one student had while hiking in the mountains. Read the essay and answer the questions after it.

¹ The Geology Field Camp had one entire day to spend in the Tetons with no lecture or "rock stops." Seven of us women decided to take a 17-mile hike up the Paintbrush Divide. Considering my unfamiliarity with the area and my inexperience climbing on snow, I was hesitant about joining the expedition. However, the leader assured me that we would stay together all the way up to the Divide.

² As soon as we started on the trail at 6:30 a.m., I could see that I was going to be the slow one. I wasn't worried about getting too far behind because I had done some hiking. However, at 9:00, I became concerned because I discovered I was alone. By 9:30 the trail the others had traveled couldn't be seen because of heavy snow that began to fall. By 10:30 I was getting pretty lonesome. I felt totally alone in the wilderness. I had fallen several times through the snow where streams had cut away the bottom and made the drift thinner. I was getting scared and a little panicky.

³ Then I slipped and fell. It took me 10 seconds to slide down to a pile of rocks 200 yards below me. Getting back up to the trail was the problem I had to face. I could take only a few steps before the slope became too steep to walk on. Fortunately, I had my rock hammer with me, so I cut footholds in the rock to pull myself up. It was exhausting, hard work. I knew that if I missed my footing I could fall all the way to the bottom, either injuring or killing myself on the way down.

⁴ After an hour of digging and climbing I reached the trail. Whether out of fear or exhaustion, I was shaking so much when I finally got there, I could hardly stand up.

a. The writer narrating her hiking experience tells us in paragraph 2 that she was first "concerned," then "pretty lonesome," and finally "scared and a little panicky." How could she have used description to *show* how her emotions increased in intensity? How much space would she need to develop her realization that she was in a dangerous situation?

b. In paragraph 3 the writer tells us that she fell 200 yards in 10 seconds. What sensory images might describe her experience in the fall? (Which of her senses would probably have been most affected?)

c. The hiker tells us that she was in a dangerous situation because she could easily fall again. List a few details she could have used to *show* the reader the seriousness of her predicament.

d. Discuss the effectiveness of the conclusion. Is there a point? What advice would you give the writer to help her improve her narrative?

# SUGGESTIONS FOR WRITING NARRATION

1. Choose an event that has a point. At one time or another each of us has had a friend or acquaintance who goes on and on about his experiences. But his stories never get anywhere. Our reaction to them is, "So what? Why are you telling me all this?" In order for you to avoid this kind of reaction from your reader, narrow your thesis so that your essay has meaning for you *and* your reader.

2. Make your experience come to life. Use dialogue, if you wish, to show an interaction or conflict between people, but don't overuse it so that your essay reads like a film script. Describe the scene or situation with detail, using sensory impressions of touch, smell, sight, hearing, and taste. Try to build some suspense if possible. Use vivid words to show emotional and physical response. (See pp. 243–244 for more advice on vivid writing.)

## PLANNING AND WRITING A NARRATIVE

Jon starts to write:

My teacher told me that when I have a conflict, I should try "writing it out." I don't have any conflict with anyone now, but I remember one that has bugged me for many years. Maybe if I think it through and try to write an essay about the experience, I will look at it from a different perspective. Now that I am more mature, writing about it can help me understand just what happened.

I had a conflict with a guy named Joe Haller when I was fifteen. We were on the same baseball team.

I can remember how I hated him, always bugging me and making me feel inferior. He used to holler at me and humiliate me in front of the other players. Why couldn't I get back at him in some way, I kept thinking. I still feel rage when I think about him. Even though I guess I got back at him a little when I caught that high pop-up, I wonder why I don't feel better about that event than I do. Perhaps I'm letting my rage get into the way of understanding the effect of that event. Maybe I should act cooler about the whole thing and look at what actually happened:

1. Joe was a perfectionist.
   He would chew out other players.
   He would humiliate me in front of people.

2. He got support from the coach, his father.

3. I was obsessed with hoping that he would make a mistake.

4. I used to dream about his making a mistake.

5. Then one day he did make a mistake:
   What did I do? Did his mistake help me to resolve my rage at him
   for humiliating me? Did I behave well or did I behave as badly as he
   had always done toward me?

Jon searches his memory for other details about his experiences with
Joe Haller, asking questions: What did the field look like? What did the ball
do? What did the crowd do? What was Haller's mistake? After he remembers some of these details, he sees that he has a basis for an essay, and a
resolution of his anger because he remembers that he behaved rather well.
He didn't gloat or humiliate Joe Haller in front of the team. He just ran
toward the dugout, head held high. Below is his final essay.

[1] When I was fifteen I played on the same baseball team with Joe Haller,
who ten years later was the batting champion of the American Association. The
year after that he played three games with the parent club before he ruined his
knee and had to retire. At fifteen, he was already a brilliant, locally famous
shortstop. He was a perfectionist, and would chew out any player who made an
error. Since I played second base, my mistakes were right under his nose, and I
got the benefit of his advice more than any other player on our team.

[2] Occasionally an opposing player would steal second base, sliding neatly
under my tag—a mistake that made Joe furious. He would shout, "That's not
how you do it!" As the baserunner left the bag to retrieve his cap, Joe would
straddle second base. He would sweep his glove across the shallow groove the
runner had just made in the dirt, crying "Get your glove *down!* Don't let him
slide *under* you!" The umpire watched respectfully. The stands were silent.
Joe's father, our coach, nodded in agreement from the dugout. Then Joe
would throw the ball to our pitcher, and the runner would take his place on
second base, and the game would resume.

[3] Joe never made a mistake that summer until one night-game late in
August. We were winning; we were in the field; the bases were empty; there
were two outs. The batter hit a very high pop-up behind the pitcher's mound,
and Joe called for it, loudly. But for some reason he didn't move from his
position deep at shortstop. The ball went so high that it almost disappeared
into the blackness of the sky. I glanced at Joe, who still stood still, peering up,
searching for the ball. Again, he called out, "I got it!" but he didn't move, and
he was at least a dozen yards away from where the ball would land. "He's lost
it," I thought, and I started running as fast as I could toward that spot behind
the mound, peering up through the haze of lights. I caught sight of the ball as it
descended, like a bullet. I went on running; I had a bead on it. But suddenly I
lost my nerve; I was afraid of crashing into another player—and I glanced
down. In that instant I saw the rows of white shirts in the stands and beyond
them the black impenetrable summer sky; and I saw how brilliantly green was
the infield grass: the stadium lights gave it a sort of electric glow. When I
looked up again the ball was *there,* an inch above my outstretched, open glove.

[4] Joe trotted toward me, smiling sheepishly. I nodded to him, and turned

my back, and, buoyed along by the bleacher-rattling crowd, I went across the gleaming grass to the dugout.

## ◆ *PRACTICE*

### *Discussion*

Read Jon's essay, and answer the following questions:

1. How does the writer set up the situation? For instance, how are Joe Haller and the writer contrasted?

2. How does paragraph 2 develop the contrast?

3. In what way does paragraph 3 contradict the first two paragraphs?

4. Do you think that the conflict is satisfactorily resolved?

5. Discuss the effectiveness of the conclusion. What would you recommend to the writer?

6. Dialogue is used sparingly in this selection. Is it sufficient or insufficient for the author's point? What *is* the point?

### *Writing*

Think about and list the details of an event that made an impression on you or one that you remember vividly. In particular, try to "relive" any conversations that occurred so that you can write the dialogue with the sound of real people talking.

Write a narrative about the event, keeping a consistent point of view. For example, if you were to narrate your experience of being locked in a fruit cellar as a child, the point of view would be affected by your being directly involved. However, if you were narrating an event from the viewpoint of a bystander, it would be more objective.

Suggestions:

—My first visit to a hospital (either as a patient or visitor)
—Walking into a house after a burglary
—The fire that nearly destroyed our house (or neighbor's, or friend's)
—My hardest assignment—giving bad news
—Selling an old car

## RON HOFF

# TO LIVE IS TO RAGE AGAINST THE DARK

*Ron Hoff has sharpened his presentation skills as a creative director and executive vice president in the fiercely competitive advertising and marketing business. For the past decade, he has coached corporate executives at the highest level and conducted presentation seminars and workshops for the American Marketing Association and dozens of communications companies throughout the United States and Canada. His bylined articles have appeared in the* New York Times, *the* Wall Street Journal, *the* Chicago Tribune, Advertising Age, *and other publications. He is a frequent keynote and banquet speaker, addressing business groups and college audiences nationally. Hoff's essay, as you will see, shows another side of a successful businessman.*

[1] It's funny how bad news makes you want to get up and get out. I'd taken all of the bad news I could take in one day—two projects canceled, another put on hold, I could hardly wait to get out of the office.

[2] Outside, it was raining and the sky was a sheet of gray. I headed for the corner, feeling the rain against my face. I had decided, as I shut my office door, to get myself a Dr Pepper—an act of self-indulgence with few, if any, redeeming virtues.

[3] As I approached the corner, I wasn't prepared for the shock of her. We got there at almost the same time, only she was moving faster than I— her cane flicking out in front of her, sweeping from side to side like radar, tapping the sidewalk with a hard, clicking sound. She was hatless in the rain, black hair that looked chopped rather than cut, and a coat as gray and sodden as the day. She seemed to be in her 30s.

[4] The cane cast a wide arc in front of her, as if it were "claiming the territory" ahead. It had a red band around the end. The rest of it was white, at least what I could see, and was discolored—bruised by countless collisions. When she reached the curbing, she stopped—holding the cane in front of her.

[5] Then, she screamed.

[6] It didn't sound like a word or a phrase. It was just a noise, cutting sharply through the wet afternoon. No, it was more than that. It was a command. Sharp, shrill, a bit scary.

[7] I started to turn the corner, moving from her. But she wasn't more than three feet away, and the rapping of the cane was so insistent.

[8] I turned back and slipped my hand gently under her elbow. "Here," I said, "this way . . ."

[9] Instantly, her arm clutched mine. I could feel the strength in it. I was no longer controlling the situation—she was. We stepped out to cross the

street. A few steps and she veered to the right—heading out of the crosswalk.

¹⁰ I tried to move her back, within the crosswalk, steering against the strength of her arm. Another few feet, and she pulled her arm away from me, angry now, and cursed. It was a familiar four-letter word, but coming from her—it seemed eerie.

¹¹ "I thought you wanted to stay on Clark, to cross the street," my words sounded feeble, even to me. She jerked herself loose from me, cane flicking in its full arc again, and continued in the direction that she obviously wanted to go.

¹² I stood in the middle of the street, rejected, watching. She headed for the double doors of a small coffee and doughnut shop on the corner— on the other side of the street. But she was moving too fast. She banged into the first set of doors and disappeared behind the second set.

¹³ Then, it dawned on me. She knew where she was. She simply wanted somebody to start her across the street when no cars were coming.

¹⁴ I saw her take a booth near the window. Suddenly, her cane rapped against the base of the table where she was sitting. I couldn't hear it, but I saw the people inside react. The young man behind the counter heard it, and reacted. He filled a cup of coffee, placed a chocolate-covered doughnut on a plate, and hurried over to her.

¹⁵ I was looking through the window at her, and she was looking out— eyes closed, scar tissue surrounding them. Her face was gray, almost purplish. She was older than I had thought. As she was looking out, unseeing, and I was looking in, seeing her really for the first time, she looked content.

¹⁶ What were the lines of Dylan Thomas? Oh yes. "Do not go gentle into that good night . . . Rage, rage against the dying of the light." They seemed right for her.

¹⁷ She looked away. I turned and headed back up Clark, toward the deli. I was walking faster now, intent on my mission and, for some reason, I did not feel the rain.


## ◆ PRACTICE

*Discussion*

1. In what way(s) does the narrator change? Would it hurt the story if he didn't change?

2. Should the woman's obscenity (paragraph 10) be recorded exactly as spoken? And was it necessary that the narrator explain his reaction as he did?

3. As the reader, you know nothing about the woman beyond what she does in a few moments in the street. Is this information sufficient?

4. What sensory images do you carry away from the narrative?

5. If you were filming the incident, where would you put your camera? Explain.

6. Does any part of the story require more compression?

7. Explain the job of paragraph 4.

8. Make a list of the things, actions, and ideas that could have been put in the narrative, but are left out.

### Vocabulary

Make a list of words in the story that could not be removed without damaging the total effect. In a sentence or two, explain each of your choices.

### Writing

1. Try outlining this story from a different point of view. (How many different points of view are possible, given the situation? Are any of them "impossible"?)

2. This is a "surprise story"; most of what happens surprises—and teaches—the narrator. Write a surprise story of your own based on occurrences in your life.

## MICHAEL BAUGHMAN

## FOOTLOOSE

*Michael Baughman spent the summers of his early childhood fishing on his great-grandfather's farm in western Pennsylvania. In 1948, when he was ten, his family moved to Hawaii, where he spearfished, surfed, and paddled in canoe races. Since 1966, he and his family have enjoyed fly-fishing, backpacking, camping, hiking, and cross-country skiing in Oregon, where he teaches English at Southern Oregon State. Baughman writes: "The fact that much of my writing deals with outdoor recreation, the environment, and a love of nature is an inevitable reflection of my life." On a lonely ski trail, Baughman finds a wolfpack trailing him to be a mystical experience—some of us might not agree.*

[1] It was a cold spell in early January, and my wife, Hilde, and I had decided to make use of the full moon to take a late-night cross-country ski tour. The drive up through the Cascade Mountains on well-cleared roads was easy, and half an hour after leaving home we were ready to ski. . . .

[2] I led the way on the downhill run, just to be sure that no trees or large limbs had fallen across the road since our last trip. The skiing was as good as I'd hoped for, even better. The bright, cold moon in the eastern sky gave plenty of light. Under the new layer of powder the frozen base was as hard as iron, which made for speed, and the three fresh inches on top made turning under control at least a possibility. Cross-country ski bindings clamp the toes of your boots down, but the heels are free, so turning is always something of a challenge when you're traveling at any kind of speed. But this night even I could manage. I'm not a good skier, don't even want to be, having never taken a lesson or read a book on the subject. If you ski a while you learn to get where you want to go, and that is sufficient for me. There's no one around to show off for. The form- and fashion-conscious downhill skiers are in another world, far away.

[3] Cross-country skis through powder snow make a lovely, muted hissing sound. That was all I heard as I gradually picked up speed down the slope, the trees dark blurs on either side, the road itself perfectly smooth and glowing white and, at night, strangely without dimension in the moonlight. About halfway down, where the run is steepest, is a very sharp left-hand turn, but it's steeply banked. Crouching low, leaning left, I negotiated it. The rest of the way to the bottom was easy, and, out of the turn, I relaxed to glide the last half mile.

[4] That was when the first coyote howled. Soon a second, then a third joined in. Then there were more. Perhaps it was the sound of skis through snow that made it happen, or it could have been the full moon.

[5] When I reached the meadow at the bottom of the road, Hilde was close behind me. The coyotes sounded very near, and she was frightened. So was I, but I didn't want to admit it. I explained to her that they couldn't possibly be as near as they seemed and that three or four coyotes can easily sound like a dozen or more.

[6] One would bark, then yip a few times in rapid succession, then start a long drawn-out howl that seemed to last at least 20 seconds, the note rising shrilly as the volume increased. The louder the howl became, the closer it seemed, and when the animals joined in chorus they sounded as near as 80 or 100 yards.

[7] I let Hilde take the lead. We kept on skiing because the route was familiar to us, and the pack of coyotes followed along. We crossed the meadow to an old homestead cabin, its roof long ago caved in, snow in drifts against the weathered logs to window level, glowing smooth and almost blue in the moonlight. Beyond the cabin a narrow creek cuts across the meadow, and when we crossed the creek we heard the water flowing far down beneath the ice and snow. Just past the creek, where a gold mine is cut into a north-facing slope, we hit another logging road and followed it south, climbing again.

[8] The coyotes stayed behind us, howling singly, then in chorus, seldom silent for more than a few seconds at a time. We looked back often enough, but of course we never saw one.

[9] The road curves two miles up through Douglas fir to a bowl that offers ideal skiing over smooth low slopes of virgin powder. We were wearing only light shirts under nylon Windbreakers, and the temperature was at least 15° below freezing, but the hard uphill skiing had us sweating by the time we reached the bowl.

[10] And at some point during the exertion of that climb we forgot to be frightened. Or perhaps it would be better to say that we remembered that we knew better. The coyote, whether alone or in company, often performs a nocturnal serenade consisting of barks, yaps and a whine that escalates into a howl. To my knowledge, there are no recorded instances of coyotes attacking humans. I reminded Hilde that the coyotes we often saw on our daytime hikes had shown us only cautious curiosity. They were every bit as shy as deer. So it wasn't really a threatening sound behind us. We had always loved coyotes, and we listened to them now for half an hour as we skied the bowl, traversing the slopes, cutting zig-zag patterns from top to bottom at moderate speed.

[11] Then we split a candy bar and started the three-mile trip back. Soon we realized that the pack had either waited in the woods for us to pass, or had made a loop to get behind us again.

[12] We skied hard to the car to stay warm, and the coyotes were with us all the way. It wasn't until the skis were lashed to the roof rack that they finally fell silent. We drank some hot coffee from a thermos, with a little bourbon in it, then ate dried fruit from a plastic bag. Even though the temperature had dropped another 5°, we were reluctant to leave. Shiver-

ing, we stood beside the car for a minute or two. Far off a lone coyote howled, and another answered. No sound on earth could be wilder, freer, lovelier than what we heard that January night. Now, whenever conditions are right for it—full moon, clear sky and new powder snow—we ski at night, and we have heard coyotes often, though never so near.

[13] Although Hilde and I are the legal owners of no land other than the lot our house sits on, we have already skied with a sense of ownership as strong as if the mountains had been deeded to us. On daytime trips, once we are well off the road, we feel that the places we ski are ours. Of course, this sense of ownership is an illusion. Coyotes really own the mountains— they have been in North America for a million years and likely will remain after we have gone—and on moonlit winter nights when they howl, the fact that we are only guests seems very clear, and quite appropriate.

## ◆ *PRACTICE*

### *Discussion*

1. Describe the viewpoint of the narrative.

2. How does Baughman set the scene?

3. Why does Baughman tell us that he is not a good skier (paragraph 2)?

4. Note the first sentence of paragraph 4. Since this narrative centers on the coyotes, why doesn't the author use this description earlier?

5. Why does Baughman interrupt the narrative with the description in paragraph 7?

6. Using two or three sentences, state the point of Baughman's narrative.

7. How does Baughman *dramatize* his point?

8. How effective, in the total sense, is Baughman's narrative?

### *Vocabulary*

| | | |
|---|---|---|
| muted | shrilly | traversing |
| dimension | nocturnal | illusion |
| coyote | serenade | |

### *Writing*

1. Write an essay describing an event that, like Baughman's, has a "double effect"; for example, of fear and awe, or pleasure and fatigue.

2. Baughman's narrative employs no dialogue. Use the scene back at the car, when the Baughmans are reliving their experience (paragraph 12). Write the scene in dialogue (making it up to express their feelings).

3. Write a narrative (your personal experience) about an event that took place in brilliant sunlight. How do your "narrative problems" differ from Baughman's?

## HARRY CREWS

# A CHILDHOOD

*Born June 7, 1935, in Alma, Georgia, Harry Crews grew up on a farm, joined the Marines at the age of eighteen, and eventually, after earning bachelor's and master's degrees from the University of Florida, became a teacher and writer. The rural South and the process of becoming a man in tune with the earth are central subjects of Crews' essays and novels, the best known of which are* Karate Is A Thing of the Spirit *(1971) and* The Hawk Is Dying *(1973). Similar themes run through* A Childhood: The Biography of a Place *(1978), from which is excerpted the following story of fearful and loving intensity. The sharp twist of a pop-the-whip line of children leads to horror and pain and to a story that also contains a number of ironic twists.*

[1] It was a bright cold day in February 1941, so cold the ground was still frozen at ten o'clock in the morning. The air was full of the steaming smell of excrement and the oily, flatulent odor of intestines and the heavy sweetness of blood—in every way a perfect day to slaughter animals. I watched the hogs called to the feeding trough just as they were every morning except this morning it was to receive the ax instead of slop.

[2] A little slop *was* poured into their long communal trough, enough to make them stand still while Uncle Alton or his boy Theron went quietly among them with the ax, using the flat end like a sledgehammer (shells were expensive enough to make a gun out of the question). He would approach the hog from the rear while it slopped at the trough, and then he would straddle it, one leg on each side, patiently waiting for the hog to raise its snout from the slop to take a breath, showing as it did the wide bristled bone between its ears to the ax.

[3] It never took but one blow, delivered expertly and with consummate skill, and the hog was dead. He then moved with his hammer to the next hog and straddled it. None of the hogs ever seemed to mind that their companions were dropping dead all around them but continued in a single-minded passion to eat. They didn't even mind when another of my cousins (this could be a boy of only eight or nine because it took neither strength nor skill) came right behind the hammer and drew a long razor-boned butcher knife across the throat of the fallen hog. Blood spurted with the still-beating heart, and a live hog would sometimes turn to one that was lying beside it at the trough and stick its snout into the spurting blood and drink a bit just seconds before it had its own head crushed.

[4] It was a time of great joy and celebration for the children. We played games and ran (I gimping along pretty well by then) and screamed and brought wood to the boiler and thought of that night, when we would have

fresh fried pork and stew made from lungs and liver and heart in an enormous pot that covered half the stove.

⁵ The air was charged with the smell of fat being rendered in tubs in the backyard and the sharp squeals of the pigs at the troughs, squeals from pure piggishness at the slop, never from pain. Animals were killed but seldom hurt. Farmers took tremendous precautions about pain at slaughter. It is, whether or not they ever admit it when they talk, a ritual. As brutal as they sometimes are with farm animals and with themselves, no farmer would ever eat an animal he had willingly made suffer.

⁶ The heel strings were cut on each of the hog's hind legs, and a stick, called a gambreling stick, or a gallus, was inserted into the cut behind the tendon and the hog dragged to the huge cast-iron boiler, which sat in a depression dug into the ground so the hog could be slipped in and pulled out easily. The fire snapped and roared in the depression under the boiler. The fire had to be tended carefully because the water could never quite come to a boil. If the hog was dipped in boiling water, the hair would set and become impossible to take off. The ideal temperature was water you could rapidly draw your finger through three times in succession without being blistered.

⁷ Unlike cows, which are skinned, a hog is scraped. After the hog is pulled from the water, a blunt knife is drawn over the animal, and if the water has not been too hot, the hair slips off smooth as butter, leaving a white, naked, utterly beautiful pig.

⁸ To the great glee of the watching children, when the hog is slipped into the water, it defecates. The children squeal and clap their hands and make their delightfully obscene children's jokes as they watch it all.

⁹ On that morning, mama was around in the back by the smokehouse where some hogs, already scalded and scraped, were hanging in the air from their heel strings being disemboweled. Along with the other ladies she was washing out the guts, turning them inside out, cleaning them good so they could later be stuffed with ground and seasoned sausage meat.

¹⁰ Out in front of the house where the boiler was, I was playing pop-the-whip as best I could with my brother and several of my cousins. Pop-the-whip is a game in which everyone holds hands and runs fast and then the leader of the line turns sharply. Because he is turning through a tighter arc than the other children, the line acts as a whip with each child farther down the line having to travel through a greater space and consequently having to go faster in order to keep up. The last child in the line literally gets *popped* loose and sent flying from his playmates.

¹¹ I was popped loose and sent flying into the steaming boiler of water beside a scalded, floating hog.

¹² I remember everything about it as clearly as I remember anything that ever happened to me, except the screaming. Curiously, I cannot remember the screaming. They say I screamed all the way to town, but I cannot remember it.

¹³ What I remember is John C. Pace, a black man whose daddy was also

named John C. Pace, reached right into the scalding water and pulled me out and set me on my feet and stood back to look at me. I did not fall but stood looking at John and seeing in his face that I was dead.

[14] The children's faces, including my brother's, showed I was dead, too. And I knew it must be so because I knew where I had fallen and I felt no pain—not in that moment—and I knew with the bone-chilling certainty most people are spared this, yes, death does come and mine had just touched me.

[15] John C. Pace ran screaming and the other children ran screaming and left me standing there by the boiler, my hair and skin and clothes steaming in the bright cold February air.

[16] In memory I stand there alone with the knowledge of death upon me, watching steam rising from my hands and clothes while everybody runs and, after everybody has gone, standing there for minutes while nobody comes.

[17] That is only memory. It may have been but seconds before my mama and Uncle Alton came to me. Mama tells me she heard me scream and started running toward the boiler, knowing already what had happened. She has also told me that she could not bring herself to try to do anything with that smoking ghostlike thing standing by the boiler. But she did. They all did. They did what they could.

[18] But in that interminable time between John pulling me out and my mother arriving in front of me, I remember first the pain. It didn't begin as bad pain, but rather like maybe sandspurs under my clothes.

[19] I reached over and touched my right hand with my left, and the whole thing came off like a wet glove. I mean, the skin on the top of the wrist and the back of my hand, along with the fingernails, all just turned loose and slid on down to the ground. I could see my fingernails lying in the little puddle my flesh made on the ground in front of me.

[20] Then hands were on me, taking off my clothes, and the pain turned into something words cannot touch, or at least my words cannot touch. There is no way for me to talk about it because when my shirt was taken off, my back came off with it. When my overalls were pulled down, my cooked and glowing skin came down.

[21] I still had not fallen, and I stood there participating in my own butchering. When they got the clothes off me they did the worst thing they could have done; they wrapped me in a sheet. They did it out of panic and terror and ignorance and love.

[22] That day there happened to be a car at the farm. I can't remember who it belonged to, but I was taken into the backseat into my mama's lap— God love the lady, out of her head, pressing her boiled son to her breast— and we started for Alma, a distance of about sixteen miles. The only thing that I can remember about the trip was that I started telling mama that I did not want to die. I started saying it and never stopped.

[23] The car we piled into was incredibly slow. An old car and very, very slow, and every once in a while Uncle Alton, who was like a daddy to me,

would jump out of the car and run alongside it and helplessly scream for it to go faster and then he would jump on the running board until he couldn't stand it any longer and then he would jump off again.

[24] But like bad beginnings everywhere, they sometimes end well. When I got to Dr. Sharp's office in Alma and he finally managed to get me out of the sticking sheet, he found that I was scalded over two-thirds of my body but that my head had not gone under the water (he said that would have killed me), and for some strange reason I have never understood, the burns were not deep. He said I would probably even outgrow the scars, which I have. Until I was about fifteen years old, the scars were puckered and discolored on my back and right arm and legs. But now their outlines are barely visible.

[25] The only hospital at the time was thirty miles away, and Dr. Sharp said I'd do just as well at home if they built a frame over the bed to keep the covers off me and also keep a light burning over me twenty-four hours a day. (He knew as well as we did that I couldn't go to a hospital anyway, since the only thing Dr. Sharp ever got for taking care of me was satisfaction for a job well done, if he got that. Over the years, I was his most demanding and persistent charity, which he never mentioned to me or mama. Perhaps that is why in an age when it is fashionable to distrust and hate doctors, I love them.)

## ◆ PRACTICE

### Discussion

1. Crews has remembered clearly many vivid, specific details from his childhood experience. But what alterations or omissions of memory, his own or others', does Crews cite in his narrative? What false conclusion is reached by John C. Pace, the other children, and Crews himself? At what points do words fail Crews as he writes of the experience? Why does he mention these failures of memory, perception, and expression in an otherwise accurate, realistic, and vivid story?

2. At what points does Crews imply or specifically draw a comparison between himself and a hog? What effect does the comparison have on the story?

3. Crews details a horrifying experience but also cites several examples of love. What are they? Do these examples blur the focus of the narrative? Explain.

4. What is the point of Crews' story? (Reflect a moment; it may be more complex than you first think. Hint: His thesis is a two-part, contrasting, balanced concept. Look to paragraphs 14, 21, 24, and 25 for help.) Where does he specifically state the dichotomy of his theme? How does Crews' organization reflect his two-part balance?

5. At what point in the story does Crews make an abrupt turn from factual description to more impressionistic observations? How does he emphasize this turn with writing techniques?

6. Although Crews does not use direct dialogue in his narrative, where does he resort to indirect dialogue (for example, "He said that . . .")? How does that indirect dialogue briefly develop the character of the indirect speakers, in addition to advancing the factual report of the experience? In what way does he create a vivid characterization of two other figures?

7. Make a list of all the phrases or images with a surprising, ironic twist that Crews employs in his narrative. Why are there so many in this particular story?

8. What is the narrator's point of view in relation to his own story here? What methods and phrases especially reinforce this point of view? How does this point of view affect the theme?

*Vocabulary*

| | | |
|---|---|---|
| flatulent | rendered | disemboweled |
| communal | defecates | interminable |
| consummate | | |

*Writing*

1. Narrate a childhood experience that led to an insight.

2. Have you ever felt such great pain or joy that it could not be expressed? Try to convey that deep emotion to a reader by narrating the story that surrounds it.

3. Crews' final line, "I love them," sums up his gratefulness to doctors as a class. Write a paper in which you describe an event in your life which made you "love" a class of people. Suggestions: firefighters, teachers, lawyers, law-enforcement officers.

# CHAPTER 11

# PROCESS

## PROCESS

If you want to tell your reader how something happens, you can use *process,* a writing strategy that describes a series of steps leading to a particular end point. Process is useful because it can be as short as a paragraph or as long as a full paper. It can also be used with other strategies.

One of the two basic kinds of process development is the *artificial* process, which traces the development of a situation or set of circumstances created by human beings. When you give directions or tell someone how to do something, you explain an artificial process. The manufacture of gasoline is such a process:

|  |  |
|---|---|
| *Steps in process* | 1. Heat the raw petroleum. |
| | 2. Cool the resulting vapor into liquid. |
| | 3. Use further refining processes. |
| *End point* | 4. Blend liquids and treat chemically to get grades of commercial gasoline. |

The second kind of process is *natural,* one which occurs in the real world around us. A natural process, for instance, may be the result of an instinctive reaction to some basic drive. Birds instinctively migrate every year. In this natural process they begin by losing some of their feathers and growing new ones, taking many trial flights, and eating a great deal to store up fat. The steps and end point in this process are:

|  |  |
|---|---|
| *Steps in process* | 1. Molting |
| | 2. Trial flights |
| *End point* | 3. Building a reserve of fat to get ready for migration |

Natural processes are also often dependent upon timing. For instance, birds migrate south in the fall of the year and north in the spring of the year.

## ✦ *PRACTICE*

### *Discussion*

Here are examples of both types of process. Read each and answer the questions at the end.

[1] The marriage flight is one of the most important days in the life of an ant colony. Its date varies according to the species but, in the case of the *rufa*, it falls between May and September. On one day—and on only one day in a single season—the reproducers must leave the nest, and workers chase out any reluctant ones.

[2] They fly out on an August morning and, in the air, they mingle with the sexed ants from neighboring nests. A pursuit begins until each female offers herself to a male on a neighboring tree. Then, in turn, the males mate with her and, in so doing, they accomplish the only act for which they were created. The next day, they all will be dead and many of the females as well. Of the surviving females, some may return to their original nests. Others will be adopted by nests in need of a queen or big enough to require more than one.

[3] Finally, others will go out alone and found a new nest. The female digs herself in about five inches below the surface of the earth and carves out a cell for herself with no exit. There she lays her eggs. Some of them will become larvae, but not all—most of them serve for food for their mother and for the larvae which she chooses to raise. If winter falls, the larvae must wait until the following spring before they become ants. On the other hand, if workers are born before the cold weather sets in, they immediately begin to dig galleries, the beginning of a future nest. They start foraging for food, and the normal life of an ant-nest has been founded.

—"Ants," *Realities* magazine

#### EXTINGUISHING AN OVEN FIRE

[1] The blazing oven is another appliance problem, although it doesn't usually indicate anything is wrong with the appliance. But it calls for a mighty quick remedy. It usually shows up first as smoke trailing out of the oven vent. If, as is usually the case, the broiler is in action, the whole kitchen may be full of smoke. If you open the oven door, all the blazes in hell seem to sail out at you. In this event, try to hang on to your nonchalance and just shut the oven door again. The chances are the big, beautiful sirloin inside isn't ruined, the house won't burn down, and the entire mess isn't as bad as it looks.

[2] First, turn off the broiler. Then yank the top off your biggest salt container. Next open the oven again and slide the broiler rack and the steak out a little with a carving fork or some other long utensil that won't burn and

doesn't make you reach in so close you get spattered with fiery fat. (Fiery fat can set your clothing afire.) Then *pile* on the salt by the fistful—at the points the flames are coming from. This salt business is a sort of old wives' tale, but it works if you have plenty of the stuff. It doesn't act chemically by creating some fancy fire-smothering gas. It simply stifles the fire by covering it up and shutting off its air supply—like a load of sand. But it's better than sand from the culinary standpoint because you can wash it off, and if a few grains remain they won't chip your teeth. Whatever you do, *don't* throw water on the fire. This blasts into steam, floats and spatters blazing grease all over the place, and can give you some very nasty burns and possibly set the kitchen on fire.

³ Actually things cool off surprisingly fast with the broiler turned off and salt piled on the conflagration. Everything usually is under complete control in a minute or two. But even with the fire out, you're likely to have a case of jitters. Just remember it's not anywhere near as horrible as it looks.

⁴ In the rare event that you can't put the fire out (most unlikely), shove the whole works back in the oven and shut the door—also the oven vent if possible. This, at least, keeps your private inferno locked up where it can do the least harm until the fire trucks arrive.—George Daniels

1. Identify the *steps* and *end point* of each process.

2. Which process is *natural,* which is *artificial*? In what ways are the processes fundamentally different?

3. In a process paper, there are usually certain transitional "signals" (*first, later, after this, before, and so on*) which help the reader discriminate among the various parts of the process. List the signals in the examples. Do most of the signals fall into any particular class or type?

4. Describe the writer's stance in each passage. The two kinds of process ordinarily have different stances. Explain why this should be so.

## SUGGESTIONS FOR WRITING PROCESS PAPERS

When you use process strategies of development, you are essentially describing how something is done, how it works, or how it "happens."

### Artificial Process

In the artificial process, you often give directions to a specific person or group (people who want to learn how to put out an oven fire, for example), and your writer's stance is clear and precise. You will probably use a time or chronological order because some steps should be done before others. For instance, when showing the process of how detergents work, it is logical to discuss adding the detergent to the water *before* you discuss what happens when water and detergent are combined. You must, therefore, give careful thought to the sequence of steps or stages when describing a process.

Keep in mind that your reader may know little about your subject and may need definitions of terms and clear signals showing how the steps or stages are separated. You may wish to speak directly to the reader and address him or her as *you*. Certain suggestions may help you to use artificial process:

1. Decide if you are giving directions or making an explanation. Then choose the writer's stance that is most appropriate.

2. Determine the end point or purpose of the process.

3. Determine the relevant, main steps of the process that lead to the end point or purpose. *State the steps clearly,* and *use transitions.*

4. If possible, keep to a clear chronological sequence of events in the process, but avoid irrelevancies.

## Natural Process

The natural process is somewhat more difficult to write because you have to look carefully at the sequence of steps in order to find them and the end point. Natural processes often involve scientific subjects, so you must be well informed in order to describe the process. However, neither you nor your reader is necessarily *in* that process. You are both standing off from it—watching it and trying to understand how it works. Instead of addressing the reader, try using the *who (or what) does what* formula:

[*Who*] The male [*does what?*] mates and dies.

## ◆ *PRACTICE*

### *Discussion*

1. Below is an artificial-process paper that uses process to inform.
   a. How does the student use the *who does what* formula to describe how she adapted to partial deafness?
   b. Note the order of steps. How long a period would you judge this process took?
   c. If you were writing a paper like this, how would you change the sequence of steps? How useful are the abstract terms *physical, mental,* and *social?*
   d. Discuss the student's use of definition.
   e. Describe her stance.

*Introduction*
*Definition by*
*classification and*
*operation*

[1] When I was eight, I had a radical mastoidectomy—a surgical procedure consisting of chiselling out the infected bone (behind the ear) called the *mastoid.* This is a serious operation, often leaving the patient with little hearing in the affected ear. Thanks to miracle drugs, mastoid operations are infrequently done today. However, since I lived in a remote area of North Dakota where the health care was not easily accessible, I developed a mastoid infection before my family realized how seriously ill I was.

*Effect*

[2] Young people are adaptable, so I didn't realize that being deaf in one ear was anything to worry about. My friends and family didn't treat me any differently. Even though the operation had been very painful and disagreeable, I was so glad to be back in school, doing the things I liked to do, that I really didn't pay much attention to the stages I went through in adapting to partial deafness. As I look back over the years, I can see that I developed a conscious process of adapting to deafness. I made physical, mental, and social adjustments.

*Introduces the*
*strategy: process*

*Thesis*

*First step:*
physical

*Four examples*

[3] The first step in adapting to deafness was physical. I had to position my body so that I could hear my friends and family. Since my right ear was my "bad" ear, I learned to tip my head to the right so that the sound entered my left or "good" ear. Over the years it has become such a habit that all my photographs show me with my head tipped to the right. Another way I found that I could position my body was to get on the right-hand side of people. Even today, when I sit on a couch or ride in the back seat of a car, I always sit on a person's right. When we walk down the street, I always get on the "outside" or right-hand side. This sometimes causes me some problems with men who think they should be on the "outside." I never talk when I drive a car because I can't hear well enough to carry on a conversation, without losing track of my concentration.

*Second step:*
mental

[4] I realized early that consciously positioning my body to the situation was not enough, so I progressed to the second step—being alert. I knew that I had to concentrate and listen very carefully to those around me. Other people were not going to go out of their way to help me hear. Besides, I wasn't willing to go around explaining that I heard with only one ear. Who cares! Therefore, I learned that by concentrating I could increase my hearing ability dramatically. By watching faces and lips, I taught myself lip-reading. Today, I can tell what is going on in television shows when the sound is off by reading the actor's lips. I also became alert to body language—unusual gestures, facial expressions and movements—that helped tell me what people were thinking.

*Two examples*

*Third and final*
*step:* social

[5] My final step was to adjust my social life to partial deafness. I couldn't have much fun at large parties because the commotion created too much "surface noise" for me to carry on conversations. However, when I was forced into large

*One example*   groups, I tried to figure out the general conversation and make suitable noises like "Oh?" "Is that so?" "Well!" and "I agree." I'm afraid there were times when I agreed when I shouldn't have. Occasionally, I received some peculiar looks when my pat answers didn't quite fit the discussion.

*Conclusion*   6 I am lucky that I became partially deaf when I was very young. I have since met older people who became deaf late in life. Instead of working on the process of hearing, they have become lazy and resentful. They make *other* people do the

*End point implied:* work. No one wants to shout while conversing. It is better to
*adaptation* answer with an occasional "I agree," even when it doesn't fit,
*successful* than to be a demanding, irritable deaf person.

2. Here is part of a magazine article written by a doctor describing a process. Is this a natural or artificial process? Identify the steps and the end point.

1 At 11 p.m. on Dec. 22, 1963 fire broke out aboard the Greek luxury liner *Lakonia* as it cruised the Atlantic near Madeira, and passengers and crew were forced into the water. The air temperature was over 60°, the sea almost 65° and rescue ships were in the area within a few hours. Nevertheless, 125 people died, 113 of these fatalities being attributed to hypothermia, the lowering of the body's inner heat, perhaps no more than 6° from the normal 98.6°. . . .

2 The moment your body begins to lose heat faster than it produces it, hypothermia threatens. As heat loss continues, the temperature of the body's inner core falls below normal. Hands and arms (the extremities most needed in order to survive) are affected first. When body temperature drops to 95°, dexterity is reduced to the point where you cannot open a jackknife or light a match.

3 According to recent research by the Mountain Rescue Association, the body reacts in a series of predictable ways when inner-core temperature falls. At 2.5° below normal, shivering begins, an automatic body process to create heat. But it takes energy to shiver—comparable to what is expended sawing wood—and the heat loss continues. The more the core temperature drops, the less efficient the brain becomes. Although you may have a pack on your back with a sleeping bag and food in it, you may not have the sense to use them.

4 If the core temperature drops to 94°, you will stop shivering but every now and then will experience uncontrollable shaking. Your system, automatically getting rid of carbon dioxide and lactic acid, also releases blood sugar and a little adrenaline, giving you a surge of energy, which causes the violent shaking. This last desperate effort by the body to produce heat utilizes a tremendous amount of energy.

5 "Now," you think, "I must be getting warmer because I am not shivering anymore." By this time you are pretty irrational. If someone were to ask you your name and telephone number, you probably wouldn't know them, for the brain has become numb.

[6] If nothing is done, death usually occurs within 1½ hours after the shivering starts. In fact, a shivering person can go from fatigue to exhaustion to cooling beyond the recovery point so quickly he may perish before rescuers can build a shelter or get a fire started.

—J. Clayton Stewart, "Growing Cold by Degrees"

# PLANNING AND WRITING A PROCESS (AN EXAMPLE)

Jack has a collection of old comic books that are becoming valuable with age. He belongs to a collector's association, which has invited him to write an article describing his process of storing comics in order to protect them from moisture, acids, and sun. He writes a paragraph on how he will plan his article:

> My comic books don't fall into just one class. I have three different kinds: run-of-the-mill, more valuable, and *very* expensive. They all require particular treatments that overlap. What is the best way to describe the storage process without confusing my audience? Perhaps I should give the basic method of storing the least valuable comics, and then build on that method in a discussion of storing the more expensive ones. My steps in the process might look like this:

|  | Run-of-the-Mill | More Valuable | Very Expensive |
|---|---|---|---|
| Step 1: | omit | use Mylar bags | same |
| Step 2: | use acid-free box | same | use acid-free notebook |
| Step 3: | use acid-free millboard | omit | omit |
| Step 4: | store in dry place | same | same |

This kind of pattern made writing his process easier than if he hadn't identified the relationship shown above.

### KEEPING COMICS

[1] Comic book collectors who are serious (like me) are known as "hard-core" collectors. There are, so one hobby magazine recently stated, tens of thousands of ordinary collectors, but only a few thousand hard-core ones. And for us, the problem is not just collecting—but keeping. Comic books were printed on very cheap paper using terrible techniques of production. Put a valuable comic book in the sun, and it may be ruined in a matter of hours. Store it improperly in a damp place, and it may be ruined in a matter of months or a few years. The answer is to store them properly and thus save your collection.

[2] Like most collectors, you probably have a large number of run-of-the-mill comics. Place these on edge (never flat) in acid-free millboard boxes. When putting them in the box, take special care of the corners. Nothing protects the

edges from bending, so put them in carefully. After packing every group of 10 or 15 comics, insert a piece of acid-free millboard. These supports will keep the comics from sagging. Bags are not necessary for these comics. Stack the boxes in a dark, cool place with relatively low humidity.

3 For your more valuable comics, an extra precaution is necessary. Place the valuable ones in three mil Mylar snugs before putting them in an acid-free box. These snugs are inert polyester bags that will last hundreds of years without decomposing. Normal polyethylene bags last only five years. When putting comics in the bags, again be careful of the edges and corners, since the corners bend easily. Mylar is quite stiff and holds the comic in a vise-like grip. This is beneficial if the comic is flat and straight in the bag, but detrimental if the corners are allowed to remain folded. Use a popsicle stick or some other blunt, flat instrument to push the corners down after the comic is in the bag. Also, watch the back cover and see that it is in straight also.

4 Store these bagged comics in small or large acid-free cartons. The small cartons are a little more expensive, but provide slightly easier access to the comics.

5 If you have *very* expensive comics costing $100 and up, give them the best treatment. Use a snug especially made for a three-ring binder. This snug, which clamps the comic like the regular snugs, is four mils rather than three mils thick. It also has an edge with punched holes for the binder. The binder, which should be well constructed and sturdy, makes it easy to display your valuable collection. The binders should also be stored in a dark, cool place.

6 Actually, any of the storage schemes for the expensive comics can be used for less expensive varieties. The best methods cost a lot of money though, up to 60 cents per stored comic. The scheme for run-of-the-mill comics costs only four cents per comic. The best rule is: Spend in proportion to what your comics are worth to you.

## ◆ *PRACTICE*

### *Discussion*

Read Jack's paper on storing comic books.

1. Outline the stance. How does the writer's *point of view* influence his *role*?

2. Where in each paragraph are the basic steps described? Discuss the applications of the steps to the three divisions (or *classes*) of comic books.

3. Discuss the importance of the materials necessary in the *process*. How is the choice of materials relevant to the *purpose* of the process?

### *Writing*

1. Think about some medical problem you or one of your family has had. Consider *one* of the following:

a. What was the process your body went through when you had your medical problem?

b. What kind of process did you develop to adjust to your problem?

You may want to interview some experts or do research in order to deal with **a** above. (You will develop a process yourself when you deal with one of these topics—search your memory, freewrite everything you can remember, group your material, identify a hook, plan your stance, and write.)

2. Choose one of the following topics. If possible, practice the process, keeping notes on what you do and in what order. Identify a suitable audience, outline your stance, and write a paper.
   a. How to write exams
   b. How to make a house burglar-proof
   c. How to pierce your ear in more than one place
   d. How to talk to an answering machine
   e. How to pack a bag for backpacking

3. Choose one of the following topics and write a process paper. If you have had no experience with any of these processes, identify one of your own.
   a. How to use psychology in dealing with _____
   b. How you defeated computer anxiety
   c. How a shopping mall changes a community
   d. How a coach taught me to _____

PETER ELBOW

# *FREEWRITING EXERCISES*

*Peter Elbow knows his way around a classroom. Educated at Williams College, Oxford, Harvard, and Brandeis universities, he has taught at the Massachusetts Institute of Technology and Franconia College. Currently he teaches at Evergreen State College in Olympia, Washington. He has directed writing programs in both academic and community settings, and his ideas have had a strong influence on teachers of writing and writing programs throughout the United States. Despite all his academic connections, the title of his 1973 writing text, from which the following piece is taken, is* Writing Without Teachers. *Teachers, Elbow writes in the preface, are more* useful *if they are not* necessary. *That philosophy of self-reliance is apparent in the very first words of the book, reproduced below.*

¹ The most effective way I know to improve your writing is to do freewriting exercises regularly. At least three times a week. They are sometimes called "automatic writing," "babbling," or "jabbering" exercises. The idea is simply to write for ten minutes (later on, perhaps fifteen or twenty). Don't stop for anything. Go quickly without rushing. Never stop to look back, to cross something out, to wonder how to spell something, to wonder what word or thought to use, or to think about what you are doing. If you can't think of a word or a spelling, just use a squiggle or else write, "I can't think of it." Just put down something. The easiest thing is just to put down whatever is in your mind. If you get stuck it's fine to write "I can't think what to say, I can't think what to say" as many times as you want; or repeat the last word you wrote over and over again; or anything else. The only requirement is that you *never* stop.

² What happens to a freewriting exercise is important. It must be a piece of writing which, even if someone reads it, doesn't send any ripples back to you. It is like writing something and putting it in a bottle in the sea. The teacherless class helps your writing by providing maximum feedback. Freewritings help you by providing no feedback at all. When I assign one, I invite the writer to let me read it. But also tell him to keep it if he prefers. I read it quickly and make no comments at all and I do not speak with him about it. The main thing is that a freewriting must never be evaluated in any way; in fact there must be no discussion or comment at all.

³ Here is an example of a fairly coherent exercise (sometimes they are very incoherent, which is fine):

I think I'll write what's on my mind, but the only thing on my mind right now is what to write for ten minutes. I've never done this before and I'm not prepared in any way—the sky is cloudy today, how's that? now I'm

afraid I won't be able to think of what to write when I get to the end of the
sentence—well, here I am at the end of the sentence—here I am again,
again, again, again, at least I'm still writing—Now I ask is there some
reason to be happy that I'm still writing—ah yes! Here comes the question
again—What am I getting out of this? What point is there in it? It's almost
obscene to always ask but I seem to question everything that way and I was
gonna say something else pertaining to that but I got so busy writing down
the first part that I forgot what I was leading into. This is kind of fun oh
don't stop writing—cars and trucks speeding by somewhere out the window, pens clittering across people's papers. The sky is cloudy—is it symbolic that I should be mentioning it? Huh? I dunno. Maybe I should try
colors, blue, red, dirty words—wait a minute—no can't do that, orange,
yellow, arm tired, green pink violet magenta lavender red brown black
green—now that I can't think of any more colors—just about done—
relief? maybe.

## ◆ *PRACTICE*

### *Discussion*

1. In what ways is freewriting completely different from the way you
   usually write a paper or a letter? In what ways is it the same?

2. Why is it so important not to get any feedback on freewriting? What is
   the point of having Elbow (or your instructor) read a freewriting
   assignment if there is to be "no discussion or comment at all"?

3. What is the most interesting point for you in the example of a freewriting exercise that Elbow gives? Why do you find that spot interesting?
   (Since the author of the piece is not here to hear your feedback, it is all
   right to coment.)

4. Does Elbow sound like a writing instructor? If not, how does his voice
   sound? What parts of this essay especially contribute to establishing his
   voice? Is that voice appropriate to the particular essay he is writing?
   Explain why it is or is not.

5. Would Elbow's essay be improved by moving his example to the beginning? Why or why not? How would such a move affect the rest of the
   essay?

6. Elbow uses a couple of incomplete sentences in his part of the essay,
   exclusive of the example. (And he calls himself a writing instructor!)
   Where are they? Rewrite them as complete sentences. What did the
   essay gain from your revisions? What did it lose?

7. Besides fragments, Elbow uses several very short sentences in the essay.
   In which paragraphs do most of them occur? They are mixed in with

some very long sentences in that same paragraph. Examine the construction of those long sentences. Does the mixture of short and long sentences vary the rhythm of the paragraph? Is the rhythm of the first paragraph the same as that of the second? Why or why not?

8. What tricks are used by the author of the freewriting exercise to keep the exercise moving? What tone do these ploys lend to the exercise?

### Vocabulary

| | | |
|---|---|---|
| freewriting | feedback | pertaining |
| babbling | coherent | clittering |
| jabbering | obscene | magenta |
| squiggle | | |

### Writing

1. Freewriting and proofreading are at opposite ends of the writing process. Write a guide to proofreading, explaining clearly to student writers how to go about proofreading a paper.

2. Freewriting is to writing as, perhaps, stretching is to running or sketching is to painting. Choose a type of exercise preparatory to something else with which you are familiar and tell someone interested in that something else about how to go about warming up. You may also want to tell your reader why he or she *should* warm up.

3. Freewrite for ten minutes. Then examine what you should have written and note any interesting spots where you might have shifted gears or become stuck, for example. Write a brief analysis of your freewriting exercise: how you got started, the steps your mind and hand took together, and how you stopped.

PATRICK McMANUS

## THE PURIST

*Patrick McManus writes a regular column for* Field and Stream *magazine. "The Purist" is one of the essays in McManus' book A* Fine and Pleasant Misery *(1978). While readers concerned with writing styles and strategies will note how McManus explains several processes and how he uses understatement, they should read through the essay once just for fun.*

¹ Twelve-year-olds are different from you and me, particularly when it comes to fishing, and most of all when it comes to fishing on Opening Day of Trout Season.

² The twelve-year-old is probably the purest form of sports fisherman known to man. I don't know why. Perhaps it is because his passion for fishing is at that age undiluted by the multitude of other passions that accumulate over a greater number of years. Say thirteen.

³ Now I am reasonably sure that I can catch a limit of trout faster on Opening Day than the average twelve-year-old, but any angler knows that speed and quantity are not true measures of quality when it comes to fishing. It's a matter of style, and here the twelve-year-old beats me hands down. You just can't touch a twelve-year-old when it comes to style.

⁴ Preparation is the big part of his secret. If Opening Day of Trout Season is June 5, the twelve-year-old starts his preparation about the middle of March. He knows he should have started earlier, but at that age he likes to put things off. With such a late start, he will be hard pressed to be ready in time.

⁵ The first thing he does is to get his tackle out and look at it. He removes from one of his shoe boxes a large snarly ball of lines, hooks, leaders, spinners, flies, plugs, weeds, tree branches, and a petrified frog. He shakes the whole mass a couple of times and nothing comes loose. Pleased that everything is still in good order he stuffs it all back into his shoe box. The next time he will look at it will be on Opening Day Eve, fifteen minutes before he is supposed to go to bed. The tackle snarl will then provide the proper degree of wild, sweaty panic that is so much a part of the twelve-year-old's style.

⁶ The next order of business is to check his bait supplies. The best time to do this is in the middle of a blizzard, when it's too cold to be outside

without a coat on or to have all the windows in the house open. The large jar of salmon eggs he has stored next to the hot-water pipes that run through his closet seems to look all right, but just to be sure he takes the lid off. He drops the lid on the floor and it rolls under something too large to move. Something must be done immediately, he knows, because uneasy murmurs are rising in distant parts of the house, and besides he won't be able to hold his breath forever. The best course of action seems to be to run the jar through every room in the building, leaving in his wake mass hysteria and the sound of windows being thrown open. Later, standing coatless with the rest of the family in the front yard while a chill north wind freshens up the house, he offers the opinion that he may need a new bottle of salmon eggs for Opening Day.

7 Occasionally the young angler will do some work on his hooks. There is, however, some diversity of opinion among twelve-year-olds whether it is better to crack off the crust of last year's worms from the hooks or to leave it on as a little added attraction for the fish. The wise father usually withholds any advice on the subject but does suggest that if his offspring decides to sharpen his hooks on the elder's whetstone, the worm crusts be removed *beforehand.* Nothing gums up a whetstone worse than oiled worm dust.

8 The twelve-year-old takes extra-special pains in the preparation of his fly rod. He gets it out, looks at it, sights down it, rubs it with a cloth, sights down it again, rubs it some more, and finally puts it away with an air of utter frustration. There is, after all, not much that you can do to a glass rod.

9 The reel is something else again. A thousand different things can be done to a reel, all of which can be grouped under the general term "taking it apart." The main reason a kid takes his reel apart is to take it apart. But most adults can't understand this kind of reasoning, so the kid has to come up with some other excuse. He says that he is taking his reel apart to clean it. No one can deny that the reel needs cleaning. It has enough sand and gravel in it to ballast a balloon. During most of the season it sounds like a miniature rock crusher and can fray the nerves of an adult fisherman at a hundred yards. For Opening Day, however, the reel must be clean.

10 There are three basic steps used by the twelve-year-old in cleaning a reel. First it is reduced to the largest possible number of parts. These are all carefully placed on a cookie sheet in the sequence of removal. The cookie sheet is then dropped on the floor. The rest of the time between March and Opening Day of Trout Season is spent looking for these parts. The last one is found fifteen minutes before bedtime on Opening Day Eve.

11 Some twelve-year-olds like to test their leaders before risking them on actual fish. Nothing is more frustrating to a kid than having a leader snap just as he is heaving a nice fat trout back over his head. Consequently, he is concerned that any weakness in a leader be detected beforehand.

There are many methods of doing this, but one of the best is to tie one end of the leader to a rafter in the garage and the other end to a concrete block. The concrete block is then dropped from the top of a stepladder. The chief drawback of this method is the cost involved in replacing cracked rafters.

[12] Eventually the big night comes—Opening Day Eve.

[13] The day is spent digging worms. Early in the season there is a surplus of worms and the young angler can be choosy. The process of worm selection is similar to that used in Spain for the selection of fighting bulls. Each worm is chosen for his size, courage, and fighting ability. One reason kids frequently have poor luck on Opening Day is that their worms can lick the average fish in a fair fight.

[14] Approximately four hundred worms are considered an adequate number. These are placed in a container and covered with moist dirt. The container is then sealed and placed carefully back in the closet by the hot-water pipes, where it is next found during a blizzard the following March.

[15] The twelve-year-old angler really peaks out, however, during that fifteen minutes before bedtime. He discovers that his tackle has become horribly snarled in his tackle box. No one knows how, unless perhaps the house has been invaded by poltergeists. The reel is thrown together with an expertise born of hysteria and panic. Four cogs, six screws, and a worm gear are left over, but the thing works. And it no longer makes that funny little clicking sound!

[16] Finally, all is in readiness and the boy is congratulating himself on having had the good sense to start his preparation three months earlier. As it was, he went right down to the last minutes. Only one major task remains: the setting of the alarm clock.

[17] Naturally, he wants to be standing ready beside his favorite fishing hole at the crack of dawn. The only trouble is he doesn't know exactly when dawn cracks. He surmises about four o'clock. If it takes him an hour to hike down to the fishing hole, that means he should set the alarm for about three. On the other hand, it may take longer in the dark, so he settles on 2:30. He doesn't have to allow any time for getting dressed since he will sleep with his clothes on.

[18] Once in bed he begins to worry. What if the alarm fails to go off? He decides to test it. The alarm makes a fine, loud clanging sound. After all the shouting dies down and his folks are back in bed, he winds up the alarm again. As a precautionary measure, he decides to set the alarm for two, thus giving himself a half-hour safety margin. He then stares at the ceiling for an hour, visions of five-pound trout dancing in his head. He shakes with anticipation. He worries. What if the alarm fails to awaken him? What if he shuts it off and goes back to sleep? The horror of it is too much to stand.

[19] Midnight. He gets up, puts on his boots, grabs his rod and lunch and brand-new bottle of salmon eggs, and heads out the door.

[20] It's Opening Day of Trout Season, and there's not a minute to spare.

# ✦ *PRACTICE*

### *Discussion*

1. On what grounds is the twelve-year-old judged the purest form of fisherman? What is the prominent feature of his inimitable style?

2. How is the whole family involved in the mystique of the pure fisherman? What emotions are felt by other family members as the pure fisherman indulges his passion?

3. What are the three basic steps used by a twelve-year-old in cleaning a reel? How are these steps each symbolic of different aspects of the ultimate fisherman's style?

4. Is the process explained by McManus an artificial or a natural process? What phrases in the essay support your answer?

5. The main process discussed in the essay contains steps that involve mini-processes. Identify every process explained in the essay.

6. Where does McManus use a delayed statement to create a humorous effect? Where does he use understatement humorously? Where does he juxtapose two completely contradictory phrases or ideas to make us laugh?

7. Spot all the ways time and dates are mentioned in the essay. Why is a concern with time appropriate to a process explanation? What does McManus do with time in this essay that one does not usually expect in a process explanation?

8. Does McManus employ dialogue anywhere in the essay? How is the voice of the twelve-year-old occasionally introduced?

### *Vocabulary*

| | | |
|---|---|---|
| diversity | ballast | cogs |
| whetstone | leaders | worm gear |
| fly rod | poltergeists | surmises |
| reel | | |

### *Writing*

1. What did you really enjoy doing as a child? Explain how you did it in such a way that the explanation also conveys your enjoyment to the reader.

2. Observe a five-year-old (or a seventy-five-year-old) performing an activity that is important to him or her. Explain how the activity is

performed. You may wish to be humorous, like McManus, but another perspective—admiring or sad, for example—may be more appropriate to your subject.

3. McManus distinguishes between style and output in fishing. Define style and, using illustration, support or refute the contention that style is a more important aspect of any activity than output.

*ROGER WELSCH*

## SHELTERS ON THE PLAINS

*Roger L. Welsch has been interested in folk architecture ever since graduate school. A professor of folklore at the University of Nebraska, Welsch would like to spend more of his time getting psychologically inside the buildings of the past—"thinking about them, feeling them, building them, tearing them down, driving nails, and cussing." As you will see in his essay, Welsch finds some unusual attitudes in the people who built the first "houses" on the American plains, people who may have been dominated by fear—but not fear of hostile Indians or marauding gunslingers.*

The hinges are of leather
And the windows have no glass;
The board roof lets the howling
   blizzards in;
I can hear the hungry coyote
As he slinks up through the grass
'Round that little old sod
   shanty on my claim.
         *Chorus of a*
     *Pioneer Plains Folksong*

¹ Even today the Great Plains crush travelers between the endless sky and a landscape that undulates like swells of the sea. But now, there are at least occasional trees and farmsteads, roads and telephone lines that delineate and articulate spaces within a land otherwise devoid of landmarks. Most of today's plains dwellers know the landscape and regard the climate and space as slight discomforts at worst, in contrast to the migrant homesteaders of the nineteenth century who had never imagined such a place in their worst dreams.

² Then there were even fewer trees than now and the grasslands were not so neatly and reassuringly divided into sizes the mind could digest. The term "prairie schooner" was only barely a metaphor. Ole E. Rölvaag, the Norwegian-born author, portrayed the life of the immigrants and described the vastness of the plains in his 1927 novel, *Giants in the Earth,*

   Bright clear sky over a plain so wide that the rim of the heavens cut down on it around the entire horizon. . . . Bright clear sky, today, tomorrow, and for all time to come. . . .
   And sun! And still more sun! It set the heavens afire every morning; it grew with the day to quivering golden light—then softened into all the shades of red

and purple as evening fell. . . . Pure color everywhere. A gust of wind, sweeping across the plain, threw into life waves of yellow and blue and green. Now and then a dead black wave would race over the scene . . . a cloud! . . .

It was late afternoon. A small caravan was pushing its way through the tall grass. The track it left behind was like the wake of a boat—except that instead of widening out astern it closed in again.

³ The agony of frontier life on the plains is immortalized on tombstones, in the lyrics of folksongs, and in journals and daybooks. But archives often do not contain information on how people responded to specific conditions. I therefore turned to a source usually ignored by those who study folk architecture—the writers of the plains. I reasoned that these poets and novelists had based their hopes of success on a sensitive perception and faithful rendering of the pioneer experience. Such subjective and creative data necessitated careful evaluation; but then so must any field-gathered information.

⁴ I reread the works of such writers as Rölvaag, Willa Cather, Mari Sandoz, and Bess Streeter Aldrich, as well as the essays of architectural historian Amos Rapoport, architectural philospher Gaston Bachelard, and demographer John Demos, looking for clues to an understanding of the nature and degree of the impact of plains geography on the mind of the migrant. The message was clear: the plains were a mysterious land of frightening, unbounded space.

⁵ The intensity of plains geography was made all the sharper by the lens through which it was first seen by the pioneers: the eyes of hopeful immigrants—from Norway, Germany, Czechoslovakia—or of settlers from other parts of the United States, such as Wisconsin, Illinois, and Connecticut, where landscapes were more manageable. These people were accustomed to a perspective foreshortened by trees, rocks, lakes, and streams—rural scenes relieved by stone or timber fences a few hundred feet apart, by farmsteads numbering two or three to an eyeful.

⁶ The German farmers were accustomed to walking in the morning to fields they could shout across and then returning in the evening to a house among other houses, where there was company and communion. On the plains they farmed areas ten times bigger than they had in the Old Country. There were no fences, trees, or rocks, few neighbors within an hour's ride, and the nearest town was days away.

⁷ The distances were only one of the brutalities the Great Plains region dished up for its challengers. The temperature range exceeded, by twenty degrees at the top of the thermometer and forty at the bottom, any they had ever experienced in their homelands. The daily range could equal the annual range in Holland. In Czechoslovakia, there had been no prairie fires racing through the tinder-dry grass faster than a man on horseback. There had been no rattlesnakes and swarms of grasshoppers in Belgium; no cacti, buffalo, or vengeful Indians in Sweden. On the plains, the wind tore the covers from wagons and thunder shook the dishes from shelves.

Hailstones, of a size that could kill horses, fell with terrifying abruptness. Trickles that would not have been worthy of a name in Germany were called rivers here, and like the Platte, they flowed—as some said—upside down, "with the sand on the top and the water underneath."

8 Thus the geography of America's northern plains region—Kansas, Nebraska, the Dakotas—offered climatic, social, and emotional violence that demanded the sturdiest of shelters. Yet, paradoxically, the plains withheld all the materials the settlers had traditionally used for building. There was little stone, even for chimneys; little wood, even for cooking. The most logical first thought would be hasty retreat.

9 Rölvaag's powerful writing grew from his own experience in the wilderness: one of his characters faces a future on the plains and cries, "How will human beings be able to endure this place? Why, there isn't even a thing that one can hide behind!" Retreat is a universal motif in plains literature and folklore. A character in Willa Cather's novel *O Pioneers!* agonizes, "The country was never meant to live in; the thing to do was to get back to Iowa, to Illinois, to any place that had been proved habitable."

10 Consider just one aspect of what the pioneers experienced as they moved westward—the change in forestation. During the nineteeth century, Indiana was almost totally forested in hardwoods—mostly oak and walnut. Forty percent of Illinois was forested; Iowa only 18 percent, hinting, perhaps, at what lay ahead. Nebraska, Kansas, and the Dakotas were 3 percent forested, mainly in a line along the Missouri River at the eastern edge of the Great Plains.

11 And yet the promise of owning land, a farm many times the size of farms in the Old Country (where the possibility of ever possessing even a small one was unlikely) steeled the settlers' resolve to stay and blurred the impact of the catalog of trials they encountered. Besides, most of them had spent everything they had, in both money and pride, to get here, and they could scarcely turn back.

12 These people had to build houses. They quickly used up the trees crowding the river and creek banks in building their traditional log houses. The next alternative, one that made homesteading on the plains a possibility, was the earth, the sod, or "Nebraska marble." And for thirty years the standard on the plains was the sod house. (How sod came to be used as a building material is uncertain. The settlers may have borrowed the idea from the Mormons, who began building with sod in the mid-1850s. The Mormons, in turn, probably got the idea from the earth lodges of the Omaha and Pawnee Indians.)

13 Today we make every effort to design houses that bring the out-of-doors indoors and take the indoors out-of-doors. Patios serve as dining rooms; huge windows provide the illusion that we are outside when we are inside. We open the house walls and break down barriers. But for nineteenth-century plains dwellers, perceptions were different. After a day of being squeezed between sky and earth, of being exposed to the withering sun or a razor-sharp wind, there was little desire on the part of the pioneers to bring the environment into their houses.

[14] The house was meant to be a fortress, a bastion for shutting out the outside. The thick walls, the few small windows and close rooms were not seen as disadvantages—as they might be now—but rather as an integral part of the sod house's advantages. Far from being discomfited by the cramped quarters, plains settlers sought the closeness of family members in the evening hours, after a day spent out of sight and hearing of each other or, for that matter, of any other human being. The close contact and association with the family took on a very special, desirable quality.

[15] Writers' words resound with echoes of this premise. To be sure, the settlers saw the plains as a source of wealth, but the riches could be won only by facing nature. The plains, with their promise of treasure and freedom, demanded an ardent suitor, one willing to face tasks and trials much like those required of fairy-tale heroes in their quest for a princess bride. The land was an adversary, an enemy, to be conquered and tamed. Sod was first and foremost an expedient response to plains geography. It not only answered the absence of conventional building materials but also countered the problems of heat, cold, wind, and defense. The two- to three-foot-thick walls kept the sod house warm in winter and cool in the summer. Neither wind nor bullets could pass through them. Grass fires, a constant threat, would sweep by the soddies, singeing the door and window frames but leaving the interiors cool. Inside the cavelike buildings, the roar of the wind and thunder was only a faint murmur.

[16] The settlers usually built their sod houses on a slight rise or hillside, never in a lowland or valley bottom where a spring flood might destroy them. They first leveled out a floor area with spades, then wetted and tamped it solid with a fence post or wagon tongue. This was the only foundation the house would have.

[17] Moist bottomlands produced the best sod. Here the grass was toughest and the soil was more likely to hold together during the processes of cutting, moving, and house construction. Preferred grasses were buffalo grass (*Buchloë dactyloides*), cordgrass (*Spartina pectinata*), and big bluestem (*Andropogon gerardii*). Only enough sod for a day's work—about a quarter acre—was cut at one time so that no sod would lie in the open overnight and dry out. A standard 12- by 14-foot soddie required about one acre of sod. Wherever possible, oxen were used to cut sod because they gave a smoother pull on the plow than horses, which tended to lurch under the heavy task.

[18] The tool used for cutting sod was not the conventional farming plow, the purpose of which was to tumble and break up the soil. Rather, a grasshopper plow, which had a horizontal blade, was used to shave away a ribbon of sod, three to four inches thick and eighteen inches wide, which passed smoothly over a rod moldboard and rolled over upside down behind the plow. Workers used sharp spades to cut this ribbon into "bricks" about two feet long. The bricks were then loaded onto a wagon or sledge and hauled to the house site.

[19] The bricks formed the walls and were laid up grass-side down (for reasons I have never been able to discover) without any sort of mortar. To

increase their stability and discourage tunneling by mice or snakes, the bricks were staggered. When the walls reached a height of two to three feet, simple board frames for the door and windows were set in place and propped with sticks. The rest of the walls then went up around them. Later, dowels were driven through the frames and into the walls to hold the windows in place.

[20] The slightly pitched roofs were made of from three to five heavy cedar beams, running from gable to gable on each side of the building. Over these beams the builders laid willow or cottonwood rods from peak to eave. Chokecherry or plum brush, then a layer of long grass—usually bluestem or prairie cordgrass—and finally, a layer of sod bricks followed. Here the sod was laid grass-side up so it would continue to grow and hold the roof together.

[21] This early, expedient form of dwelling, often as much cave as house, had severe shortcomings, however. As the lyrics of "Starving to Death on a Government Claim," a folksong of the period, depict it,

> My house it is built out of
>   national soil,
> The walls are erected according
>   to Hoyle;
> The roof has no pitch, it is level
>   and plain,
> But I never get wet—unless
>   it happens to rain.

[22] Even after a rain had ended, water from the thick sod roof would continue to drip inside a house for several days.

[23] Before many years this *ad hoc* house type began to undergo the polishing processes of tradition. A technology of sod construction quickly developed; within twenty years it had transformed the miserable sod hovel into the sometimes elegant sod home. The walls of these more elaborate dwellings were shaved with a spade, giving them clean, sharp lines. Window frames were slanted to permit more light to come through. Commercial or homemade plaster and stucco covered the house inside and out to increase its durability and reduce a major problem of sod houses—fleas. These insects infested the porous walls and plagued the occupants.

[24] Windows, the most expensive component of the house (and one required by many homesteading laws), often cracked or broke with the uneven settling of the heavy walls. Builders ingeniously solved the problem by leaving a four- to-six inch gap above the window during construction. This space was stuffed with paper or grass; as the walls settled, the gap simply closed.

[25] Leaking roofs—the perpetual bane of sod houses—were made watertight either by adding a layer of plaster on the thatch under the roof sod or by using commercial cedar shingles brought in by railroad. Most houses

still retained a sod covering over the shingles for insulation and to add enough weight to hold the roof on during high winds.

[26] At the end of the nineteenth century, the suitability of the sod house for plains conditions became most apparent. The Nebraska State Historical Society's photographic collection of sod houses reveals ample amounts of milled lumber lying near the dwellings. Those who had settled on the plains during the early part of this century told me that while frame construction was fine for animals, sod was best for people. Wood burns, rots, warps, swells, and shrinks; insects and mice chew through it; and the cold penetrates it. The large number of still standing, and frequently still occupied, sod houses that are fifty to eighty years old offers further substantiation of the durability of sod.

[27] Why then did plains dwellers almost universally abandon sod for frame construction during the late nineteenth century? The primary cause was class consciousness. Those who had achieved financial security could advertise their success through the frame house.

[28] As another reason, the initial impact of plains geography had begun to wear off. As a familiar plains' line goes, "Living in Nebraska is a lot like being hanged; the initial shock is a bit abrupt but once you hang there for a while you sort of get used to it." In the demise of sod houses, the forbidding mystery of the plains had dissipated to the extent that inhabitants no longer felt the need for the physical and psychological security that these dwellings offered.

[29] Sod houses still dot the plains. Some are still lived in, but most are just derelicts—abandoned, their roofs overgrown, their door and window frames sagging. These ghosts, however, are more than merely abandoned houses. They are reminders of the grip the plains had on their early settlers. Behind their dark sod, these houses offered protection from a lonely and inhospitable land. They also offer another reminder—their abandonment and replacement by wood frames are symbolic of a reversal in attitude. Now, it appears that plains dwellers have a grip on the land instead of the other way around. Thus the sod house was as much a product on the impact of the plains on the human mind as it was a product of the geography of the plains.

[30] A farmer friend of mine commented a short time ago, "We seem to forget that we may have made this land what it is, but first it made us what we are."

[31] It also made the plains' houses of our parents and grandparents.

## ◆ *PRACTICE*

### *Discussion*

1. Is the process the author describes *natural* or *artificial*?

2. Is the author giving directions or making an explanation?

3. List and explain the major *transitional signals* (p. 75).

4. How many paragraphs does the author take to get to the description of the process? (Why is the introduction so long?)

5. State the thesis of Welsch's essay. Is the thesis directly related to the process he describes?

6. In your opinion, has the author overstated his case about the psychological effects of living on the plains?

7. Give the *steps* of the process and its *end point.*

8. Explain the structure of paragraph 7.


*Vocabulary*

| | | |
|---|---|---|
| delineate | discomfited | substantiation |
| devoid | resound | derelicts |
| demographer | expedient | |


*Writing*

1. Consider the last sentence to paragraph 29. Write a paper on a similar theme as applied to something else in your own culture. For example: *The family van is as much a product of American lifestyle as it is a method of getting from one place to another.*

2. Welsch used *process* because he wanted to show how a certain group of people adapted to negative forces on them. Write a process paper in which you show how a group or individual you are aware of undergoes a process for a similar reason. Sample topic: *the process my brother created to adapt to the demands placed by our ambitious parents on his meager athletic skills.*

3. If you were under house arrest for a year (no visitors allowed), what major process would you create to combat your loneliness and boredom? You can use everything in your house but phone, radio, and TV, which have been removed.

*CHAPTER 12*

# CAUSE AND EFFECT (CAUSATION)

## CAUSE AND EFFECT (CAUSATION)

*Cause and effect* (or simply causation) refers to a specific relationship between events in time. If you fail to look both ways before crossing a street and get hit by a car, the *cause* is failing to look and the *effect* is getting hit. If a doctor tells you that you have a broken leg from the accident, the broken leg is the effect of getting hit by the car, which is the cause. An event (in this case, the accident) can be *both* a cause and an effect of other events.

As a strategy of development, *causation* answers the question "Why did it happen?" You will find causation useful not only by itself but also combined with other strategies. It is often used with *process* because *how* something happened (process) is often related to *why* something happened (causation).

For many subjects—particularly those related to social and political matters—causes and effects are ambiguous or indistinct, leaving you unsure about the truth of the situation. Therefore, you must be very careful when you discuss causes and effects. For many subjects you also have the reactions of your reader to worry about because your analysis of a cause-and-effect relationship might be controversial, and your reader may not agree with you. For example, in discussions about causes and effects in certain social issues—such as crime or government spending—some readers may object to your analysis. Therefore, stance is very important in this strategy.

### Recognizing the Signs of Causation

In order to identify and determine whether or not a cause-and-effect relationship is logical, you should look for certain signs. Two of the most common are:

*The Sign of Association.* Suppose you find two events, A and B, in association. Their being together could imply that A causes B, or vice versa. However, B must ordinarily occur whenever A does—otherwise you probably don't have a genuine cause-and-effect relationship. For instance, hair should bleach when a strong solution of peroxide is applied to it; the cook should burn his hand every time he touches a very hot skillet handle.

*The Sign of Time-Sequence.* If B comes after A in time, this fact may imply a causal relationship. If a student stays up all night studying, the fatigue he suffers the next day is an effect signaled by time. But determining time-sequence is so tricky that a special name has been given to the fallacy of misinterpreting it. The fallacy is called *post hoc* (short for *post hoc, ergo propter hoc*—"after this, therefore because of this"). You create the *post hoc* fallacy if you say that A causes B merely because B comes after A. In other words, if the 8:30 train comes after the 8:15 train, you cannot say that the earlier train "causes" the later one.

In brief, the signs of causation are no more than signs—they are not proofs. To avoid making fallacies in thinking about causation, you must take each sign and investigate it carefully. Never assume that a causal relationship exists until you find proof.

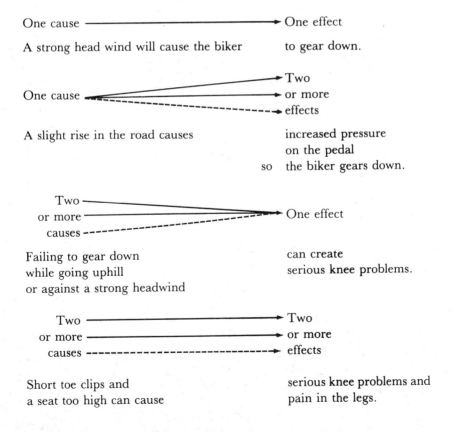

The diagram on p. 196 shows four types of cause-and-effect sequences that you should be aware of. (The examples support the thesis: *Proper gearing and equipment may help a biker avoid leg and knee problems.*)

In most situations, more than one cause or effect is involved. Drug addiction, for example, may have several causes, and these causes may have more than a single effect.

Following is an annotated cause-and-effect paper written by a student. Notice the writer's use of transitions, examples, and summary statements, making the cause-and-effect relationship clear.

| | |
|---|---|
| *Definition of term by negation* | [1] Student-watchers have long identified a common type on campus—the "Joiner." I don't mean the woman who belongs to the band and the Pi Phis, and maybe in her junior year joins an accounting honorary. Nor do I mean the engineer who belongs to a mere three organizations. Nothing so limiting works for the true Joiner, who may belong to six or eight organizations, and who may pop up in student government as well. What makes Joiners join? |
| *Question posed; answered by succeeding pars.* | |
| *First cause, supported by three examples* | [2] First, Joiners like the limelight. Most of the groups they belong to are visible. On the dorm council they write petitions, or collect the petitions of others. In the marching band they perform before thousands of people. In fraternities, they are the treasurers who hound people for money and make long reports in meetings on the state of fraternal economy. |
| *Transition, introducing second cause with one example* | [3] As these remarks imply, Joiners like to run things. My sister is a Joiner, and one can be sure that any group she belongs to, she is president or leader of it. If the group has no important office to fill, she will run it by indirection, volunteering to do this or that job, writing any necessary letters or memos, being the first one at the meeting and the last to leave. No job is too small for her to take on cheerfully. By the end of the semester, any group she joins discovers that she has become its chief bottle-washer and major spokesman. She has fulfilled her desire to control events and people. |
| *Summary statement, explaining effect of cause* | |
| *Last cause with transition, finally* | [4] Finally, Joiners join because they must have something to do with themselves. They are usually hyperactive. Have you ever seen a Joiner sitting alone, perhaps in the Union, just reading a book? Sam, on the men's side of my dorm, is a Joiner; and for all the time I have known him, he has never been alone. People in the dorm say that Sam even goes to the bathroom with somebody. He belongs to eight organizations, and will someday be president of the country—if he can just decide which political party to join. |
| *Example* | |
| *Surprise ending* | |

Occasionally, it is necessary and rhetorically useful to organize a cause-and-effect essay or paragraph by introducing the effect first, then giving an explanation of the causes. Note how the writer in the following exerpt explains why the poor have more garbage than the rich.

*Effect*      [1] . . . low-income neighborhoods in Tucson discard 86 percent more garbage per week per household than do high-income areas, and 40 percent more waste than medium-income districts. There is a trick to that statistic. There are more people per household in low-income areas. But, even dividing on a per person basis, the poor produce more garbage than the middle class and only slightly less than the rich.

Question: *why?*      [2] Why? It's not so hard to figure out. The rich buy antiques, the poor buy and throw away cheap or used furniture. The rich give their old clothes to the "Goodwill," the poor buy them there, wear them out and throw them away. And it is the poor and the working people who discard most of the packaging waste. They are the ones who drink soft drinks and beer and eat low-cost canned vegetables and canned stews, fish sticks,

*Causes*      pot pies, and T.V. dinners. And, if they eat out at all, it is at McDonalds or Burger King or Kentucky Fried Chicken, with the packaging which that entails. It is the rich who have their food flown in fresh daily from Florida or Spain. It is the rich who eat in the fancy French restaurants with all those superb dishes prepared from scratch, sans packaging and sans disposable dinner ware.

—Judd Alexander, "Truth and Consequences"

# SUGGESTIONS FOR WRITING CAUSE-AND-EFFECT PAPERS

When describing causation, remember this advice:

1. *Investigate your subject thoroughly, either from your own firsthand knowledge or from research.* Identifying the causes and effects in a subject that you know firsthand can be easy to do. Your dissatisfaction with your roommate, for instance, may be based on the fact that he won't do his share in keeping the apartment clean. The *cause* is his laziness or carelessness. The *effect* is your anger and frustration. But identifying the causes of pollution in Los Angeles is much more difficult because pollution is a complex problem, and without doing research, you will not know enough to write about the subject.

2. *Qualify your generalizations carefully when you draw cause-and-effect relationships.* Do not hesitate to use qualifiers such as "it seems to me," "it may be," or "the evidence points to." In most cause-and-effect relationships, you deal in probabilities rather than certainties, particularly when you get out of the realm of scientific subjects.

3. *Be sure that your time-sequence is accurate and inclusive.* This is especially true when you are explaining scientific causes and effects. You should present the chronology of the steps as they actually occur, and you should include every important link in the chain of events in order to ensure the accuracy of your paper. Here is an effective explanation of why Mexican jumping beans jump:

> [1] A simple explanation reveals the secret of the fascinating twisting, turning and jumping of the beans. Inside each bean is a tiny yellow caterpillar, the larvae of a small moth. How does it get there? The moth lays an egg in the flower of the spurge shrub. In time the eggs hatch and the larvae are said to work their way deep into the blossom, where they are eventually encased in the seeds.
>
> [2] The caterpillar devours a large part of the inside of the seed, so that it occupies about one-fifth of the interior of its little home. To move the bean, the caterpillar grasps the silken wall of the bean with its legs and vigorously snaps its body, striking its head against the other end of the bean and sending it this way or that. The bean may actually travel several inches at a time, or leap in the air. Some people call them bronco beans because of the way they jump.
>
> [3] A jumping bean may keep up its antics for as long as six months. Then the caterpillar finally emerges from its house and becomes a moth.
> —"Why Mexican Jumping Beans Jump," *Awake!*

4. *Separate "sufficient" from "contributory" causes.* An event may contribute to a cause, but it will not be sufficient in itself to create an effect. Failing to add baking powder or soda to biscuit dough is *sufficient* cause for the dough's failure to rise. A *contributory* cause to the flat biscuits might be a distracting phone call you had just when you were about to add the leavening agent. However, it isn't the phone call that caused the biscuits to be flat, but rather your forgetting to add the soda or baking powder. So you separate the phone call (*contributory* cause) from the lack of leavening agent (*sufficient* cause).

5. *Do not ignore immediate effects in a chain of multiple effects.* Note this description of the multiple effects of the cholera organism:

> For centuries, men had known that cholera was a fatal disease, and that it caused severe diarrhea, sometimes producing as many as thirty quarts of fluid a day. Men knew this, but they somehow assumed that the lethal effects of the disease were unrelated to the diarrhea; they searched for something else: an antidote, a drug, a way to kill the organism. It was not until modern times that cholera was recognized as a disease that killed through dehydration primarily; if you could replace a victim's water losses rapidly, he would survive the infection without other drugs or treatment.
> —Michael Crichton, *The Andromeda Strain*

A diagram of this chain of cause and effect might look like this:

Cholera organism (first cause)
    ↘diarrhea (first immediate effect)
       ↘dehydration (second immediate effect)
          ↘death (ultimate effect)

In this case, the failure to investigate the implications of an important immediate effect led to disastrous consequences.

6. *Much of what we loosely call "cause and effect" is actually "correlation."* In the process of identifying causation, researchers study samples to see if they can establish a pattern from which a generalization can be drawn about why something occurred. For example, from many medical experiments, researchers have discovered that there is a *correlation* between high cholesterol level and heart disease. They do not conclude that high cholesterol level *causes* heart disease but that a significant *correlation* exists between the two. You may use correlation in an analysis of cause and effect, but do not identify as causes what may only be correlations.

## *PLANNING AND REVISING CAUSE AND EFFECT (AN EXAMPLE)*

Jana writes:

Irritationnnn. Illritatatat . . . irrittt. IRITIATION what did I do, s hit the sf shift key?

This is the most . . . . ok back to electric typewriter.

The keyboard is unfamiliar. The screen hurts my eyes. The printer goes clack, brzzt, clack. If you punch the wrong button, the whole thing disappears. The screen talks back to me: ARE YOU SURE YOU WANT TO LOG OUT, JANA?

I say: Yes, you monster, LOG ME OUT OF THIS THING!!!

It says dutifully, JANA LOGGED OUT MONDAY OCTOBER 20, 1987, 2:35 PM.

Phooey.

Now Jana has it out of her system. Her mother, a free-lance writer, has a new computer with a word processor and letter-quality printer added on. Jana can log into the computer whenever her mother isn't using it. But as you can see from her brainstorming above, her early experience on the new and unfamiliar equipment was not a pleasant one.

After two days and hours of practice with the computer and word processor, Jana decides to write a cause-effect paper based in part on the brainstorming material quoted above.

What I want to show [she writes in her plan of attack on the paper] is that when you first use the computer and word processor, all the causes lead to one effect: confusion and anger—most of which are UNNECESSARY. That is my hook: *unnecessary.*
Writer: me.
Point: I just said it.
Reader: Anybody just starting out on a word processor.

Here's my order of main ideas:

> *Makes no sense, partic. keyboard*
> *Machine confusing — commands?*
> *Printer noise*
> _____
> *But now they don't seem to bother me as much. (?)*

And here I go!

Jana's draft

1. All right monster, I have logged in. And I have named you . . . ZARKON. (Wasn't Zarkon a villain on STAR TREK?) Well irregardless, ZARKON, you are now (and forever will be) a villain.

2. The first thing about you, ZARKON, is that you're crazy. Look at your keyboard. The asterisk is above the 8 where the apostrophe ought to be; so I keep writing Mother*s Manuscript, Jack*s foot, etc. On the left side of the keyboard are 10 buttons numbered F1 through F10. On the right side are buttons called Num Lock and Scroll Lock, End, Ins,

and so on. My favorite button is nanmed PrtSc. Didn't she win the Derby last year?

3. When I put my fingers on the keys, I inevitably place them wrong because there are extra keys where no keys should be. Also the key shift for capitals is one key too far to the left, so I keep hitting the wrong key when I want to make a capital. The result is I can't type decently and spend too much time correcting.

4. On top of that, ZARKON, you are too hard to use when I try to take the WordPerfect lessons. I log in, punch the buttons your manual tells me to, and then you say WRONG COMMAND. How could it be the wrong command when you told me to do it? Now I just sit there with the cursor flashing at me. My lesson is gone from the screen—how do I get it back? I punch the ESC [escape] button and nothing happens. Listen, ZARKON, If I say escape, I mean escape. Let me out! I called the dealer. He said, write in DIR for directory. Ok, now I am back to the lesson. But how did I get there?

5. Now, ZARKON, a few words about your printer. It goes clack, brzzt, clack; and now and then whirrpp. Your daisy wheel is a real flower, too. It goes in two directions, almost at once. The noise this printer makes is awful, and in Mom's little office it scrapes on my ear like a fingernail noise on a blackboard. Then, ZARKON, you jammed your paper. When I got up to unjam your paper , I tripped over the plug and pulled it out of the wall and ERASED ALL MY WORK.

6. ZARKON, you are an idiot and a bore and noisy . . . two days ago. Now, for some reason you seem docile and even pleasant. Even dare

I say it, even a little easy to use? Is it possible you have spiked my diet

cola with a little outer-space dumb drug?

7. I am not yet ready to believe that the two ZARKONS are one

and the same, that just because I get a little used to you, you are sud-

denly a pussy cat.

8. ZARKON—are you trying to tell me that all the pain and irrita-

tion were unnecessary?

9.. Brrzt, clack.

## ◆ *PRACTICE*

### *Discussion*

1. Remember that Jana's paper on the computer (and word processor)
   consists at this point of (a) a short piece of brainstorming, (b) a scratch
   outline of topics to cover, and (c) a first draft.
   Go back over these three materials and make direct suggestions to
   Jana for her next draft, which we will assume will be her final one.
   Consider every part of her writing problem: hook, point of her paper,
   organization of draft, paragraphing, sentences, words, choice of detail,
   grammar. Do you recommend that she make many changes in her
   draft?
   Describe the cause-effect patterns implicit in the paper.

2. Discuss the accuracy and validity of the cause-and-effect relationships
   in these statements:
   a. The state's experiment in the abolition of capital punishment is
      going badly. During the first six months of the trial period, murders
      are up an estimated 20 percent and there has been a rash of sex
      crimes against children. Two child rapists last week got life im-
      prisonment—which practically means, in this state, parole after
      twenty years.
   b. *Statistic:* If you change jobs very often, your chance of having a heart
      attack is two or three times greater than if you stay at one job for a
      long time.
   c. Why do people who in private talk so pungently often write so
      pompously? There are many reasons: tradition, the demands of
      time, carelessness, the conservative influence of the secretary.
      Above all is the simple matter of status. Theorem: the less estab-

lished the status of a person, the more his dependence on jargon. Examine the man who has just graduated from pecking out his own letters to declaiming them to a secretary and you are likely to have a man hopelessly intoxicated with the rhythm of businessese. Conversely, if you come across a blunt yes or no in a letter, you don't need to glance further to grasp that the author feels pretty firm in his chair.

—William H. Whyte, "The Language of Business," Fortune magazine

d. The dog [as a pet] has advantages in the way of uselessness as well as in special gifts of temperament. He is often spoken of, in an eminent sense, as the friend of man, and his intelligence and fidelity are praised. The meaning of this is that the dog is man's servant and that he has the gift of an unquestioning subservience and a slave's quickness in guessing his master's mood. Coupled with these traits, which fit him well for relation of status—and which must for the present purpose be set down as serviceable traits—the dog has some characteristics which are of a more equivocal aesthetic value. He is the filthiest of the domestic animals in his person and the nastiest in his habits. For this he makes up in a servile, fawning attitude towards his master, and a readiness to inflict damage and discomfort on all else. The dog, then, commends himself to our favour by affording play to our propensity for mastery, and as he is also an item of expense, and commonly serves no industrial purpose, he holds a well-assured place in men's regard as a thing of good repute. The dog is at the same time associated in our imagination with the chase—a meritorious employment and an expression of the honorable predatory impulse.

—Thorstein Veblen, The Theory of the Leisure Class

### Writing

1. Choose one of the following hypothetical situations that could be appropriate for you. (If you don't have a car, situation **a** wouldn't fit your life.) If none of the situations suit you, develop one of your own, using the format: "If I . . . then . . ."

   Make a list of all the possible effects of your taking such an action. Classify or group the effects, develop a generalization for each class or group, and use the generalizations as paragraph topic leads (or topic sentences) in a discussion of causation.
   a. If I decide to sell my car, then . . .
   b. If I get married this month, then . . .
   c. If I decide to quit school and go to work full-time, then . . .
   d. If my parents are unable to help pay my tuition next fall, then . . .
   e. If I can move into an apartment, then . . .
   f. If I change majors, then . . .

2. Pick a subject concerning your hometown. Write a paper discussing the possible cause-and-effect relationships in the subject. Possible broad subjects: crime, education, religion, prosperity, government, sports, race relations, culture, economics. (Be sure to narrow your topic.)

3. Develop a cause-and-effect essay on one of the following familiar topics:
   a. The effect of children on a family, or the effect of not having children.
   b. The effect of the change of seasons on your behavior.
   c. The effect of paperback books on reading.
   d. The effect of compulsory attendance laws on education.
   e. The effect of the Beatles on popular music.
   f. The effect of moving a child from one community to another.
   The following topics are more specialized and may take some research:
   g. the effect of salt on automobiles.
   h. The effect of extreme cold or extreme heat on a machine or animal.
   i. The effect of loss of electricity, due to a storm, on a household.
   j. The effect of public opinion polls on the news.
   k. The effect of allergies on the body.

You may find a combination of process and cause-effect useful for some of the above. For example, the *process* of salting the streets in the winter has an *effect* on automobiles.

*PENNY WARD MOSER*

## TIME OUT FOR FANDANGOS

*Penny Ward Moser, a contributing writer to* Sports Illustrated, *is a you-name-it, I've-written-on-it writer. She has done scientific pieces on cats, cockroaches, and television for* Discover, *the science magazine. She has appeared on the "Today" show to expound on the mechanics of dust balls. She is a bird watcher about to sight her 300th species, and an ardent Washington Redskins fan—once dying her hair a bright Redskins burgundy in honor of the team. And, yes, she has danced on the hood of a Chevrolet, with a picture to prove it.*

[1] For some time now I have experienced a sudden depression on Sunday nights just as *60 Minutes* starts to "tick, tick, tick," signaling the end of six hours of football on TV. It's not that I'm sad the games are over or that my team has lost; six hours is enough, and my team usually does fine. It's not even that the *60 Minutes* folks are about to chronicle the awfulness of the human condition. Rather, I get a horrible feeling that I don't dance enough. This is the chief symptom of what I think of as the everybody-in-sports-commercials-is-having-more-fun-than-I syndrome.

[2] When I wake up Sunday morning, everything's O.K. I have a nice husband, a good job, a station wagon and a solid little house in the capital of the free world. But by about halftime of the first game, I begin to sense that my life is lacking.

[3] We don't dance enough. The Coors people dance. The Budweiser and Pontiac people dance, the Chevy people dance. They dance with a passion around their cars, even on top of their cars. I don't recall ever dancing around the old blue wagon.

[4] These commercials, with their desperately hot music and pretty people, make me feel like I'm not leading an interesting life. At first I thought it was creeping middle age. Now I think it could be genetic. Never once did my mother, like the woman in the Cadillac commercial, dress up in a swingy ball gown and crawl over the roof of the car to kiss my father as he opened the door.

[5] A friend of mine says I have "Pepsi generation malaise." There we boomers all were some years back, the "think young, think smart" people swilling colas. Now we have done everything right, but we see all these new people—who don't seem to be thinking at all—having a better time than we are. The men shave in bathrooms as big as my living room, and the women have bodies that support strapless dresses even when they're

dancing madly. Sometimes a man opens his hands and slides, oh, say, $350,000 worth of diamonds over a woman's arm.

6 In football land, at seemingly every change of possession, the Wrangler jeans folks come on the screen having a ball. Sometimes they're just euphorically skipping past bright lights. Other times they appear to be walking away from a steel mill having fun. They do all this in slow motion. The message seems to be that they have done an honest day's work and now it's time to play hard.

7 Such commercials make me feel sorry for myself and my colleagues. In my office building I have yet to see a group of flannel-shirted, macho Americans jitterbugging toward a frosty cold one at the Duck Inn before tearing off in the pickup. It's more the kind of place where a stressed-out lawyer can be seen at 8 P.M., clutching a bag of soggy McNuggets. All he has to look forward to is later, maybe much later, creeping home in his Volvo.

8 Commercials tell me that even where I live is wrong. Just when I'm happy Ali Haji-Sheikh made the extra point for my beloved Redskins, the tube blinks and those gorgeous people out to "light up the night" are dancing around their cars over empty, steaming city streets. Where I live the streets only steam when the sewers back up, and the only people dancing around in the steam are communicating with aliens or asking for spare change.

9 To judge by commercials, almost everyone but me spends most of the time taking fast curves through Big Sur or sailing over the long hard blacktops of Texas or the Montana high country. These folks seem to be wheat farmers and the like. My father was a wheat farmer, but I don't recall him tearing off the road, popping airborne over hilltops and barreling through rivers in any vehicle.

10 I suppose I should be pleased that Mad Ave. sees us sports fans as good Americans who like to have fun. Certainly I would rather watch these fast-dancing, hard-driving folks unwind at a bar than cringe in front of those body orifice spots for denture glue and hemorrhoid remedies that appear on the evening news. But then just when I the sports fan am feeling smug that advertisers think I have money to give some high-profile invest-ment firm, the Great Western Champagne couple, dressed in black tie, run across the front lawn of their mansion. Our row house's front yard is exactly 17 feet wide. Unless we run in tight circles, it hardly seems worth the effort.

11 Here's the crux of my depression. Where can I find this life? Where is this land of ever-dancing people and bars without any sloppy, sad drunks? With big bathrooms and garages that hold only cars? Where no one sits for five minutes trying to make a left-hand turn out of the 7-Eleven?

12 Maybe one of these days I'll just glue on a black strapless ball gown and cartwheel into my station wagon and drive until I find it. But first, I would have to get my husband into black tie. Maybe I'll just settle in and watch basketball.

## ✦ *PRACTICE*

### *Discussion*

1. What does the title mean? Does it fit the essay?

2. This essay can be called a "disguised cause-effect" piece. Explain.

3. Moser's reactions (the *effects* of the commercials on her) seem exaggerated. Why?

4. Is there any danger that readers will think Moser is serious?

5. We remark on p. 194 that causation may be "combined with other strategies." Does this occur in Moser's essay?

6. Discuss the organization of paragraph 11.

7. The editor of Moser's piece used a boldfaced description of her essay: "Folks have a damnably swell time in NFL game commercials." Look up the words *damnably* and *swell* in your dictionary. How appropriate is the editor's comment?

### *Vocabulary*

| | | |
|---|---|---|
| syndrome | swilling | orifice |
| malaise | euphorically | crux |
| boomers | jitterbugging | |

### *Writing*

1. Write a paper explaining why companies would buy expensive TV time to sell products (using glamour) during football games. Why would they get the *effects* they want during football and not, say, during prime-time news?

2. Reread paragraph 8. Note the *contrast* device the author uses here and in other paragraphs. Using the same device with other commercials, write a satiric paper showing the cause-effect reality behind certain famous commercials; for example, the ones showing the toughness of certain pickups (remember the pickup dropped from ten feet in the air?).

3. Write a memo from the head of a TV advertising agency to its client, a company which wants to use the glamourizing technique described by Moser. As the ad man, how do you explain the *effects* you want your ads to have for the company product? (Designate your own product.)

CLAUDIA DOWLING

# THE RELATIVE EXPLOSION

*The following article by journalist Claudia Dowling appeared in the April 1983 issue of* Psychology Today. *Dowling speaks from experience when she writes about the relative explosion of the nuclear family. She is both a mother and a stepmother. Most recently published in* Life Magazine, *Dowling has been working on a book entitled* A Working Parents' Guide to Baby Care. *In "The Relative Explosion," Dowling takes for her subject a very complex sociological phenomenon and its attendant issues and uses the associations of cause and effect as the means to unravel a few of the complexities.*

[1] There is a new family in America, riddled with ex-spouses and half siblings, stepchildren and former in-laws, lovers and their children, not to mention an unprecedented collection of other relationships. In family law, according to the *New York Times,* "concepts unheard of a decade ago—joint custody of children . . . visiting rights for grandparents, and so-called habitation contracts between those not married but living together—have become commonplace in the courts." Today, a four-member "nuclear family" can boast as many surnames; to sort out the ties that bind might faze a genealogist for whom *Debrett's Peerage* is light reading. Not surprisingly, these complicated connections of blood and lust have left many men, women, and children floundering, for no clear social rules exist to guide them through the forms of modern serial monogamy.

[2] The tangled web of new relationships is arguably the legacy of the 60s. Almost anyone who lived through that era without suffering a chemically induced memory burnout can embark on a recitation of who lived with whom and then subsequently with whomever else, an account that would be as dull as the begats. In this chain of connections, moreover, all the people usually knew one another, often in the biblical sense. "One thing you can say about our friends," comments a survivor, "we didn't sleep with strangers."

[3] That, in a sense, was the problem—or if not the problem, the ingredient that was to change everything. The so-called sexual revolution led these bedfellows to act out their loves and passions one after the other in something of a round-robin manner. Risqué types had been doing that in Hollywood for years, but actors and actresses usually married the people whom they went to bed with. The 60s kids did not. At first. But they grew up. They waited a little longer than their parents, but eventually they did marry. Then some of them got unmarried and did it again. Every relationship—legal and otherwise—was played out against the backdrop of

who had lived with whom before. And as the various unions have been blessed with progeny. things have become really complex.

4 Perhaps as an extension of that charming but outmoded exhortation to "love everybody," the members of the 60s generation do not sever past ties with ease. Indeed, they take pleasure and sometimes pride in maintaining all their ties, à la Bo and John and Ursula and Linda. Divorced partners no longer cut each other dead as a matter of course, particularly when there are children in the picture. Child-rearing has become an activity for both parents, especially when the parents are no longer married. Fathers are demanding, and taking, an active role, a rarity in the past. Equal parenting is made easier by the fact that divorces are by and large less acrimonious and certainly less beset by social stigma than even a decade ago. After all, these marriages were just legal chapters in the continuing serial. Besides, these days everybody's doing it: One out of two couples eventually hits the matrimonial skids. Children have become virtually communal property.

5 The effects of this shared responsibility are only beginning to be felt by the new generation, but the unprecedented technical difficulties for their fathers and mothers—and their grandparents—are already enormous. For one thing, each child is the beneficiary of at least two complete sets of holidays, in some instances divided by hours of solitary plane flights. A mitigating factor for the young travelers is that the holidays are all accompanied by presents. For another thing, each child, in all likelihood, now has two sets of parents, each with an arithmetically expanding flock of satellite relatives—uncles, aunts, and cousins, some of whom have also been married more than once—in addition to two sets of grandparents and at least one set of stepgrandparents. This is the Relative Explosion.

6 In the interests of simplicity, some divorced parents have found it advisable to combine forces. This is possible only for those of enlightened sensibilities, and even then it can lead to situations that are the stuff of television comedies. One modern man reports: "In the past three years, I have spent two Thanksgivings, one Christmas, one New Year's Eve, three spring breaks and two weeks at the shore with my present wife, my son from my first marriage, and my ex-wife. Plus her present mate and his child and various combinations of my parents and my present wife's parents. It made our heads spin at first. We all thought that we were being incredibly mature. But now we just think it's normal . . ."

7 Obviously, the skills appropriate to life in the Relative Explosion have yet to be defined. The most critical need is for large portions of forbearance and tolerance—what some circles call "keeping cool" and others call "being laidback." Certain groups may find that large quantities of alcohol or other depressants are stopgap aids for New Family gatherings. But such artificial de-stimulation was an Old Family gathering standby too, so it can hardly be considered ground-breaking.

8 Coming to a comfortable *modus operandi* requires, first of all, an ordering of priorities. Top priorities should be one's current partner and

one's children by birth, marriage, or whatever. If some of the children are the result of a previous relationship, the demands may conflict. A parent will have to deal with his or her ex, which may annoy, anger, or frighten the current partner.

[9] One way to defuse the threat of an ex is to include his or her present mate in any necessary gathering. Such coupling is particularly desirable if the occasion requires an overnight stay; it removes much of the awkwardness of bedtime for everyone. And if one is the guest ex, one feels much less like a marauder in enemy territory. An additional benefit is that the *status quo* is graphically illustrated for children who, however, accepting of their new circumstances, may still harbor a latent desire to see their parents get back together. Seeing each parent with his or her separate partner helps a child accept the original break.

[10] In regard to children and exes, most parents and many of those *in loco parentis* are willing to put their own emotional games aside in a child's interest. If a child feels better knowing that his or her estranged parents are on speaking terms—and most do—mature adults will bow gracefully to their needs. Children need not, indeed should not, suffer the torment of divided loyalties. On the other hand, if it seems to make children uncomfortable to see their parents together, there is obviously no need to pursue conviviality for its own sake.

[11] Stepparents will find that it is best in most cases to refrain from forcing a spouse's child to "think of me as your own father." The child already has parents and, if our own experiences are anything to go by, doesn't need any more. Loaded appellations like "Dad" or "Mama Sue" will not help children cope. First names are best, indicating intimacy but not family ties. This also goes for well-meaning step-uncles, -aunts, -grand-parents, and so on. How many relatives can one youngster deal with?

[12] All this suggests that the New Family is perhaps the most difficult of all for children. They may have half siblings who spend much more time with one parent than they themselves can. A child of a first marriage may view the child of a second as an interloper, stealing the attention of the father or mother. A child of the second marriage may be threatened by the older half sibling who comes like an invader for the summer and seems to have some prior claim on the parent. Fortunately, left to themselves, children are eminently capable of sorting out their own differences and will quickly arrive at a working relationship. The worst possible thing a parent can do is to disparage the absent parent of one child in the presence of another. "I can see where you got your temper, and it wasn't from me—little Johnny doesn't talk that way." Such remarks are unfair to both children and cast the parent in the role of a hanging judge. And who can trust a hanging judge?

[13] It is particularly important to use self-control when embarked on New Family voyages. The one shoal to steer absolutely clear of is allusion to the past. "Before your mother and I were divorced . . ." or "You always used to . . ." are unwise beginnings to any sentence. With those former ties

of love and lust omnipresent in the air, all reminiscences are emotionally volatile. Even if they don't offend the children or the ex, they will assuredly offend the current partner.

14 After all, we made our beds. And if we suffer a restless night or two coping with the perplexing intricacies, we have ourselves to blame, and we can find the way to resolve them. These struggles to integrate the past with the present are the growing pains of a new design for society. What the result of the struggle may be in emotional, social, linguistic, legal, and political terms, no one knows. But in striving to make their lives and relationships workable in an entirely new context, many of today's young adults are pioneers. Their performance will be measured by coming generations.

## ✦ *PRACTICE*

*Discussion*

1. What is the cause or causes of the relative explosion according to Dowling? What are the effects? Can you think of other causes and effects that Dowling has not mentioned?

2. What advice does Dowling give for coping with the effects of the relative explosion? Is hers a definitive guide? Why or why not?

3. Where do Dowling's sympathies and concerns in this article seem most to lie—with men, women, current spouses, ex-spouses, or children? How can you tell?

4. Dowling uses a number of foreign terms or references. Compile a list of all that you can find. What does this choice of words tell you about Dowling's expected audience?

5. This article appeared in *Psychology Today,* a popular magazine. Why could it never have appeared in its current form in a scholarly journal for professional psychologists? Cite specific examples that support your answer. What paragraph or paragraphs could have been published unchanged in such a journal? Is that paragraph or paragraphs inappropriate for *Psychology Today?*

6. Which type or types of cause-and-effect sequence does Dowling use to construct her essay? (Refer to your answer to the earlier question on causes and effects.)

7. Where does Dowling use dialogue in the essay? Is it used successfully? Explain your answer.

8. How carefully does Dowling qualify her generalizations about cause and effect? Find as many examples as you can of qualification.

## Vocabulary

| | | |
|---|---|---|
| faze | risqué | mitigating |
| monogamy | progeny | *modus operandi* |
| begats | acrimonious | *status quo* |
| round-robin | stigma | *in loco parentis* |

## Writing

1. Are you a member of an exploded nuclear family or do you know someone well who is? Drawing on your experience or knowledge, write an essay delving further into the effects of the relative explosion. For example, Dowling deals mostly with effects on young children. What are the effects on teenagers and college students whose parents are divorced and, perhaps, remarried?

2. How do television and the movies depict the contemporary family? Are the media's family portraits causes or effects of the social changes Dowling describes? Write an essay presenting your ideas on these questions.

3. What other effects, besides the relative explosion, have resulted from the sexual revolution of the 60s? Write an essay exploring one or several related effects that you think are significant.

RICHARD CONNIFF

# *WHY GOD CREATED FLIES*

*Richard Conniff writes on the natural world and on its unnatural opposite, everyday American life, for* Time, Smithsonian, Audubon, Sports Illustrated, *the* New York Times Magazine, *and other publications in this country and abroad. A collection of his natural history pieces will be published soon under the title* Sleeping with Snapping Turtles. *He is also the author of* Irish Walls, *about the Irish landscape, and of* The Devil's Book of Verse, *an anthology of poison penmanship from Catullus to Kingsley Amis. Conniff was born in Jersey City, New Jersey, in 1951. At the age of 18, he got a job at a local newspaper writing obituaries. After graduation from Yale University, he returned to newspaper work briefly and later served as a staff writer at several magazines, and as managing editor of* Geo. *He now lives in Connecticut with his wife and three children.*

¹ Though I have been killing them for years now, I have never tested the folklore that, with a little cream and sugar, flies taste very much like black raspberries. So it's possible I'm speaking too hastily when I say there is nothing to like about houseflies. Unlike the poet who welcomed a "busy, curious, thirsty fly" to his drinking cup, I don't cherish them for reminding me that life is short. Nor do I much admire them for their function in clearing away carrion and waste. It is, after all, possible to believe in the grand scheme of recycling without liking undertakers.

² A fly is standing on the rim of my beer glass as I write these words. Its vast, mosaic eyes look simultaneously lifeless and mocking. It grooms itself methodically, its forelegs entwining like the arms of a Sybarite luxuriating in bath oil. Its hind legs twitch across the upper surface of its wings. It pauses, well fed and at rest, to contemplate the sweetness of life.

³ We are lucky enough to live in an era when scientists quantify such things, and so as I type and wait my turn to drink, I know that the fly is neither busy nor curious. The female spends 40.6 percent of her time doing nothing but contemplating the sweetness of life. I know that she not only eats unspeakable things, but spends an additional 29.7 percent of her time spitting them back up and blowing bubbles with her vomit. The male is slightly less assiduous at this deplorable pastime but also defecates on average every four and a half minutes. Houseflies seldom trouble us as a health threat anymore, at least in this country, but they are capable of killing. And when we are dead (or sooner, in some cases), they dine on our corrupted flesh.

⁴ It is mainly this relentless intimacy with mankind that makes the housefly so contemptible. Leeches or dung beetles may appall us, but by

and large they satisfy their depraved appetites out of our sight. Houseflies, on the other hand, routinely flit from diaper pail to dinner table, from carrion to picnic basket. They are constantly among us, tramping across our food with God-knows-what trapped in the sticky hairs of their half-dozen legs.

5 Twice in this century, Americans have waged war against houseflies, once in a futile nationwide "swat the fly" campaign and again, disastrously, with DDT foggings after World War II. The intensity of these efforts, bordering at times on the fanatic, may bewilder modern Americans. "Flies or Babies? Choose!" cried a headline in the *Ladies Home Journal* in 1920. But our bewilderment is not due entirely to greater tolerance or environmental enlightenment. If we have the leisure to examine the fly more rationally now, it is primarily because we don't suffer its onslaughts as our predecessors did. Urban living has separated us from livestock, and indoor plumbing has helped us control our own wastes and thus control houseflies. If that changed tomorrow, we would come face to face with the enlightened, modern truth: With the possible exception of *Homo sapiens*, it is hard to imagine an animal as disgusting or improbable as the housefly. No bestiary concocted from the nightmares of the medieval mind could have come up with such a fantastic animal. If we want to study nature in its most exotic permutations, the best place to begin is here, at home, on the rim of my beer glass.

6 In this country, more than a dozen fly species visit or live in the house. It is possible to distinguish among some of them only by such microscopic criteria as the pattern of veins in the wings, so all of them end up being cursed as houseflies. Among the more prominent are the blue- and green-bottle flies, with their iridescent abdomens, and the biting stable flies, which have served this country as patriots, or at least as provocateurs. On July 4, 1776, their biting encouraged decisiveness among delegates considering the Declaration of Independence. "Treason," Thomas Jefferson wrote, "was preferable to discomfort."

7 The true housefly, *Musca domestica*, does not bite. (You may think this is something to like about it, until you find out what it does instead.) *M. domestica*, a drab fellow of salt-and-pepper complexion, is the world's most widely distributed insect species and probably the most familiar, a status achieved through its pronounced fondness for breeding in pig, horse, or human excrement. In choosing at some point in the immemorial past to concentrate on the wastes around human habitations, *M. domestica* made a major career move. Bernard Greenberg of the University of Illinois at Chicago has traced human representations of the housefly back to a Mesopotamian cylinder seal from 3000 B.C. But houseflies were probably with us even before we had houses, and they spread with human culture.

8 Like us, the housefly is prolific, opportunistic, and inclined toward exploration. It can adapt to a diet of either vegetables or meat, preferably somewhat ripe. It will lay its eggs not just in excrement but in rotting lime peels, bird nests, carrion, even flesh wounds that have become infected and

malodorous. Other flies aren't so flexible. For instance, *M. autumnalis,* a close relative, prefers cattle dung and winds up sleeping in pastures more than in houses or yards.

⁹ Although the adaptability and evolutionary generalization of the housefly may be admirable, they raise one of the first great questions about flies: Why is there this dismaying appetite for abomination?

¹⁰ Houseflies not only defecate constantly but do so in liquid form, which means they are in constant danger of dehydration. The male can slake his thirst and get most of the energy he needs from nectar. But fresh manure is a good source of water, and it contains the dissolved protein the female needs to make eggs. She also lays her eggs in excrement or amid decay so that when the maggots hatch, they'll have a smorgasbord of nutritious microorganisms on which to graze.

¹¹ Houseflies bashing around the kitchen or the garbage shed thus have their sensors attuned to things that smell sweet, like flowers or bananas, and to foul-smelling stuff like ammonia and hydrogen sulfide, the products of fermentation and putrefaction. (Ecstasy for the fly is the stink-horn fungus, a source of sugar that smells like rotting meat.)

¹² The fly's jerky, erratic flight amounts to a way of covering large territories in search of these scents, not just for food but for romance and breeding sites. Like dung beetles and other flying insects, the fly will zigzag upwind when it gets a whiff of something good (or, more often, bad) and follow the scent plume to its source.

¹³ Hence the second question about the housefly: How does it manage to fly so well? And the corollaries: Why is it so adept at evading us when we swat it? How come it always seems to land on its feet, usually upside-down on the ceiling, having induced us to plant a fist on the spot where it used to be, in the middle of the strawberry trifle, which is now spattered across tablecloth, walls, loved ones, and honored guests?

¹⁴ The housefly's manner of flight is a source of vexation more than wonder. When we launch an ambush as the oblivious fly preens and pukes, its pressure sensors alert it to the speed and direction of the descending hand. Its wraparound eyes are also acutely sensitive to peripheral movement, and they register changes in light about ten times faster than we do. (A movie fools the gullible human eye into seeing continuous motion by showing it a sequence of twenty-four still pictures a second. To fool a fly would take more than 200 frames a second.) The alarm flashes directly from the brain to the middle set of legs via the largest, and therefore fastest, nerve fiber in the body. This causes so-called starter muscles to contract, simultaneously revving up the wing muscles and pressing down the middle legs, which catapult the fly into the air.

¹⁵ The fly's wings beat 165 to 200 times a second. Although this isn't all that fast for an insect, it's more than double the wingbeat of the speediest hummingbird and about twenty times faster than any repetitious movement the human nervous system can manage. The trick brought off by houseflies and many other insects is to remove the wingbeat from direct

nervous system control, once it's switched on. Two systems of muscles, for upstroke and downstroke, are attached to the hull of the fly's midsection, and they trigger each other to work in alternation. When one set contracts, it deforms the hull, stretching the other set of muscles and making it contract automatically a fraction of a second later. To keep this seesaw rhythm going, openings in the midsection stoke the muscles with oxygen that comes directly from the outside (flies have no lungs). Meanwhile the fly's blood (which lacks hemoglobin and is therefore colorless) carries fuel to the cells fourteen times faster than when the fly is at rest. Flies can turn a sugar meal into usable energy so fast that an exhausted fly will resume flight almost instantly after eating. In humans . . . but you don't want to know how ploddingly inadequate humans are by comparison.

[16] An airborne fly's antennae, pointed down between its eyes, help regulate flight, vibrating in response to airflow. The fly also uses a set of stubby wings in back, called halteres, as a gyroscopic device. Flies are skillful at veering and dodging—it sometimes seems that they are doing barrel rolls and Immelmann turns to amuse themselves while we flail and curse. But one thing they cannot do is fly upside-down to land on a ceiling. This phenomenon puzzled generations of upward-glaring, strawberry-trifle-drenched human beings, until high-speed photography supplied the explanation. The fly approaches the ceiling rightside up, at a steep angle. Just before impact, it reaches up with its front limbs, in the manner of Superman exiting a telephone booth for takeoff. As these forelegs get a grip with claws and with the sticky, glandular hairs of the footpads, the fly swings its other legs up into position. Then it shuts down its flight motor, out of swatting range and at ease. . . .

[17] Here is the final great question about flies: What awful things are they inoculating us with when they flit across our food or land on our sleeping lips to drink our saliva? Over the years, authorities have suspected flies of spreading more than sixty diseases, from diarrhea to plague and leprosy. As recently as 1951, the leading expert on flies repeated without demurring the idea that the fly was "the most dangerous insect" known, a remarkable assertion in a world that also includes mosquitoes. One entomologist tried to have the housefly renamed the "typhoid fly."

[18] The hysteria against flies early in this century arose, with considerable help from scientists and the press, out of the combined ideas that germs cause disease and that flies carry germs. In the Spanish-American War, easily ten times as many soldiers died of disease, mostly typhoid fever, as died in battle. Flies were widely blamed, especially after a doctor observed particles of lime picked up in the latrines still clinging to the legs of flies crawling over army food. A British politician argued that flies were not "dipterous angels" but "winged sponges speeding hither and thither to carry out the foul behests of Contagion." American schools started organizing "junior sanitary police" to point the finger at fly breeding sites. Cities sponsored highly publicized "swat the fly" campaigns. In Washington, D.C., in 1912, a consortium of children killed 343,800 flies and won a $25

first prize. (This is a mess of flies, 137.5 swatted for every penny in prize money, testimony to the slowness of summers then and the remarkable agility of children—or perhaps to the overzealous imagination of contest sponsors. The figure does not include the millions of dead flies submitted by losing entrants.)

[19] But it took the pesticide DDT, developed in World War II and touted afterwards as "the killer of killers," to raise the glorious prospect of "a flyless millennium." The fly had by then been enshrined in the common lore as a diabolical killer. In one of the "archy and mehitabel" poems by Don Marquis, a fly visits garbage cans and sewers to "gather up the germs of typhoid, influenza, and pneumonia on my feet and wings" and spread them to humanity, declaring that "it is my mission to help rid the world of these wicked persons/i am a vessel of righteousness."

[20] Public health officials were deadly serious about conquering this arch fiend, and for them DDT was "a veritable godsend." They recommended that parents use wallpaper impregnated with DDT in nurseries and playrooms to protect children. Believing that flies spread infantile paralysis, cities suffering polio epidemics frequently used airplanes to fog vast areas with DDT. Use of the chemical actually provided some damning evidence against flies, though not in connection with polio. Hidalgo County in Texas, on the Mexican border, divided its towns into two groups and sprayed one with DDT to eliminate flies. The number of children suffering and dying from acute diarrheal infection caused by *Shigella* bacteria declined in the sprayed areas but remained the same in the unsprayed zones. When DDT spraying was stopped in the first group and switched to the second, the dysentary rates began to reverse. Then the flies developed resistance to DDT, a small hitch in the godsend. In state parks and vacation spots, where DDT had provided relief from the fly nuisance, people began to notice that songbirds were also disappearing.

[21] In the end, the damning evidence was that we were contaminating our water, ourselves, and our affiliated population of flies with our own filth (not to mention DDT). Given access to human waste through inadequate plumbing or sewage treatment, flies can indeed pick up an astonishing variety of pathogens. They can also reproduce at a godawful rate: In one study, 4,042 flies hatched from a scant shovelful, one-sixth of a cubic foot, of buried night soil. But whether all those winged sponges can transmit the contaminants they pick up turns out to be a tricky question, the Hidalgo County study being one of the few clearcut exceptions. Of polio, for instance, Bernard Greenberg writes, "There is ample evidence that human populations readily infect flies . . . But we are woefully ignorant whether and to what extent flies return the favor."

[22] Flies probably are not, as one writer declared in the throes of the hysteria, "monstrous" beings "armed with horrid mandibles . . . and dripping with poison." A fly's body is not, after all, a playground for microbes. Indeed, bacterial populations on its bristling, unlovely exterior tend to decline quickly under the triple threat of compulsive cleaning, desiccation,

and ultraviolet radiation. (Maggots actually produce a substance in their gut that kills off whole populations of bacteria, which is one reason doctors have sometimes used them to clean out infected wounds.) The fly's "microbial cargo," to use Greenberg's phrase, reflects human uncleanliness. In one study, flies from a city neighborhood with poor facilities carried up to 500 million bacteria, while flies from a prim little suburb not far away yielded a maximum count of only 100,000.

[23] But wait. While I am perfectly happy to suggest that humans are viler than we like to think, and flies less so, I do not mean to rehabilitate the fly. Any animal that kisses offal one minute and dinner the next is at the very least a social abomination. What I am coming around to is St. Augustine's idea that God created flies to punish human arrogance, and not just the calamitous technological arrogance of DDT. Flies are, as one biologist has remarked, the resurrection and the reincarnation of our own dirt, and this is surely one reason we smite them down with such ferocity. They mock our notions of personal grooming with visions of lime particles, night soil, and dog leavings. They toy with our delusions of immortality, buzzing in the ear as a memento mori (a researcher in Greenberg's lab assures me that flies can strip a human corpse back to bone in about a week, if the weather is fine). Flies are our fate, and one way or another they will have us.

[24] It is a pretty crummy joke on God's part, of course, but there's no point in getting pouty about it and slipping into unhealthy thoughts about nature. What I intend to do, by way of evening the score, is hang a strip of flypaper and cultivate the local frogs and snakes, which have a voracious appetite for flies (flycatchers don't, by the way; they seem to prefer wasps and bees). Perhaps I will get the cat interested, as a sporting proposition. Meanwhile, I plan to get a fresh beer and sit back with my feet up and a tightly rolled newspaper nearby. Such are the consolations of the ecological frame of mind.

## ◆ PRACTICE

### Discussion

1. Suppose someone asks you: "What is that article you're reading *about*?" Give an answer as if you were speaking to the person.

2. The same person asks you, "I thought you said that the essay is a cause-effect; it doesn't sound like cause-effect to me." Defend your earlier statement that the essay basically deals with a broad kind of causation.

3. Where is the thesis of the essay?

4. Explain the *positioning* of the thesis.

5. "There are two major cause-effect patterns in the essay." Explain.

6. Explain the organizational techniques of paragraphs 13–16, particularly as they are related to cause-effect.

7. Discuss the cause-effect pattern in paragraphs 9–12.

8. As you read the essay, were you aware that the *question* was fairly often being used to organize parts of it? Was this question technique obtrusive?

*Vocabulary*

| | | |
|---|---|---|
| carrion | dipterous | consortium |
| bestiary | pathogens | voracious |
| iridescent | offal | |

*Writing*

1. Besides the fly, what insect, animal, or "fish" do we find repellent? Write a cause-effect paper explaining why.

2. Write a brief cause-effect paper showing how an insect, animal, "fish," or plant does something; for example, how a goldfish reproduces, how weeds respond to weed killer. Use Conniff's *question* technique to organize your discussion.

3. Use writing exercise **1,** but replace the word *repellent* with *attractive* or *lovable.* Concentrate on physical details and images that are the exact opposite of Conniff's.

# CLASSIFICATION

## CLASSIFICATION

Classifying or grouping things is a natural way to think. Young children playing with rocks separate large ones from small ones, rough ones from smooth ones. As they grow older, they become more sophisticated in their classifying, and they begin to group their playmates into those they like to play with and those they don't. When they enter school, they separate their school clothes from their play clothes. Then as they learn to use abstractions in their thinking, they identify subjects in school that they are interested or successful in. In every one of these classifications, the grouping is made according to a *ruling principle:* rocks classified according to *size* or *smoothness;* friends classified according to *amiability;* clothes classified according to *use;* school subjects classified according to *success* or, perhaps, *interest.*

Although classifying is a process "natural" to human beings, it is useful to remember that classes as such do not exist in nature itself. We create classes and systems of classification to help us understand our world.

### The "Ruling Principle" in Classification

*Classifying* is the act of grouping things, persons, activities, ideas, and so on, according to their similarities and differences. By the time you are of college age you are so accustomed to classifying and to being classified that you are scarcely aware of the process. Yet classification affects nearly every part of your life. To mention only a few of the possibilities, you may be classified in religion as a believer, nonbeliever, or agnostic; a Christian or non-Christian; a Protestant, Jew, or Catholic; a Methodist, Baptist, or Episcopalian; etc. In politics, you are Republican, Democrat, or Independent. In school, you are a freshman, sophomore, junior, senior (or un-classified). In a university, you may be placed in the College of Arts and Sciences, Engineering, Education, etc. If you are in Arts and Sciences, you may be classified as an English major, math major, or psychology major, etc. (In classifying, the *et cetera* is important because the classifier must be sure that all the members of the class are included. However, listing all the possible options may be boring and unnecessary.)

A *classification,* to define the term more accurately, is a significant and informative grouping of things, persons, activities, ideas, etc. The key words here are *significant* and *informative.* We classify in order to use information, and the most informative classifications are those based upon significant groupings. If, in order to understand them, we separate the students in a particular composition class into two groups, men and women, we have made a classification, but it does not seem significant nor does it satisfy our curiosity about the students.

To make such a classification useful, we must apply a significant *ruling principle,* which is a unifying idea or point of view used in the act of classifying. The division of a composition class into men and women is based upon a ruling principle of *gender,* which is not a particularly significant grouping here, and thus will not prove to be very informative. Other ruling principles of varying significance might be *athletic ability, religion, major field, interest in composition,* etc.

In the following passage, observe that there are two ruling principles, cloud *formation* and *altitude*:

1 Clouds are classified according to how they are formed. There are two basic types: (1) Clouds formed by rising air currents. These are piled up and puffy. They are called "cumulus" which means piled up or accumulated. (2) Clouds formed when a layer of air is cooled below the saturation point without vertical movement. These are in sheets or foglike layers. They are called "stratus," meaning sheetlike or layered.

2 Clouds are further classified by altitude into four families: high clouds, middle clouds, low clouds, and towering clouds. The bases of the latter may be as low as the typical low clouds, but the tops may be at or above 75,000 feet.

—Paul E. Lehr, R. Will Burnett, and Herbert S. Zim, *Weather*

As with the other strategies of development, classification is created by the writer *for a specific reason.* In the classification of clouds, the writers' aim was to explain cloud formations to a reader who is not a scientist and who knows very little about clouds.

A diagram of another classification may help you visualize how this strategy works. Note how the following discussion of different types of kisses might be diagrammed.

If one wishes to classify the kiss, then one must consider several principles of classification. One may classify kissing with respect to sound. Here the language is not sufficiently elastic to record all my observations. I do not believe that all the languages in the world have an adequate supply of onomatopoeia to describe the different sounds I have learned to know at my uncle's house. Sometimes it was smacking, sometimes hissing, sometimes hollow, sometimes squeaky, and so on forever. One may also classify kissing with regard to contact, as in the close kiss, the kiss *en passant* [in passing], and the clinging kiss. . . . One may classify them with reference to the time element, as the brief and the prolonged. With reference to the time element, there is still another classification, and this is the only one I really care about. One makes a difference between the first kiss and all others. That which is the subject of this reflection is incommensurable with everything which is included in the other classifications; it is indifferent to sound, touch, time in general. The first kiss is, however, qualitatively different from all others.

—Soren Kierkegaard, *Either/Or*

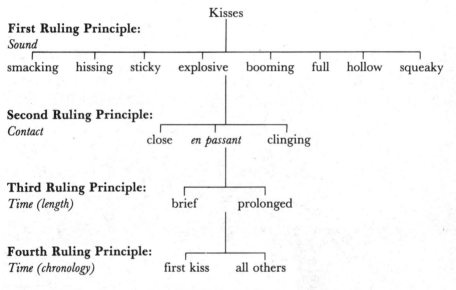

**First Ruling Principle:**
*Sound*

Kisses

smacking  hissing  sticky  explosive  booming  full  hollow  squeaky

**Second Ruling Principle:**
*Contact*

close  *en passant*  clinging

**Third Ruling Principle:**
*Time (length)*

brief  prolonged

**Fourth Ruling Principle:**
*Time (chronology)*

first kiss  all others

*Point of classification:* The first kiss is different .

# SUGGESTIONS FOR WRITING A CLASSIFICATION PAPER

Here are some suggestions for writing the classification paper that you should find useful.

1. The first step in classifying is to list your evidence. The evidence you collect is from your experience or reading. Your evidence may be the answer to a question such as "What kinds of . . . ?" or "What are the facts about . . . ?" After you have collected the evidence in order

to answer the question, you have a list. Once you have your list, you should be able to see relationships, keep the evidence that is pertinent, and ignore the rest. Then you can identify your ruling principle and develop categories.

2. Next, remember to avoid artificial overlapping or illogical classifications. Simply chopping your subject into parts will not necessarily give you a valid classification. If you divide your composition class into (a) men and (b) good students, you have made a classification that is artificial and probably useless.

3. Be consistent with your ruling principle. You may change your principle if, after having investigated your subject thoroughly from one angle, you wish to investigate it from another. Note that the classification of clouds used two ruling principles. If you were studying political systems, for example, you might use several different ruling principles: (a) time-sequence or history, (b) causes and effects, (c) types of systems, (d) philosophies of systems, (e) success of systems, to name just a few.

4. Make sure your classification has a point. Don't try to write a classification paper without a specific stance.

5. Avoid most either-or classifications. For instance:

> Voters are either left-wing or right-wing.
> Financiers are either successful or unsuccessful.
> Rhetoric students are either good writers or poor writers.

By its very structure, each of these either-or classifications probably distorts the truth because it omits certain members of the total group—those who would fall somewhere between the extremes of "left" or "right," "successful" or "unsuccessful," and "good" or "poor." Among a group of rhetoric students, for example, there are likely to be writers who are "excellent," "good," "fair," "poor," and (perhaps) "terrible."

# WRITING AND REVISING A CLASSIFICATION PAPER (AN EXAMPLE)

To understand more clearly how the process of classification works in the contexts of thinking and writing, let's follow a student named Tom who wants to understand the *behavior* of the fifteen eight-year-old boys that he supervised in summer camp. His purpose in using classification is to get some ideas for dealing with these boys when he returns to his counselling job next summer. He has made some scratch notes, and from those notes he writes the rough draft of a paragraph.

### KIDS AT A SUMMER CAMP

Most campers fall into at least one emotional category that reveals a lot about the way they think about life. Every counselor should expect at least one of the following. *The Homesick Kid* is normally the one in his bunk while everyone else is playing soccer outside. Odds are he's writing home (at least three times a day). This kid has probably never been away from home much before, and normally he wishes that he is anywhere but camp. But at the end of camp, he'll cry even harder because he doesn't want to leave. *The Whiner* complains about everything. At meals, the food is always too gloppy, runny, bland, or spicy. At night, the bed is too hard or too soft, and the games are always too hard or too boring. Some kids are *Non-Existent,* and as their counselor you never meet them until their parents come to pick them up. They tend to be lethargic, hard to find, and exceptionally quiet—meaning that they sometimes end up being a counselor's favorite. *The Jock* is the all-around athlete, able to beat anyone in camp (including his counselors) in tetherball, football, soccer, etc. They're great to have around, though, if you need something heavy (a trunk, bed, or person) lifted. *The Super-Jock* is another story. He thinks he can do anything well, but his prime attribute is normally making excuses (sun too bright, glove too big or small, field too rough, not the way we play at home). Along these same lines is *the Veteran*—the kid who has done it all "many times," and is an expert at absolutely everything. Unfortunately for him, the camp never seems to do anything "his way," and he normally learns some big lessons in humility by the time the summer is over.

After Tom reviews what he has written, he discovers that he has failed to follow the steps for developing a clear classification system: He has no *ruling principle* and no *categories.* Instead, he has treated each boy as a separate class; consequently his grouping overlaps: a *homesick boy* can be a *whiner;* a *veteran camp-goer* can be a *jock.* Tom reconsiders his ruling principle. What each boy "thinks about life" is pretty vague, so he decides that a more important *ruling principle* would be to consider how various classes of boys contribute to the success of the camp, thereby helping the counselor run a better program. Tom believes that the classification system should be useful for the counselors, so he changes his system to include three categories: *leader, follower,* and *obstructionist.* His definitions help him to place the boys in these categories:

A *leader* is a boy who takes initiative and has certain qualities that make other boys respect and follow him.

A *follower* is a boy who does what the leader expects, but seldom acts on his own initiative.

An *obstructionist* is a boy who exerts no positive leadership but hinders the day-by-day progress of the camp with unacceptable behavior.

Keeping these three categories in mind, Tom can now see that whether or not a boy is homesick is irrelevant. It is the way his homesickness keeps him from being a *leader* or causes him to be a *follower* or *obstructionist* that is important. It isn't whether or not a boy is selfish or generous that is the important thing, but how these traits affect his behavior and his leadership qualities.

Next Tom develops a *stance:*

| | |
|---|---|
| *Role:* | A college freshman who supervised a group of eight-year-old boys at YMCA summer camp the summer after graduating from high school. |
| *Audience:* | Other counselors of the YMCA camp or any other boys' camp. |
| *Thesis:* | If you want to succeed as a camp counselor, you should recognize that eight-year-old boys fall into three categories—*leaders, followers,* and *obstructionists.* (It will make your life easier if you know how to get cooperation from the members of each class.) |

Here is Tom's completed paper.

### CAN EIGHT-YEAR-OLD BOYS BEHAVE RESPONSIBLY?

[1] When I took a job as counselor at the YMCA camp, I had hoped to work with older boys because I had experience with a twelve-year-old brother and his friends. Consequently, I was disappointed to be assigned to a group of eight-year-olds, an age I considered too child-like to interest me. I knew, however, that it was my job to understand the boys who come to the camp with varying backgrounds and personalities. It was apparent that I would be expected to teach, counsel, and clean up after these boys, so I had to learn something about them fast. Eight weeks—the length of the camp—isn't very long.

[2] During the summer I learned that there are three kinds of eight-year-old boys—*leaders, followers,* and *obstructionists.* I knew that my life would be easier if I could get the best from each class of boy because I could make use of their abilities to lead or follow. The *leaders* I define as those boys who take initiative, and have certain qualities that make other boys respect and follow them. The *followers* are boys who do what the leader expects but who show no initiative. A *follower* seldom acts on his own initiative to help make camp successful. The *obstructionist* is a boy who exerts no positive leadership but hinders the day-by-day progress of the camp with unacceptable behavior.

[3] The *leader* class may consist of only one or two boys. If a camp counselor can find any boy who others will look up to and one who will also support the counselor, he is lucky. A *leader* is usually self-confident, but not overbearing. He may be a good athlete, so he understands what team-work means. Other boys look up to athletes because they can beat other teams in tetherball, football, or soccer, making the camp team look good. The boys in the leader class have usually been to summer camp before, so they know the procedures and are not likely to be homesick. It is a good idea to identify any leaders in your group early because they can make your life as a camp counselor infinitely easier. They can cooperate with you by rounding up the followers at the end of a day, and they can get *followers* to cooperate with you.

4 The next largest class is *followers*, subclassified into *retreating* and *eager* boys. The *retreating boy* is usually homesick. He may stay in his bunk writing home every day. Sometimes he won't eat, so he is lethargic. A *retreater* will usually comply with directions because he is frightened. *Retreaters* are often generous. If a retreater gets a package of cookies from his parents, he shares it with the whole cabin. This kind of sharing helps to form a cohesive group.

5 *Eager* boys make good followers, particularly if they believe that they are lucky to be at any camp at all. Most boys' camps try to admit each summer a few children from orphanages or foster homes. Their fees are usually paid by the YMCA or a service club like the Kiwanis or Rotary. Since these boys have no family and are used to institutional life, they think the camp food is great, the beds comfortable, and the counselor a good guy.

6 The largest class—and the biggest problem for a camp counselor—is the *obstructionist*. Perhaps eight-year-olds become *obstructionists* when they are away from home because they have to accommodate to a new environment. Consequently, they are complainers. They whine about the food being too runny, bland, or spicy. Their beds are too hard or too soft. The games are boring. Some boys who fancy themselves good athletes complain when they don't succeed: the sun is too bright, the baseball glove is too small, the field is too rough, and the camp team doesn't play by the rules that they know. Some of the obstructionists are selfish because they are used to having people wait on them. They can't get used to doing the everyday chores of washing dishes, making beds, and sweeping floors. A selfish boy may draw a line around his bunk, padlock his food packages from home, and even steal food from other boys.

7 A counselor must put a great deal of effort into getting the obstructionists to accept responsibility for the group. One way of dealing with these boys is to be abrupt and order them about. However, this will probably make them even less cooperative than they were before. I have found a better way: Make them feel important. They are usually very insecure and frightened of a new experience, so they show their insecurity by aggressive and selfish behavior. I try to treat obstructionists as I treat my little brother when he displays similar behavior. I pay attention to him and make him think I'm interested in what he does. If I treat *obstructionists* as I treat my brother, by the end of eight weeks they usually become more cooperative—not completely cooperative—but *more* so!

8 Other counselors may find my classification incomplete, and they may not agree with my solutions. But these are the kinds of boys that I found in the YMCA camp. Knowing what I learned last summer will help me next year when I face another group of boys whose parents happily shipped their kids off to summer camp for me and my friends to civilize.

## ◆ PRACTICE

### Discussion

1. Study Tom's final draft. How well do the details and examples support each of his categories? Discuss the point of the paper. Is it clear enough that another counselor could follow Tom's advice? What suggestions do you have for improvements in the paper? Improvements in the classification system?

2. For class discussion, make a significant classification of the following items. You may need to subdivide to complete your classification. *Hint:* One of the category *names* may be in some of the lists. Give the ruling principle of your classification. Use the heading *Etc.* if an item doesn't fit your classifying system.
   a. *Time,* table, book, chair, magazine, divan, *Sports Illustrated,* newspaper, bookcase, *Fortune.*
   b. Truck, station wagon, automobile, luxury car, "semi," convertible, pickup, sports car, compact, economy car.
   c. Left-winger, Southern Democrat, socialist, communist, right-winger, Democrat, Republican, independent, middle-of-the-roader.
   d. Poet, novelist, journalist, editorial writer, TV commentator, textbook author, social philosopher, newspaper columnist, writer for *The National Enquirer,* writer on college paper, literary critic.
   e. Thugs, robbers, rascals, killers, arsonists, scoundrels, shoplifters, murderers, burglars, assassins, car thieves, rapists, traitors, villains.
   f. Various kinds of *rights:* moral, natural, political, original, acquired, absolute, relative, property, liberty, equality.
   g. Presidents, governors, prime ministers, mayors, kings, princes, queens, despots, princesses, commissars, dictators, rulers, wardens, magistrates.

3. For purposes of research, a major university has classified "human subjects" in the following categories. Discuss the accuracy of the classification. What is the ruling principle? Are all classes represented? Do any of the classes overlap?

TYPE OF SUBJECT:

A. _____ Adult, non-student

_____ University student

_____ Minor

_____ Other (explain)

B. _____ Normal volunteer

_____ In-patient

_____ Out-patient

_____ Mentally retarded

_____ Mentally disabled

_____ Individual with limited civil freedom

_____ Pregnant women, fetuses, and the dead

4. Discuss the following ideas for classification papers. Identify any flaws in the ruling principle.
   a. In her first classification exercise, a seventh-grader wrote, "I classify my friends by their loyalty, manners, or indifference toward me."
   b. Harp strings are classified according to the materials they are made of—cat gut, springs, or nylon—because the different materials influence the tone of the sound.
   c. When I put my stamp collection in order, I separate the stamps first by country, then by series and date.
   d. From a U.S. government questionnaire: Check your nationality—(a) white, (b) black, (c) Asian, (d) Hispanic, (e) Cuban.
   e. People: There are two main categories, significant people and outsiders. Significant people include family, friends and business associates; outsiders may be anyone from the cashiers at the local supermarket to pedestrians on the street. People can be considered significant even when they have a negative impact. Prison guards, for example, would be extremely important to a prisoner.
      —Shannon Brownlee
   f. Casey Stengel, famous manager of the New York Yankees: "All right you guys, line up alphabetically according to size."
   g. Looters belong to three categories. There are everyday thieves—men and women of no conscience—who would steal wherever and whenever no authority existed to restrain them.

      In the second group are those who feel deprived and frustrated and seize the opportunity to express their grievances at being unemployed, hungry, angry at society, their bosses or spouses, and who feel they have little chance for revenge. These individuals are easily galvanized into action by watching others behave wantonly.

      The third category interests psychiatrists the most because any of us could potentially become looters. In the wake of a disaster, impulses usually contained—greed, naked aggression, lust for power, etc.—often flow unchecked. The carnival atmosphere reigns, while the impulses to help and to heal may be given short shrift.—*Wall Street Journal*


*Writing*

1. Write a paper in which you classify your reactions to "things" around you. Be sure to identify the significance of your classification. Examples:
   a. Things you worry about.
   b. Things you keep secret from your family.
   c. Things you celebrate.
   d. Things you laugh about.
   e. Things you feel guilty about.

2. Choose a topic that can be classified, and write an essay. Be sure to keep in mind the following: (1) choose the ruling principle(s) by which you plan to classify; (2) identify your purpose in classifying (your reader should not read your classification and say, "So what?"); (3) choose a writer's stance that suits the ruling principle and the purpose of the classification; (4) write the paper.

Here are some possible topics (modify when necessary):

a. There are distinct kinds of people who patronize laundromats/sporting-goods stores/pizzerias/delicatessens; *therefore* . . .

b. I have encountered many types of people/ideas since coming to college. *My conclusions are* . . .

c. The subjects in my major field can be divided into several categories; *consequently* . . .

d. The parents of successful children fall into several categories, but *the most important category is* . . .

e. The summer and part-time jobs available to a college student have certain characteristics, *so when you look for a job* . . .

FRAN LEBOWITZ

# THINGS

*Fran Lebowitz is a perfect example of the native New Yorker, although she was actually born in Morristown, New Jersey, somewhere in the vicinity of 1951. Classified as an American essayist, she claims to have supported herself prior to the fame of* Metropolitan Life *(1978) by working as a bulk mailer, taxi driver, cleaning person (apartments only), and advertising salesperson. Her columns and reviews have appeared regularly in Andy Warhol's* Interview *magazine,* Mademoiselle, *and* Changes *magazine. Citing Oscar Wilde as her own favorite writer, Lebowitz is herself a favorite contemporary satirist of many and a popular guest on television talk shows. Reviewers call her cranky only slightly less often than they call her funny, and her stylish brand of humorous irritability has sold an impressive number of books. In "Things" from* Social Studies *(1981), Lebowitz organizes an impressive number of things ("all of the things in the world," in fact) into two very manageable categories. Manageable, that is, to a young curmudgeon like Lebowitz.*

¹ All of the things in the world can be divided into two basic categories: natural things and artificial things. Or, as they are more familiarly known, nature and art. Now, nature, as I am only too well aware, has her enthusiasts, but on the whole, I am not to be counted among them. To put it rather bluntly, I am not the type who wants to go back to the land; I am the type who wants to go back to the hotel. This state of affairs is at least partially due to the fact that nature and I have so little in common. We don't go to the same restaurants, laugh at the same jokes or, most significant, see the same people.

² This was not, however, always the case. As a child I was frequently to be found in a natural setting: playing in the snow, walking in the woods, wading in the pond. All these things were standard events in my daily life. But little by little I grew up, and it was during this process of maturation that I began to notice some of nature's more glaring deficiencies. First of all, nature is by and large to be found out of doors, a location where, it cannot be argued, there are never enough comfortable chairs. Secondly, for fully half of the time it is day out there, a situation created by just the sort of harsh overhead lighting that is so unflattering to the heavy smoker. Lastly, and most pertinent to this discourse, is the fact that natural things are by their very definition wild, unkempt and more often than not crawling with bugs. Quite obviously, then, natural things are just the kind of things that one does not strive to acquire. *Objets d'art* are one thing; *objets d'nature* are not. Who, after all, could possibly want to own something that even the French don't have a word for?

³ In view of all this I have prepared a little chart designed to more

graphically illustrate the vast superiority of that which is manufactured over that which is not.

| NATURE | ART |
|---|---|
| The sun | The toaster oven |
| Your own two feet | Your own two Bentleys |
| Windfall apples | Windfall profits |
| Roots and berries | Linguini with clam sauce |
| Time marching on | The seven-second delay |
| Milk | Butter |
| The good earth | 25 percent of the gross |
| Wheat | Linguini with clam sauce |
| A man for all seasons | Marc Bohan for Dior |
| Ice | Ice cubes |
| Facial hair | Razor blades |
| The smell of the countryside after a long, soaking rain | Linguini with clam sauce |
| TB | TV |
| The mills of God | Roulette |
| A tinkling mountain brook | Paris |

⁴ Now that you have had an opportunity to gain an overview of the subject, it is time to explore things more thoroughly, time to ask yourselves what you have learned and how you can best apply your new-found knowledge. Well, obviously, the first and most important thing you have learned is that linguini with clam sauce is mankind's crowning achievement. But as this is a concept readily grasped, it is unnecessary to linger over it or discuss it in greater detail.

⁵ As to the question of how you can best apply what you have learned, I believe that it would be highly beneficial to you all were we to examine the conventional wisdom on the subject of things in order to see what it looks like in the light of your new-found knowledge:

*THE CONVENTIONAL WISDOM ON THE SUBJECT OF THINGS*
*AS SEEN IN THE LIGHT OF YOUR NEW-FOUND KNOWLEDGE*

*All good things come to those who wait.* This is a concept that parallels in many respects another well-known thought, that of the meek inheriting the earth. With that in mind, let us use a time-honored method of education and break the first statement into its two major component parts: a) All good things; b) come to those who wait. Immediately it is apparent that thanks to our previous study we are well informed as to which exactly the good things are. It is when we come to "those who wait" that we are entering virgin territory. Educators have found that in cases like this it is often best to use examples from actual life. So then, we must think of a place that from our own experience we know as a place where "those who wait" might, in fact, be waiting. Thus I feel that the baggage claim area of a large metropolitan airport might well serve our purpose.

⁶ Now, in addressing the fundamental issue implied by this question— i.e., the veracity of the statement "All good things come to those who wait"—we are in actuality asking the question, "Do, in fact, all good things come to those who wait? In breaking our answer into *its* two major component parts, we find that we know that: a) among "all good things" are to be found linguini with clam sauce, the Bentley automobile and the ever-fascinating city of Paris.

⁷ We also know that: b) "those who wait" are waiting at O'Hare. We then think back to our own real-life adventures, make one final check of our helpful chart and are sadly compelled to conclude that "No, all good things do *not* come to those who wait"—unless due to unforeseeably personal preferences on the part of "those who wait," "all good things" are discovered to include an item entitled *SOME OF YOUR LUGGAGE MISSING ALL OF ITS CONTENTS.*

*A thing of beauty is a joy forever:* this graceful line from a poem written by John Keats is not so much inaccurate as it is archaic. Mr. Keats, it must be remembered, was not only a poet but also a product of the era in which he lived. Additionally, it must not be forgotten that one of the salient features of the early nineteenth century was an inordinate admiration for the simple ability to endure. Therefore, while a thing of beauty is a joy, to be sure, we of the modern age, confined no longer by outmoded values, are free to acknowledge that nine times out of ten a weekend is long enough.

*Each man kills the thing he loves:* and understandably so, when he has been led to believe that it will be a joy forever.

*Doing your own thing:* the use of the word "thing" in this context is unusually precise, since those who are prone to this expression actually do *do* things as opposed to those who do work—i.e., pottery is a thing—writing is a work.

*Life is just one damned thing after another:* and death is a cabaret.

## ◆ *P R A C T I C E*

### *Discussion*

1. Relying strictly on the explicit and implicit evidence contained in the essay, describe the kind of person Fran Lebowitz seems to be (or, perhaps, just pretends to be).

2. Does Lebowitz' classification fit the precise definition of "classification" given by the authors of this text? Does it have a ruling principle? Does it have a point? Explain your answers.

3. Lebowitz' explications of "conventional wisdom on the subject of things" are not simply jokes. She makes some serious—or, perhaps, mildly serious—points. Delve into her comments on *"Doing your own thing."* What observations can you make about her meaning there?

4. Study the chart comparing nature and art. Is there a method to the madness; that is, can you perceive a pattern or patterns in the way examples are chosen? If so, what is it or what are they? If not, why doesn't Lebowitz need a pattern? Continue her chart with a few examples of your own chosen according to her method or lack of method.

5. What is the relationship, if any, between the first half of the essay (through the chart) and the second half? Is the essay a coherent, unified whole? Does it need to be?

6. What voice does Lebowitz establish in the essay or, another way to ask the question, like whom does she sound? Is that voice heard consistently throughout the essay? How does that voice contribute to the humor of the piece?

7. Lebowitz is usually labelled a satirist by her reviewers. What is satire? Whom or what is Lebowitz satirizing in this essay? How is the voice that you identified in the previous question especially suited to satire?

8. Many critics have said that Lebowitz has a "New York style," characterized by a love of language and elegant, often witty, phrases. Where do you find witty phrasing in this essay? Does she use puns? Are puns elegant?

### *Vocabulary*

| | | |
|---|---|---|
| maturation | *objets d'art* | archaic |
| pertinent | linguini | salient |
| discourse | metropolitan | inordinate |
| unkempt | veracity | cabaret |

*Writing*

1. Try your hand (and your sense of humor) at dividing "all of the things in the world" into two (and only two) basic categories that reflect your preferences and prejudices. Do not attempt to take this impossible task nor yourself too seriously. Do write a humorous essay about your method of classification.

2. How would you divide all the people in the world (or in your school or at work) into *three* basic categories? Write an essay explaining your classification. A humorous approach is entirely acceptable but not required.

3. Some very serious and persuasive essays have been written about the superiority of art over nature. Write a serious essay that classifies things and/or actions as belonging to nature or to art and defend the superiority of one class over the other. You may consider art as including manufacture.

JAMES T. BAKER

# HOW DO WE FIND THE STUDENT IN A WORLD OF ACADEMIC GYMNASTS AND WORKER ANTS?

*Professor of history and director of the honors program at Western Kentucky University, James T. Baker is a graduate of Baylor University. He earned his Ph.D. at Florida State University. Baker has published biographies of Thomas Merton, Ayn Rand, Eric Hoffer, Jimmy Carter, and Broooks Hays. His latest book is about Studs Terkel. The recipient of two Fulbright Senior Lectureships, Baker has taught or studied in Florence, Italy; Seoul, Korea; Taipei, Taiwan; and Oxford, England. Here he describes students particularly and generally. Perhaps you can find yourself somewhere in his description.*

[1] Anatole France once wrote that "the whole art of teaching is only the art of awakening the natural curiosity of young minds." I fully agree, except I have to wonder if, by using the word "only," he thought that the art of awakening such natural curiosity was an easy job. For me, it never has been—sometimes exciting, always challenging, but definitely not easy.

[2] Robert M. Hutchins used to say that a good education prepares students to go on educating themselves throughout their lives. A fine definition, to be sure, but it has at times made me doubt that my own students, who seem only too eager to graduate so they can lay down their books forever, are receiving a good education.

[3] But then maybe these are merely the pessimistic musings of someone suffering from battle fatigue. I have almost qualified for my second sabbatical leave, and I am scratching a severe case of the seven-year itch. About the only power my malaise has not impaired is my eye for spotting certain "types" of student. In fact, as the rest of me declines, my eye seems to grow more acute.

[4] Has anyone else noticed that the very same students people college classrooms year after year? Has anyone else found the same bodies, faces, personalities returning semester after semester? Forgive me for violating my students' individual "personhoods," but reality makes it so tempting to see them as types. Doubtless you will recognize at least some of them. They have twins, or perhaps clones, on your campus, too.

[5] There is the eternal Good Time Charlie (or Charlene), who makes every party on and off the campus, who by November of his freshman year has worked his face into a case of terminal acne, who misses every set of examinations because of "mono," who finally burns himself out physically

and mentally by the age of 19 and drops out to go home and recuperate, and who returns at 20 after a long talk with Dad to major in accounting.

[6] There is the Young General Patton, the one who comes to college on an R.O.T.C. scholarship and for a year twirls his rifle at basketball games while loudly sniffing out pinko professors, who at midpoint takes a sudden but predictable, radical swing from far right to far left, who grows a beard and moves in with a girl who refuses to shave her legs, who then makes the just as predictable, radical swing back to the right and ends up preaching fundamentalist sermons on the steps of the student union while the Good Time Charlies and Charlenes jeer.

[7] There is the Egghead, the campus intellectual who shakes up his fellow students—and even a professor or two—with references to esoteric formulas and obscure Bulgarian poets, who is recognized by friend and foe alike as a promising young academic, someday to be a professional scholar, who disappears every summer for six weeks ostensibly to search for primeval human remains in Colorado caves, and who at 37 is shot dead by Arab terrorists while on a mission for the C.I.A.

[8] There is the Performer—the music or theater major, the rock or folk singer—who spends all of his or her time working up an act, who gives barely a nod to mundane subjects like history, sociology, or physics, who dreams only of the day he or she will be on stage full time, praised by critics, cheered by audiences, who ends up either pregnant or responsible for a pregnancy and at 30 is either an insurance salesman or a housewife with a very lush garden.

[9] There is the Jock, of course—the every-afternoon intramural champ, smelling of liniment and Brut, with bulging calves and a blue-eyed twinkle, the subject of untold numbers of female fantasies, the walking personification of he-man-ism—who upon graduation is granted managerial rank by a California bank because of his golden tan and low golf score, who is seen five years later buying the drinks at a San Francisco gay bar.

[10] There is the Academic Gymnast—the guy or gal who sees college as an obstacle course, as so many stumbling blocks in the way of a great career or a perfect marriage—who strains every moment to finish and be done with "this place" forever, who toward the end of the junior year begins to slow down, to grow quieter and less eager to leave, who attends summer school, but never quite finishes those last six hours, who never leaves "this place," and who at 40 is still working at the campus laundry, still here, still a student.

[11] There is the Medal Hound, the student who comes to college not to learn or expand any intellectual horizons but simply to win honors— medals, cups, plates, ribbons, scrolls—who is here because this is the best place to win the most the fastest, who plasticizes and mounts on his wall every certificate of excellence he wins, who at 39 will be a colonel in the U.S. Army and at 55 Secretary of something or other in a conservative Administration in Washington.

[12] There is the Worker Ant, the student (loosely rendered) who takes 21 hours a semester and works 49 hours a week at the local car wash, who sleeps only on Sundays and during classes, who will somehow graduate on time and be the owner of his own vending-machine company at 30 and be dead of a heart attack at 40, and who will be remembered for the words chiseled on his tombstone:

All This Was Accomplished Without Ever Having So Much As Darkened The Door Of A Library.

[13] There is the Lost Soul, the sad kid who is in college only because teachers, parents, and society at large said so, who hasn't a career in mind or a dream to follow, who hasn't a clue, who heads home every Friday afternoon to spend the weekend cruising the local Dairee-Freeze, who at 50 will have done all his teachers, parents, and society said to do, still without a career in mind or a dream to follow or a clue.

[14] There is also the Saved Soul—the young woman who has received, through the ministry of one Gospel freak or another, a Holy Calling to save the world, or at least some special part of it—who majors in Russian studies so that she can be caught smuggling Bibles into the Soviet Union and be sent to Siberia where she can preach to souls imprisoned by the Agents of Satan in the Gulag Archipelago.

[15] Then, finally, there is the Happy Child, who comes to college to find a husband or wife—and finds one—and there is the Determined Child, who comes to get a degree—and gets one.

[16] Enough said.

[17] All of which, I suppose, should make me throw up my hands in despair and say that education, like youth and love, is wasted on the young. Not quite.

[18] For there does come along, on occasion, that one of a hundred or so who is maybe at first a bit lost, certainly puzzled; who may well start out a Good Timer, an Egghead, a Performer, a Jock, a Medal Hound, a Gymnast, a Worker Ant; who may indeed have trouble settling on a major, who will be distressed by what sometimes passes for education, who might even be a temporary dropout; but who has a vital capacity for growth and is able to fall in love with learning, who acquires a taste for intellectual pleasure, who becomes in the finest sense of the word a Student.

[19] This is the one who keeps the most jaded of us going back to class after class, and he or she must be oh-so-carefully cultivated. He or she must be artfully awakened, given the tools needed to continue learning for a lifetime, and let grow at whatever pace and in whatever direction nature dictates.

[20] For I try always to remember that this student is me, my continuing self, my immortality. This person is my only hope that my own search for Truth will continue after me, on and on, forever.

# ◆ *PRACTICE*

## *Discussion*

1. Describe Baker's *role* as a writer. How soon do you understand his role fully? Who is his *reader*?

2. What is the *ruling principle* of Baker's classification?

3. Are Baker's classifications *significant* and *informative*?

4. What is Baker's purpose in making the classification?

5. Baker uses the *representative example* (see *illustration,* pp. 249–250). Where does he use it, and why?

6. Several descriptions of individual students begin one way and end another—for example, the egghead who ends up being killed while working for the CIA. Explain the technique.

7. Discuss the sentence construction of the paragraph *leads* (the first sentence in each paragraph) in the body of the essay. Explain particularly that of paragraph 18.

8. Respond to the final paragraph of the essay.

## *Vocabulary*

| | | |
|---|---|---|
| sabbatical | primeval | plasticizes |
| pinko | mundane | Gulag Archipelago |
| esoteric | lush | |

## *Writing*

1. Reread paragraph 4. In the first line, substitute another clause for *the very same students people college classrooms.* Examples: *The very same professors people . . . ; same janitors . . . ; same secretaries people department offices; same columnists people the student paper;* etc.

2. Write a paper explaining why you agree or disagree (or partly agree) with Baker's *point* in writing the essay.

3. Write a classification paper explaining the motives of your high-school friends who decided to go to college.

JAMES H. AUSTIN

# CHANCE

*As a neurologist involved in biomedical research, James H. Austin has had many opportunities to observe the four varieties of chance he explores in the following essay. Austin was born in Cleveland, Ohio, on January 4, 1925. A graduate of Brown University, he received his medical degree from Harvard Medical School in 1948. Doctor and teacher, the combination has made him especially well suited to explain abstruse scientific issues to laymen, which he has done in his book on the psychology of creativity,* Chase, Chance, and Creativity: The Lucky Art of Novelty. *The essay here is adapted from his article in* Executive Health Reports *that anticipated Austin's book. While one appreciates the scientific clarity of his classification of chance, one is also informed by Austin's definitions, his examples, and his enthusiasm.*

¹ I am reminded of George Bernard Shaw's comment: "Never lose a chance: it doesn't come every day."

² Of course, you get lucky sometimes. Everyone does! But is there something you can learn about the structure of chance that might improve your percentage?

³ As a physician-investigator, I began to wonder about these questions some years ago. What started me were some astonishing "happy accidents" . . . chance events that were completely unpredictable. Now, being a neurologist, raised in the conventional work ethic, I still believe that success in research comes from being hard-working, persistent, curious, imaginative, intuitive, and enthusiastic. . . . But when this is said and done, it still turns out that many of our lucky breaks will still be decided by our extracurricular activities—by those pivotal events that come only when we have reached out in a spirit of adventure and jousted at chance. Like the lowly turtle, man, too, lurches forward only if he first sticks his neck out and chances the consequences.

⁴ What is chance? Dictionaries define chance as something fortuitous that happens unpredictably without discernible human intention. *La cheance,* in old French, is derived from the Old Latin, *cadere,* to fall, implying that it is in the nature of things to fall, settle out, or happen by themselves.

⁵ Chance is unintentional, it is capricious, but we needn't conclude that chance is immune from human intervention. Indeed, chance enters in four different ways when we react creatively with one another and with our environment. You and I are each affected by the principles involved, and it is time we examine them more carefully.

⁶ The four kinds of chance each have a different kind of motor exploratory activity and a different kind of sensory receptivity. The varieties of

chance also involve distinctive personality traits and differ in the way you, as a person, interact with them.

[7] Chance I is the pure blind luck that comes with no effort on your part. If, for example, you are sitting playing bridge at a table of four, it's "in the cards" for you to receive a hand of thirteen spades, but statisticians tell us it will occur on an average only once in 635 billion deals. You will ultimately draw this lucky hand, but it may involve a rather longer wait than most have time for.

[8] Chance II evokes the kind of luck Charles Kettering, the automotive engineer, had in mind when he said: "Keep on going and the chances are you will stumble on something, perhaps when you are least expecting it. I have never heard of anyone stumbling on something sitting down."

[9] Consistent motion is what distinguishes Chance II; its premise is that *un*-luck runs out if you persist. An element of the chase is also implicit in Chance II, but action is still your primary goal, not results. The action is ill-defined, restless, driving, and it depends on your basic need to release energy, not on your conscious intellect. Of course, if you move around in more likely areas, Chance II may enter in to influence your results more fruitfully. For example, if orchids were your only goal, you wouldn't want to go tramping looking for them in the harsh desert.

[10] So Chance II springs from your energetic, generalized motor activities, and, with the above qualification, the freer they are the better. A certain basal level of action "stirs up the pot," brings in random ideas that will collide and stick together in fresh combinations in your brain, lets chance operate. When someone, *anyone,* does swing into motion and keeps on going, he will increase the number of collisions between events. If you link a few events together, you can then exploit some of them, but many others, of course, you cannot. Kettering was right. Press on. Something will turn up. We may term this kinetic principle the Kettering Principle.

[11] In our two previous examples, a unique role of the individual person was either lacking or minimal. Now, as we move on to Chance III, we see blind luck tiptoeing in softly and dressed in camouflage. Chance presents the clue, the opportunity exists, but it would be missed except by that *one person* uniquely equipped to recognize it, visualize it conceptually, and fully grasp its significance. Chance III involves a special receptivity and discernment unique to the recipient. Louis Pasteur characterized it for all time when he said: "Chance favors only the prepared mind."

[12] Pasteur himself had it in full measure. But the classic example of his principle occurred in 1928, when Alexander Fleming's mind instantly fused at least five elements into a conceptually unified nexus. He was in the laboratory at the bench one day, when his mental sequences went something like this: (1) I see that a mold has fallen by accident into my culture dish; (2) the staphylococcal colonies residing near it failed to grow; (3) therefore, the mold must have secreted something that killed the bacteria; (4) this reminds me of a similar experience I had once before; (5) if I could separate this new "something" from the mold, it could be used to kill staphylococci that cause human infections.

[13] Actually, Fleming's mind was exceptionally well prepared for the penicillin mold. Nine years earlier, while he was suffering from a cold, his own nasal drippings had found their way onto a culture dish, for reasons not made entirely clear. He noted that bacteria around this mucus were killed, and astutely followed up the lead. His observations then led him to discover a bactericidal enzyme lysozyme, present in nasal mucus and tears. Lysozyme proved too weak to be of medical use, but imagine how receptive Fleming's mind was to the penicillin mold when nine years later it happened on the scene!

[14] One word evokes the quality of the operations involved in the first three kinds of chance. It is *serendipity*. The term describes the facility for encountering unexpected good luck, as the result of: accident (Chance I), general exploratory behavior (Chance II), or sagacity (Chance III). Serendipity was coined by the English-man-of-letters, Horace Walpole, in 1754. He used it with reference to the legendary tales of the Three Princes of Serendip (Ceylon), who quite unexpectedly encountered many instances of good fortune on their travels. In today's parlance, we have usually watered down serendipity to mean the good luck that comes solely by accident. We think of it as a result, not an ability. We have tended to lose sight of the element of sagacity, by which term Walpole wished to emphasize that some distinctive personal receptivity is involved. The archaic meaning of sagacity is acuteness of smell, if we need further testimony of the word's entirely *sensory* connotation.

[15] But now something is lacking—the motor counterpart to sagacity. The English Prime Minister Benjamin Disraeli summed up the principle underlying Chance IV when he noted that "we make our fortunes and we call them fate." Disraeli, the practical politician, appreciated that by our actions we each forge our own destiny, at least to some degree. One might restate the principle as follows: *Chance favors the individualized action. This is the fourth element in good luck . . . an active, but unintentional, subtle personal prompting of it.*

[16] Chance IV is the kind of luck that develops during a probing action which has a distinctive personal flavor. It comes to you because of who you are and how you behave. It is one-man-made, and is as personal as your signature. Being highly personal, it is not easily understood by someone else the first time around. The outside observer may have to go underground to see Chance IV, for here we probe into subterranean recesses that autobiographers know about, biographers rarely. Neurologists may be a little more comfortable with the concept because so much of the nervous system we work with exists as anatomically separate sensory and motor divisions. So, some natural separation does exist and underlies the distinction: Chance III concerned with personal *sensory receptivity;* its counterpart, Chance IV involved with personal *motor behavior.*

[17] Unlike Chance II, Chance IV connotes no generalized activity, as bees might have in the anonymity of a hive. Instead, like a highly personal hobby, it comprehends a kind of discrete behavioral performance. Anyone

might complete the lucky connections of Chance II as a happy by-product of a kind of circular stirring of the pot. But the links of Chance IV can be drawn together and fused only by *one* quixotic rider cantering in on his own home-made hobby horse to intercept the problem at an odd angle. Chance IV does resist straight logic and takes on something of the eccentric flavor of Cervantes' Spanish fiction.

[18] Indeed, something about the quality of Chance IV is as elusive as a mirage. Like a mirage, it is difficult to get a firm grip on, for it tends to recede as we pursue it and advance as we step back. But we still accept a mirage when we see it, because we vaguely understand the basis for the phenomenon: a strongly heated layer of air, less dense than usual, lies next to the earth, and it bends the light rays as they pass through.

[19] What psychological determinants enter into the varieties of chance? Chance I is completely impersonal. You can't influence it. Personality traits only start to enter in the other forms of chance. To evoke Chance II, you will need a persistent curiosity about many things coupled with an energetic willingness to experiment and explore. To arrive at the discernment involved in Chance III, you must have a sufficient background of firm knowledge plus special abilities in observing, remembering, recalling, and quickly forming significant new associations. Chance IV may favor you if you have distinctive, if not eccentric hobbies, personal life styles, and motor behaviors. The farther apart your personal activities are from the other area you are pursuing, the more strikingly novel will be the creative product when the two meet.

[20] Many examples of luck exist in medical research, but if we return to the life of Alexander Fleming, we can see all four varieties of chance illustrated in one man.

[21] Good examples of Chance I (pure blind luck) do not leap out from the medical literature because researchers feel guilty about mentioning luck when it replaces their more rational thought processes. However, Fleming tells us with refreshing candor how it was to be visited by Chance I. He said: "There are thousands of different molds, and there are thousands of different bacteria, and that chance put that mold in the right spot at the right time was like winning the Irish Sweepstakes."

[22] Many investigators, like Fleming, are as energetic as bees, so their fast mental and physical pace stirs up a certain amount of Chance II for this reason alone. Examples of Chance II are surely all around us, but it is difficult to prove with scientific certainty that they exist, because studies of twins would be required. No medical researcher seems to have a twin who is indolent, but equal in all other abilities, to serve as a basis for comparison.

[23] We have already considered Fleming's receptivity under Chance III, and we can also rely on him to serve as an example of the subtle workings of the personality in Chance IV. In Fleming's background was a boyhood shaped by the frugal economy of a Scottish hill farm in Ayrshire. Later, we find that much of his decision to train and work at old St. Mary's Hospital in London was not based on the excellence of its scientific facilities. Labora-

tories there were primitive by today's standards, damp and readily contaminated by organisms swirling in out of the London fog. Instead, Fleming's decision hinged on the fact that he liked to play water polo, and St. Mary's had a good swimming pool. Without the *hobby*—swimming—that drew him to St. Mary's, Fleming would never have gone on to discover penicillin! Among the several elements that entered into the penicillin story, this is one crucial personal item usually lost sight of.

[24] Still later, when he is 47, let us observe this same thrifty Scot in his laboratory at St. Mary's. His bench stands beneath a window open to the outside air, covered by a clutter of old culture dishes, for Fleming won't throw any dish out until he is certain that everything possible has been learned from it. He then picks up one culture dish of staphylococci that, with ingrained thrift, he has hoarded for many days. The delay has been critical. Had he thrown the dish out earlier, on schedule like the rest of us, the penicillin mold might not have had the opportunity to grow. But there the mold is now, growing in the over-age culture dish, and he alone also has the prepared mind, the sagacity, to realize its implications.

[25] We now have seen Sir Alexander Fleming's modest comment about his Irish Sweepstakes luck under Chance I, and can infer that Chance II entered his life by virtue of his many industrious years in the laboratory. We later observed how receptive he was (Chance III) and finally how both his swimming hobby and his thrifty habits coalesced in Chance IV. In Fleming's life, then, we see a fusion of all four forms of chance, and from there follows a simple conclusion: *The most novel, if not the greatest, discoveries occur when several varieties of chance coincide.* Let us name this unifying observation the Fleming Effect. His life exemplifies it, and it merits special emphasis.

[26] Why do we still remember men like Fleming? We cherish them not as Nobel Prize winning scientists alone. There is more to it than that. The fact is that, as men, their total contribution transcends their scientific discoveries. Perhaps we remember them, too, because their lives show us how malleable our own futures are. In their work we perceive how many loopholes fate has left us—how much of destiny is still in our hands. In them we see that nothing is predetermined. Chance can be on our side, if we but stir it up with our energies, stay receptive to its every random opportunity, and continually provoke it by individuality in our hobbies, attitudes, and our approach to life.

## ◆ *PRACTICE*

### *Discussion*

1. What are the four kinds of *chance* Austin describes?

2. What ruling principle does Austin use to classify chance? Where does he tell you? Does he use the ruling principle consistently?

3. What is the "Fleming Effect"? Why is it important in a discussion of *chance*? Is this more an essay about Fleming than a classification of *chance*?

4. What purpose do paragraphs 20 through 26 fulfill? What would be the effect of ending the essay after paragraph 19?

5. Why did Austin present the four kinds of *chance* in the order he used? Could they be arranged in a different sequence? Why or why not?

6. Outline Austin's pattern of organization, taking into account the relationship between his classes and his examples.

7. James Austin is a doctor and no doubt has a large technical vocabulary. What "language" does he use for writing this essay? Why?

8. What distinctions and relationships does Austin draw among the words *luck, chance,* and *serendipity*?

## Vocabulary

| | | |
|---|---|---|
| fortuitous | nexus | candor |
| discernible | sagacity | indolent |
| capricious | parlance | implications |
| intervention | discrete | coalesced |
| camouflage | quixotic | malleable |
| conceptually | | |

## Writing

1. Write an essay in which you describe how you have experienced at least three kinds of *chance* as classified here.

2. Using Austin's essay as a model, write a paper in which you classify an abstraction. Show how one person you know exemplifies each of your classes. Suggested topics: morality, intelligence, frugality, temperance, affection.

3. According to Austin, Disraeli suggested that "we each forge our own destiny, at least to some degree." Write a paper classifying the events in your life in which you "shaped your own destiny."

# ILLUSTRATION

## ILLUSTRATION

*Illustration,* as one dictionary says, is the "act of clarifying or explaining." It also refers to the material used to clarify or explain: the details, facts, or examples a writer employs to communicate specifics. Any time you support a generalization with evidence in the form of specific examples and details, you are using *illustration.* You can have a generalization at the paragraph-topic level, or a generalization that acts as your thesis for a paper. In either case, you must support those generalizations. But it isn't *where* you should use specifics that is important; rather it is that your evidence should be specific and convincing. As readers, we are often bored and put off by general or abstract statements. We enjoy examples and details because these give us a chance to picture situations for ourselves and to understand quickly what the writer is talking about.

### Using Specific Examples and Details

Here are a few statements—written by a student—that give a reader little to understand and nothing to picture:

> I learned very quickly last summer that there was one thing you had to understand immediately when you worked around a waterhole drilling rig: safety was the watchword. Rigs are dangerous. I had to be careful and watch my step. One of the other roustabouts forgot this, and he got badly hurt.

The student gives us a general statement: "Rigs are dangerous." However, he doesn't specify *how* they are dangerous. Why was "safety" the "watchword"? How and why did another roustabout get hurt? Here in a second draft is the passage rewritten for specificity: Notice how the writer states a generalization first, then moves to more specific examples, finally ending with a statement about *one* roustabout.

| | |
|---|---|
| *Generalization* | During the drilling operation, a *rig* is dangerous at *three times:* when the *head driller* is *breaking out, putting pipe on,* or *drilling hard.* Take *breaking out (removing pipe),* for instance. The driller *signals* when he wants his *helper* to put his *wrench* on the *pipe.* When he is ready, he will *clutch-out* and throw the *rotary table* into *reverse.* After the table begins to turn, if the helper does not take his *hands* off the *wrench* he will get his *fingers cut off* because the wrench *slams* against the *drilling mast* with the force of 200 *horsepower* behind it. One *roustabout, Billy Lawe,* got careless one day and lost *three fingers* on his *left hand.* |
| *Specific details* | |
| *Application to one person— Billy Lawe* | |

Let's look at another example of dull, uninformative writing that lacks specific material:

The Model T Ford was versatile. It could do lots of things on the farm. It provided necessary power for emergencies and other things farmers needed to do.

By contrast, Reynald M. Wik uses illustrative *specific* detail to describe the versatility of the Model T:

| | |
|---|---|
| *Generalization* | [1] On the farm the Model T proved extremely versatile. In the fall when sparks from railroad locomotives often set prairie fires, farmers would use a car to pull a walking plow to make a fire guard to control the flames. Model Ts were used as early as 1913 to fight forest fires. In butchering hogs, the power from a car could be utilized to hoist the pig out of the hot water in the scalding barrel. In the fields, Model Ts pulled hay rakes, mowers, grain binders, harrows, and hay loaders. Pickup trucks stretched woven wire, hauled water to livestock, and distributed supplies where needed. Ford trucks hauled grain to elevators, brought cattle and hogs to market, and returned from town with coal, flour, lumber, and feed. |
| *Specific details* | |
| *Specific details* | [2] To secure belt power, farmers attached pulleys to the crankshaft, or bolted them to a rear wheel to utilize the 20-horsepower motor for grinding grain, sawing wood, filling silos, churning butter, shearing sheep, pumping water, elevating grain, shelling corn, turning grindstones, and washing clothes. One ingenious fellow used the spinning rear wheel to knock the shells off walnuts. One farmer said his Model T would do everything except rock the baby to sleep or make love to the hired girl. |
| *One fellow* | |
| *One farmer* | |

Sometimes, however, specific examples and details alone do not stimulate the reader's interest. The material must also be presented vividly and vigorously so that the reader can identify with the person writing the essay. Consider Richard Wright's account of his early life. Notice how Wright uses a single example to support his paragraph lead: *My first lesson in how to live as a Negro came when I was quite small.*

1 My first lesson in how to live as a Negro came when I was quite small. We were living in Arkansas. Our house stood behind the railroad tracks. Its skimpy yard was paved with black cinders. Nothing green ever grew in that yard. The only touch of green we could see was far away, beyond the tracks, over where the white folks lived. But cinders were good enough for me and I never missed the green growing things. And anyhow cinders were fine weapons. You could always have a nice hot war with huge black cinders. All you had to do was crouch behind the brick pillars of a house with your hands full of gritty ammunition. And the first woolly black head you saw pop out from behind another row of pillars was your target. You tried your very best to knock it off. It was great fun.

2 I never fully realized the appalling disadvantages of a cinder environment till one day the gang to which I belonged found itself engaged in a war with the white boys who lived beyond the tracks. As usual we laid down our cinder barrage, thinking that this would wipe the white boys out. But they replied with a steady bombardment of broken bottles. We doubled our cinder barrage, but they hid behind trees, hedges, and the sloping embankments of their lawns. Having no such fortifications, we retreated to the brick pillars of our homes. During the retreat a broken milk bottle caught me behind the ear, opening a deep gash which bled profusely. The sight of blood pouring over my face completely demoralized our ranks. My fellow combatants left me standing paralyzed in the center of the yard and scurried for their homes. A kind neighbor saw me and rushed me to a doctor, who took three stitches in my neck.

3 I sat brooding on my front steps, nursing my wound and waiting for my mother to come from work. I felt that a grave injustice had been done me. It was all right to throw cinders. The greatest harm a cinder could do was leave a bruise. But broken bottles were dangerous; they left you cut, bleeding, and helpless.

4 When night fell, my mother came from the white folks' kitchen. I raced down the street to meet her. I could just feel in my bones that she would understand. I knew she would tell me exactly what to do next time. I grabbed her hand and babbled out the whole story. She examined my wound, then slapped me.

5 "How come yuh didn't hide?" she asked me. "How come yuh awways fightin'?"

6 I was outraged and bawled. Between sobs I told her that I didn't have any trees or hedges to hide behind. There wasn't a thing I could have used as a trench. And you couldn't throw very far when you were hiding behind the brick pillars of a house. She grabbed a barrel stave, dragged me home, stripped me naked, and beat me till I had a fever of one hundred and two. She would

smack my rump with the stave, and while the skin was still smarting, impart to me gems of Jim Crow wisdom. I was never to throw cinders any more. I was never to fight any more wars. I was never, never, under any conditions, to fight *white* folks again. And they were absolutely right in clouting me with the broken milk bottle. Didn't I know she was working hard every day in the hot kitchens of the white folks to make money to take care of me? When was I ever going to learn to be a good boy? She couldn't be bothered with my fights. She finished by telling me that I ought to be thankful to God as long as I lived that they didn't kill me.

[7] All that night I was delirious and could not sleep. Each time I closed my eyes I saw monstrous white faces suspended from the ceiling, leering at me.

[8] From that time on, the charm of my cinder yard was gone. The green trees, the trimmed hedges, the cropped lawns grew very meaningful, became a symbol. Even today when I think of white folks, the hard, sharp outlines of white houses surrounded by trees, lawns, and hedges are present somewhere in the background of my mind. Through the years they grew into an overreaching symbol of fear. —Richard Wright, *Black Boy*

The word picture Wright draws of his life as a child is so distinct and strikingly alive that readers get the impression that they are there at the scene hearing the mother's tirade and feeling the boy's pain and frustration.

No writer can create reality. He can only create the illusion of reality by choosing details, examples, and words that are strikingly alive—*vivid*. As the novelist Joseph Conrad wrote: "My task which I am trying to achieve is, by the power of the written word, to make you hear, to make you feel—it is, before all, to make you *see*."

A basic strategy in writing vividly is: Don't just *tell* your readers—*show* them, too. General statements can explain a great deal, but they are often flat and colorless in comparison to the examples and details that *show* the reader what you have in mind.

## The Representative Example

Magazines and newspapers are full of essays with titles like "The Typical College Student of the '80s," "The Workaholic in You," and "The Senior Citizen Today." In these essays, the writer gives a representative picture of a class. The writer understands that no person has all the traits described, but that it is often useful and informative to give the reader a composite picture of a particular group. We like to read such essays to see if we fit the picture. The writer of a representative example must be a keen observer of human behavior; otherwise, the picture will be unrepresentative and faulty. Following is an excerpt from an essay by Studs Terkel on the obstinate "hunger" for pride in one's work. Terkel gives three representative examples:

[1] Conditions may be horrendous, tensions high, and humiliations frequent, yet Paul Dietch finds his small triumphs. He drives his own truck, interstate, as a steel hauler. "Every load is a challenge. I have problems in the morning with heartburn. I can't eat. Once I off-load, the pressure is gone. Then I can eat anything. I accomplished something."

[2] Yolanda Leif graphically describes the trials of a waitress in a quality restaurant. They are compounded by her refusal to be demeaned. Yet pride in her skills helps her through the night. "When I put the plate down, you don't hear a sound. When I pick up a glass, I want it to be just right. When someone says, 'How come you're just a waitress?' I say, 'Don't you think you deserve being served by me?'"

[3] Peggy Terry has her own sense of pride and beauty. Her jobs have varied with geography, climate, and the ever-felt pinch of circumstance. "What I hated worst was being a waitress, the way you're treated. One guy said, 'You don't have to smile, I'm gonna give you a tip anyway.' I said, 'Keep it, I wasn't smiling for a tip.' Tipping should be done away with. It's like throwing a dog a bone. It makes you feel small."

## SUGGESTIONS FOR USING ILLUSTRATION

As you plan an essay using illustration, keep the following suggestions in mind:

1. Make sure that you use specific details and examples in your illustrations.

2. Use appropriate examples. If you are trying to show that student shoplifting exists on your campus, do not use examples of nonstudents who shoplift. Do not describe shoplifting that occurs off-campus in the downtown stores—unless that is part of your thesis.

3. Use appropriate and varied signals for your examples, but don't oversignal. You do not have to use "for example" or "another example of this is . . ." every time you introduce a new illustration. If you think your reader doesn't realize that another illustration is coming up, use a variety of signals:

> For instance . . .
> Hence . . .
> Thus . . .
> Another case . . .
> Additional evidence . . .

4. Develop some kind of order in your use of illustration.

# WRITING AND REVISING ILLUSTRATION (AN EXAMPLE)

One day, when Kathryn was out jogging, she took a rest in an old cemetery close to her college. It was a lovely fall day, so she decided to walk around and read the inscriptions on some of the gravestones and monuments. When she returned to her dormitory, she wrote about her impressions:

1 Mount Hope Cemetery was a very enjoyable place. I expected the graveyard to be less than pleasing, but I was surprised. Instead of seeing a piece of earth with dead bodies underneath and gravestones lined up like seats in a movie theatre, I found a place that made me think more of life than of death. Each gravestone, or at least each family plot, had its own personality. This gave me a feeling for the people who had died. They didn't seem like generic corpses, but rather people who had lived and done certain, unique things in their lives. This is what I caught myself thinking about as I walked through the cemetery.

2 There was a lot of life in the cemetery to take notice of. Though the trees screened the cemetery from the outside, out of the corner of my ear I could still hear traffic. Life existed inside the cemetery as well. I saw squirrels, chipmunks, birds, and insects galore. People were there jogging, and even doing their rhetoric assignments for their college course. I wouldn't say that the graveyard was absolutely bustling or anything, but it was more energetic than I expected. The foliage, too, was healthy and alive looking. The grass was green and thick, and the trees were plentiful.

3 The placement of the bushes, gravel roads, and land slopes gently separated the cemetery into small, semi-private areas. Each family had its own place which was private, yet part of the rest of the graveyard community. Each family's place had its own feeling, its own personality. One spot I remember very well. In a hollow were several graves covered by a large, old maple. The grass grew in long, thin clumps the way it does under large, old trees, and dirt predominated. All the stones in this area were dark charcoal grey, and somewhat old. It made me think of an old, sad family who perhaps had no more children who would ever visit their graves.

4 The Paro family of tree stumps was one of my favorite groups. The family name was written on a huge stone shaped like a tree trunk with an anchor leaning up against it. Surrounding this was a forest of stubby little tree-stump stones for individual members of the Paro family. The anchor interested me. What seafaring family would live in Illinois?

5 The Campbell family had a stone shaped like the Eiffel Tower which almost shone. It looked more like a monument than a gravestone. I wondered if this family had anything to do with Campbell Hospital; they seemed to be flaunting their money. Even if they couldn't take it with them, they could still show it off.

6 Other areas were more touching. A family buried a 29-year-old daughter under a Greek temple ruin. The Waters family buried a child, their "darling,"

under a small stone shaped like a scroll, covered with lichen and discolored. An ornate stone, carved to look like a tree with day lilies, trillium, lily of the valley, and ivy winding around it, covered another grave. It was green with moss, and discolored with time. I found this to be the saddest stone of all. It was small, like a child's grave, and whispered sad things about death when young. This stone was sad and depressing, and didn't have much to do with life at all, but it had the right to be sad, if someone who died young was buried beneath it. At first I reacted the same way when I saw other stones with "mother" or "father" on them, but then I realized that although I personally would not like to be remembered only as the mother of someone, at least epitaphs like this made each grave different from the others. The epitaphs showed that people had done something that others, at least, considered unique and worthwhile in their lives.

7 Mount hope was a cemetery that allowed the people buried there to retain something of their personalities. While death may make everyone equal, in Mount Hope death did not make everyone the same. Pieces of people's lives showed, even if they were very small, making each person different from the rest. I think this made the cemetery less sad. I felt better knowing that people can make a lasting impression on others. It seems to me that one of the saddest things about death is that people and what they did are so easily forgotten.

After reading her draft, Kathryn sees that not all of her paragraphs support her main point—that each gravestone or family plot in the Mount Hope cemetery gives the impression that a person who was unique is buried there.

For example, paragraph 2 is a pleasant description of a cemetery, but it doesn't do much to support her main point. Some of paragraph 3 needs to be better focused. Paragraphs 4–6 are really the only paragraphs that support her point, but they don't support it well.

As a result of her analysis, Kathryn goes back to revise the paper, tying her illustrations to her main point in a more organized, convincing fashion.

1 I expected a visit to a cemetery to be less than pleasing, but I was surprised. Paradoxically, I discovered that the cemetery made me think more about the people when they lived—in other words, think more about life than death. Each gravestone or family plot had its own "personality," giving me a feeling for the people buried there, that they had been unique in some way.

2 Mount Hope cemetery is an attractive, well-kept place. Trees, bushes, and small slopes separate the cemetery into semi-private areas. Each family has its own private place, and each family plot has its own personality. In an older part of the cemetery, a little hollow is covered by a large, old maple tree. The grass grows in long, thin clumps, typical of shady areas. All of the family stones in this area are in old, dark charcoal-grey marble. The plot is not well-kept—weeds grow among the stones, and it is evident that no one has visited for many years. The area has been neglected and makes me think of a sad family made up of two old people with no children to visit their graves.

3 At another spot in the older area of the cemetery, I saw this simple phrase

on a gravestone: "She lived for others." I could imagine a woman who was plump and rosy-cheeked, with many children to care for. Her death must have caused grief for those who had known and loved her.

⁴ Family names are important in some areas of the cemetery. Sometimes a grouping of gravestones with the family name makes a distinctive display. An example of this is the Paro family plot whose name is written on a huge stone shaped like a tree trunk. However, a peculiar addition to the tree trunk makes the monument most unusual—leaning against the trunk is an anchor. Surrounding the trunk is a forest of stubby little stone tree stumps designating the graves of individual members of the Paro family. I wondered if the anchor was a metaphorical symbol for stability and security of the main trunk of the family.

⁵ The Campbell family had a monument shaped like the Eiffel Tower that stood much higher than any other family gravestone in the cemetery. Compared with the other stones it seemed to be an ostentatious flaunting of wealth. One got the impression that the family believed if they couldn't take it with them, they could at least show it off.

⁶ One family buried a 29-year-old daughter under a monument that looked like the ruin of a Greek temple. Another family buried their child, called their "darling," under a small scroll-shaped tombstone. A small child was buried under the stone carving of a little tree with day lilies, trillium, lily of the valley, and ivy winding around it.

⁷ At first I was sad when I saw stones with "mother" or "father" carved on them. I thought that I wouldn't want to be remembered only as "the mother." However, I realized that designations like these made each grave different from the others, showing that these people had been considered special and worthwhile by their families or loved ones.

⁸ Mount Hope cemetery allows the people buried there to retain something of their uniqueness. While death may make everyone equal, in this cemetery death does not make everyone the same. I felt better knowing that people can make a lasting impression on others. It seems to me that one of the saddest things about death is that it is too easy to forget the specialness of the individual. A gravestone or burial plot may be the last place where people can be made special for those of us left behind.

## ◆ PRACTICE

### Discussion

1. Study the rewritten paper about the cemetery.
   a. Discuss the writer's use of *signals* and *examples*.
   b. Discuss the appropriateness of the examples.
   c. In what way(s) could Kathryn's essay be about other cemeteries? How is this cemetery different from others? How does the choice of examples indicate the difference or similarity?
   d. How does Kathryn use description as a means of exemplification or illustration?

*Writing*

1. Revise a paper of yours by adding vivid illustration: facts, details, and examples. Insofar as you can, avoid *telling* your readers; *show* them with specific detail—but avoid mere storytelling.

2. Write a paragraph giving a composite picture of the typical yearbook, autograph book, or picture album.

3. Write an essay in which you give at least four specific illustrations to support one of the following topics:
   a. In spite of efforts to abolish cheating, it still occurs on our campus.
   b. Photography is an expensive hobby.
   c. Collecting _____ satisfies my need for accumulating things.
   d. Old descriptions of my family do not reflect the present situation.

4. Write an essay in which you give a representative picture of a typical place or event. Suggestions:

   Amusement parks
   Recreation on campus
   Decorations in my dorm/rooming house/apartment complex
   The use of cosmetics in the 1980s

JOHN LEO

# A POX ON ALL OUR HOUSES

*John Leo is a highly respected senior writer for* U.S. News & World Report, *writing essays and cover stories on a wide range of social issues. Leo earned a B.A. with honors from the University of Toronto in 1957. He has been an associate editor for* Commonweal, *a reporter for the* New York Times, *and—before joining* U.S. News—*a senior writer for* Time *magazine for fourteen years. In more than thirty years of reporting the news, Leo has seen just about every stigma mankind has to offer—yet he has a kind word for (some) stigmas. Why?*

¹ Ed Koch, the former mayor of New York City, came out in favor of stigma the other day. He said we should probably try to revive the stigma against unwed mothers (he might have suggested a new one against absent unwed fathers, as well). This bold pro-stigma stance is a rare one. Since the Spanish Inquisition, at least, stigmatizing has had a terrible press. A Nexis computer search of recent newspapers turned up hundreds of awful stigmas, from the one against AIDS patients to the somewhat less revolting one against major-league pitchers who go only five innings. The computer uncovered stigmas against overly ignorant college jocks, careless home decoration and people with whiny voices. But there was only one stigma so positive that we can all get behind it: The stigma against chemical warfare.

² In truth, stigmatization is the normal stuff of politics, from John Tower's troubles to former President Reagan's attempts to stigmatize and then destigmatize the "Evil Empire." Stigma contests, which clarify and define social values, go on all the time in every community, at every level.

³ An example of a recently concluded stigma contest is smoking. The battle is over and the antismokers have won. The burning and inhaling of dead plant matter will continue, but it is now a defiant, rear-guard activity, best undertaken in a spirit of sheepishness or shame. Now officially stigmatized, smokers are exposed to a level of harassment that would have been considered shocking three or four years ago. Ashtrays are vanishing. Lighting up anywhere is likely to draw a withering glance. Studies will continue to find that smoking a cigar, even in an open field on a breezy day, endangers the lives of innocent children for miles around. More and more pressure and regulations will be brought to bear on tobacco addicts. That is the way stigma works. And in this case, it will save many thousands of lives.

⁴ Another duel that is currently going well for the stigmatizers revolves around animal rights. The fur industry is very vulnerable because it is not in a position to mount a serious counterargument. Furs are not necessities,

just status symbols, and such symbols change with blinding speed in America. Yesterday's glamorous mink wearer is tomorrow's accomplice in the mass murder of tiny furry creatures. Even though the issue has not yet burst full-blown upon the nation's consciousness, chances are that the animal-rights folks will win this contest fairly quickly, maybe in two or three years. Designers such as Bill Blass have already stopped making things with fur. Wealthy women are sneaking out the back of fur salons. How long can such furtive departures be associated with high status?

5 The main reason that the animal-rights people will win big is that the cause plays well on television. Researchers who experiment on animals have a serious case to make, but it is an abstract one: Your child's life may be saved by this dead monkey. Their arguments won't be able to stand up to all that horrendous film of bound animals, convulsed and screaming. Small-game hunting will very likely survive the animal-rights victory, and a drastically reduced amount of animal experimentation will take place under severe restriction, but prepare for a moving *Zeitgeist.* The '90s will not be a good time to invest in mounted animal heads, start a circus or even plan a municipal zoo. Stigma will forbid it.

6 Mothers Against Drunk Driving has taken a light stigma and converted it into a very heavy one. Alcohol may or may not be losing its glamour, but drunkenness has been stigmatized rather quickly, going from something humorous or cute just a decade ago to a strange loss of control. It is hard to watch the old Thin Man movies in quite the same way. William Powell's dawn-to-dusk martini drinking, played for laughs, now just seems pathetic.

7 Gay activists have turned a severe stigma into a much milder one. This long-running contest has now stabilized. On the whole, the straight majority has no stomach for isolating or penalizing gays, but it is not willing to grant that homosexual behavior has the same value and meaning as normal heterosexual sex. A gay male wrote to the *Village Voice* that he wants people to smile when they see him holding hands with his lover on the street. Smiles like this are unlikely to be extracted from most straights for the foreseeable future. The logic of this position, which offers tolerance but not approval, is a faint stigma. Gay-rights laws are now controversial only because many straights consider them exercises in stigma removal.

8 Efforts to stigmatize drug taking have always run afoul of the '60s generation and its tendency to identify drugs with liberation and, now, nostalgia. At the moment, the issue is not greatly relevant. The drug destroying us is crack, and it is consumed by people not known to respond well to middle-class stigma contests. For what it's worth, however, the snorting of cocaine may be about to join freebasing and heroin use as stigmatized pursuits. When the party-going novelist Jay McInerney says he no longer knows anybody who uses coke, this can be taken as a bulletin from the coke frontier.

9 Abortion is the most dramatic stigma contest now being fought. But there are also dozens of low-level skirmishes going on, such as attempts to

restigmatize debt and to invent a brand-new stigma to cover the more rapacious expressions of greed. The first order of business, though, is to destigmatize stigma. In a sensible world, Ed Koch and opponents of poison gas should not be out there all alone defending this perfectly natural and healthy process. Any behavior that weakens and disorders social life is ripe for reform. And the first step is often sticking it with stigma.

## ◆ PRACTICE

### Discussion

1. The term *stigma* in the essay is all-important. What does it mean? A fact that you won't find explained in detail in some dictionaries is that originally the word referred to a brand in the flesh of a criminal, slave, or prisoner. It could be cut into the flesh or burned in with an iron.

2. Explain the structure of paragraphs 2 and 3.

3. At the end of paragraph 1, Leo says that "only one stigma [is] so positive that we can all get behind it: The stigma against chemical warfare." Can you think of any other stigmas in America that are equally positive?

4. What and where is the thesis of the essay? Defend or attack its location.

5. Do the illustrations in the essay support the thesis? Explain.

6. Explain the job of the paragraph *leads* in paragraphs 3–4 and 6–8. (The lead is the first sentence of a paragraph.)

7. In his introduction, Leo seems to imply that this essay will be about unwed mothers and fathers—but it isn't. Did Leo mislead his readers?

8. Leo does not use a *representative example* (p. 249) in his essay. Why?

### Vocabulary

| | | |
|---|---|---|
| sheepishness | stomach (par. 7) | skirmish |
| furtive | nostalgia | rapacious |
| *Zeitgeist* | freebasing | |

### Writing

1. Pick (a) a topic (an idea, activity, or type of person) that you would like to see stigmatized; or (b) an idea, etc., that you would like to see destigmatized. Write a paper supporting your point of view. Use illustration as much as you can.

2. What stigma in America is presently undergoing change? Explain your answer, using illustrations.

3. Despite the many angry calls by Americans for a stigma against violence and sex in movies and TV, no real national stigma has formed against their use. Explain why this is true.

BOB GREENE

# UNWRITTEN RULES CIRCUMSCRIBE OUR LIVES

*Born in 1947 in Columbus, Ohio, Bob Greene writes a daily column for the* Chicago Tribune *which is widely syndicated in the United States and abroad. His regular column for* Esquire *magazine, where he is contributing editor, is called "American Beat," and he has been featured in* Newsweek *and* Rolling Stone *as well as on network radio and television. Among his books are* Running: A Nixon-McGovern Campaign Journal *(1973) and* Johnny Deadline, Reporter: The Best of Bob Greene *(1976). The following essay, one of Greene's* Chicago Tribune *columns, typifies Greene's accustomed stance and subject: the factual, yet broadly emotional Midwesterner looking around at his fellow Americans.*

[1] The restaurant was almost full. A steady hum of conversation hung over the room; people spoke with each other and worked on their meals.

[2] Suddenly, from a table near the center of the room, came a screaming voice:

[3] "Damn it, Sylvia. . . ."

[4] The man was shouting at the top of his voice. His face was reddened, and he yelled at the woman sitting opposite him for about 15 seconds. In the crowded restaurant, it seemed like an hour. All other conversation in the room stopped, and everyone looked at the man. He must have realized this, because as abruptly as he had started, he stopped; he lowered his voice and finished whatever it was he had to say in a tone the rest of us could not hear.

[5] It was startling precisely because it almost never happens; there are no laws against such an outburst, and with the pressures of our modern world you would almost expect to run into such a thing on a regular basis. But you don't; as a matter of fact, when I thought about it I realized that it was the first time in my life I had witnessed such a demonstration. In all the meals I have had in all the restaurants, I had never seen a person start screaming at the top of his lungs.

[6] When you are eating among other people, you do not raise your voice; it is just an example of the unwritten rules we live by. When you consider it, you recognize that those rules probably govern our lives on a more absolute basis than the ones you could find if you looked in the lawbooks. The customs that govern us are what make a civilization; there

would be chaos without them, and yet for some reason—even in the disintegrating society of the 80s—we obey them.

7 How many times have you been stopped at a red light late at night? You can see in all directions; there is no one else around—no headlights, no police cruiser idling behind you. You are tired and you are in a hurry. But you wait for the light to change. There is no one to catch you if you don't, but you do it anyway. Is it for safety's sake? No; you can see that there would be no accident if you drove on. Is it to avoid getting arrested? No; you are alone. But you sit and wait.

8 At major athletic events, it is not uncommon to find 80,000 or 90,000 or 100,000 people sitting in the stands. On the playing field are two dozen athletes; maybe fewer. There are nowhere near enough security guards on hand to keep the people from getting out of their seats and walking onto the field en masse. But it never happens. Regardless of the emotion of the contest, the spectators stay in their places, and the athletes are safe in their part of the arena. The invisible barrier always holds.

9 In restaurants and coffee shops, people pay their checks. A simple enough concept. Yet it would be remarkably easy to wander away from a meal without paying at the end. Especially in these difficult economic times, you might expect that to become a common form of cheating. It doesn't happen very often. For whatever the unwritten rules of human conduct are, people automatically make good for their meals. They would no sooner walk out on a check than start screaming.

10 Restrooms are marked "Men" and "Women." Often there are long lines at one or another of them, but males wait to enter their own washrooms, and women to enter theirs. In an era of sexual egalitarianism, you would expect impatient people to violate this rule on occasion; after all, there are private stalls inside, and it would be less inconvenient to use them than to wait. In Cleveland—why Cleveland I don't know—this custom has begun to change. At public events in Cleveland it is not unusual to find women getting out of line at the women's restroom and walking into the men's room. Elsewhere it just isn't done. People obey the signs.

11 Even criminals obey the signs. I once covered a murder which centered around that rule being broken. A man wanted to harm a woman— which woman apparently didn't matter. So he did the simplest thing possible. He went to a public park and walked into a restroom marked "Women"—the surest place to find what he wanted. He found it. He attacked with a knife the first woman to come in there. Her husband and young child waited outside, and the man killed her. Such a crime is not commonplace, even in a world grown accustomed to nastiness. Even the most evil elements of our society generally obey the unspoken rule: If you are not a woman, you do not go past a door marked "Women."

12 I know a man who, when he pulls his car up to a parking meter, will put change in the meter even if there is time left on it. He regards it as the right thing to do; he says he is not doing it just to extend the time

remaining—even if there is sufficient time on the meter to cover whatever task he has to perform at the location, he will pay his own way. He believes that you are supposed to purchase your own time; the fellow before you purchased only his.

[13] I knew another man who stole tips at bars. It was easy enough; when the person sitting next to this man would depart for the evening and leave some silver or a couple dollars for the bartender, this guy would wait until he thought no one was looking and then sweep the money over in front of him. The thing that made it unusual is that I never knew anyone else who even tried this; the rules of civility stated that you left someone else's tip on the bar until it got to the bartender, and this man stood out because he refused to comply.

[14] There are so many rules like these—rules we all obey—that we think about them only when that rare person violates them. In the restaurant, after the man had yelled "Damn it, Sylvia" and had then completed his short tirade, there was a tentative aura among the other diners for half-an-hour after it happened. They weren't sure what disturbed them about what they had witnessed; they knew, though, that it violated something very basic about the way we are supposed to behave. And it bothered them—which in itself is a hopeful sign that things, more often than not, are well.

## ◆ PRACTICE

### Discussion

1. Is Greene too optimistic? Among the basic rules that Greene uses as examples, can you spot any that you think are broken more often than he suggests? What examples can you give of their being broken?

2. Several of Greene's examples occur in the same sort of place. What is it? Why do you think we tend to behave ourselves there?

3. What additional examples can you offer of unwritten rules that circumscribe our lives? What examples can you offer of similar rules, formerly unbroken, that are now flagrantly ignored? Does your second list alarm you as much as Greene suggests it might? Explain.

4. What is the ratio of paragraphs containing illustrations to those explaining Greene's theory? What would be the effect of reversing the ratio? Of balancing the ratio?

5. Where does Greene move smoothly from one paragraph to the next? How does he do it in each case? Where does he not even try? How does he get away with it there without seeming abrupt?

6. An illustration may also, within itself, employ another strategy of de-

velopment. Which of Greene's illustrations is also a narration? Which is an explanation of a process? Which discusses cause and effect? What other strategies can you spot in the essay?

7. Does Greene use simple sentences, compound sentences, or complex sentences most often? Does this general habit change in the final paragraph? Does it vary anywhere else?

8. How does Greene use the first, second, and third person pronouns in his essay? How does his *I/you* contribute to his thesis of social agreement?

### Vocabulary

| | | |
|---|---|---|
| disintegrating | civility | tentative |
| en masse | tirade | aura |
| egalitarianism | | |

### Writing

1. Write the mirror image of Greene's essay—that is, using mostly illustration—showing that our breaking of unwritten social rules presages the break-up of our civilization.

2. Use illustrations from a variety of contemporary experiences to present a theory you hold about today's society.

3. Rewrite Greene's essay so that it addresses the same issue of social order but set in the context of (for example) Rome just before the fall, America just before the Revolution, or your particular school now.

*JAN HAROLD BRUNVAND*

# URBAN LEGENDS

*In 1966, Jan Harold Brunvand was still wet behind his folklorist's ears, as he acknowl-edges in "Urban Legends." That year he began teaching folklore at the University of Utah in Salt Lake City, where he is currently professor of English. He is also editor of the* Journal of American Folklore *and has written three books on the subject, so his ears have dried out but his enthusiasm for folklore clearly flourishes. A longer version of "Urban Legends," adapted from his book* Urban American Legends, *appeared in* Psychology Today *magazine in June 1980. The illustrations that Brunvand scatters liberally throughout his essay are like salted peanuts: They whet your appetite for more.*

[1] "A man in California saw an ad for an 'almost new' Porsche, in excellent condition—price, $50. He was certain the printers had made a typographical error, but even at $5,000 it would be a bargain, so he hurried to the address to look at the car. A nice-looking woman appeared at the front door. Yes, she had placed the ad. The price was indeed $50. 'The car is in the garage,' she said. 'Come and look at it.' The fellow was over-whelmed. It was a beautiful Porsche and, as the ad promised, nearly new. He asked if he could drive the car around the block. The woman said, 'of course,' and went with him. The Porsche drove like a dream. The young man peeled off $50 and handed it over, somewhat sheepishly. The woman gave him the necessary papers, and the car was his. Finally, the new owner couldn't stand it any longer. He had to know why the woman was selling the Porsche at such a ridiculously low price. Her reply was simple: with a half-smile, she said, 'My husband ran off with his secretary and left a note instructing me to sell the car and send him the money.'"

[2] This story, which has been in circulation for years, turned up in a recent Ann Landers colunn. It was sent in by a reader who claimed to have seen it in the *Chicago Tribune*. Ann Landers accepted the story as true, and many of her readers probably did also. But when she checked with the *Chicago Tribune*, the paper could find no actual record of it.

[3] The story seems believable at first, but when you stop to think about it, wouldn't a man running off with his secretary do so in his own Porsche? And if not, would he really trust his abandoned wife to sell such a car to help finance his departure?

[4] Many people have heard stories of this kind and accepted them as true accounts of actual experiences. But scholars of contemporary Ameri-can folklore recognize tales like "The Philanderer's Porsche" as charac-teristic examples of what they call "urban legends." ("Urban," as used by folklorists in this case, means "modern," and is not specifically related to

cities.) Other widely known urban legends have titles such as "The Boyfriend's Death," "The Snake in the K-Mart," and "The Solid Cement Cadillac."

[5] Urban legends are realistic stories that are said to have happened recently. Like old legends of lost mines, buried treasure, and ghosts, they usually have an ironic or supernatural twist. They belong to a subclass of folk narratives that (unlike fairy tales) are believed—or at least believable—and (unlike myths) are set in the recent past, involving ordinary human beings rather than extraordinary gods and demigods.

[6] Unlike rumors, which are generally fragmentary or vague reports, legends have a specific narrative quality and tend to attach themselves to different local settings. Although they may explain or incorporate current rumors, legends tend to have a longer life and wider acceptance; rumors flourish and then die out rather quickly. Urban legends circulate, by word of mouth, among the "folk" of modern society, but the mass media frequently help to disseminate and validate them. While they vary in particular details from one telling to another, they preserve a central core of traditional themes. In some instances, these seemingly fresh stories are merely updatings of classic folklore plots, while other urban legends spring directly from recent conditions and then develop their own traditional patterns in repeated retellings. For example, "The Vanishing Hitchhiker," which describes the disappearance of a rider picked up on a highway, has evolved from a 19th-century horse-and-buggy legend into modern variants incorporating freeway travel. A story called "Alligators in the Sewers," on the other hand, goes back no further than the 1930s and seems to be a New York City invention. Often, it begins with people who bring pet baby alligators back from Florida and eventually flush them down the drains.

[7] What most interests the modern folklorist is *why* these stories recur. We suspect that the reasons will tell us something about the character of the society in which they circulate.

[8] One genre of urban legend is the horror story, which seems to appeal particularly to American adolescents. Consider the well-known legend that folklorists have named "The Boyfriend's Death." The version below might typically be told in a darkened college dormitory room with fellow students sprawled on the furniture and floor:

[9] *"This happened just a few years ago out on the road that turns off Highway 59 by the Holiday Inn. This couple was parked under a tree out on this road. Well, it got to be time for the girl to be back at the dorm, so she told her boyfriend that they should start back. But the car wouldn't start, so he told her to lock herself in the car and he would go down to the Holiday Inn and call for help. Well, he didn't come back and he didn't come back, and pretty soon she started hearing a scratching noise on the roof of the car. Scratch, scratch . . . scratch, scratch. She got scareder and scareder, but he didn't come back. Finally, when it was almost daylight, some people came along and stopped and helped her out of the car, and she looked up and there was her boyfriend hanging from the tree, and his feet were scraping against the roof of the car."*

[10] Here is a story that has rapidly achieved nationwide oral circulation, in the process becoming structured in the typical manner of folk narratives. The traditional and fairly stable elements in it are the parked couple, the abandoned girl, the mysterious scratching, the daybreak rescue, and the horrible climax. The precise location, the reason for her abandonment, the nature of the rescuers, and the murder details may vary. For example, the rescuers may be the police, who are either called by the missing teens' parents or simply appear on the scene in the morning to check the car. In a 1969 variant from Maryland, the police utter this warning: "Miss, please get out of the car and walk to the police car with us, but don't look back." Of course the standard rule of folk-narrative plot development now applies: the taboo must be broken. The girl *does* always look back, à la Orpheus in the Underworld, and her hair may turn white from the shock of what she sees.

[11] The style in which such oral narratives are told deserves attention, for a telling that is dramatic, fluid and possibly quite gripping in actual performance before a sympathetic audience may seem stiff, repetitious, and awkward when simply read. The setting of the legend-telling also plays a vital role, along with the storyteller's vocal and facial expression, gestures, and the audience's reactions.

[12] However, even the bare texts retain some earmarks of effective oral performance. In "The Boyfriend's Death," notice the artful use of repetition (typical of folk-narrative style): "Well, he didn't come back and he didn't come back. . . ." The repeated use of "well" and the building of lengthy sentences with "and" are also hallmarks of oral style that give the narrator control over his performance and tend to squeeze out interruptions or lapses in attention among listeners. The scene that is set for the incident—lonely road, night, a tree looming over a car out of gas—and the sound effects—scratches or bumps on the car—all contribute to the style.

[13] Many urban legends preserve the basic shock effect of classic ghost stories or horror tales. They play on the fears of physical assault or of contamination. Another significant group of legends depends on soap-opera plots rather than on scare stories. In these tales, the characters are merely threatened with the discovery of a supposed infidelity or with having their naked bodies exposed, both of which they fear will amount to public proof of their foolishness.

[14] Sometimes the situation is clearly one of dalliance, with someone getting caught in the act—or at least caught in preparing for the act. So realistic are the plots and so ordinary the characters that it seems completely possible not only that such adventures *could* have happened but also that they could in fact happen again to anyone.

[15] I was taken in by one of these stories myself when I was still wet behind my folklorist's ears: I eventually christened it "The Solid Cement Cadillac." One day in the early summer of 1961, proud of my freshly earned Ph.D. in folklore, I lounged on a beach along Lake Michigan with family and friends and daydreamed about my first teaching job. A neigh-

bor of my parents began to tell us about a funny incident that she said had happened recently to a cement-truck driver in Kalamazoo. Her story soon had my full attention:

16 *"It seems that the truck driver was delivering a load of wet mix to an address near his own neighborhood one day when he decided to detour slightly and say hello to his wife. When he came in sight of his home, he saw a shiny new Cadillac in the driveway, and so he parked the ready-mix truck and walked around the house to check things out. Voices were heard coming from the kitchen; when he peeped in through the window, there was his wife talking to a strange man. Without checking any further, and certainly without alerting the couple inside, the truck driver proceeded to lower a window of the new Cadillac, and he emptied the entire load of wet cement into it, filling the car completely. But when he got off work that evening and returned home, his tearful wife informed him that the new (now solid cement) car was for him—bought with her own hardearned savings—and that the stranger was merely the local Cadillac dealer who had just delivered the car and was arranging the papers on it with her."*

17 I made a mental note of the story, for even though it seemed to have some details that could be corroborated (police had been called, a wrecking company towed the car away, the name of the cement company had been mentioned), it surely had the ring of other urban legends I had heard and studied. For example, I wondered how one of those big, noisy, ready-mix trucks could have parked right outside a house—let alone unloaded—without attracting attention from the two people who were chatting quietly inside.

18 Later that summer, I received the first issue of the *Oregon Folklore Bulletin* and read this notice: "An interesting story is presently circulating in all parts of the United States. It is told as if it were right out of last week's newspaper, and concerns a cement-truck driver who stops by his own house for a midmorning cup of coffee while on the way to deliver a load. But when he drives down his street he notices a flashy car parked in front of his house, and . . ."

19 The only variation is the story as reported from Oregon turned out to be that the driver "finds his wife and a strange man in a compromising situation and sees that he is a bit too late to intervene successfully." In the next two issues of the *Oregon Folklore Bulletin*, the editor reported on his findings about the cement-truck driver story. He described "a plethora of versions mailed from all over the country," and in the third issue of the *Bulletin* provided a summary of 43 versions then on file. The majority of the accounts contained supposed authenticating details about police, tow trucks, or newspaper reports, but no really solid documentation was ever offered. The make and model of the car varied, of course, but only two other significant changes were reported: a Utah version had it that the car belonged to the company boss who had come around to set up a surprise party for the driver for faithful service to the company; in Massachusetts the car was said to be one that the wife had just won in a raffle.

<sup>20</sup> American folklorists did not pay much further attention to the story, except to record it regularly from their students and acquaintances. Like many urban legends, it tends to run in unpredictable cycles of popularity. Its continued appeal clearly derives from the belief that philandering spouses should "get what they deserve," a viewpoint tempered with the warning that a person ought to be absolutely sure of the evidence before doing something drastic. Thus, the truck driver, who looks like a decisive, aggressive, he-man hero at first, is shown up finally as an impulsive dummy who jumped to an incomplete conclusion before making his move.

<sup>21</sup> A great mystery of folklore research is where oral traditions originate and who invents them. One might expect that, at least in modern folklore, we could come up with answers to such questions, but that is seldom, if ever, the case. Most leads pointing to possible authors or original events lying behind urban legends simply fizzle out.

<sup>22</sup> Whatever their origins, the dissemination process is no mystery. Groups of age-mates, especially adolescents, form one important legend channel; other paths of transmission include gatherings of office workers and club members, or religious, recreational, and regional groups, like the Ozark hill folk or the Pennsylvania Dutch. Some people seem to specialize in knowing every recent rumor or tale and can enliven any coffee break, party, or trip with the latest supposed news. The telling of one episode inspires other people to share what they have read or heard, and in a short time, a lively exchange of details occurs, with new variants often created.

<sup>23</sup> The difficulties in tracing a story can be illustrated by "The Snake at K-Mart," an urban legend involving a modern suburban discount store. A dangerous creature is discovered in an unexpected place; this time it's a poisonous snake which supposedly strikes an unaware shopper who is looking at some imported rugs, blankets, or sweaters in the store.

<sup>24</sup> Although there are dozens of oral versions of "The Snake at K-Mart," a news story in the *Dallas Morning News* (1970) illustrates the hopeless circular quest for origins that anyone hoping to track down such an urban legend as this is likely to undergo:

<sup>25</sup> *"'I'd like some information,' a male caller told the* Dallas News *City Desk some weeks ago. It seems he'd heard about a woman who had gone to a local discount store to look at some fur coats imported from Mexico. When the woman put her hand in the coat pocket, she felt a sudden, sharp pain. A few minutes later her arm supposedly had started turning black and blue.*

<sup>26</sup> *"'Well,' the man continued, 'they rushed her to the hospital. It seems that pain was a snake in the coat pocket. The woman's arm had to be amputated.'*

<sup>27</sup> *"The reporter said he'd check the story. About that time a woman called with the same story, only she'd heard the woman had died right in Presbyterian Hospital's emergency ward. Presbyterian Hospital said it had no such case on record.*

<sup>28</sup> *"'My brother is a doctor,' another caller explained. 'He's on the staff at Baylor Hospital, and he was present when they brought the woman in.'*

<sup>29</sup> *"Baylor Hospital said it had no such case on record. Nor did the police or the*

*health department. When the doctor was questioned, he said it wasn't actually he who was present but a friend. The friend explained that he had not been present either, but that he had just overheard two nurses talking about it.*

[30] *"After about 10 calls from other 'interested' persons the fur coat turned into some material that had come in from India.*

[31] *"One man gave the name of the insurance company that was handling the case. The insurance man said it wasn't actually his company, but his next door neighbor's cousin's company.*

[32] *"Finally, a caller came up with the victim's name. The* News *called and the supposed victim answered the phone. She said she had never been in better health. Someone must have confused her with someone else, but she had heard the rumor. Only she had heard the snake was found in a basket of fruit."* (Probably only in Texas would so many people believe that fur coats may be purchased in discount stores.)

[33] For a folklorist—unlike a journalist—the purpose of trying to trace an urban legend is not merely to validate or debunk a good story. For us, collecting a story's variations and tracing its dissemination and change through time and across space are only the beginning of an analysis. The larger theme in "The Snake at K-Mart" is the fear of danger or contamination of commercial products, as with "The Mouse in the Coke Bottle" or "The Rat in the Fried Chicken." This theme seems to grow out of the widespread anxiety about a multitude of health risks in our environment, many of them possibly caused by individual or corporate negligence. The legend sounds plausible and serves effectively as a warning against the dangers that may be lurking in terrific bargains, fast-food restaurants, and cheap goods from underdeveloped countries.

[34] Along with the best-known urban legends, which circulate over a wide territory (including other countries) in various well-wrought versions, there are numerous other fragmentary rumors and stories going around—sometimes only within a specific folk group. Some of these are takeoffs on older traditional themes that come alive again suddenly after years of inactivity. Others may have intense local or regional life for a time, but fail to catch on with the general public, usually because they are too much the esoteric possession of a particular ethnic or occupational group.

[35] It is tempting to take one or two of the most typical examples of urban legends as inclusive symbols of distinctive aspects of our recent history. "The Snake in the K-Mart," some have suggested, draws on our guilt stemming from the war in Vietnam and implies that the venomous intentions we fear Asian peoples may feel toward us take the form of revenge via imported goods. Personally, I see the story simply as a new twist on the old theme of xenophobia.

[36] Without denying that such themes may be implied, I believe that a great deal of the legends' continuing popularity might be explained much more simply. Goods *are* imported in quantity from some countries that

have tropical climates: what if a snake or snake eggs got into them (as insects sometimes stow away in fruit shipments)?

[37] In any age or with any subject, when a skilled oral storyteller begins to play around with such ideas and when members of the audience respond, repeat the stories, and begin to add their own flourishes, such legends will begin to be formed and to circulate. I expect to hear many more examples of the old favorite urban legends in the coming years and to hear many more new ones as well. And I expect that these stories will continue to suggest how people believe things have happened, or how they either hope—or fear—that things *could* happen.

# ◆ PRACTICE

### Discussion

1. How are urban legends different from other categories of folklore? What characteristics do they share with all folklore?

2. Why are folklorists interested in studying urban legends? How do they go about their work and share their findings? How is it significant that this essay appeared in *Psychology Today*?

3. What part do the media play in the urban legends? How do reporters and folklorists differ in their approaches to stories?

4. Although this essay appears in the section on illustration, Brunvand uses several strategies of development. Name three other strategies and cite the section of the essay where each is used.

5. What general categories of urban legends does Brunvand's essay explore? List the categories in order. What ordering principle can you perceive? Is the first illustration in or out of order? Would you change it? Why?

6. Brunvand speaks in several voices in this essay. Where does he sound like a college student? Like a teacher? Like a sociologist? Where does he use a traditional folk saying to give a lively introduction to a story about himself? How does he prevent all these voices from confusing the reader?

7. Which is more important, setting or characterization, in "The Philanderer's Porsche"? In "The Boyfriend's Death"? In "The Solid Cement Cadillac"? In each case, why? What stylistic device do they share?

8. Compare the length of and number of illustrations in this essay and the one by Bob Greene. How do you account for the differences?

*Vocabulary*

| | | |
|---|---|---|
| typographical | genre | plethora |
| philanderer | Orpheus | debunk |
| demigods | dalliance | esoteric |
| disseminate | corroborated | xenophobia |

*Writing*

1. Write out three or four urban legends with which you are familiar. Be a skilled storyteller. As Brunvand describes in his final paragraph, "play around with [the] ideas . . . and [your] own flourishes."

2. Identify a theme in some of the graffiti you have seen or can gather, and write an essay on the ideas or feelings that drive those particular scribblings. Illustrate liberally.

3. Examine folklore publications and identify some common interests of folklorists besides urban legends. Write an essay about the work of folklorists. Use illustrations from the publications you studied.

# *DEFINITION*

## *DEFINITION*

Any example of how you intend to use a word or phrase can be called a *definition*. If you clarify a usage which is common or customary, as in dictionary definitions, you give what is called a *reported definition*. The reported definition of *follower* is someone who believes (or follows) another's creed, doctrine, or teachings. If, on the other hand, you give the term a special usage in the context of your discussion, you have created a *stipulative definition*. Tom, the student who classified boys as *leaders, followers,* and *obstructionists* (see p. 225), stipulated his use of *followers* to mean *those boys attending summer camp who do what the leader expects, but who seldom act on their own initiative.*

It is often necessary to define terms beyond a one-sentence definition. Abstract terms, for example, require more attention. Sometimes you may want to deal with traditional ideas in a different way. Or you may wish to take a special view of a subject—and will then need to clarify your terms. So used, definition becomes one of the major methods of developing a subject, and can even be a full-length paper, if you find that the subject is large enough to warrant that much space. *Definition* can be both a method of developing a subject and a subject itself.

Consider this paragraph:

> Mysteries are about *understanding;* thrillers are about *winning.* In a mystery you are never really sure who the villain is or what he is up to until the end of the book (and sometimes not even then if you have not read carefully). In a thriller you usually know what the villain wants and how he plans to get it. Often you know perfectly well how the story will end—Germany will lose World War II, de Gaulle will not be assassinated, New York will not be destroyed by the nuclear device in the closet in the Pan Am Building. The

tension comes from trying to figure out how the hero will avert disaster and survive. The task of the mystery-writer is to make you share a detective's curiosity, whereas the thriller-writer must make you share a hero's fear.

—Ken Follett, "A Moscow Mystery"

In this paragraph, we find many of the typical characteristics and uses of definition:

1. Definition works in a context of an event, situation, problem, etc. Ken Follett, in his book review of a mystery novel, clarifies his position on the differences between a mystery and a thriller in order to make his review more persuasive.

2. Definition clarifies an ambiguous situation by explaining the key term (or terms) your essay is based on. You ordinarily define in order to support a thesis convincingly and to get your reader to see the point you are making. In the article from which the paragraph is taken, Follett adopts the role of a book reviewer who tries to persuade his readers that this book is, indeed, a mystery novel, not a thriller, as the book's publishers have advertised it.

3. Definition explains, limits, and specifies. The rest of this section shows you how this is done.

4. Definition is a part of the writer's attempt to give a truthful account of what a thing, act, or idea is really like. Defining is another strategy for getting at the truth.

## Techniques of Defining

Now that you know something about definition, here are five practical techniques for getting the ordinary jobs of defining done. We will keep our discussion of each quite brief. All of them could be expanded by adding more examples and details.

### Definition by Classification (Logical Definition)

In defining by classification, you put the term to be defined in its *class* (of things, people, activities, or ideas). Then you explain how the term *differs* from other terms in the same class. Examples:

| *Term* | *Class* | *Differences* |
|---|---|---|
| Epic [is] | narrative poetry | "of exalted style, celebrating heroic ventures, mythical or historical, in poems of considerable length." |
| | | —*Oxford Companion to Classical Literature* |

| Bucket [is] | a domestic carrying utensil | deep and round, with a curved handle that fits into the hand, used for carrying fluids, especially water or milk. |
|---|---|---|
| Liberty [is] | a human condition, mainly political and mainly negative | that has to do with those freedoms that are neither social, nor religious, nor private; it consists simply of being let alone by the people who have the temporary powers of government. |

For logical definitions to be useful, neither class nor differences should be too broadly stated. The class for epic is *narrative poetry*, not simply *poetry*. The class for bucket is *domestic carrying utensil*, not just *domestic utensil* or *carrying utensil*. The list of differences should be complete enough so that the term is clearly distinguished from other terms.

## Definition by Negation

This method of definition explains what something is not. A *bucket* is not a "scoop." *Cool* is not "hot." *Liberty* does not mean "license." *Education* has little to do with "training." Negative definitions are useful because they allow you to narrow your general area of definition. You can use them at the beginning of an extended definition to cut out areas of meaning you do not want to deal with, as the student-writer does in this definition of the slang term *rhubarb:*

> Anyone who has ever attended a major league baseball game knows what a *rhubarb* is. For those of you who are not sports fans, you must understand that a rhubarb is not the plant from the buckwheat family. Neither is it the stalk of the pie plant from which your grandmother made sauce or pastries. Instead, it is a term used to describe the heated discussion that occurs between a baseball player (or the manager) and the umpire over a close call in baseball.

## Definition by Illustration or Example

You can sometimes employ, implicitly or explicitly, *illustration* or *example* to aid in your definition. That is, you can define a thing by giving an example of it. What is an epic poem? *The Iliad, The Odyssey,* and *Paradise Lost* are examples. What do I mean by "a great baseball player"? I mean someone like Joe DiMaggio or Fernando Valenzuela. Defining by illustration or example gives you a simple but incomplete meaning; consequently, you should use this method with at least one of the others.

## Definition by Synonym

There are no perfect synonyms. Every word is at least slightly different from every other word. But it is possible to define a word by using another word that is similar in meaning. Examples: A *herald* is a "forerunner." *Honor,* in various senses, may be "homage," "reverence," or "deference." *Cool* may mean "composed," "collected," "unruffled," "nonchalant," "unfriendly," or "not warm." Like defining by illustration or example, this is a specialized approach that you should ordinarily use with at least one of the other methods.

### Definition by Operation

You define by operation when you state what something does or how it works: A bucket is a round, deep container, hung from a curved handle, that is used for carrying water, milk, or other materials. Liberty allows one to say or do what he pleases without injuring others. Education is an attempt to discipline the mind so that it can act intelligently on its own.

If sufficiently detailed, the operational definition is valuable because it gives you a practical check on the reality or truth behind a definition. For example, the word *traitor* has been defined as "someone who deserts his country." This is a limited operational definition. But the definition does not take into account the possibility that one's country might be, like certain dictatorships, deserving of desertion. This last idea gives us an *operational check* on the definition of *traitor* and allows us to add a clause to the definition: A traitor "is someone who deserts his country when his country both needs and deserves his allegiance." Observe that the added clause is itself operational. If someone does not accept our operational check on the definition of *traitor,* we can ask him to provide his own check, and then we can argue the matter with him.

## Avoiding Errors in Defining

Many errors are caused by the writer's not limiting a definition sufficiently. Consider this definition, which is both logical and operational: "A belt is a thing that a man wears around his waist to keep his trousers up." As a class, *thing* is not limited enough, for it does not take into account what sort of "thing" a belt may be. One can hold up his pants with rope, but that fact does not make the rope a belt. On the other hand, the rest of the definition is too limited because it does not take into account that women often wear belts to hold up "trousers" and that belts have many other uses. The process of limiting in the logical definition should be done in two steps—first limit the *class,* then limit the *differences.*

Perhaps the commonest errors in defining are made by writers who do not realize that their definitions must fit reality. The final question to ask yourself is: Am I telling the truth about this word? If you define *monarchy* as a "contemporary government ruled by a king for his own selfish purposes," you are in danger of being untruthful; for this definition would fit badly, to give only one example, the English constitutional monarchy. The writer who defined *individualism* as "the need of every person to be honored by others" not only blurred the meaning of *individualism* but also stated an untruth about the nature of an important idea. If a student defines *fraternity* epigrammatically as "a snob co-op," is he really being truthful about the fraternities on his campus and about fraternity life in general? The fraternity man may answer that the definition does not fit fraternity life as he knows it, that the definition is not "true." This does not mean that the point is unarguable; it means rather that the students are going to have to agree on the reality behind their definitions before they can get anywhere with their debate.

Observe how a student used a variety of techniques of defining to help her explain the term *ad-lib:*

| | |
|---|---|
| **Introduction** | [1] There is nothing more frightening to the amateur in the theater—at least to me—than to forget my lines. After weeks of rehearsal, with my lines seemingly embedded forever in my subconscious, I cannot conceive of forgetting them. However, all actors occasionally forget a line. Then what they do is to think up another one, called an *ad-lib*. An ad-lib is a made-up response to a cue when the actor has forgotten the playwright's words. It is not part of the script. Ad-libbing requires instant extemporizing—or improvising. The word comes from the Latin *ad libitum,* which means "as one pleases." An actor usually does not "please" to forget a line, but if one is clever the made-up lines will please the other members of the cast who may be waiting for their cues. |
| *Definition by* classification | |
| *Definition by* negation | |
| *Definition by* operation | [2] When I realize I have forgotten a line, my mind races frantically over the lines I *do* know. If I can't remember, I think of a replacement which fits the context of the scene. All of this activity is carried out in the space of about five seconds, although it may seem ten or twenty times longer to the actor. In the meantime, most of the audience may be totally oblivious to what is going on, especially if the actors are cool about the situation. |
| | [3] For the amateur, the situation is terrifying. I break out in a cold sweat, the silence is interminable, and the stage lights blinding. I feel dizzy. The other actors are in a panic, also. They try to concentrate on the forgotten line in the hope that they can transmit it by mental telepathy. When the actor finally ad-libs, everyone heaves a sigh of relief and the play continues smoothly until another actor drops a line. |
| *Definition by* example | [4] The ad-lib requires a certain amount of creativity. Other actors may interject an ad-lib to cover for the one who has forgotten the line. It may also be used when someone has forgotten to enter. The actor who is on stage alone may say something mundane such as, "I wonder where John is?" or "John must be late," or "Perhaps John didn't receive my invitation." |
| | [5] The ad-lib is an important part of performance. Actors must be trained to make up lines in order to fill those gaps that inevitably will occur when a group of amateurs get on stage to play someone else's speeches. |

# SOME FINAL SUGGESTIONS FOR DEFINING

In most instances, you will use definition in one of two ways. In the first way, you define a term at the beginning of a paper and then go on to develop your ideas by different methods. In the second, you devote much of your paper to an extended definition, part of which may actually supply your thesis. Sometimes you will need to combine these two ways.

Common to both of them are certain useful practices you should follow:

1.  If a term you use is likely to cause confusion, define it when you first use it. If the term is important to your theme and its thesis, define it in the introduction. Don't make your reader guess at what you mean by a particular word or phrase.

2.  Look to your dictionary for help, but don't use it as a crutch. Do not merely quote dictionary definitions because they are easy to copy into a paper. Before using them, make sure that they apply to your paper and to the situation you are discussing.

3.  Understand the techniques of defining and how they work. Keep in mind, for example, that defining by negation is particularly useful for cutting out inapplicable areas of word meanings.

4.  Make your definitions reasonably complete by using as many techniques of defining as are necessary. Remember that the techniques work very well in combination.

5.  Run an "operational check" on your definition. Be sure that the definition fits reality—that it is *true*.

Most of your defining will be rather informal. Perhaps for many papers you will need no more than a few words in the first or second paragraph stating how you are using a particular word or phrase. For example: "By *teachers' union* I mean an organization similar to a trade union in which the workers organize to protect their economic interests."

# WRITING AND REVISING A DEFINITION PAPER (AN EXAMPLE)

After she had been studying human behavior in her psychology 101 course, Jenine wrote some comments about *competition* in her journal.

> *Competition* is a common form of aggression. Competitiveness usually exists between two or more people. It is the basis for all of our games and sports. All sports pit one or many persons against one or many other persons. Some sports also produce competition against oneself. Runners, bikers, and swimmers

attempt to better their own scores, times, or distances. Competition may also be found in more subtle forms. For example, students strive to better their grades or, more importantly, to achieve better grades than their peers. Many students try to "stick" their teachers by getting high grades. This seems to be a healthy outlet for competitive aggression. In general, we all strive to exceed others in our social or age group in whatever way possible. Competitiveness, therefore, while not the most obvious, is the most common form of aggression, because most everything we do is an attempt to know more, have more, or do more in school, business, and sports, respectively.

Therefore, aggression, in these forms, and its many others too numerous to mention here, seems to be the greatest facet of human nature. All of our modern problems, from the arms race to the starving Cambodians, have aggression at their roots. This may be debated, as indeed it will be. But this, I feel, is positively fundamental, if I know anything about human nature.

Rereading her journal, Jenine wasn't happy with what she wrote. For one thing, she didn't limit her definition well enough. It is true that she could define *competition* as "a common form of aggression," but she saw that she hadn't distinguished *competitive aggression* from other kinds of *aggression*. So she made some notes:

> *Competition* is *good aggression* unless it gets out of hand. I talk a lot about competition in sports, but I really don't show how the rules of sports dictate a "healthy outlet for competitive aggression." I must get some examples to prove that point.

Jenine continued an analysis of her journal entry, noting how many things she had omitted. When she was through she had two pages of ideas from which she planned and wrote a paper.

### DEFINITION OF COMPETITION

[1] Competition is a form of aggression, but aggression controlled and channelled—not antisocial, in other words. We think of pure aggression as being one-sided and anti-social: people band together and attack someone else, who may or may not deserve the attack. The attack itself may be one of several kinds, from the merely verbal to full-scale war.

[2] Unlike pure aggression, competition adds a second (and balancing) side to the human equation, so that the forces of aggression are more or less equalized and each side has rights. These rights are formalized in "rules of play," which may be written down in books or simply agreed on when the competition starts. In vacant lots, you will hear young children shout: "That tree is second base. This bare spot will be home plate." And: "Any ball hit into the street is a double." As play begins, shouts of "NO FAIR!" tell us that the agreed-upon rules of aggressive play have been violated by someone.

[3] In addition, competitions are usually made for a reason apart from mere aggression, especially for a prize. And there are many kinds of prizes. You can win the game, lead the league in batting, get the highest pass completion

average in the conference, become the best chess player north of Division Street, win an encyclopedia, be first in your class and graduate *cum laude*.

4 Yet despite all this, the competitive person is still driven to a great extent by aggression. Indeed if he is not, he may not be successfully competitive. Something burns within the competitive person. Like quarterback Joe Montana, the true competitor never gives up. (Montana is a particularly good example because he is so controlled, even polite—his aggression is masked by good manners.)

5 What burns most in the competitive person is a fanatical desire to win. I knew a checkers champion who wanted to win so badly that when he lost he threw up. My father was so naturally competitive that if his neighbor was mowing his lawn at the same time Dad was mowing his, Dad would try to finish first—to win at lawn mowing. Dad quit playing softball in his late forties because he could no longer "win" in his own eyes, meaning he thought that he could not play aggressively enough to compete.

6 It is curious to watch how many competitive people "give off" aggressive signals in almost every direction. When they drive they shout at other drivers. In school, they are the ones who stop you in the hall after a quiz is returned to utter the cliché: "Whatja get?" You tell them. Then they say: "Oh, *I* did better than that!" The expensive car is still a major signal of successful aggression. It means: "I won in the competition of the business world, and this Cadillac (or Mercedes or whatever) is my prize."

7 Why do we accept competitiveness in men and women? Possibly for the very reason that its aggressiveness is controlled and channelled in fairly positive ways. Competition in business provides opportunity and jobs for workers. Competition in sports and films provides entertainment. Only when the aggressive instinct gets out of hand, when individuals no longer agree to play by certain rules, whether written or not, do we worry about what happens when human beings have that sharp "competitive edge."

## ✦ *P R A C T I C E*

### *Discussion*

1. For class discussion, read the second draft of Jenine's paper, and answer the following questions:
   a. Jenine followed the conventions for good defining by classifying *competition* as a form of *aggression*. Next she limited her use of the term *aggression* to particular kinds. For instance in paragraph 1, she calls *competition* "controlled aggression." Identify other limits she has placed on her use of *aggression* in the context of her definition. Discuss the effectiveness of these limits.
   b. Compare the use of examples in her journal entry and in her final paper.

2. For class discussion write a brief analysis of each definition given below. What are the techniques of defining being used? Do you see any errors in defining? How would you improve and rewrite any definition that

you consider weak or unrealistic? (You may wish to check your dictionary as you go along.)

a. *Shortening* is something you put in a cake to make it better.

b. *Marriage* is the ceremony of uniting two people in holy wedlock.

c. A *dog* is a canine.

d. *Integration* is the getting of people together for political freedom.

e. A *thermocouple* is a temperature-sensing instrument made of two
dissimilar metals.

f. *Tree-skiing* is a dangerous and exciting winter sport. It is not cross-
country, slalom, or downhill skiing, and it is not the sport of skiing
between two trees! Some people call it *woods winding* or *trailing*.

g. A book is *obscene* if it is totally without redeeming social importance
and appeals entirely to the reader's prurient interest.

h. When we come to accurate measurement, we find that the word
"hard" has dozens of slightly different meanings. The most usual
tests of hardness in steels is that of Brinell. A very hard steel ball of
10 millimetres diameter is pressed onto a steel plate for 30 seconds
with a load of 3 tons. The hardness number decreases with the
depth of the indentation.
    —J. B. S. Haldane, *A Banned Broadcast and Other Essays*

i. [What is meant by *life*? A thing *is alive* when] it does a minimum of
four things: it eats "foreign" substances which differ to a greater or
lesser degree from its own body tissue. Then it "digests" these
substances, and assimilates them into its body, which produces some
waste material that is ejected. Furthermore, it "grows": it increases
in size and bulk up to a certain point, which is different for different
life forms. Finally, it "propagates": it produces, or reproduces, its
own kind.—Willy Ley, "Life on Other Planets"

j. The idea that, since democracy is defective, it ought to be abolished,
is an example of the commonest error in political philosophy, which
I call "utopianism." By "utopianism" I mean the idea that there is a
perfect constitution, and politics could be perfect. The last of our
democratic duties which I shall mention is to avoid utopianism.
Politics are and always will be a creaking, groaning, lumbering,
tottering wagon of wretched make-shifts and sad compromises and
anxious guesses; and political maturity consists in knowing this in
your bones.—Richard Robinson, *An Atheist's Values*

## Writing

1. Definition skills are especially important when you must write a discussion of something that you know well but your reader does not. For
instance, if you are writing a proposal for insulating a house, you will
have to define *loose-fill, foam,* and *blanket* insulation methods so that the
owner will know what the choices are.

Pick a subject you know fairly well and write a paper on it in which
you define terms that the ordinary reader may not be familiar with—
your subject can be anything from clarinet playing to fixing engines.
Pick a stance, and convince your reader to do or believe something. At
the beginning, define any terms necessary to your thesis.

2. Choose one of the following terms (or pick your own). Define the term
   in as many ways as possible, using the methods described on pp. 272–
   274. Choose a subject that you have some feelings about or some experience with so that you can define by a long narrative example. Group
   your definitions, develop a thesis, and write an extended definition
   paper.

   —home
   —pond
   —anger
   —noun
   —ingratitude
   —tennis
   —yellow
   —surgeon
   —hypnotism

PICO IYER

# IN PRAISE OF THE HUMBLE COMMA

*In July of 1990, Pico Iyer could be seen in a* Time *magazine photo standing before the ruins of his Santa Barbara home and clutching the book manuscript he had saved. His house burned completely in one of the worst brush fires in California history. For Iyer even to have been at home to save his manuscript was remarkable, for he travels a good deal in his search for stories, recently finding himself in Japan, the Himalayas, and China. "I try to catch the inner stirrings of a country," he says. "Over the past year I observed the summer solstice in Iceland, attended the Wimbledon tennis matches, and went to Cuba for Carnaval." In the article you are about to read, Iyer turns Lilliputian, trying to catch the "inner stirrings" of that tiny squiggle, the comma.*

¹ The gods, they say, give breath, and they take it away. But the same could be said—could it not?—of the humble comma. Add it to the present clause, and, of a sudden, the mind is, quite literally, given pause to think; take it out if you wish or forget it and the mind is deprived of a resting place. Yet still the comma gets no respect. It seems just a slip of a thing, a pedant's tick, a blip on the edge of our consciousness, a kind of printer's smudge almost. Small, we claim, is beautiful (especially in the age of the microchip). Yet what is so often used, and so rarely recalled, as the comma—unless it be breath itself?

² Punctuation, one is taught, has a point: to keep up law and order. Punctuation marks are the road signs placed along the highway of our communication—to control speeds, provide directions and prevent head-on collisions. A period has the unblinking finality of a red light; the comma is a flashing yellow light that asks us only to slow down; and the semicolon is a stop sign that tells us to ease gradually to a halt, before gradually starting up again. By establishing the relations between words, punctuation establishes the relations between the people using words. That may be one reason why schoolteachers exalt it and lovers defy it ("We love each other and belong to each other let's don't ever hurt each other Nicole let's don't ever hurt each other," wrote Gary Gilmore to his girlfriend). A comma, he must have known, "separates inseparables," in the clinching words of H.W. Fowler, King of English usage.

³ Punctuation, then, is a civic prop, a pillar that holds society upright. (A run-on sentence, its phrases piling up without division, is as unsightly as a sink piled high with dirty dishes.) Small wonder, then, that punctuation was one of the first properties of the Victorian age, the age of the corset, that the modernists threw off: the sexual revolution might be said to have begun when Joyce's Molly Bloom spilled out all her private thoughts in 36 pages of unbridled, almost unperioded and officially censored prose; and

another rebellion was surely marked when E.E. Cummings first felt free to commit "God" to the lower case.

[4] Punctuation thus becomes the signature of cultures. The hot-blooded Spaniard seems to be revealed in the passion and urgency of his doubled exclamation points and question marks (*¡Caramba! ¿Quien sabe?"*), while the impassive Chinese traditionally added to his so-called inscrutability by omitting directions from his ideograms. The anarchy and commotion of the '60s were given voice in the exploding exclamation marks, riotous capital letters and Day-Glo italics of Tom Wolfe's spray-paint prose; and in Communist societies, where the State is absolute, the dignity—and divinity—of capital letters is reserved for Ministries, Sub-Committees and Secretariats.

[5] Yet punctuation is something more than a culture's birthmark; it scores the music in our minds, gets our thoughts moving to the rhythm of our hearts. Punctuation is the notation in the sheet music of our words, telling us when to rest, or when to raise our voices; it acknowledges that the meaning of our discourse, as of any symphonic composition, lies not in the units but in the pauses, the pacing and the phrasing. Punctuation is the way one bats one's eyes, lowers one's voice or blushes demurely. Punctuation adjusts the tone and color and volume till the feeling comes into perfect focus: not disgust exactly, but distaste; not lust, or like, but love.

[6] Punctuation, in short, gives us the human voice, and all the meanings that lie between the words. "You aren't young, are you?" loses its innocence when it loses the question mark. Every child knows the menace of a dropped apostrophe (the parent's "Don't do that" shifting into the more slowly enunciated "Do not do that"), and every believer, the ignominy of having his faith reduced to "faith." Add an exclamation point to "To be or not to be . . ." and the gloomy Dane has all the resolve he needs; add a comma, and the noble sobriety of "God save the Queen" becomes a cry of desperation bordering on double sacrilege.

[7] Sometimes, of course, our markings may be simply a matter of aesthetics. Popping in a comma can be like slipping on the necklace that gives an outfit quiet elegance, or like catching the sound of running water that complements, as it completes, the silence of a Japanese landscape. When V.S. Naipaul, in his latest novel, writes, "He was a middle-aged man, with glasses," the first comma can seem a little precious. Yet it gives the description a spin, as well as a subtlety, that it otherwise lacks, and it shows that the glasses are not part of the middle-agedness, but something else.

[8] Thus all these tiny scratches give us breadth and heft and depth. A world that has only periods is a world without inflections. It is a world without shade. It has a music without sharps and flats. It is a martial music. It has a jackboot rhythm. Words cannot bend and curve. A comma, by comparison, catches the gentle drift of the mind in thought, turning in on itself and back on itself, reversing, redoubling and returning along the course of its own sweet river music; while the semicolon brings clauses and thoughts together with all the silent discretion of a hostess arranging guests around her dinner table.

⁹ Punctuation, then, is a matter of care. Care for words, yes, but also, and more important, for what the words imply. Only a lover notices the small things: the way the afternoon light catches the nape of a neck, or how a strand of hair slips out from behind an ear, or the way a finger curls around a cup. And no one scans a letter so closely as a lover, searching for its small print, straining to hear its nuances, its gasps, its sighs and hesitations, poring over the secret messages that lie in every cadence. The difference between "Jane (whom I adore)" and "Jane, whom I adore," and the difference between them both and "Jane—whom I adore—" marks all the distance between ecstasy and heartache. "No iron can pierce the heart with such force as a period put at just the right place," in Isaac Babel's lovely words; a comma can let us hear a voice break, or a heart. Punctuation, in fact, is a labor of love. Which brings us back, in a way, to gods.

## ◆ PRACTICE

### Discussion

1. Iyer says that lovers "defy" punctuation (paragraph 2). Do you agree? Why might this be so?

2. The author believes that punctuation is related to propriety. (See paragraph 3.) Do you agree? Can you find examples in, say, an issue of *Time* (in which this essay appeared)?

3. Iyer's essay is about how one *feels* about a subject that most people don't feel anything about. After reading the essay, how do you feel about these little scrabbles on the page: ,.?';-- :!()?

4. Reread carefully the third sentence of the first paragraph. How does it exemplify Iyer's comment in the first sentence of the paragraph?

5. Explain the metaphor in paragraph 2, sentence 2. Is it appropriate?

6. Discuss the function of the first sentence in paragraph 3. Why could this sentence *not* be the first one in Iyer's paper?

7. What is the overall organization of Iyer's essay? *Hint:* Where do you first learn its main point? Why has Iyer arranged the essay in this fashion?

8. Iyer's main intention is to define. What technique(s) of defining does he use most? Why would he use these rather than others?

### Vocabulary

| | | |
|---|---|---|
| pedant | demurely | [the] resolve |
| civic | ignominy | precious |
| proprieties | gloomy Dane | jackboot |
| [the] pacing | | |

*Writing*

1. Reread paragraph 2. Then write a short note to a dearly loved one. How is it punctuated? Why?

2. See Discussion question **3.** Write an essay explaining your feelings on a particular mark of punctuation; for example, "The semicolon is a stuffy old gentleman always standing in my way."

3. The first sentence of paragraph 6 is a classic "lead" that controls the paragraph as a topic sentence. The material following this sentence gives supporting detail. Write a paragraph employing the same topic sentence but using different details and examples. Use your own experience with punctuation.

BARBARA LYLES

# WHAT TO CALL PEOPLE OF COLOR

*Barbara Lyles is associate professor of human development and personality in the Howard University School of Education, where she has been teaching for more than a quarter century. She received her B.S. in zoology from Marietta College, Marietta, Ohio, in 1951 and her Ph.D. in human development from the University of Maryland in 1971. She has been named Professor of the Year at Howard on four occasions and received the Howard University Teacher-Scholar Award in 1981. She is presently at work on a book, the core of which is derived from the essay we reprint below. In her letter to us, Dr. Lyles mentions that she is the mother of three children.*

[1] While some influential black leaders ponder the continuing relevance of "black" as a reference for people of color, I am led to recall the words of a wise old black man. "When I was a boy," said he, "I was poor. As the years passed I became 'destitute,' 'impoverished,' 'economically disadvantaged,' and 'psychosocially and culturally deprived.' Now I'm an old man and though what they call it has changed many times, I'm still poor."

[2] Like the old gentleman, I've been through a number of semantic name changes over the last half century plus. As a kid, I was a "negro." My father often admonished us that "colored people" were never to be referred to in his house as "niggers." Daddy required that we familiarize ourselves with Carter G. Woodson, W.E.B. Du Bois, George Washington Carver, Paul Laurence Dunbar, Countee Cullen and lots of other renowned "negroes." I now realize that, having been exposed to "negroes" in history and "people of color" in antiquity, I had had a prefashionable instruction in the positive meaning of being colored.

[3] Somewhere, in the '40s, I guess, the argument began that "negro" should be capitalized and the standard English translation of "negro" became "Negro." In 1947 I got called "nigger" for the first time by some poor white kids who probably saw my blackwatch plaid skirt and white bucks as too good for me. But I was a "Negro" with a capital letter; I passed on. The typewriter, the books, the monogrammed leather notebook, the no name calling and no slang in Daddy's house had made their mark. There never was much money; what there was was devoted to Paul Robeson's "Othello," Marian Anderson's concerts, Jackie Robinson's baseball debut, the Hayden Planetarium, Nedick's orange juice and cream-cheese-and-olive sandwiches from the Automat. The point is also to be made that Daddy was *there:* colored? negro? Negro?; a male image with undeniable positive influence.

⁴ All my life, standardized tests were given without recourse to the fact that being a "Negro" had probably damaged my mind. Nobody seemed to care; you passed or you failed. Period. Test moratoria were unknown. Daddy's notion was if you have it to do—Do it. No excuses. Sure, I've had my bruises, grades that would have been white A's were Negro B's or maybe even C's. Maybe I was naive but I just sort of plodded on. Maybe the fact that I didn't call attention to my difference made it difficult for anyone in authority to mount a sustained attack on my efforts.

⁵ One marriage, two degrees and one doctoral candidacy later found me in the rhetorical '60s. Washington was burning, the Kennedys were dead, Martin Luther King was dead and the horror of unbridled human rage and frustration was upon us. By now, a college professor, I found it necessary to stand up to a student activist who had decided that he had the authority to cancel my class in midlecture. Never given then to verbal obscenity, I found myself spouting words that he could understand. "This is my damn class and it will be over when I say so." Maybe he was so shocked at my nerve that he slinked away. Sure, black was beautiful. Whoever said it wasn't? Foot-wide Afros were there and a puzzle to me; they were so hard to groom when they were so long. Lots of people in my youth had worn their hair natural. So what.

⁶ And now we've come full circle. Our "popular" departed president suggested that black leaders are getting rich and keeping their organizations viable by claiming that prejudice exists. That sounds as if he thinks that discrimination is in the minds of black leaders. From 1981 to 1989, he implied that homelessness was a matter of personal preference and that jobless workers were unemployed by their own choice; anyone could see the homeless on the heating grates a few blocks away from the White House. Perhaps President Bush will find the poor and admit that black economic and social progress has begun to move backwards into the '60s.

⁷ There is something inherently obtuse about attempting to apply a name to 29 million Americans. Emergent individualism and a refusal to be bound by semantic trivialization may yet force the majority culture to perceive people of color as having the diversity necessary to escape a label. It may also force the minority culture to assert itself to explore the American dream with an unlabeled right to access without the need for excuse or permission.

⁸ "Colored," "negro," "Negro," "black," "Black," "Africanamerican," "Afro American," "Afro Amerikan," "American." No matter what people of color call themselves or are called—achievement, education and economic growth are what count. But people of color have had subliminal and mean-spirited training in learning self-contempt. The idea of working together for the common good has generally been unsuccessful because historically we have been torn apart by the majority group's need to assure itself that we will never be able to unify ourselves for a concerted thrust against an oppressive and repressive system.

⁹ Maybe the best way to lose the stigma attached to whatever one calls people of color is not to call attention to difference by changing names. Let's change the strategy. Forget the semantic absurdity of what to call people of color and get on with the business of achieving. If attention is drawn to what is done rather than who does it, names won't matter. We did not ask to be Americans in the 1600s. Now that it is clear that we will not return en masse to Africa, we may as well be called Americans.

## ◆ *PRACTICE*

### Discussion

1. What is the *context* of Lyles' definition?

2. Why doesn't Lyles use a dictionary definition of any of her synonyms for *black?*

3. Is Lyles trying to "clarify an ambiguous situation" (point 2, p. 272)?

4. Which of the techniques of defining is Lyles employing in her essay?

5. "There is something inherently obtuse about attempting to apply a name to 29 million Americans" (paragraph 7). Discuss.

6. What term, exactly, is Lyles intending to define?

7. We emphasize in the text that a definition must fit reality. One reader has said that Lyles' essay "is almost entirely about reality." Discuss.

### Vocabulary

| | | |
|---|---|---|
| semantic | automat | stigma |
| admonished | moratoria | en masse |
| antiquity | subliminal | |

### Writing

1. Write a response to Lyles, arguing that *black* or *Afroamerican* (or a different name) should be used for people of color.

2. "If attention is drawn to what is done rather than who does it, names won't matter." Write an argument based on the quotation. Agree or disagree.

3. ". . . Achievement, education, and economic growth are what count." Respond specifically to the quotation.

NANCY MAIRS

## ON BEING A CRIPPLE

*Feminist poet and essayist Nancy Mairs was born in Long Beach, California, in 1943; grew up and attended college in New England (A.B. in English literature, Wheaton College, 1964); and now lives in Tucson, Arizona, where she earned her Ph.D. in English literature from the University of Arizona in 1984. She has worked as a technical editor, as a teacher of high school and college composition, and as a project director for the Southwest Institute for Research on Women. Her most recent publication (1990) is a collection of essays, fittingly titled* Essays. *The following essay, published in her 1986 collection,* Plaintext, *uses definition as a springboard to an inspiring exploration of the human condition.*

[1] The other day I was thinking of writing an essay on being a cripple. I was thinking hard in one of the stalls of the women's room in my office building, as I was shoving my shirt into my jeans and tugging up my zipper. Preoccupied, I flushed, picked up my book bag, took my cane down from the hook, and unlatched the door. So many movements unbalanced me, and as I pulled the door open I fell over backward, landing fully clothed on the toilet seat with my legs splayed in front of me: the old beetle-on-its-back routine. Saturday afternoon, the building deserted, I was free to laugh aloud as I wriggled back to my feet, my voice bouncing off the yellowish tiles from all directions. Had anyone been there with me, I'd have been still and faint and hot with chagrin. I decided that it was high time to write the essay.

[2] First, the matter of semantics. I am a cripple. I choose this word to name me. I choose from among several possibilities, the most common of which are "handicapped" and "disabled." I made the choice a number of years ago, without thinking, unaware of my motives for doing so. Even now, I'm not sure what those motives are, but I recognize that they are complex and not entirely flattering. People—crippled or not—wince at the word "cripple," as they do not at "handicapped" or "disabled." Perhaps I want them to wince. I want them to see me as a tough customer, one to whom the fates/gods/viruses have not been kind, but who can face the brutal truth of her existence squarely. As a cripple, I swagger.

[3] But, to be fair to myself, a certain amount of honesty underlies my choice. "Cripple" seems to me a clean word, straightforward and precise. It has an honorable history, having made its first appearance in the Lindisfarne Gospel in the tenth century. As a lover of words, I like the accuracy with which it describes my condition: I have lost the full use of my limbs. "Disabled," by contrast, suggests any incapacity, physical or mental.

And I certainly don't like "handicapped," which implies that I have deliberately been put at a disadvantage, by whom I can't imagine (my God is not a Handicapper General), in order to equalize chances in the great race of life. These words seem to me to be moving away from my condition, to be widening the gap between word and reality. Most remote is the recently coined euphemism "differently abled," which partakes of the same semantic hopefulness that transformed countries from "undeveloped" to "underdeveloped," then to "less developed," and finally to "developing" nations. People have continued to starve in those countries during the shift. Some realities do not obey the dictates of language.

⁴ Mine is one of them. Whatever you call me, I remain crippled. But I don't care what you call me, so long as it isn't "differently abled," which strikes me as pure verbal garbage designed, by its ability to describe anyone, to describe no one. I subscribe to George Orwell's thesis that "the slovenliness of our language makes it easier for us to have foolish thoughts." And I refuse to participate in the degeneration of the language to the extent that I deny that I have lost anything in the course of this calamitous disease; I refuse to pretend that the only differences between you and me are the various ordinary ones that distinguish any one person from another. But call me "disabled" or "handicapped" if you like. I have long since grown accustomed to them; and if they are vague, at least they hint at the truth. Moreover, I use them myself. Society is no readier to accept crippledness than to accept death, war, sex, sweat, or wrinkles. I would never refer to another person as a cripple. It is the word I use to name only myself.

⁵ I haven't always been crippled, a fact for which I am soundly grateful. To be whole of limb is, I know from experience, infinitely more pleasant and useful than to be crippled; and if that knowledge leaves me open to bitterness at my loss, the physical soundness I once enjoyed (though I did not enjoy it half enough) is well worth the occasional stab of regret. Though never any good at sports, I was a normally active child and young adult. I climbed trees, played hopscotch, jumped rope, skated, swam, rode my bicycle, sailed. I despised team sports, spending some of the wretchedest afternoons of my life, sweaty and humiliated, behind a field-hockey stick and under a basketball hoop. I tramped alone for miles along the bridle paths that webbed the woods behind the house I grew up in. I swayed through countless dim hours in the arms of one man or another under the scattered shot of light from mirrored balls, and gyrated through countless more as Tab Hunter and Johnny Mathis gave way to the Rolling Stones, Creedence Clearwater Revival, Cream. I walked down the aisle. I pushed baby carriages, changed tires in the rain, marched for peace.

⁶ When I was twenty-eight I started to trip and drop things. What at first seemed my natural clumsiness soon became too pronounced to shrug off. I consulted a neurologist, who told me that I had a brain tumor. A battery of tests, increasingly disagreeable, revealed no tumor. About a year and a half later I developed a blurred spot in one eye. I had, at last, the

episodes "disseminated in space and time" requisite for a diagnosis: multiple sclerosis. I have never been sorry for the doctor's initial misdiagnosis, however. For almost a week, until the negative results of the tests were in, I thought that I was going to die right away. Every day for the past nearly ten years, then, has been a kind of gift. I accept all gifts.

⁷ Multiple sclerosis is a chronic degenerative disease of the central nervous system, in which the myelin that sheathes the nerves is somehow eaten away and scar tissue forms in its place, interrupting the nerves' signals. During its course, which is unpredictable and uncontrollable, one may lose vision, hearing, speech, the ability to walk, control of bladder and/or bowels, strength in any or all extremities, sensitivity to touch, vibration, and/or pain, potency, coordination of movements—the list of possibilities is lengthy and, yes, horrifying. One may also lose one's sense of humor. That's the easiest to lose and the hardest to survive without.

⁸ In the past ten years, I have sustained some of these losses. Characteristic of MS are sudden attacks, called exacerbations, followed by remissions, and these I have not had. Instead my disease has been slowly progressive. My left leg is now so weak that I walk with the aid of a brace and a cane; and for distances I use an Amigo, a variation of the electric wheelchair that looks rather like an electrified kiddie car. I no longer have much use of my left hand. Now my right side is weakening as well. I still have the blurred spot in my right eye. Overall, though, I've been lucky so far. My world has, of necessity, been circumscribed by my losses, but the terrain left me has been ample enough for me to continue many of the activities that absorb me: writing, teaching, raising children and cats and plants and snakes, reading, speaking publicly about MS and depression, even playing bridge with people patient and honorable enough to let me scatter cards every which way without sneaking a peek.

⁹ Lest I begin to sound like Polyanna, however, let me say that I don't like having MS. I hate it. My life holds realities—harsh ones, some of them—that no right-minded human being ought to accept without grumbling. One of them is fatigue. I know of no one with MS who does not complain of bone-weariness; in a disease that presents an astonishing variety of symptoms, fatigue seems to be a common factor. I wake up in the morning feeling the way most people do at the end of a bad day, and I take it from there. As a result, I spend a lot of time *in extremis* and, impatient with limitation, I tend to ignore my fatigue until my body breaks down in some way and forces rest. Then I miss picnics, dinner parties, poetry readings, the brief visits of old friends from out of town. The offspring of a puritanical tradition of exceptional venerability, I cannot view these lapses without shame. My life often seems a series of small failures to do as I ought.

¹⁰ I lead, on the whole, an ordinary life, probably rather like the one I would have led had I not had MS. I am lucky that my predilections were already solitary, sedentary, and bookish—unlike the world-famous French cellist I have read about, or the young woman I talked with one long

afternoon who wanted only to be a jockey. I had just begun graduate school when I found out something was wrong with me, and I have remained, interminably, a graduate student. Perhaps I would not have if I'd thought I had the stamina to return to a full-time job as a technical editor; but I've enjoyed my studies.

[11] In addition to studying, I teach writing courses. I also teach medical students how to give neurological examinations. I pick up freelance editing jobs here and there. I have raised a foster son and sent him into the world, where he has made my two grandbabies, and I am still escorting my daughter and son through adolescence. I go to Mass every Saturday. I am a superb, if messy, cook. I am also an enthusiastic laundress, capable of sorting a hamper full of clothes into five subtly differentiated piles, but a terrible housekeeper. I can do italic writing and, in an emergency, bathe an oil-soaked cat. I play a fiendish game of Scrabble. When I have the time and the money, I like to sit on my front steps with my husband, drinking Amaretto and smoking a cigar, as we imagine our counterpart in Leningrad and make sure that the sun gets down once more behind the sharp childish scrawl of the Tucson Mountains.

[12] This lively plenty has its bleak complement, of course, in all the things I can no longer do. I will never run again, except in dreams and one day I may have to write that I will never walk again. I like to go camping, but I can't follow George and the children along the trails that wander out of a campsite through the desert or into the mountains. In fact, even on the level I've learned never to check the weather or try to hold a coherent conversation: I need all my attention for my wayward feet. Of late, I have begun to catch myself wondering how people can propel themselves without canes. With only one usable hand, I have to select my clothing with care not so much for style as for ease of ingress and egress, and even so, dressing can be laborious. I can no longer do fine stitchery, pick up babies, play the piano, braid my hair. I am immobilized by acute attacks of depression, which may or may not be physiologically related to MS but are certainly its logical concomitant.

[13] These two elements, the plenty and the privation, are never pure, nor are the delight and wretchedness that accompany them. Almost every pickle that I get into as a result of my weakness and clumsiness—and I get into plenty—is funny as well as maddening and sometimes painful. I recall one May afternoon when a friend and I were going out for a drink after finishing up at school. As we were climbing into opposite sides of my car, chatting, I tripped and fell, flat and hard, onto the asphalt parking lot, my abrupt departure interrupting him in mid-sentence. "Where'd you go?" he called as he came around the back of the car to find me hauling myself up by the door frame. "Are you all right?" Yes, I told him, I was fine, just a bit rattly, and we drove off to find a shady patio and some beer. When I got home an hour or so later, my daughter greeted me with "What have you done to yourself?" I looked down. One elbow of my white turtleneck with the green froggies, one knee of my white trousers, one white kneesock

were blood-soaked. We peeled off the clothes and inspected the damage, which was nasty enough but not alarming. That part wasn't funny: The abrasions took a long time to heal, and one got a little infected. Even so, when I think of my friend talking earnestly, suddenly, to the hot thin air while I dropped from his view as though through a trap door, I find the image as silly as something from a Marx Brothers movie.

14 I may find it easier than other cripples to amuse myself because I live propped by the acceptance and the assistance and, sometimes, the amusement of those around me. Grocery clerks tear my checks out of my checkbook for me, and sales clerks find chairs to put into dressing rooms when I want to try on clothes. The people I work with make sure I teach at times when I am least likely to be fatigued, in places I can get to, with the materials I need. My students, with one anonymous exception (in an end-of-the-semester evaluation), have been unperturbed by my disability. Some even like it. One was immensely cheered by the information that I paint my own fingernails; she decided, she told me, that if I could go to such trouble over fine details, she could keep on writing essays. I suppose I became some sort of bright-fingered muse. She wrote good essays, too.

15 The most important struts in the framework of my existence, of course, are my husband and children. Dismayingly few marriages survive the MS test, and why should they? Most twenty-two and nineteen-year-olds, like George and me, can vow in clear conscience, after a childhood of chicken pox and summer colds, to keep one another in sickness and in health so long as they both shall live. Not many are equipped for catastrophe: the dismay, the depression, the extra work, the boredom that a degenerative disease can insinuate into a relationship. And our society, with its emphasis on fun and its association of fun with physical performance, offers little encouragement for a whole spouse to stay with a crippled partner. Children experience similar stresses when faced with a crippled parent, and they are more helpless, since parents and children can't usually get divorced. They hate, of course, to be different from their peers, and the child whose mother is tacking down the aisle of a school auditorium packed with proud parents like a Cape Cod dinghy in a stiff breeze jolly well stands out in a crowd. Deprived of legal divorce, the child can at least deny the mother's disability, even her existence, forgetting to tell her about recitals and PTA meetings, refusing to accompany her to stores or church or the movies, never inviting friends to the house. Many do.

16 But I've been limping along for ten years now, and so far George and the children are still at my left elbow, holding tight. Anne and Matthew vacuum floors and dust furniture and haul trash and rake up dog droppings and button my cuffs and bake lasagna and Toll House cookies with just enough grumbling so I know that they don't have brain fever. And far from hiding me, they're forever dragging me by racks of fancy clothes or through teeming school corridors, or welcoming gaggles of friends while I'm wandering through the house in Anne's filmy pink babydoll pajamas. George generally calls before he brings someone home, but he does just as

many dumb thankless chores as the children. And they all yell at me, laugh at some of my jokes, write me funny letters when we're apart—in short, treat me as an ordinary human being for whom they have some use. I think they like me. Unless they're faking. . . .

¹⁷ Faking. There's the rub. Tugging at the fringes of my consciousness always is the terror that people are kind to me only because I'm a cripple. My mother almost shattered me once, with that instinct mothers have— blind, I think, in this case, but unerring nonetheless—for striking blows along the fault-lines of their children's hearts, by telling me, in an attack on my selfishness, "We all have to make allowances for you, of course, because of the way you are." From the distance of a couple of years, I have to admit that I haven't any idea just what she meant, and I'm not sure that she knew either. She was awfully angry. But at the time, as the words thudded home, I felt my worst fear, suddenly realized. I could bear being called selfish: I am. But I couldn't bear the corroboration that those around me were doing in fact what I'd always suspected them of doing, professing fondness while silently putting up with me because of the way I am. A cripple. I've been a little cracked ever since.

¹⁸ Along with this fear that people are secretly accepting shoddy goods comes a relentless pressure to please—to prove myself worth the burdens I impose, I guess, or to build a substantial account of good will against which I may write drafts in times of need. Part of the pressure arises from social expectations. In our society, anyone who deviates from the norm had better find some way to compensate. Like fat people, who are expected to be jolly, cripples must bear their lot meekly and cheerfully. A grumpy cripple isn't playing by the rules. And much of the pressure is self-generated. Early on I vowed that, if I had to have MS, by God I was going to do it well. This is a class act, ladies and gentlemen. No tears, no recriminations, no faint-heartedness.

¹⁹ One way and another, then, I wind up feeling like Tiny Tim, peering over the edge of the table at the Christmas goose, waving my crutch, piping down God's blessing on us all. Only sometimes I don't want to play Tiny Tim. I'd rather be Caliban, a most scurvy monster. Fortunately, at home no one much cares whether I'm a good cripple or a bad cripple as long as I make vichyssoise with fair regularity. One evening several years ago, Anne was reading at the dining-room table while I cooked dinner. As I opened a can of tomatoes, the can slipped in my left hand and juice spattered me and the counter with bloody spots. Fatigued and infuriated, I bellowed, "I'm so sick of being crippled!" Anne glanced at me over the top of her book. "There now," she said, "do you feel better?" "Yes," I said, "yes, I do." She went back to her reading. I felt better. That's about all the attention my scurviness ever gets.

²⁰ Because I hate being crippled, I sometimes hate myself for being a cripple. Over the years I have come to expect—even accept—attacks of violent self-loathing. Luckily, in general our society no longer connects deformity and disease directly with evil (though a charismatic once told me

that I have MS because a devil is in me) and so I'm allowed to move largely at will, even among small children. But I'm not sure that this revision of attitude has been particularly helpful. Physical imperfection, even freed of moral disapprobation, still defies and violates the ideal, especially for women, whose confinement in their bodies as objects of desire is far from over. Each age, of course, has its ideal, and I doubt that ours is any better or worse than any other. Today's ideal woman, who lives on the glossy pages of dozens of magazines, seems to be between the ages of eighteen and twenty-five; her hair has body, her teeth flash white, her breath smells minty, her underarms are dry; she has a career but is still a fabulous cook, especially of meals that take less than twenty minutes to prepare; she does not ordinarily appear to have a husband or children; she is trim and deeply tanned; she jogs, swims, plays tennis, rides a bicycle, sails, but does not bowl; she travels widely, even to out-of-the-way places like Finland and Samoa, always in the company of the ideal man, who possesses a nearly identical set of characteristics. There are a few exceptions. Though usually white and often blonde, she may be black, Hispanic, Asian, or Native American, so long as she is unusually sleek. She may be old, provided she is selling a laxative or is Lauren Bacall. If she is selling a detergent, she may be married and have a flock of strikingly messy children. But she is never a cripple. . . .

21 At the beginning, I thought about having MS almost incessantly. And because of the unpredictable course of the disease, my thoughts were always terrified. Each night I'd get into bed wondering whether I'd get out again the next morning, whether I'd be able to see, to speak, to hold a pen between my fingers. Knowing that the day might come when I'd be physically incapable of killing myself, I thought perhaps I ought to do so right away, while I still had the strength. Gradually I came to understand that the Nancy who might one day lie inert under a bedsheet, arms and legs paralyzed, unable to feed or bathe herself, unable to reach out for a gun, a bottle of pills, was not the Nancy I was at present, and that I could not presume to make decisions for that future Nancy, who might well not want in the least to die. Now the only provision I've made for the future Nancy is that when the time comes—and it is likely to come in the form of pneumonia, friend to the weak and the old—I am not to be treated with machines and medications. If she is unable to communicate by then, I hope she will be satisfied with these terms.

22 Thinking all the time about having MS grew tiresome and intrusive, especially in the large and tragic mode in which I was accustomed to considering my plight. Months and even years went by without catastrophe (at least without one related to MS), and really I was awfully busy, what with George and children and snakes and students and poems, and I hadn't the time, let alone the inclination, to devote myself to being a disease. Too, the richer my life became, the funnier it seemed, as though there were some connection between largesse and laughter, and so my tragic stance began to waver until, even with the aid of a brace and a cane, I couldn't hold it for very long at a time.

23 After several years I was satisfied with my adjustment. I had suffered my grief and fury and terror, I thought, but now I was at ease with my lot. Then one summer day I set out with George and the children across the desert for a vacation in California. Part way to Yuma I became aware that my right leg felt funny. "I think I've had an exacerbation," I told George. "What shall we do?" he asked. "I think we'd better get the hell to California," I said, "because I don't know whether I'll ever make it again." So we went on to San Diego and then to Orange, up the Pacific Coast Highway to Santa Cruz, across to Yosemite, down to Sequoia and Joshua Tree, and so back over the desert to home. It was a fine two-week trip, filled with friends and fair weather, and I wouldn't have missed it for the world, though I did in fact make it back to California two years later. Nor would there have been any point in missing it, since in MS, once the symptoms have appeared, the neurological damage has been done, and there's no way to predict or prevent that damage.

24 The incident spoiled my self-satisfaction, however. It renewed my grief and fury and terror, and I learned that one never finishes adjusting to MS. I don't know now why I thought one would. One does not, after all, finish adjusting to life, and MS is simply a fact of my life—not my favorite fact, of course—but as ordinary as my nose and my tropical fish and my yellow Mazda station wagon. It may at any time get worse, but no amount of worry or anticipation can prepare me for a new loss. My life is a lesson in losses. I learn one at a time.

25 And I had best be patient in the learning, since I'll have to do it like it or not. As any rock fan knows, you can't always get what you want. Particularly when you have MS. You can't, for example, get cured. In recent years researchers and the organizations that fund research have started to pay MS some attention even though it isn't fatal; perhaps they have begun to see that life is something other than a quantitative phenomenon, that one may be very much alive for a very long time in a life that isn't worth living. The researchers have made some progress toward understanding the mechanism of the disease: It may well be an autoimmune reaction triggered by a slow-acting virus. But they are nowhere near its prevention, control, or cure. And most of us want to be cured. Some, unable to accept uncurability, grasp at one treatment after another, no matter how bizarre: megavitamin therapy, gluten-free diet, injections of cobra venom, hypothermal suits, lymphocytopharesis, hyperbaric chambers. Many treatments are probably harmless enough, but none are curative.

26 The absence of a cure often makes MS patients bitter toward their doctors. Doctors are, after all, the priests of modern society, the new shamans, whose business is to heal, and many an MS patient roves from one to another, searching for the "good" doctor who will make him well. Doctors too think of themselves as healers, and for this reason many have trouble dealing with MS patients, whose disease in its intransigence defeats their aims and mocks their skills. Too few doctors, it is true, treat their patients as whole human beings, but the reverse is also true. I have always

tried to be gentle with my doctors, who often have more at stake in terms of ego than I do. I may be frustrated, maddened, depressed by the incurability of my disease, but I am not diminished by it, and they are. When I push myself up from my seat in the waiting room and stumble toward them, I incarnate the limitation of their powers. The least I can do is refuse to press on their tenderest spots.

27 This gentleness is part of the reason that I'm not sorry to be a cripple. I didn't have it before. Perhaps I'd have developed it anyway— how could I know such a thing?—and wish I had more of it. But I'm glad of what I have. It has opened and enriched my life enormously, this sense that my frailty and need must be mirrored in others, that in searching for and shaping a stable core in a life wrenched by change and loss, change and loss, I must recognize the same process, under individual conditions, in the lives around me. I do not deprecate such knowledge, however I've come by it.

28 All the same, if a cure were found, would I take it? In a minute. I may be a cripple, but I'm only occasionally a loony and never a saint. Anyway, in my brand of theology God doesn't give bonus points for a limp. I'd take a cure; I just don't need one. A friend who also has MS startled me once by asking, "Do you ever say to yourself, 'Why me, Lord?'" "No, Michael, I don't," I told him, "because whenever I try, the only response I can think of is 'Why not?'" If I could make a cosmic deal, who would I put in my place? What in my life would I give up in exchange for sound limbs and a thrilling rush of energy? No one. Nothing. I might as well do the job myself. Now that I'm getting the hang of it.

## ◆ PRACTICE

### Discussion

1. Why does Mairs dislike the terms "handicapped," "disabled," and "differently abled"? Why do some people prefer them to "crippled"?

2. What problems for the families of an MS victim are listed? Which of these has Mairs experienced in her own family? How have she and her family escaped so many?

3. What is Mairs' attitude towards the first doctor who treated her? Towards subsequent doctors? How can she say that she doesn't need a cure?

4. List the major terms related to her disease that Mairs defines in her essay. What technique or techniques are used to define each? Does the essay employ an introductory definition, an extended definition, or both?

5. Mairs refers to herself in the first person throughout most of the essay. Does the first person voice give the essay a more formal or informal

tone? When would an essay on MS be inappropriately written in the first person? Where does Mairs vary from the first person in speaking of herself? Why is that shift appropriate to the content at that point in the essay?

6. What technique or techniques does Mairs use in paragraph 5 to define a normal child and young adult? The definition is arranged in the form of a list. Where else is listing employed in the essay? Under what circumstances might the use of lists in an essay get out of hand? Does Mairs run into any of these problems?

7. In paragraph 22, Mairs writes, "The richer my life became, the funnier it seemed, as though there were some connection between largesse and laughter, and so my tragic stance began to waver until, even with the aid of a brace and a cane, I couldn't hold it for very long at a time." Now that is a sentence to admire for many reasons. What are they?

8. What role do questions play in Mairs' essay? What do they reveal about her relationship with her family and friends? With herself?

*Vocabulary*

| | | |
|---|---|---|
| semantics | remissions | vichyssoise |
| degeneration | *in extremis* | charismatic |
| neurologist | venerability | shamans |
| disseminated | scurvy | incarnate |

*Writing*

1. Do you or someone you know have a physical handicap? Define the condition using more than one technique and continue your essay into a further exploration of the condition and how it affects everyday life, plans for the future, and family and friends.

2. Choose a term that you think describes an important part of who you are: artist, athlete, homemaker, manager, analyst, teacher, student, etc. Define that term. Use the library; research its origin and development in language. Then explore it in the context of your life. Your essay, like Mairs', should illuminate both the term and its author.

3. Mairs writes about being both happy and sad about her condition and certain events connected with her condition. How can she feel both ways at once? Write an essay about the term "bittersweet" or about the term "tragi-comedy" or about a term of your choice that expresses a combination of happiness and sadness. Explore both the term and the condition.

*C H A P T E R   16*

# COMPARISON AND CONTRAST

## COMPARISON AND CONTRAST

*Comparing* means "showing likenesses"; *contrasting*, "showing differences." Classification (or grouping) is an important step in comparison and contrast because, when you classify, you usually group pieces of information by the principle of similarity. However, when you compare and contrast, you identify those qualities that distinguish members of a class from each other by their individual differences. Therefore, when you make a comparison and contrast, you show *likenesses* and *differences* between two or more (but usually only two) persons, ideas, actions, things, or classes—*for the purpose of making a point*. We emphasize "making a point" because you customarily employ the strategy of comparison and contrast to convince the reader of an idea you have—that A is better than B; more interesting than B; more useful than B; and so on. You may show the likenesses or the differences between two things at the paragraph level or in a longer paper.

## Planning a Comparison and Contrast

For several reasons, a comparison and contrast requires particularly strong control of your point and organization. First, you usually have more material to work with—two subject areas instead of the customary one. Consequently, you should rigorously narrow your point—or thesis—for a longer comparison and contrast so that you can cover the subjects in the number of words you have allotted. Next, you have to know a good deal about both subjects. Finally, your comparison and contrast must do more than just show similarities or likenesses. This is a trap that students often fall into. They describe the two subject areas, giving plenty of detail for both but omitting the point, thus leaving the reader wondering why the paper was written in the first place.

Note how a student uses comparison and contrast for the purpose of making a decision, and thereby communicating his *point*. His comparison and contrast is not only useful for himself but also for a reader who might be interested in learning about motorcycles and mopeds.

### MOTORCYCLES AND MOPEDS

*Purpose for comparison/ contrast*

[1] When I go back to school next semester, I will need a more reliable means of transportation than buses, bicycles or friends' cars. So I'm going to buy a vehicle which will take me when and where I want to go. After examining the various advantages and disadvantages of cars, buses, taxicabs, airplanes, trains, and submarines, I have found that either a motorcycle or a moped will best suit my need for an inexpensive and convenient means of transportation. The problem is to find out which one is better suited for me.

*First consideration: cost*

[2] My first problem in considering a means of transportation is its cost, including the initial investment, insurance, and gas. The lowest starting price for a new motorcycle is usually around $600, which is definitely out of my price range at the moment. On the other hand, I find that new mopeds, priced at around $320, are more nearly what I can afford. Since drivers of motorcycles in my state are required to carry liability insurance, I would have to pay an additional $45 to $50 if I bought a motorcycle. In my state mopeds can be driven without liability insurance.

[3] I will have to pay for my own gas, which means that I will need a vehicle that will run on the least amount of gas possible. Motorcycles average 50 to 75 mpg, while a moped can get from 80 to 150 mpg.

*Second consideration: speed*

[4] I do not need a vehicle capable of high speeds. What I want is one that can keep up with city traffic, which usually travels (on the streets I wish to use) between 20 and 35 mph. Motorcycles have large motors with complicated transmissions that allow them to travel at speeds of at least 45 to 50 mph. Mopeds run on a simple two-horsepower motor. The state law limits them to a maximum speed of 25 to 35 mph, which is fast enough for me.

*Third consideration: parking*

[5] Since parking places are hard to find in the university lots, the motorcycle would be less convenient than a moped because I can park a moped in a bicycle rack. Furthermore, I can ride the moped on the university bicycle paths. For getting to and from classes easily, the moped would definitely be more convenient than the motorcycle. Another convenience of the moped is that in my state I don't need a special license, an automobile license being adequate.

*Result: Moped is better choice*

⁶ After comparing the motorcycle and the moped as a means of inexpensive and convenient transportation, I think that the moped better suits my needs. I would advise any student in my position to buy one instead of a motorcycle.

The writer of the essay on motorcycles and mopeds has strong control of his thesis and organization. He makes the comparison-contrast in order to consider his need for better transportation, and that purpose is made clear. Note that he does not try to include irrelevant items such as bicycles and automobiles. He covers both items under consideration completely so that the paper is not primarily about mopeds even though that vehicle is his final choice. His transitional devices (such as *on the other hand* and *furthermore*) help the reader to follow the organization of the material.

## ORGANIZING COMPARISON AND CONTRAST

There are three basic methods of organizing *comparison and contrast*. In the "block" method, you first discuss one item thoroughly, then go on to the second, giving about equal space to each. In the second method, you list all the similarities between the two items, then all the differences. In the third "point-by-point" method, you discuss one point or feature of each item, then go on to the next, and so on. The following lists show how the three methods are organized. A and B stand for the two items being compared.

| *Block* | *Similarities–Differences* | *Point-by-Point* |
|---|---|---|
| 1. introduce subject | introduce subject | introduce subject |
| 2. discuss A (transition) | discuss similarities between A and B (transition) | discuss point 1 of A and B (transition) |
| 3. discuss B | discuss differences between A and B | discuss point 2 of A and B |
| 4. conclude | conclude | conclude |

In the three models on the following pages, you will see how the writers used these methods for organizing their writing. The second and third examples are student essays.

### BLOCK METHOD

*Introduction*

¹ I think there's something wrong here, but I can't exactly put my finger on it. I recently bought quantities of two fluids.

*Discussion of A (gasoline)*

*1. Source*

² The first fluid was gasoline. Gasoline is derived from crude oil, which is found deep under the ground in remote sections of the earth. Enormous amounts of money are risked in the search for oil. Once it's found, a great deal more money is expended to extract it from the earth, to ship it to distant

refineries, to refine it, to ship it via pipeline to regional distribution points, to store it, to deliver it to retail outlets and then to make it available to the retail consumer. . . .

*2. Supply*

³ As far as we know, the earth's supply of crude oil is limited. Once it's gone, it's gone. There may be other substances fermenting under the soil that will prove of value to future civilizations, but for the here and now our oil supplies are finite. . . .

*Discussion of B (soda pop)*

⁴ The other fluid was sweetened, carbonated water, infused with artificial fruit flavoring. Some call it soda pop. It's made right here in town. As far as we know, the raw materials exist in unlimited supply. Most of it falls from the heavens at regular intervals. . . .

*1. Source*

*2. Supply*

⁵ Almost all of it, by processes chemical and natural, will recycle back into the system. It will become sewage, will cleanse itself, will evaporate and will rain down again from the heavens at some undetermined time and place. It will come back. We can't really get rid of it. . . .

*Conclusion*
*Thesis*

⁶ When you further consider that roughly a third of the cost of gasoline is taxes, that means that soda pop costs almost three times as much per gallon as does gasoline.

—Robert Rosefsky, *Chicago Daily News*

## SIMILARITIES-DIFFERENCES METHOD

*Introduction*

¹ What was it like for a girl to be brought up by two bachelors? When I was ten, my mother (a widow) died, and I had no one to look after me except her two brothers, Arthur and Alan. Both were in their early forties at the time. Arthur had been married once, long ago, and his wife had left him; Alan had never married and was, people said, a woman hater. Being brothers, they had several traits in common; but they were also very different. And that fact showed up in their treatment of me.

*Thesis implied*

*Similarities between A (Alan) and B (Arthur)*

² For instance, neither of them wanted me to work while I was going to high school. They were brought up to believe that a woman's place is in the home or, at least, in the trailer at the edge of town where we all lived. When they found out I took a job at a local drive-in, Alan bawled me out and made me quit, while Arthur, the more sociable of the two, made a personal visit to the manager to give him hell for hiring such a young kid. Both of them could not understand why I could not get by on the $5.00 a week they gave me for spending money. And besides, they said that the job was interfering with my "schooling."

*1. Attitude toward work*

*2. Attitude toward school*

³ School was another thing they were concerned about, and probably with good reason. They always wanted to see my grade reports, although they were never quite sure when they were issued. And I tried to keep them in the dark about that as much as possible. Arthur, who thought he was better educated

than Alan, always wanted to help me with my homework. Just to get him off my back, I sometimes let him. About the only thing he seemed to remember from his school days were the names of the capital cities of all the states, which, of course, did not help me much. Alan was always concerned with long-term results, continually asking, "Are you going to pass this term?" "Are you going to graduate?" I think he was a little surprised when I did. But, if it had not been for their concern, I probably would not have made it past my junior year.

*Differences between*
*A and B*

*1. Attitude toward*
*dating*

⁴ But in other matters involving me, they had quite different attitudes. Alan was very protective of me as far as boys and dating were concerned. Arthur, however, encouraged me to date because he wanted me to have a good time while I was young. Alan treated me like a young Farrah Fawcett who was luring every male for miles around. When male friends would stop by, he would always grill them as if they were sex maniacs, while Arthur offered them a beer and talked sports, always managing to put in a good word for his niece. Alan was so protective that he sometimes would drive me to parties or dances, and sit outside a teen den in his pickup, waiting until I came out after the last song died away.

*2. Attitude toward*
*drinking*

⁵ Their concern for me also showed itself in their attitude toward drinking. Alan did not drink much, but Arthur was an alcoholic. He not only drank, he liked other people drinking. He made me my first salty dog. He taught me that any sort of sweet stuff with bourbon was the devil's idea. Alan disapproved greatly of all this, but he was incapable of attacking his own brother, who could charm people with ease. Alan would, when I was seventeen, take a beer out of my hand if I was drinking one—only one!—with Arthur, and pour it down the sink. After Alan had gone to bed, Arthur would go to the refrigerator and get me another one. I was never more than mildly interested in alcohol, however; the sight of Arthur drunk and sick was enough to make anyone cautious.

*Conclusion*
*(with an anecdote*
*that emphasizes*
*their similarities*
*and differences)*

⁶ Even though they were alike in some things and different in others, my uncles took care of me. When I graduated from high school last year, they came to the ceremony in the pickup. Alan wore his best and only suit, which had been out of style twenty years ago. Arthur was dressed like a king, and was so drunk he had to be carried out in the middle of "Pomp and Circumstance." A strange "family," but they are all I have—and many times all I need.

## POINT-BY-POINT METHOD

¹ Since I came to the United States from the mainland of China in 1985, I have been to church services, Bible studies, circle meetings, church organized picnics, family dinners, parties, and sales. I have learned more about the American culture and felt less lonely through these activities, thanks to

all who invited me there. But at the same time I am present in these religious situations, I cannot help comparing the worship of God to that of Mao in the Cultural Revolution. Yes, that Revolution made Mao an almighty figure to us Chinese. He was worshiped before meals; in classrooms, offices, factories, train stations, the fields; and at bus stops. Now, even though this excessive Mao worship is gone, the memory of it still haunts me. When I think about whether I should become a Christian, I ask myself: "Am I going to accept another figure like Mao? Will the worship of God one day become as ridiculous as Mao worship did?"

*Point 1:*
*The Bible vs.*
*Mao's Red Book*
*(pars. 2–3)*

² As the one holy book at home and the church, the Bible reminds me of the red copy of Mao's works. It was called the treasured book. There were four volumes of his works in all sizes, and a pocket book of his quotations. Most times, one got these copies free. They were the books one brought to evening studies from 1966 to 1976. Seldom now can I think of meetings without the memory of those studies. In America, when I was at the church (in Bible studies) turning to pages in the Bible, I felt as if I were turning to pages in Mao's red book.

³ The format of some Bible studies resembles that of Mao studies. I was in grade school during the Cultural Revolution in China. I remember that for some time the school began and ended with our reading of Mao's quotations line by line to examine what we had done on a particular day and promise what we should do the next day.

*Point 2:*
*Self-criticism in*
*Bible studies and*
*worship of Mao*
*(pars. 4–6)*

⁴ One morning, after I stood up in class and read this quotation of Mao, "Fight selfishness and repudiate revisionism," I told the class that the day before when the ice-cream cart came by, several kids and I (who were playing in the neighborhood) all wanted the red-bean icebar. But there was only one left. As I ran to the cart first, I got that bar and sucked it contentedly in front of other kids. Mao's quotation made me realize that I was being selfish. I promised to the class that next time such things happened, I would give that icebar to others. This was my simple understanding and application of Mao's quotation. I could not comprehend the latter part of the quotation, but I read it anyway.

⁵ The morning study of Mao's teachings usually lasted 30–50 minutes, in which time other students took turns reading a quotation of Mao and criticizing themselves just as I did. I heard then that the older kids in Chinese high schools did the same thing, except that their self-criticisms were more complicated than ours. The last period of class would repeat the format of the morning session. As each day thus repeated itself, many times I could not find any fault with myself; yet feeling I should still say something to criticize myself, I lied or exaggerated things.

⁶ I almost forgot this type of self-criticism until I went to Bible studies in America. At some of these studies, people

would read the Bible line by line, discuss the meanings, and criticize themselves for having failed at times to do what God commands them to do. (I am not criticizing the Bible studies themselves.) At one study, for example, after we read lines 14–16 in Matthew 5 where Jesus asks his disciples to shine their light before people like a lamp on a stand, one person criticized herself for sometimes being too shy to tell non-Christians that she is a Christian and pass God's teachings to them. Immediately I thought about the exaggerated self-criticisms I had made during our Mao studies.

*Point 3: Celebrations in Mao's China and the Western Church (pars. 7–8)*

7 Saying grace before meals and singing songs of Jesus in the church and at Bible studies remind me of the late 1960s in China when we would sing songs in worship of Mao, read aloud his quotations, or do both before meals at camps, in the dining-halls or other public eating places. Mao was the sun, the savior, in those songs. The radio was broadcasting them all day long. The theatres were staging choirs of those songs, revolutionary operas, and dances. In fact, songs in worship of Mao or of a revolutionary nature were the only songs taught in schools. They were also the only songs the whole nation was allowed to sing during the Cultural Revolution.

8 Last Christmas Eve, I attended the midnight service at a Baptist Church. I was impressed with the solemn decorations of the church, the special dresses of the choir, and the way they sang their songs. Yet afterwards, all this brought back to me the memory of the celebration of Mao's birthday, which is Dec. 26, a day so close to the birthday of Jesus. For some years during the Cultural Revolution, there were special performances and gatherings in celebration of Mao's birthday in many theatres and music halls. On that particular day, there would be a long front-page editorial dedicated to Mao in the *People's Daily*. The title was always printed in big red characters.

*Conclusion*

9 As a child, I truly respected Mao and enjoyed participating in the songs and dances. But now that I have grown up and realized the excessiveness of Mao worship, it becomes hard for me to accept any new worship. I have discussed my feelings with some other Chinese, and they all feel the same. Perhaps it is because Mao was the first God-figure I believed in (and later on I found myself cheated) that I doubt how long the worship of God can last. Certainly, if I remain only an observer of God worship, I will not feel guilty or be laughed at when God loses His favor.—Ming Xiao, "God and Mao"

# WRITING AND REVISING A COMPARISON AND CONTRAST (AN EXAMPLE)

Rachel, a member of the track team, has just returned from a strenuous training session in which the coach told her, "Pain is your friend." She thinks about his statement, wondering if he is really correct. She begins freewriting:

¹ I would say that some kinds of physical pain are good for me. Note that I distinguish *physical* pain from other kinds. There is another kind of pain: mental. Mental pain is much worse than physical pain. It lasts longer, and instead of diminishing in a relatively short time like physical pain, it can eat at you for days, months, or perhaps an entire lifetime. If unresolved, it can build up and drive you mad.

² Mental pain hurts. It can come from any number of situations. A friend or relative may have gone, a girlfriend or boyfriend may have broken off a relationship, you may have been under a lot of stress, or a misunderstanding may have come between friends. There is a great difference between mental and physical pain—misunderstandings can cause much mental anguish and grief, but you will never hear of a "misunderstood broken leg."

³ Coach says, "Pain is your friend." Of course, he means the physical pain caused by running. This pain while running or exercising in other ways can be your friend by telling you that you are really working. This pain should not be confused with injury, which is a definite sign that something is wrong. Injury can be caused by too much physical work, or an accident. Sometimes injury is difficult to distinguish from soreness. Soreness is another kind of pain caused by physical work. It generally occurs when you have not exercised in a while, and have just started. You may then have soreness for a few days.

⁴ Mental and physical pain have different effects and are caused by different things. For me, mental pain is much more unpleasant because it can linger on, while physical pain fades relatively quickly.

Later, Rachel studies her freewriting. She is now more critical of what she wrote. She sees two problems that are reflected in her freewriting:

She notes that she has a problem with her terms. She is satisfied with the term *training pain*, but she knows she can't compare that kind of pain with every kind of *mental pain*. Therefore, she reviews her experiences with runners and other athletes. She decides to limit *mental pain* to the *emotional pain* caused by losing, or from having to stay off the team as a result of injury.

As a result of thinking about her terms, she sees that she needs clearer definitions of the two kinds of pain because the terms will form the basis for her *comparison and contrast*.

After she has tied down her terms, she develops a preliminary outline in which the coverage of two kinds of pain falls naturally in a block organization (see pp. 300–301).

I. Training pain helps to condition the body.
   A. If the athlete trains carefully, the training pain will go away.
   B. Training pain is not caused by an injury.
II. Emotional pain connected with athletics affects the spirit.
   A. Emotional pain lasts longer than training pain.
   B. Emotional pain is connected with losing and with injury.

Rachel's stance:

> *Role:*     A student member of the women's track team.
> *Audience:*   Other runners and athletes who might be interested in an analysis of pain.
> *Thesis:*    Emotional pain is worse for an athlete than physical pain.

### ATHLETES AND PAIN

[1] Recently a few members of the women's track team were comparing notes on their aches and pains. I am not a masochist, but I think that the kind of pain that comes from training is good for me (and for other athletes) because it doesn't last long, and also conditions the body. But athletes sometimes suffer another kind of pain—the emotional pain that is nearly always related to losing or being taken off the team as a result of injury. Emotional pain can last longer than training pain and sometimes affects an athlete's self-esteem.

[2] Our track coach often says, "Pain is your best friend." Of course he means training pain—the pain caused by intense physical conditioning. This pain is my friend because it tells me that I am really working hard and getting better at my sport. For example, the first month of training for long-distance running is the most difficult. In this period, I must establish a vigorous stride that can be maintained without pain. Before I can establish that stride, I must break through a wall of pain—a physical barrier that will finally disappear if I continue to push myself beyond it. Getting over that wall can be gratifying because I know that I am not going to experience quite as much pain in the future. In my first month of training, I was preparing for the three-hundred. As I neared the two-hundred mark, the pain became excruciating. It came from inside as though something had exploded, and my legs required all the energy and concentration I could muster.

[3] However, training pain should not be confused with pain from injury. If runners are not careful to establish a schedule for running, or if they attempt long distances too soon, they will get shin splints, a bone and tendon irritation that disables runners. Any pressure on the ankles, knees, and shins will be so painful that a runner will not be able to run for weeks. Other injuries such as stress fractures, bursitis, and tendonitis will not disappear like training pain but will keep an athlete from running.

[4] Emotional pain hurts too, but it is the spirit, not the body, that suffers. And emotional pain lasts longer than training pain. Emotional pain is different from training pain because the discomfort isn't transmitted through the nervous system. However, emotional pain caused by disappointment or anxiety can cause an athlete anguish and grief that will affect the spirit for weeks, months, or even years.

[5] The desire to win is strong in athletes. Runners, in particular, suffer emotional pain when they lose. They usually don't have people in the stands to cheer them on, so they must depend on their own team members for emotional support. I was in a race when three of us moved neck-and-neck toward the finish tape. As I leaned for the tape, I stumbled. Lying on the track, too exhausted to get up, I learned that I had come in second, not first as I had hoped. My desire had not been enough to win. As a result of my stumble, I believed that I had let my team down because we lost the meet. My friends on

the team didn't treat me differently, but I believed that I had not done my best. As a result I was disconsolate for weeks. It was only after I won the next race that my self-esteem was renewed.

6 Suffering a physical injury which keeps athletes from competing may affect the spirit. A friend of mine broke his collarbone while training for basketball. He told me that the break caused physical pain while doing the most routine tasks: dressing, lying down, or even sneezing. But the emotional pain was the most difficult to bear. The day after he suffered his injury, he watched his team practicing in a full-court scrimmage. He said that watching his friends practice the one sport he loves more than anything else made him feel left out and abandoned. Since basketball is one of the few things he looks forward to during the year, having an injury that locked him out of the team caused him more emotional pain than physical pain.

7 Athletes are bound to suffer pain, but they hope that it is training pain, not the pain from losing or the pain from staying off the team. An athlete's self-esteem is tied up with being part of a team and any fluctuation in the team as an entity or group influences an athlete's self-esteem.

# ◆ *PRACTICE*

## *Discussion*

Read the final version of "Athletes and Pain." Prepare the following questions for class discussion.

1. How well has Rachel supported the main points of her comparison and contrast? What recommendations would you make for improvements in her paper and support of her thesis?

2. List Rachel's transitions. How well do they help to advance her comparison and contrast? Could her use of transitions be improved?

3. You followed Rachel through the process of identifying her terms and developing a thesis. Now review her freewriting. Are there any points in her freewriting that could have been used in her second draft?

## *Writing*

1. Pick two words or phrases that are often used in comparable ways. Write a comparison-contrast in which you show the likenesses and the differences between the meanings of the two. Suggestions:

   Fashion—Style
   Pathetic—Tragic
   Persuasion—Force
   Stink—Odor
   Civil disobedience—Dissent
   Amateur—Professional

Politician—Civil servant
Appetite—Hunger
Pacify—Appease
Practical—Practicable
Exercise—Drill
Movie—TV program
Blocking—Tackling
Housewife—Career woman

2. Choose two people you know well—friends or relatives. Make two separate lists, identifying all the qualities that are distinctive for *each* person. Analyze and group the characteristics that these two people share (or do not share). Draw a generalization about each group of characteristics. Develop a thesis or a point, and choose an organizational method. Write a comparison-contrast, trying to keep an appropriate balance between the two people so that you don't cover one more thoroughly than the other.

*MARK TWAIN*

# THE FACE OF THE WATER

*Samuel Langhorne Clemens (1835–1910) took his pen name, Mark Twain, from the term for "safe water" used on Mississippi riverboats. Born in Hannibal, Missouri, along the Mississippi River, Twain traveled around the country and, later, the world as a journalist and lecturer, but the great river was a central thread in his life and works. He was, for a while, a riverboat pilot, as he explains in the excerpt included here from* Life on the Mississippi *(1883). Among his many famous novels and stories are* Tom Sawyer *(1876) and the classic American novel* Huckleberry Finn *(1885). Twain's skillful use of exaggeration, irreverence, and deadpan seriousness is not so apparent in the following excerpt as it is in much of his writing. What can be seen here is his sensitivity to the sound of language and colloquial American speech.*

[1] The face of the water, in time, became a wonderful book—a book that was a dead language to the uneducated passenger, but which told its mind to me without reserve, delivering its most cherished secrets as clearly as if it uttered them with a voice. And it was not a book to be read once and thrown aside, for it had a new story to tell every day. Throughout the long twelve hundred miles there was never a page that was void of interest, never one that you could leave unread without loss, never one that you would want to skip, thinking you could find higher enjoyment in some other thing. There never was so wonderful a book written by man; never one whose interest was so absorbing, so unflagging, so sparklingly renewed with every reperusal. The passenger who could not read it was charmed with a peculiar sort of faint dimple on its surface (on the rare occasions when he did not overlook it altogether); but to the pilot that was an *italicized* passage; indeed, it was more than that, it was a legend of the largest capitals, with a string of shouting exclamation points at the end of it; for it meant that a wreck or a rock was buried there that could tear the life out of the strongest vessel that ever floated. It is the faintest and simplest expression the water ever makes, and the most hideous to a pilot's eye. In truth, the passenger who could not read this book saw nothing but all manner of pretty pictures in it, painted by the sun and shaded by the clouds, whereas to the trained eye these were not pictures at all, but the grimmest and most dead-earnest of reading matter.

[2] Now when I had mastered the language of this water and had come to know every trifling feature that bordered the great river as familiarly as I knew the letters of the alphabet, I had made a valuable acquisition. But I had lost something, too. I had lost something which could never be restored to me while I lived. All the grace, the beauty, the poetry had gone

out of the majestic river! I still keep in mind a certain wonderful sunset which I witnessed when steamboating was new to me. A broad expanse of the river was turned to blood; in the middle distance the red hue brightened into gold, through which a solitary log came floating, black and conspicuous; in one place a long, slanting mark lay sparkling upon the water; in another the surface was broken by boiling, tumbling rings, that were as many-tinted as an opal; where the ruddy flush was faintest, was a smooth spot that was covered with graceful circles and radiating lines, ever so delicately traced; the shore on our left was densely wooded, and the somber shadow that fell from this forest was broken in one place by a long, ruffled trail that shone like silver; and high above the forest wall a clean-stemmed dead tree waved a single leafy bough that glowed like a flame in the unobstructed splendor that was flowing from the sun. There were graceful curves, reflected images, woody heights, soft distances; and over the whole scene, far and near, the dissolving lights drifted steadily, enriching it, every passing moment, with new marvels of coloring.

[3] I stood like one bewitched. I drank it in, in a speechless rapture. The world was new to me, and I had never seen anything like this at home. But as I have said, a day came when I began to cease from noting the glories and the charms which the moon and the sun and the twilight wrought upon the river's face; another day came when I ceased altogether to note them. Then, if that sunset scene had been repeated, I should have looked upon it without rapture, and should have commented upon it, inwardly, after this fashion: This sun means that we are going to have wind tomorrow; that floating log means that the river is rising, small thanks to it; that slanting mark on the water refers to a bluff reef which is going to kill somebody's steamboat one of these nights, if it keeps on stretching out like that; those tumbling "boils" show a dissolving bar and a changing channel there; the lines and circles in the slick water over yonder are a warning that the troublesome place is shoaling up dangerously; that silver streak in the shadow of the forest is the "break" from a new snag, and he has located himself in the very best place he could have found to fish for steamboats; that tall dead tree, with a single living branch, is not going to last long, and then how is a body ever going to get through this blind place at night without the friendly old landmark?

[4] No, the romance and the beauty were all gone from the river. All the value any feature of it had for me now was the amount of usefulness it could furnish toward compassing the safe piloting of a steamboat. Since those days, I have pitied doctors from my heart. What does the lovely flush in a beauty's cheek mean to a doctor but a "break" that ripples above some deadly disease? Are not all her visible charms sown thick with what are to him the signs and symbols of hidden decay? Does he ever see her beauty at all, or doesn't he simply view her professionally, and comment upon her unwholesome condition all to himself? And doesn't he sometimes wonder whether he has gained most or lost most by learning his trade?

◆ *P R A C T I C E*

*Discussion*

1. What is the advantage of reading the river as a novice? The disadvantage? What are the advantages of reading the river as a professional? The disadvantages?

2. To what kind of book is the Mississippi River compared? List the qualities mentioned in the essay. Name a book you have read that has many of these same qualities for you.

3. Has the pilot gained most or lost most by learning his trade? How about the doctor? Give the answer you think is implicit in the essay and explain why you are influenced that way.

4. What analogy is drawn in the first paragraph? In the last? Which one is literal and which figurative? What other strategy of development is used whenever an analogy is drawn?

5. What comparison is at the heart of the essay? How is it structured? Try reshaping it into a structure that moves back and forth.

6. Compare the sentence structures and rhythms of the second paragraph to those in the third paragraph. What differences do you see and hear? How are the structures and rhythms appropriate for the view being presented in each case?

7. Look again at the opening analogy and track it through the essay, noting all the points of comparison that contribute to it. Where is it finally dropped? Is the final analogy developed as extensively?

8. What type of sentence predominates in the final paragraph? How are the sentences of this type distributed? What is the effect of such an arrangement? What would be the effect of moving the first sentence of that paragraph to the end, possibly revised to read: "The romance and the beauty are all gone"?

*Vocabulary*

| | | |
|---|---|---|
| reperusal | hue | reef |
| italicized | ruddy | bar |
| trifling | rapture | shoaling |
| acquisition | bluff | snag |

*Writing*

1. If you are skilled in a specific field, explain how you view your field differently than a novice would. What have you gained and lost?

2. Compare your first impression of someone you came to love with the way you see that person today.

3. Describe a scene from two different points of view—for example, a child's room from the perspective of the child and its mother, or a football field from the perspective of a coach and a player or a fan and his or her date.

E. B. WHITE

# ONCE MORE TO THE LAKE

*Many good prose writers wish they could write like E. B. White, and his popular revision of William Strunk's* Elements of Style *(1979) has helped many student prose writers to write better. Born in 1899, educated at Cornell University, White was for many years associated with the* New Yorker *magazine. His deep caring for precision and clarity of language, along with his personal style and humor, set standards of excellence for the American essay. Children and adults alike treasure his stories for children:* Stuart Little *(1945),* Charlotte's Web *(1952), and* The Trumpet of the Swan *(1970). Publication of White's collected letters in 1976 and essays in 1977 put him again on the bestseller lists. "Once More to the Lake" was written in 1941 for White's "One Man's Meat" column in* Harper's. *As White compares past and present times in the essay, the future is also there.*

[1] One summer, along about 1904, my father rented a camp on a lake in Maine and took us all there for the month of August. We all got ringworm from some kittens and had to rub Pond's Extract on our arms and legs night and morning, and my father rolled over in a canoe with all his clothes on; but outside of that the vacation was a success and from then on none of us ever thought there was any place in the world like that lake in Maine. We returned summer after summer—always on August 1st for one month. I have since become a salt-water man, but sometimes in summer there are days when the restlessness of the tides and the fearful cold of the sea water and the incessant wind which blows across the afternoon and into the evening make me wish for the placidity of the lake in the woods. A few weeks ago this feeling got so strong I bought myself a couple of bass hooks and a spinner and returned to the lake where we used to go, for a week's fishing and to revisit old haunts.

[2] I took along my son, who had never had any fresh water up his nose and who had seen lily pads only from train windows. On the journey over to the lake I began to wonder what it would be like. I wondered how time would have marred this unique, this holy spot—the coves and streams, the hills that the sun set behind, the camps and the paths behind the camps. I was sure the tarred road would have found it out and I wondered in what other ways it would be desolated. It is strange how much you can remember about places like that once you allow your mind to return into the grooves which lead back. You remember one thing, and that suddenly reminds you of another thing. I guess I remembered clearest of all the early mornings, when the lake was cool and motionless, remembered how the bedroom smelled of the lumber it was made of and of the wet woods whose scent entered through the screen. The partitions in the camp were

thin and did not extend clear to the top of the rooms, and as I was always the first up I would dress softly so as not to wake the others, and sneak out into the sweet outdoors and start out in the canoe, keeping close along the shore in the long shadows of the pines. I remembered being very careful never to rub my paddle against the gunwale for fear of disturbing the stillness of the cathedral.

[3] The lake had never been what you would call a wild lake. There were cottages sprinkled around the shores, and it was in farming country although the shores of the lake were quite heavily wooded. Some of the cottages were owned by nearby farmers, and you would live at the shore and eat your meals at the farmhouse. That's what our family did. But although it wasn't wild, it was a fairly large and undisturbed lake and there were places in it which, to a child at least, seemed infinitely remote and primeval.

[4] I was right about the tar: it led to within half a mile of the shore. But when I got back there, with my boy, and we settled into a camp near a farmhouse and into the kind of summertime I had known, I could tell that it was going to be pretty much the same as it had been before—I knew it, lying in bed the first morning, smelling the bedroom, and hearing the boy sneak quietly out and go off along the shore in a boat. I began to sustain the illusion that he was I, and therefore by simple transposition, that I was my father. This sensation persisted, kept cropping up all the time we were there. It was not an entirely new feeling, but in this setting it grew much stronger. I seemed to be living a dual existence. I would be in the middle of some simple act, I would be picking up a bait box or laying down a table fork, or I would be saying something, and suddenly it would be not I but my father who was saying the words or making the gesture. It gave me a creepy sensation.

[5] We went fishing the first morning. I felt the same damp moss covering the worms in the bait can, and saw the dragonfly alight on the tip of my rod as it hovered a few inches from the surface of the water. It was the arrival of this fly that convinced me beyond any doubt that everything was as it always had been, that the years were a mirage and there had been no years. The small waves were the same, chucking the rowboat under the chin as we fished at anchor, and the boat was the same boat, the same color green and the ribs broken in the same places, and under the floor-boards the same fresh-water leavings and debris—the dead helgramite, the wisps of moss, the rusty discarded fishhook, the dried blood from yesterday's catch. We stared silently at the tips of our rods, at the dragonflies that came and went. I lowered the tip of mine into the water, tentatively, pensively dislodging the fly, which darted two feet away, poised, darted two feet back, and came to rest again a little farther up the rod. There had been no years between the ducking of this dragonfly and the other one—the one that was part of memory. I looked at the boy, who was silently watching his fly, and it was my hands that held his rod, my eyes watching. I felt dizzy and didn't know which rod I was at the end of.

<sup>6</sup> We caught two bass, hauling them in briskly as though they were mackerel, pulling them over the side of the boat in a businesslike manner without any landing net, and stunning them with a blow on the back of the head. When we got back for a swim before lunch, the lake was exactly where we had left it, the same number of inches from the dock, and there was only the merest suggestion of a breeze. This seemed an utterly enchanted sea, this lake you could leave to its own devices for a few hours and come back to, and find that it had not stirred, this constant and trustworthy body of water. In the shallows, the dark, watersoaked sticks and twigs, smooth and old, were undulating in clusters on the bottom against the clean ribbed sand, and the track of the mussel was plain. A school of minnows swam by, each minnow with its small individual shadow, doubling the attendance, so clear and sharp in the sunlight. Some of the other campers were in swimming, along the shore, one of them with a cake of soap, and the water felt thin and clear and unsubstantial. Over the years there had been this person with the cake of soap, this cultist, and here he was. There had been no years.

<sup>7</sup> Up to the farmhouse to dinner through the teeming, dusty field, the road under our sneakers was only a two-track road. The middle track was missing, the one with the marks of the hooves and the splotches of dried, flaky manure. There had always been three tracks to choose from in choosing which track to walk in; now the choice was narrowed down to two. For a moment I missed terribly the middle alternative. But the way led past the tennis court, and something about the way it lay there in the sun reassured me; the tape had loosened along the backline, the alleys were green with plaintains and other weeds, and the net (installed in June and removed in September) sagged in the dry noon, and the whole place steamed with midday heat and hunger and emptiness. There was a choice of pie for dessert, and one was blueberry and one was apple, and the waitresses were the same country girls, there having been no passage of time, only the illusion of it as in a dropped curtain—the waitresses were still fifteen; their hair had been washed, that was the only difference—they had been to the movies and seen the pretty girls with the clean hair.

<sup>8</sup> Summertime, oh summertime, pattern of life indelible, the fade-proof lake, the woods unshatterable, the pasture with the sweetfern and the juniper forever and ever, summer without end; this was the background, and the life along the shore was the design, the cottages with their innocent and tranquil design, their tiny docks with the flagpole and the American flag floating against the white clouds in the blue sky, the little paths over the roots of the trees leading from camp to camp and the paths leading back to the outhouses and the can of lime for sprinkling, and at the souvenir counters at the store the miniature birch-bark canoes and the post cards that showed things looking a little better than they looked. This was the American family at play, escaping the city heat, wondering whether the newcomers in the camp at the head of the cove were "common" or "nice," wondering whether it was true that the people who drove up for Sunday

dinner at the farmhouse were turned away because there wasn't enough chicken.

⁹ It seemed to me, as I kept remembering all this, that those times and those summers had been infinitely precious and worth saving. There had been jollity and peace and goodness. The arriving (at the beginning of August) had been so big a business in itself, at the railway station the farm wagon drawn up, the first smell of the pine-laden air, the first glimpse of the smiling farmer, and the great importance of the trunks and your father's enormous authority in such matters, and the feel of the wagon under you for the long ten-mile haul, and at the top of the last long hill catching the first view of the lake after eleven months of not seeing this cherished body of water. The shouts and cries of the other campers when they saw you, and the trunks to be unpacked, to give up their rich burden. (Arriving was less exciting nowadays, when you sneaked up in your car and parked it under a tree near the camp and took out the bags and in five minutes it was all over, no fuss, no loud wonderful fuss about trunks.)

¹⁰ Peace and goodness and jollity. The only thing that was wrong now, really, was the sound of the place, an unfamiliar nervous sound of the outboard motors. This was the note that jarred, the one thing that would sometimes break the illusion and set the years moving. In those other summertimes all motors were inboard; and when they were at a little distance, the noise they made was a sedative, an ingredient of summer sleep. They were one-cylinder and two-cylinder engines, and some were make-and-break and some were jump-spark, but they all made a sleepy sound across the lake. The one-lungers throbbed and fluttered, and the twin-cylinder ones purred and purred, and that was a quiet sound too. But now the campers all had outboards. In the daytime, in the hot mornings, these motors made a petulant, irritable sound; at night, in the still evening when the afterglow lit the water, they whined about one's ears like mosquitoes. My boy loved our rented outboard, and his great desire was to achieve singlehanded mastery over it, and authority, and he soon learned the trick of choking it a little (but not too much), and the adjustment of the needle valve. Watching him I would remember the things you could do with the old one-cylinder engine with the heavy flywheel, how you could have it eating out of your hand if you got really close to it spiritually. Motor boats in those days didn't have clutches, and you would make a landing by shutting off the motor at the proper time and coasting in with a dead rudder. But there was a way of reversing them, if you learned the trick, by cutting the switch and putting it on again exactly on the final dying revolution of the flywheel, so that it would kick back against compression and begin reversing. Approaching a dock in a strong following breeze, it was difficult to slow up sufficiently by the ordinary coasting method, and if a boy felt he had complete mastery over his motor, he was tempted to keep it running beyond its time and then reverse it a few feet from the dock. It took a cool nerve, because if you threw the switch a twentieth of a second too soon you would catch the flywheel when it still had speed enough to go

up past center, and the boat would leap ahead, charging bull-fashion at the dock.

[11] We had a good week at the camp. The bass were biting well and the sun shone endlessly, day after day. We would be tired at night and lie down in the accumulated heat of the little bedrooms after the long hot day and the breeze would stir almost imperceptibly outside and the smell of the swamp drift in through the rusty screens. Sleep would come easily and in the morning the red squirrel would be on the roof, tapping out his gay routine. I kept remembering everything, lying in bed in the mornings—the small steamboat that had a long rounded stern like the lip of a Ubangi, and how quietly she ran on the moonlight sails, when the older boys played their mandolins and the girls sang and we ate doughnuts dipped in sugar, and how sweet the music was on the water in the shining night, and what it had felt like to think about girls then. After breakfast we would go up to the store and the things were in the same place—the minnows in a bottle, the plugs and spinners disarranged and pawed over by the youngsters from the boys' camp, the fig newtons and the Beeman's gum. Outside, the road was tarred and cars stood in front of the store. Inside, all was just as it had always been, except there was more Coca-Cola and not so much Moxie and root beer and birch beer and sarsaparilla. We would walk out with a bottle of pop apiece and sometimes the pop would backfire up our noses and hurt. We explored the streams, quietly, where the turtles slid off the sunny logs and dug their way into the soft bottom; and we lay on the town wharf and fed worms to the tame bass. Everywhere we went I had trouble making out which was I, the one walking at my side, the one walking in my pants.

[12] One afternoon while we were there at that lake a thunderstorm came up. It was like the revival of an old melodrama that I had seen long ago with childish awe. The second-act climax of the drama of the electrical disturbance over a lake in America had not changed in any important respect. This was the big scene, still the big scene. The whole thing was so familiar, the first feeling of oppression and heat and a general air around camp of not wanting to go very far away. In midafternoon (it was all the same) a curious darkening of the sky, and a lull in everything that had made life tick; and then the way the boats suddenly swung the other way at their moorings with the coming of a breeze out of the new quarter, and the premonitory rumble. Then the kettle drum, then the snare, then the bass drum and cymbals, then crackling light against the dark, and the gods grinning and licking their chops in the hills. Afterward the calm, the rain steadily rustling in the calm lake, the return of light and hope and spirits, and the campers running out in joy and relief to go swimming in the rain, their bright cries perpetuating the deathless joke about how they were getting simply drenched, and the children screaming with delight at the new sensation of bathing in the rain, and the joke about getting drenched linking the generations in a strong indestructible chain. And the comedian who waded in carrying an umbrella.

[13] When the others went swimming my son said he was going in too. He

pulled his dripping trunks from the line where they had hung all through the shower, and wrung them out. Languidly, and with no thought of going in, I watched him, his hard little body, skinny and bare, saw him wince slightly as he pulled up around his vitals the small, soggy, icy garments. As he buckled the swollen belt suddenly my groin felt the chill of death.

## ✦ PRACTICE

### Discussion

1. What reasons does White give for returning to the lake instead of going to the seashore? Does he fulfill his purpose? What does he discover that is most unexpected?

2. In what ways has the modern world of 1941 encroached on the backwoods area? Does White seem to be very surprised or upset by this encroachment? What aspect of change bothers him most?

3. What actions of his son remind White of himself as a boy? When does White feel like his own father? Why does he feel "the chill of death" at the end?

4. How does White prepare us for the morbid shock of the final insight?

5. What phrase does White keep repeating to stress his sense of connectedness in time? How is the use of this repetition especially effective in paragraph 12?

6. What method of comparison-contrast does White use for this essay? Would another method have been as effective? Explain.

7. How does White manage to make his memories so vivid to his readers, as well as to himself? Find examples of his appeal to each of the five senses.

8. Where does White describe an artificial process? Why does he include this section?

### Vocabulary

| | | |
|---|---|---|
| incessant | helgramite | petulant |
| placidity | pensively | imperceptibly |
| gunwale | undulating | moorings |
| primeval | indelible | premonitory |
| mirage | tranquil | languidly |
| debris | | |

## Writing

1. Write an essay comparing a place where you have lived or visited at two different points in time.

2. Write an essay comparing your perspective of an experience with that of your mother or father.

3. Describe the process you follow to make, run, or fix something and your interest in the process, and compare these with the process followed and the interest felt by an earlier generation.

PERRI KLASS

# A WORLD WHERE TOO MANY CHILDREN DON'T GROW UP

*Perri Klass earned her bachelor's degree from Radcliffe College in 1979 and her medical degree from Harvard Medical School in 1986. She completed a residency in pediatrics at The Children's Hospital in Boston. Author as well as doctor, Klass has a collection of short stories,* I Am Having An Adventure, *a novel,* Recombinations, *and a new collection of essays,* Other Women's Children, *to her credit. She has written for* Discover *magazine and contributed articles to the* New York Times, Vogue, Esquire, *and* Mademoiselle. *The following account of her experience with Indian pediatrics was written when Klass was a fourth-year medical student at Harvard. The culture shock sent Klass sharply back to basics. In an earlier part of the article, not included in the excerpt that follows, Klass tells of questioning an obvious diagnosis because she mistook a ten-year-old boy for a girl. She was unfamiliar with the Sikh custom of long coiled braids for boys. Klass' article, which appeared in the April 1986 issue of* Discover, *illustrates the narrowness of the personal perspective with which we view the world.*

¹ Recently I spent some time in India, working in the pediatric department of an important New Delhi hospital. I wanted to learn about medicine outside the U.S., to work in a pediatric clinic in the Third World, and I suppose I also wanted to test my own medical education, to find out whether my newly acquired skills are in fact transferable to any place where there are human beings, with human bodies, subject to their range of ills and evils.

² But it wasn't just a question of my medical knowledge. In India, I found that my cultural limitations often prevented me from thinking clearly about patients. Everyone looked different, and I was unable to pick up any clues from their appearance, their manners of speech, their clothing. This is a family of Afghan refugees. This family is from the south of India. This child is from a very poor family. This child has a Nepalese name. All the clues I use at home to help me evaluate patients, clues ranging from what neighborhood they live in to what ethnic origin their names suggest, were hidden from me in India.

³ The people don't just look different on the outside, of course. It might be more accurate to say *the population is different.* The gene pool for example: there are some genetic diseases that are much more common here than there, cystic fibrosis, say, which you have to keep in mind when evaluating patients in Boston, but which would be a showoffy and highly unlikely diagnosis-out-of-a-book for a medical student to suggest in New Delhi (I know—in my innocence I suggested it).

⁴ And all of this, in the end, really reflects human diversity, though

admittedly it's reflected in the strange warped mirror of the medical profession; it's hard to exult in the variety of human genetic defects, or even in the variety of human culture, when you're looking at it as a tool for examining a sick child. Still, I can accept the various implications of a world full of different people, different populations.

[5] *The diseases are different.* The patient is a seven-year-old boy whose father says that over the past week and a half he has become progressively more tired, less active, and lately he doesn't seem to understand everything going on around him. Courteously, the senior doctor turns to me, asks what my assessment is. He asks this in a tone that suggests that the diagnosis is obvious, and as a guest, I'm invited to pronounce it. The diagnosis, whatever it is, is certainly not obvious to me. I can think of a couple of infections that might look like this, but no single answer. The senior doctor sees my difficulty, and offers a maxim, one that I've heard many times back in Boston. Gently, slightly reprovingly, he tells me, "Common things occur commonly. There are many possibilities, of course, but I think it is safe to say that this is almost certainly tuberculous meningitis."

[6] Tuberculous meningitis? Common things occur commonly? Somewhere in my brain (and somewhere in my lecture notes) "the complications of tuberculosis" are filed away, and, yes, I suppose it can affect the central nervous system, just as I vaguely remember that it can affect the stomach, and the skeletal system . . . To tell the truth, I've never even seen a case of straightforward tuberculosis of the lungs in a small child, let alone what I would have thought of as a rare complication.

[7] And hell, it's worse than that. I've done a fair amount of pediatrics back in Boston, but there are an awful lot of things I've never seen. When I'm invited to give an opinion on a child's rash, I come up with quite a creative list of tropical diseases, because guess what? I've never seen a child with measles before. In the U.S., all children are vaccinated against measles, mumps, and rubella at the age of one year. There are occasional outbreaks of measles among college students, some of whom didn't get vaccinated 20 years ago, but the disease is now very rare in small children. ("Love this Harvard medical student. Can't recognize tuberculous meningitis. Can't recognize measles or mumps. What the hell do you think they teach them over there in pediatrics?")

[8] And this, of course, is one of the main medical student reasons for going to study abroad, the chance to see diseases you wouldn't see at home. The pathology, we call it, as in "I got to see some amazing pathology while I was in India." It's embarrassing to find yourself suddenly ignorant, but it's interesting to learn all about a new range of diagnoses, symptoms, treatments, all things you might have learned from a textbook and then immediately forgotten as totally outside your own experience.

[9] The difficult thing is that these differences don't in any way, however tortured, reflect the glory of human variation. They reflect instead the sad partitioning of the species, because they're almost all preventable diseases, and their prevalence is a product of poverty, of lack of vaccinations, of malnutrition and poor sanitation. And therefore, though it's all very educa-

tional for the medical student (and I'm by now more or less used to parasitizing my education off of human suffering), this isn't a difference to be accepted without outrage.

¹⁰ *The expectations are different.* The child is a seven-month-old girl with diarrhea. She has been losing weight for a couple of weeks, she won't eat or drink, she just lies there in her grandmother's arms. The grandmother explains: one of her other grandchildren has just died from very severe diarrhea, and this little girl's older brother died last year, not of diarrhea but of a chest infection . . . I look at the grandmother's face, at the faces of the baby's mother and father, who are standing on either side of the chair, where the grandmother is sitting with the baby. All these people believe in the possibility of death, the chance that the child will not live to grow up. They've all seen many children die. These parents lost a boy last year, and they know that they may lose their daughter.

¹¹ The four have traveled for almost sixteen hours to come to this hospital, because after the son died last year, they no longer have faith in the village doctor. They're hopeful, they offer their sick baby to this famous hospital. They're prepared to stay in Delhi while she's hospitalized, the mother will sleep in the child's crib with her, the father and grandmother may well sleep on the hospital grounds. They've brought food, cooking pots, warm shawls because it's January and it gets cold at night. They're tough, and they're hopeful, but they believe in the possibility of death.

¹² Back home, in Boston, I've heard bewildered, grieving parents say, essentially, "Who would have believed that in the 1980s a child could just die like that?" Even parents with terminally ill children, children who spend months or years getting sicker and sicker, sometimes have great difficulty accepting that all the art and machinery of modern medicine is completely hopeless. They expect every child to live to grow up.

¹³ In India, it isn't that parents are necessarily resigned, and certainly not that they love their children less. They may not want to accept the dangers, but poor people, people living in poor villages or in urban slums, know the possibility is there. If anything, they may be even more terrified than American parents, just because perhaps they're picturing the death of some other loved child, imagining this living child going the way of that dead one.

¹⁴ I don't know. This is a gap I can't cross. I can laugh at my own inability to interpret the signals of a different culture, and I can read and ask questions and slowly begin to learn a little about the people I'm trying to help care for. I can blush at my ignorance of diseases uncommon in my home territory, study up in textbooks, and deplore inequalities that allow preventable diseases to ravage some unfortunate populations, while others are protected. I can try to become more discriminating in my appreciation of medical technology and its uses, understanding that the best hospital isn't the one that does the most tests. But I can't draw my lesson from this grandmother, these parents, this sick little girl. I can't imagine their awareness, their accommodations of what they know. I can't understand

how they live with it. I can't accept their acceptance. My medical training has taken place in a world where all children are supposed to grow up, and the exceptions to this rule are rare horrible diseases, disastrous accidents. This is the attitude, the expectation, I demand from patients. I'm left most disturbed not by the fact of children dying, not by the different diseases from which they die, or the differences in the medical care they receive, but by the way their parents look at me, at my profession. Perhaps its only in this that I allow myself to take it all personally.

## ◆ *PRACTICE*

### *Discussion*

1. What three misdiagnoses does Klass make? Why is she mistaken in each case? Is she a poor medical student?

2. What insights are particularly difficult or disturbing to Klass?

3. What difference does Klass discover between the way American and Indian parents look on the death of their children? Does she find any similarities?

4. Into what three major sections is the essay divided? What method of organization is used? Why are the three parts arranged in just that order? How are the three sentences that conclude the three sections related?

5. How has Klass provided for transitions in her essay? Are her transitions clear? smooth? effective?

6. Klass takes her subject seriously, but she doesn't always take herself seriously. What differences of diction or construction does she employ to cut herself down to size? In which section does she not employ these methods? Why not?

7. Study paragraph 13. Can you suggest a rearrangement of its sentences or phrases that might improve its interior logic as well as its transitions from paragraph 12 and to paragraph 14? Explain.

8. How does Klass build up emotion in her final paragraph? Look for similarities in words and structures and their relative placement in the paragraph. Look for short and long sentences.

### *Vocabulary*

| | | |
|---|---|---|
| pediatric | maxim | pathology |
| gene pool | tuberculosis | prevalence |
| cystic fibrosis | meningitis | parasitizing |
| exult | rubella | deplore |

*Writing*

1. Describe an experience that you have had performing a familiar activity in an unfamiliar setting.

2. Have you had the experience of visiting a foreign country with a radically different culture from your own? another section of your own country with a radically different lifestyle? Write an essay comparing and contrasting the two cultures or lifestyles. Give your essay focus and purpose.

3. Interview another person about his or her views on death, funerals, or immortality. Choose someone whose age, ethnic background, or religion is different from yours. Write an essay comparing and contrasting your views and those of the person you interview.

# C H A P T E R   17

# ANALOGY

## ANALOGY

Definition: An analogy is an *extended* comparison between two "things"—ideas, actions, processes, and so on. An analogy is more than just saying A is like B. It also says (in *extending* the point) that A is like B in certain important ways and for significant reasons. Analogies are used for two major purposes: (1) to help make an argument, and (2) to help readers understand something *unknown* by reference to a *known*.

Let's look at an example of purpose (1). In the passage below, Professor Joseph Weizenbaum, Professor of Computer Science at MIT, argues that educating children in computer science is a "delusion."

[1] We in the United States are in the grip of a mass delusion with respect to the education of kids with computers. The belief that it is urgent that we put computers in primary and secondary schools is based on a number of premises, of which only one is true. The true premise is that the whole world is becoming increasingly pervaded by computers. . . .

[2] I would like to draw an analogy to something that is ubiquitous in our society—the electric motor. There are undoubtedly many more electric motors in the United States than there are people, and almost everybody owns a lot of electric motors without thinking about them. They are everywhere, in automobiles, food mixers, vacuum cleaners, even watches and pencil sharpeners. Yet, it doesn't require any sort of electric-motor literacy to get on with the world, or, importantly, to be able to use these gadgets.

[3] Another important point about electric motors is that they're invisible. If you question someone using a vacuum cleaner, of course they know that there is an electric motor inside. But nobody says, "Well, I think I'll use an electric motor programmed to be a vacuum cleaner to vacuum the floor."

⁴ The computer will also become largely invisible, as it already is to a large extent in the consumer market. I believe that the more pervasive the computer becomes the more invisible it will become. We talk about it a lot now because it is new, but as we get used to the computer, it will retreat into the background. How much hands-on computer experience will students need? The answer, of course, is not very much. The student and the practicing professional will operate special-purpose instruments that happen to have computers as components.

⁵ If Johnny can't read and somebody writes computer software that will improve Johnny's reading score a little bit for the present, then the easiest thing to do is to bring in the computer and sit Johnny down at it. This makes it unnecessary to ask why Johnny can't read. In other words, it makes it unnecessary to reform the school system, or for that matter the society that tolerates the breakdown of its schools.

—Joseph Weizenbaum, "Another View from MIT"

In this analogy, you observe that Weizenbaum does more than just compare the electric motor to the computer. He also extends the comparison, talking about the electric motor in vacuum cleaners and automobiles, and its invisibility in such machines. He points out that the computer will also be invisible in machinery of various kinds; indeed it is invisible already "to a large extent in the consumer market." Weizenbaum uses the analogy to *argue* that students do not need to be taught in school to use an invisible mechanical servant. And he concludes that computer study wastes time which would be better spent on other educational endeavors.

The second purpose of typical analogies is to help a reader understand an *unknown* by reference to a *known*. Here is such an analogy from a student paper:

¹ A tank truck usually holds between 4,000 and 6,000 gallons of gasoline. Depending on the tanker and the oil company, there are three to six individual compartments which hold 600 to 900 gallons of gasoline apiece. The tank that contains the compartments is elliptically shaped to distribute the pressure equally and to allow a more complete flow of air when the gasoline is delivered.

² Until recently the only way to load a tanker was to climb up on top, where the openings to the compartments are located. You can easily picture this by visualizing six pop bottles lined up in single file on a table. A man wants to fill up bottle three, so he takes the cap off. He then inserts a small hose into the neck of the bottle and turns on a faucet which is connected to the hose.

³ A gasoline tanker is loaded in a similar way, but on a much larger scale. A man climbs on top of the tanker and opens a particular compartment by removing the cap. He then takes a hose with a four-foot metal pipe extension, about three and a half inches in diameter, and inserts the pipe down into the "bottle" (the compartment hole), which measures four inches in diameter. A pump is then turned on, allowing the gasoline to flow into the compartment.

In this analogy, an engineering student explains something relatively *unknown* (loading a tanker) by using her knowledge of something *known* (filling pop bottles). If you, the reader, think that a tanker consists of one long compartment, then the engineer's analogy is valuable and useful. If, however, you knew before reading the analogy how tankers were constructed and loaded, the analogy might not be particularly informative. That means, of course, that you should base your use of analogy on the knowledge of your audience.

All of us know many things that we can use to help a reader understand an idea better. Here a geology major helps to understand how the oil seismograph works by comparing it to shouting at a cliff wall.

| | |
|---|---|
| *Introduction*<br><br>*Definition* | ¹ For over twenty years, my father has worked on an oil seismograph crew. We all know about the big seismographs that detect and measure earthquakes. The oil seismograph is a small portable electronic instrument that detects and measures artificial earthquakes. The purpose of the instrument is to find geological structures that may contain oil. I have worked for the past two summers on a seismograph crew. In that period of time I have learned that the oil seismograph instrument is not mysterious because it can be compared to shouting at a cliff wall. |
| *First analogy:*<br>*Echo, and*<br>*relationship to*<br>*distance* | ² Let me begin with an occurrence that should be familiar. Imagine yourself standing near the base of a large cliff. If you shout at the cliff face, you will get an echo because the sound waves bounce back from the so-called "interface" where air meets rock. The sound waves travel at 1100 feet per second. You can find out how far you are standing from the cliff by measuring the time it takes for your shout to travel from you to the cliff and back again, and then by solving a simple formula for distance. |
| *Echo analogy*<br>*applied to*<br>*seismograph* | ³ The function of the oil seismograph is to find out how far down in the earth the horizontal layers of rock are. To discover this distance, the oil seismologist digs a deep hole (usually 100–200 feet) in the surface of the ground—the purpose of the hole I will explain later. At the bottom of the hole, he explodes a heavy charge of dynamite. Ground waves travel from the explosion down to the layers of rock. At each major interface between the layers, the waves bounce back to the surface. The explosion is similar to shouting at the cliff. Just as sound travels through the air at a certain speed, ground waves travel through the earth, although much faster. Ground waves bounce from rock interfaces as sound waves bounce from a cliff face. And the seismologist can determine distance just as you can determine the distance between you and the cliff. |
| | ⁴ Why does the seismologist dig a hole to explode the dynamite? Much of the ground surface is covered with what geologists call *weathering,* that relatively loose covering of soil, sand, clay, etc., that usually goes down to the water table. This weathering has a disastrous effect upon seismic waves in the ground; it slows them up and even disperses them. To explode |

*Second analogy:* a dynamite charge on top of the ground would be like shout-
*Weathering of* ing at a cliff face through a bowl of mush—no matter how
*ground like mush* loud you shouted, little of your voice would get through. So
the seismologist drills through the weathering and plants the
dynamite charge below it. Usually the weathering has a bad
effect only on the waves at the point of explosion; the *reflected*
waves will travel through the weathering to the instruments on
the surface.

*Differences* 5 In the interests of accuracy, I should add that the analogy
between air waves and seismic waves is partly literal and partly
figurative. The principles are similar but the conditions are
different. Air waves are relatively constant in speed because
the medium varies little. Seismic waves, by contrast, increase in
speed with depth, and the increase is irregular and difficult to
measure. Also, seismic reflections vary in ways that no one
completely understands. But the analogy is, in a basic sense,
revealing and accurate enough to explain to a beginner how an
oil seismograph works.

We can diagram the first basic analogy here as follows:

|  | *Shouting at cliff face* | | *Using a seismograph* |
|---|---|---|---|
| Point A | shout | ⟶ | set off dynamite |
| Point B | creates sound waves in air | ⟷ | creates seismic waves in earth |
| Point C | waves travel at set rate | ⟷ | waves travel at certain rates |
| Point D | waves bounce back from cliff | ⟷ | waves bounce back from rock interface |
| Point E | distance can be measured | ⟷ | distance can be measured |

When you construct an analogy, make sure that the compared points
*are* comparable. Cut out or explain any points that cannot be logically
compared and be certain that the familiar or known side of the analogy is
really familiar and known to your reader. It is useless to explain a mineral's
crystal-lattice structure by reference to analytic geometry if your reader
knows nothing about analytic geometry. Do not try to stretch an analogy
too far. Like the fabled camel which first put his nose in the man's tent,
then his head, and finally his whole body, pushing the man out of the tent,
metaphor tends to creep into analogies. What starts out to be literally
explanatory can become as unreal and metaphorical as a fairy tale, and no
more convincing.

Sometimes you may choose to develop analogies by using figures of
speech. Figurative language can help you to clarify, dramatize, or sharpen
your comparison. The function of such analogies is not so much to explain
one "side" of the extended comparison, but to help the reader see the
whole thing in a new and fresh way. For instance, we all know what war and
cancer are; they are known to us. But observe how Sydney Harris uses

metaphor to argue that war is like cancer; both must be eradicated to save the species.

*Introduction*
*The term "self-preservation" introduced*

[1] We say that the aim of life is self-preservation, if not for the individual, at least for the species. Granted that every organism seeks this end, does every organism know what is best for its self-preservation?

[2] Consider cancer cells and noncancer cells in the human body. The normal cells are aimed at reproducing and functioning in a way that is beneficial to the body. Cancer cells, on the other hand, spread in a way that threatens and ultimately destroys the whole body. Normal cells work harmoniously, because they "know," in a sense, that their preservation depends upon the health of the body they inhabit. While they are organisms in themselves, they also act as part of a substructure, directed at the good of the whole body.

*Contrast between cancer cells and normal cells*

*Beginning of analogy: "Cancer cells [like warriors] do not know about self-preservation"*

[3] We might say, metaphorically, that cancer cells do not know enough about self-preservation; they are, biologically, more ignorant than normal cells. The aim of cancer cells is to spread throughout the body, to conquer all the normal cells—and when they reach their aim, the body is dead. And so are the cancer cells.

[4] For cancer cells destroy not only all rival cells, in their ruthless biological warfare, but also destroy the large organization—the body itself—signing their own suicide warrant.

*Extension of analogy: War and cancer both kill*

[5] The same is true of war, especially in the modern world. War is the social cancer of mankind. It is a pernicious form of ignorance, for it destroys not only its "enemies," but also the whole superstructure of which it is a part—and thus eventually it defeats itself. Nations live in a state of anarchy, not in a state of law. And, like cancer cells, nations do not know that their ultimate self-interest lies in preserving the health and harmony of the whole body (that is, the community of man), for if that body is mortally wounded, then no nation can survive and flourish.

*Argument stated in an "if . . . then" analogy*

[6] If the aim of life is self-preservation—for the species as well as for the individual—we must tame or eradicate the cancer cells of war in the social organism. And this can be done only when nations begin to recognize that what may seem to be "in the national interest" cannot be opposed to the common interest of mankind, or both the nation and mankind will die in this "conquest."

*Analogy continued*

*Conclusion*

[7] The life of every organism depends upon the viability of the system of which it is a member. The cancer cells cannot exist without the body to inhabit, and they must be exterminated if they cannot be re-educated to behave like normal cells. At present, their very success dooms them to failure—just as a victorious war in the atomic age would be an unqualified disaster for the dying winner.

—Sydney J. Harris, "When Winning Is Losing"

When using metaphor in an analogy, keep in mind C. S. Lewis' advice:

1. The figures [of speech] or metaphors should be well chosen by the writer.
2. The reader must be able to understand the figures.
3. Both writer and reader should understand that figurative language is being used.

## WRITING AND REVISING AN ANALOGY (AN EXAMPLE)

Gerry Kinder starts to write an extended analogy. He begins with a title:

*IS THE GREEK LETTER ORGANIZATION JUST A COUNTRY CLUB?*

This Gerry follows with a scratch outline:

1. Me and the Greeks
   — they're OK

2. Snobbery
   and exclusiveness

3. The great life — in both country club
   and Greek house

4. Business deals
   country club
   frat house

Gerry now begins his first draft:

[1] I'm neither for nor against Greeks. My sister went through rush here two years ago and pledged Tri-Delt. She is now a happy sorority girl. I have shown some interest my first year in going Greek and have visited some of the houses and been involved in some of the entertainments. I've played football against Greeks in Touch League. I know and like many Greeks of both sexes. But

something bothers me about them—even though I am not "politically" against their organization. (I am not a devout Independent either.)

² There is too much snobbery in the Greek system. They remind me of the people I used to caddy for in the country club at home. Their major idea is to be exclusive. Exclusive. The One and Only. Their motto is: Keep others out. Otherwise, why join either the country club or a fraternity/sorority?

³ Another advantage of both is that you get to live better. In a Greek house you eat better and have a better place to sleep and have fun. Similarly a country club is the place to eat great dinners, and swim in a luxurious swimming pool. There is something very similar about the people sitting around the pool watching the golfers come in at dusk and their counterpart: the boys sitting on the front steps watching the students coming back from their late afternoon classes, the sun shining through the trees. Glamor.

⁴ And the deals. How many deals are completed over golf and drinks at the country club? How many friendships are cemented in the fraternity, friendships that later are used in furthering business relationships?

At this point Gerry stops. For him, this has been a "letting loose" draft, one that provides ideas and material, a rambling outline of sorts. Now he needs to think hard about the ordering of ideas and shape the whole paper more carefully. He puts down a new order of elements in the basic analogy:

1. Deals (business, etc.)
2. Live better
3. Exclusiveness: *the whole pt.*

Now he begins on the new draft. He cuts the first paragraph entirely because it starts the paper too slowly, and he wants to see how short a paper he can write that still does the job. How vivid—yet economical—can he be? He chooses a new title and writes two new opening paragraphs that set analogous scenes. Having finished these, he simply keeps writing:

### GOLDEN GHETTOES

¹ They sit quietly, handsome wives beside them; drinks in their hands, the setting sun glimmering beautifully on their tanned faces. There are muted sounds of traffic from the highway a mile away and sounds of splashing from the pool a few feet away. "I parred the last one!" says a happy man walking toward the club house. He is about fifty, his fine-looking hair glowing silver in the setting sun.

² Two-hundred miles from this scene, their sons and daughters sit quietly, tanned faces turned toward the street. A convertible pulls up in the driveway, and a young man with the arms of a sweater tied around his throat vaults gracefully over the side of the car. A girl drinks from a beer can, tilts it high, drops it carefully into a wastebasket. Another girl strides by on the sidewalk, her long legs carrying her smoothly along. "I aced the geology exam!" she calls out happily. A murmur follows her down the street.

3 Here are two sides of the good life, American style. In the country club, affluent Americans play and enjoy themselves: this is what life is meant to be. In the fraternity and sorority, their sons and daughters play and enjoy themselves: practicing their skills for the life that will be theirs—some day.

4 But there is more to the uses of Greek organization and country club besides just the good life. It is well known that thousands of business deals every year are made in country clubs. On the golf course, people agree to buy this or sell that. Plans are made: "Let's talk to old Freddy about his work on the downtown mall." (As a caddy I would stand and listen; they ignored me as if I were a 19th-century slave, present but invisible.) At lunch they pull out pens and pencils and draw on napkins and add up figures. "Waiter—more napkins!" The lawyers talk to engineers, who talk to city council members, who shout across the room: "Hey, Sam, are you going to handle the Lions' Antique Show this year?"

5 In the frats, the same kind of scenes occur. The same names, the same ignoring of waiters, similar deals. But little money is involved usually, except for festive occasions. Jack Windsor chairs the Homecoming program. "Can we get THE FILTHY FIVE this year? I heard they were great at Purdue." A senior, graduating at midterm, tells his roommate: "Listen, next year call up Selkirk in my Dad's office; he may be hiring then." Meanwhile, over in a sorority, two girls plot an attack on a favored law school. "I know what you should write in your Statement on the application," says one. "They *love* to hear that you're big on sports."

6 All this is real enough, the good life and the business deals. Yet what keeps both country club and Greek organization permanently alive is more deeply psychological. It is a sense of being different by choice and warming your whole self in that choice. Members of both organizations swim happily in exclusivity. Not everybody can get in; they are the chosen few. Both organizations come with a dozen privileges that not even a Phi Beta Kappa key can get for you. The key won't allow you to ignore the slave carrying forty pounds of golf clubs; or to eat de-boned trout and drink champagne with the mayor of the city; or to date the star quarterback who (after graduation) will be worth two million dollars on June 1st. Greek house and country club: the golden ghettoes of American life.

## ✦ *PRACTICE*

### *Discussion*

1. Read Gerry's final draft and prepare for discussion the following questions:
   a. Diagram the analogy, following the form on p. 328. Discuss the diagram in relation to the paper's organization.
   b. What is the writer's point? Is there a "known" side of the analogy?
   c. How is the organization similar to one of the *comparison and contrast* patterns?
   d. Discuss the use of dialogue in the paper.

    e. Study the discussion of the *representative example* on pp. 249–250. How has Gerry used that kind of illustrative material in his paper?

    f. How well does Gerry fulfill his goal: to write a vivid, economical paper that "does the job"?

2. Discuss each of the analogies below. Do any of them depend on figures of speech? Is the extended comparison consistently made? Do the differences between the two elements being compared weaken the analogy? Is the "known side" of the analogy familiar enough to you? How could the analogy be improved (if at all)?

    a. For a long time now, since the beginning, in fact, men and women have been sparring and dancing around with each other, each pair trying to get it together and boogie to the tune called Life. For some people, it was always a glide, filled with grace and ease. For most of us, it is a stumble and a struggle, always trying to figure out the next step, until we find a partner whose inconsistencies seem to fit with ours, and the two of us fit into some kind of rhythm. Some couples wind up struggling and pulling at cross purposes; and of course, some people never get out on the floor, just stand alone in the corners, looking hard at the dancers.

       That's the way it's always been, and probably, always will be. The only difference now is that for the past few years a group of noisy people have been standing over next to the band and yelling above it, "Hey, listen everybody! You don't have to dance to the old tune any more! You can make up your own tune! You can make up your dance steps! *The man doesn't even have to lead any more!* Forget the band! This is a whole new movement! It's called *you can make your Life whatever you want!*"—Jay Molishever, "Marriage"

    b. In practice, showing "respect" for machines means learning not to look on them simply as slaves. When a slave owner sees that his slaves are stronger, faster, and more efficient than himself, he is likely to fear that someday these slaves will realize their power and revolt. In the same way, so long as human beings see machines as slaves, they will continue to regard any machine that is stronger, faster, or "smarter" than themselves as a potential threat. It is only when the stereotypes are broken and an individual human being makes the effort to become thoroughly familiar with a particular machine—however complex or powerful it may be—that this fear is overcome and the machine becomes a partner rather than a slave. Just as truckers get to know their "rigs," sailors their ships, and musicians their instruments, so ordinary people in the near future may get to know their computers.

       —Jennings Lane, "Computer Chess"

    c. Our dependence on uncertain energy sources to power our big cars and our recreational vehicles, to heat and cool our oversized houses and ill-designed office buildings, may be as deadly in the long run as an addict's dependence on dope.—William Raspberry

d. Probably you have to go down several coal mines before you can get much grasp of the processes that are going on around you. This is chiefly because the mere effort of getting from place to place makes it difficult to notice anything else. In some ways it is even disappointing, or at least is unlike what you have expected. You get into the cage, which is a steel box about as wide as a telephone box and two or three times as long. It holds ten men, but they pack it like pilchards in a tin, and a tall man cannot stand upright in it. The steel door shuts upon you, and somebody working the winding gear above drops you into the void. . . . When you crawl out at the bottom you are perhaps four hundred yards under ground. That is to say you have a tolerable-sized mountain on top of you; hundreds of yards of solid rock, bones of extinct beasts, subsoil, flints, roots of growing things, green grass and cows grazing on it—all this suspended over your head and held back only by wooden props as thick as the calf of your leg.

—George Orwell, *The Road to Wigan Pier*

e. It would sound ridiculous to ask, "Should robbery be studied in our schools?" Yet, if academic freedom is the sole issue rather than national survival, such a question is consistent and in order. If carpentry, why not burglary? Both are ways and means of getting a living. But carpentry is socially constructive and robbery is socially destructive. Communism is likewise socially destructive for its methods frankly include robbery, murder, arson, lying, and incitement to violence. These it defends and advocates on the basis of its working slogan that the "ends justify the means."

We protect our young people from harmful epidemic diseases of a physical nature such as smallpox, by quarantining them. We expose our young people to harmful epidemic diseases of an ideological nature, such as Communism, by a false suicidal interpretation of academic freedom. What youth does when it reaches maturity is something else again. At that time, in the interest of national security, adults should study Communism to be able to recognize it and fight it for dear life whenever and under whatever disguise it rears its hideous head.

—Ruth Alexander,
"Should Communism Be Studied in Our Schools?"

## ◆ PRACTICE

### Writing

1. Write a paragraph or essay using one of the following theses and the analogy that it suggests; or you may use a thesis and analogy of your own choice. Specify your stance.

a.　　*Thesis:*　The theater department should produce some older, less contemporary plays.

*Analogy:*　A theater that produces only new plays is like a library that stocks only new books

—Martin Gottfried

b.　　*Thesis:*　Man should colonize space.

*Analogy:*　Saying that man should not colonize space because it is too dangerous is like refusing to leave a sinking ship and board a lifeboat because the open sea is too dangerous.

c.　　*Thesis:*　Smoking should not be allowed in public buildings.

*Analogy:*　A person who smokes (or who breathes other people's cigarette smoke) takes in a small dose of poison each day.

d.　　*Thesis:*　Being able to drive a car makes a young person feel like an adult.

*Analogy:*　Passing one's first driving test is similar to an initiation rite.

e.　　*Thesis:*　Every citizen should make an effort to avoid littering the nation's roadsides, parks, and cities.

*Analogy:*　Destroying the nation's environment is like burning down your house.

2. The powerful and prosperous Roman empire was said to have fallen for the following reasons: (a) the rise of despotic one-man rule; (b) the lowering of the prestige of the government; (c) the devaluing of the currency and increasing taxation; (d) the creation of a welfare state; (e) the rise of military control over civil government; (f) the expansion of bureaucracy; (g) the lowering of public morality; (h) the inability of the military to repulse foreign invaders. Write a paper in which you argue by using analogy that the United States is (or is not, or partly is) going the way of ancient Rome.

3. Write a figurative analogy in which you define a term by comparing it to something else. Suggestions:

Hysteria is like a fire.
Human opposites are like two magnets.
Social welfare multiplies like yeast cells.
Pets are like children.

SYDNEY J. HARRIS

# WHAT TRUE EDUCATION SHOULD DO

*Veteran newspaperman Sydney J. Harris wrote his syndicated column "Strictly Personal" from 1941–first for the* Chicago Daily News *and then for the* Chicago Sun-Times— *until his death in 1986. Although Harris was born in England in 1917, he was a thorough Chicagoan, having lived there since he was five. He attended the University of Chicago before launching a career that resulted in many honors and several books, among them* Strictly Personal *(1953), a collection of his early columns, and* The Best of Sydney J. Harris *(1975), a later counterpart. Harris wrote about American life in particular, about human nature in general. As the following selection from his "Strictly Personal" column illustrates, he knew how to draw a striking analogy to make the reader see a general point.*

[1] When most people think of the word "education," they think of a pupil as a sort of animate sausage casing. Into this empty casing, the teachers are supposed to stuff "education."

[2] But genuine education, as Socrates knew more than two thousand years ago, is not inserting the stuffings of information *into* a person, but rather eliciting knowledge *from* him; it is the drawing out of what is in the mind.

[3] "The most important part of education," once wrote William Ernest Hocking, the distinguished Harvard philosopher, "is this instruction of a man in what he has inside of him."

[4] And, as Edith Hamilton has reminded us, Socrates never said, "I know, learn from me." He said, rather, "Look into your own selves and find the spark of truth that God has put into every heart, and that only you can kindle to a flame."

[5] In the dialogue called the "Meno," Socrates takes an ignorant slave boy, without a day of schooling, and proves to the amazed observers that the boy really "knows" geometry—because the principles and axioms of geometry are already in his mind, waiting to be called out.

[6] So many of the discussions and controversies about the content of education are futile and inconclusive because they are concerned with what should "go into" the student rather than with what should be taken out, and how this can best be done.

[7] The college student who once said to me, after a lecture, "I spend so much time studying that I don't have a chance to learn anything," was succinctly expressing his dissatisfaction with the sausage-casing view of education.

[8] He was being so stuffed with miscellaneous facts, with such an indi-

gestible mass of material, that he had no time (and was given no encouragement) to draw on his own resources, to use his own mind for analyzing and synthesizing and evaluating this material.

[9] Education, to have any meaning beyond the purpose of creating well-informed dunces, must elicit from the pupil what is latent in every human being—the rules of reason, the inner knowledge of what is proper for men to be and do, the ability to sift evidence and come to conclusions that can generally be assented to by all open minds and warm hearts.

[10] Pupils are more like oysters than sausages. The job of teaching is not to stuff them and then seal them up, but to help them open and reveal the riches within. There are pearls in each of us, if only we knew how to cultivate them with ardor and persistence.

## ◆ *PRACTICE*

### *Discussion*

1. What are the responsibilities of a teacher, according to Harris? What are the responsibilities of a student? How do current discussions of education fail to address these responsibilities?

2. Who are Hocking, Hamilton, and Socrates? What does their presence in Harris' essay tell you about his value system?

3. Is Harris' view of education a bit too simple? What limitations do you perceive in his approach? Can you expand the pearl analogy to illustrate a broader view?

4. Are Harris' analogies figurative or literal? If you said figurative, suggest a literal analogy for education. If you said literal, suggest a figurative one. How might you take either of these analogies too far?

5. Is Harris still using the sausage-casing analogy in paragraph 8? Explain.

6. List every repetition of the term *put into* or a variation of that phrase that you can find in the essay. Do the same with *draw out*. Why is the variation important? How can repetition be effective? Has Harris overdone the two?

7. What is the composition of the audience at which this essay is most probably aimed? To what part of that audience are the references in paragraphs 3 and 4 likely to appeal? To what part of the audience is the reference in paragraph 7 likely to appeal?

8. What figurative analogy is Socrates quoted as drawing? What literal analogy does he make? Why is analogy a strategy particularly well suited to Harris' thesis?

## *Vocabulary*

| | | |
|---|---|---|
| animate | futile | latent |
| casing | succinctly | assented |
| [Socratic] dialogue | synthesizing | cultivate |
| axioms | elicit | ardor |

## *Writing*

1 Use a fresh analogy to explain your sense of what your education was like in elementary or secondary school compared to what it is like in college.

2. Describe a former teacher who treated you like an oyster or a sausage casing. Explain how you reacted.

3. Define the proper role and responsibilities of a student. Try to use analogy to make your definition clear.

ANN H. ZWINGER

# BECOMING MOM TO AN INFANT WORD PROCESSOR

*Nature writer Ann H. Zwinger was born in Muncie, Indiana, in 1925. She earned a B.A. degree from Wellesley College in 1946 and an M.A. from Indiana University in 1950. Mother of three daughters as well as an infant word processor, she currently lives in Colorado Springs. Her books include* Land Above the Trees: A Guide to the American Alpine Tundra *(1970), which was nominated for the National Book Award;* Run, River, Run: A Naturalist's Journey Down One of the Great Rivers of the West *(1975);* A Conscious Stillness: Two Naturalists on Thoreau's River *(1982); and* A Desert Country Near the Sea *(1983). The latter two created the need for a computer. The essay that follows, which appeared in the February 1982 issue of* Smithsonian *magazine, was, presumably, written on a word processor.*

¹ A decade ago I graduated to an electric typewriter which, since I type my own manuscripts, was a godsend. Within the last year, however, I found myself with two books to finish almost simultaneously, and when my agent sent me an article about the growing number of writers using word processors, working with one seemed the answer to endless hours of arduous typing when you've just run out of available hours.

² But becoming the mother of a word processor is not simple. It is like adopting a child. First there were preliminary interviews which, I suspect, may have indicated my fitness for leasehood, such as: Will this person be able to "think computer"? Will she take the time to train it in the way it ought to go?

³ After the order was placed (I refrained from saying I didn't care if it were a boy or girl), my workroom was checked to see if I had the proper environment for the new infant. My work desk had proper triple-pronged sockets, but cagily I did not let anyone see my pack rat's dream of a back room in which old and new manuscripts, shells and rocks, account book, index cards, unlabeled Diptera, *Gourmet* magazines back to 1970, and dictionaries all coexist in tottering equilibrium.

⁴ Finally the thing in question arrived. No young mother ever as proudly removed her first child from the hospital as I did the word processor from its packing, plugging numbered plugs into numbered sockets. When I turned it on the CRT (for cathode ray tube) hummed gently, a *most* satisfactory child.

⁵ But not the printer. The printer balked and I had to call the pedia— sorry, repairman—who spent almost a whole afternoon adjusting, tickling

its rollers, and offering lollipops, until it, too, sprang into proper configuration with a triumphant whirl.

[6] Then began the training period. Mine, not its. Immediately the inevitable occurred: a whole sentence simply kept spacing to the right, running down into the next line. And it simply would not come back. I chased it by cursor and by scatological comment. Neither worked. Finally I "thought computer." I won, but not without some scars on my ego.

[7] I soon discovered that I simply needed to apply a little parental guidance and all would work well. When I requested "MOVE" it queried "MOVE WHAT?" and then "WHERE TO?" And when I chucked it under the cursor it made typing an uninterrupted flowing delight; it moved paragraphs, created intriguing juxtapositions, and even enhanced the opportunity for creative play. And, *mirabile dictu,* it even corrected my spelling!

[8] The printer got clean ribbons when necessary and was fed paper when hungry. We developed a working relationship of considerable satisfaction to all of us. Or so *I* thought.

[9] Then came growing pains. The CRT spit out petulantly, "Printer error, printer error!" And the other machine grated "Ratchety ratchety BLAT!" The CRT flashed accusingly: "Printer reprinting. Check output." So, I checked.

[10] After that, the inevitable: adolescence. Having been through it with assorted children, I should have been prepared. But somehow one never is. The CRT took three chapters and ran. Absconded. Three hard-worked chapters. Gone into the ether.

[11] And the printer. When I stood beside it, it behaved. But let me step out of the room and, like a greedy teenager, it stuffed paper onto its roller as fast as it could. And jammed.

[12] Well, what can you do but forgive, forget—and (sigh) retype? Hope your patience and forbearance will be rewarded? And at last I do believe I see signs of real maturity in the CRT. Giving a little. Seeing things my way once in a while. Not losing things so much. Growing up.

[13] And just lately I've been able to fix a sandwich in relative serenity while the printer bleeps and burrs out Chapter 5. The CRT is even getting not to mind a little mayonnaise on its keys, and on arduous days, is not averse to a chocolate bar alongside.

[14] I wonder: has anyone written a diet program for a matronly WP?


## ✦ PRACTICE

*Discussion*

1. To what specific steps in a child's development does Zwinger liken her learning to use her word processor? Where does she begin a step in the analogy, pretend to hesitate, and then roll into the analogy full-tilt? Why does she pretend to hesitate?

2. How much previous experience does the author have with machines? How much experience does she have with children? How do her two types of experiences help her with her word processor?

3. What does Zwinger mean by the term "think computer"? What scars do you think she acquired on her ego in the process of learning to "think computer"?

4. How does Zwinger order the steps of her analogy? What advantages might she gain by using a different organization of points? What might she lose?

5. What is amusing about the use of dialogue in the essay? You have been advised by the authors of this text to "avoid unnecessary repetition of the speakers' names or unnecessary descriptions of the way they speak." Should Zwinger get a "D" for dialogue? Explain.

6. In general, the longer sentences in the essay deal with what kind of content? With what content do the shorter sentences and fragments generally deal? Point out a good example of each.

7. Run a "transition check" on Zwinger's essay, i.e., list all the first words of every paragraph after the first. What interesting patterns do you perceive in the list? Are Zwinger's transitions smooth? clear?

8. In the last two paragraphs, Zwinger switches from figurative to literal analogy. Explain what happens there. Is Zwinger in trouble by mixing the two types of analogy?

### Vocabulary

| | | |
|---|---|---|
| godsend | configuration | *mirabile dictu* |
| arduous | cursor | petulantly |
| Diptera | scatological | absconded |
| cathode ray tube | chucked | ether |

### Writing

1. Pull a reversal on Zwinger's article and write an essay on "Becoming a Child to a Parental Computer."

2. Write an essay showing how using a computer is like playing a sport of your choice.

3. For those who do not now and have never used a computer, write an essay about a human activity that has, in your opinion, become overly regimented and mindlessly mechanized (registering for courses, perhaps, or seeing a doctor). Use an analogy to a machine, a factory, or a mechanized process to make your point.

## A. M. ROSENTHAL

# LEGALIZING ADDICTIVE DRUGS LIKE BRINGING BACK SLAVERY

*A. M. Rosenthal is best known as a* New York Times *reporter and editor. As a reporter, he filed stories from the United Nations, Warsaw, Geneva, and Tokyo. He won the Pulitzer Prize for international reporting in 1960. Rosenthal rose through the ranks of various editorships at the* Times, *until he was made executive editor in 1977. He is now a highly respected syndicated columnist for the newspaper. His wide experience in the world does not let him take certain subjects lightly, nor does he tend to care for "on the other hand, I see my opponent's point" arguments. Those who would legalize drugs, he believes, are simply wrong.*

[1] Across the country, a scattered but influential collection of intellectuals is intensely engaged in making the case for slavery. With considerable passion, these Americans are repeatedly expounding the benefits of not only tolerating slavery but legalizing it.

[2] Legalization, they say, would make life less dangerous for the free. It would save a great deal of money. And since the economies could be used to improve the lot of the slaves, in the end they would be better off. The new anti-abolitionists, like their predecessors in the 19th century, concede that those now in bondage do not themselves see the benefits of legalizing their status. But in time they will, we are assured, because the beautiful part of legalization is that slavery would be designed so as to keep slaves pacified with the very thing that enslaves them!

[3] The form of slavery under discussion is drug addiction. It does not have every characteristic of more traditional forms of bondage. But they have enough in common to make the comparison morally valid—and the campaign for drug legalization morally disgusting.

[4] Like the plantation slavery that was a foundation of American society for so long, drug addiction largely involves specifiable groups of people. Most of the enchained are children and adolescents of all colors and black and Hispanic adults. Like plantation slavery, drug addiction is passed on from generation to generation. And this may be the most important similarity: like plantation slavery, addiction will destroy among its victims the social resources most valuable to free people for their own betterment—family units, family traditions, family values.

[5] Anti-abolitionists argue that legalization would make drugs so cheap and available that the profit for crime would be removed. Well-supplied addicts would be peaceful addicts. We would not waste billions for jails. We could spend some of the savings helping the addicted become drug-free.

That would happen at the very time that new millions of Americans were being enticed into addiction by legalization.

 [6] Are we really foolish enough to believe that tens of thousands of drug gang members would meekly steal away, foiled by the marvels of the free market? Not likely. The pushers would cut prices, making more money than ever from the ever-growing mass market. They would immediately increase the potency and variety beyond anything available at any government-approved narcotics counters. Crime would increase. Crack produces paranoid violence. More permissiveness equals more use equals more violence. And what will legalization do to the brains of Americans drawn into drug slavery by easy availability?

 [7] Earlier this year, an expert drug pediatrician told me that after only a few months babies born with crack addiction seemed to recover. Now we learn that stultifying behavioral effects last at least through early childhood. Will they last forever? How long will crack affect neurological patterns in the brains of adult crack users? Dr. Gabriel Nahas of Columbia University argues in his new book, *Cocaine: The Great White Plague,* that the damage may be irreversible. Would it not be an act of simple intelligence to drop the legalization campaign until we find out?

 [8] Then why do a number of writers and academicians, left to right, support it? I have discussed this with anti-drug leaders like Jesse Jackson, Dr. Mitchell Rosenthal of Phoenix House and William Bennett, who search for answers themselves.

 [9] Perhaps the answer is that the legalizers are not dealing with reality in America. I think the reason has to do with class. Crack is beginning to move into the white middle and upper classes. That is a tragedy for those addicted. However, it has not yet destroyed the communities around which their lives revolve, not taken over every street and doorway. It has not passed generation to generation among them, killing the continuity of family. But in ghetto communities poverty and drugs come together in a catalytic reaction that is reducing them to social rubble.

 [10] The anti-abolitionists, virtually all white and well-to-do, do not see or do not care. Either way, they show symptoms of the callousness of class. That can be a particularly dangerous social disorder.


## ◆ PRACTICE

### Discussion

1. Check again the *diagram* of an analogy (p. 328). Make a similar diagram of Rosenthal's analogy.

2. Looking at your diagram, do you find any flaw in the extended comparison (analogy)?

3. Explain the *order* of points in the analogy.

4. Which side of the analogy is *known* (see p. 325)? Why does the author use *this* known side, rather than some other? Suggest two or three different knowns, of varying effectiveness, that the author might have used.

5. Is the whole essay an analogy? Explain your answer.

6. What is the job of paragraphs 5–10?

7. Why does the author wait until paragraph 3 to make his main point: "The form of slavery under discussion is drug addiction"?

8. Explain the purpose of the last two sentences of paragraph 3.

*Vocabulary*

| | | |
|---|---|---|
| abolitionists | enticed | permissiveness |
| bondage | foiled | paranoid |
| pacified | potency | |

*Writing*

1. Write a brief paper in which you *expand* Rosenthal's analogy, using more points of comparison.

2. Write an attack on Rosenthal's argument, pointing out any weaknesses you see in the analogy.

3. Write an argument using Rosenthal's historical technique of comparison on other American social problems. *Examples:* abortion, day care, America as peacekeeper for the world, crime, punishment, sex and violence, etc.

# ARGUMENTATION

## ARGUMENTATION

Situation One:

"I got gas for my car today—those *prices*! The big oil companies are sure out to get all they can out of the consumer."

"Well, it's not the oil companies' fault. They can't get enough oil for their refineries."

"I bet they've got *plenty* of oil! They just know they have the consumer where they want him. We've got to have fuel for our cars and houses, and they'll jack up the prices in this fake shortage, and then keep them there after the shortage is over."

"How do you know it's a fake shortage—are you an expert on the oil business or something?"

Situation Two:

Dear Sir:

I read your recent editorial in which you attacked the patriotic organization "Freedom Ringers" that calls people on the telephone and tells them how bad communism is.

I don't understand your point at all. Isn't telephoning a voluntary act? Who pays for the call? Not the man who owns the phone. Who is forced to listen? Any man has a recognized right of not listening to a Freedom Ringer.

Why does the telephone company yield to pressure? Is freedom of speech coming to an end in America?

Very truly yours,

Each of these situations involves *argument*, which is an attempt to convince or persuade. But neither situation represents a *formal argument*, as we use the phrase here. A *formal argument* is an orderly arrangement of carefully defined terms and properly qualified statements (backed by evidence) which support a single thesis. A formal argument is a written attempt to *convince* or *persuade* the reader that he should *believe* something or *do* something (or both).

It is possible to argue two or three theses in a long formal argument. But in practice, a well-made formal argument tends to have its own unity, so that even if you are arguing two or three theses, you will find that there is an implicit single thesis underlying or supporting them. It is important that a formal argument have evidence. Formally speaking, assertions such as these are not arguments:

> "The big oil companies are sure out to get all they can out of the consumer."
> "Any person has a recognized right of not listening to a Freedom Ringer."

The formal argument requires you to manage your stance with unusual care. When such an argument is successful, both you and your reader feel that you have arrived at a conclusion more or less together, having agreed to believe in the thesis of the argument. As the writer, you *lead* your reader to agree with you not by force or deception but by the legitimate power of your persuasion.

What makes a formal argument *persuasive?* In most genuinely persuasive arguments there are five elements. We will discuss each of these elements in the pages that follow.

1. *A human approach.* The writer strikes the reader as an honest, believable person who has a genuine interest in his material and in his reader.

2. *Solid evidence.* The writer does not rely on mere assertion; he uses pertinent facts, details, statistics, or testimony from authorities to back up his statements.

3. *Good logic.* The writer makes the right *connections* between his pieces of evidence; he creates accurate generalizations and draws proper conclusions. If the evidence warrants, the writer makes use of the thinking and organization strategies of *cause and effect, comparison and contrast, analogy,* etc.

4. *An avoidance of fallacy.* The writer not only avoids logical errors, he also avoids irrelevancies, false appeals to emotion, or question begging. (These and other fallacies are explained in this chapter.)

5. *A clear argumentative organization.* The writer organizes his argument so that his reader can understand all its parts and how the parts relate to each other and to the thesis.

# USE A HUMAN APPROACH

The *human approach* in argument involves a special adaptation of the writer's stance, particularly the relationship between the writer and reader. The human approach has two basic aspects, closely interrelated. The first deals with the writer's *character* (his "ethical proof"), the second with the writer's *feeling for his reader* (his "you-attitude").

## Ethical Proof

From the time of the ancient Greeks, authorities in rhetoric have pointed out that the arguer's character is very important. The Greek word for "character" was *ethos,* and a writer (or speaker, in ancient times) whose work showed him to be honest, fair, and reasonable was said to be employing *ethical proof.* As Cato, a Roman, put it, an orator should be "a good man skilled in speaking."

When your good character appears in a written formal argument to your advantage, you too are employing the very old device of ethical proof. But such proof is not to be artificially displayed in an argument. Rather, you should emphasize your natural good qualities, and at the same time suppress any qualities—such as a tendency to jump to conclusions—that might injure your character or your believability in the eyes of your reader. Such suppression is not dishonest if it improves the truth and effectiveness of your argument.

As an example of ethical proof, consider these paragraphs from the end of John Kennedy's inaugural address:

*Modesty and patriotism*
1 In your hands, my fellow citizens, more than mine, will rest the final success or failure of our course. Since this country was founded, each generation of Americans has been summoned to give testimony to its national loyalty. The graves of young Americans who answered the call to service surround the globe.

2 Now the trumpet summons us again—not as a call to bear arms, though arms we need—not as a call to battle, though embattled we are—but a call to bear the burden of a long twilight struggle, year in and year out, "rejoicing in hope, patient in tribulation"—a struggle against the common enemies of man: tyranny, poverty, disease and war itself.

*Concern for others*
3 Can we forge against these enemies a grand and global alliance, North and South, East and West, that can assure a more fruitful life for all mankind? Will you join in that historic effort?

4 In the long history of the world, only a few generations have been granted the role of defending freedom in its hour

*Courage*

*Selfless dedication*

of maximum danger. I do not shrink from this responsibility—I welcome it. I do not believe that any of us would exchange places with any other people or any other generation. The energy, the faith, the devotion which we bring to this endeavor will light our country and all who serve it—and the glow from that fire can truly light the world.

5 And so, my fellow Americans: Ask not what your country can do for you—ask what you can do for your country.

6 My fellow citizens of the world: Ask not what America will do for you, but what together we can do for the freedom of man.

*High religious and moral standards*

7 Finally, whether you are citizens of America or citizens of the world, ask of us here the same high standards of strength and sacrifice which we ask of you. With a good conscience our only sure reward, with history the final judge of our deeds, let us go forth to lead the land we love, asking His blessing and His help, but knowing that here on earth God's work must truly be our own.

In this brief passage, the admirable qualities of President Kennedy's character shine through *as an integral part of the argument.* This ethical proof, which really cannot be precisely described in the marginal notes, is woven into the texture of honest, clear arguments.

## The "You-Attitude"

The *you-attitude* can be summed up like this: "As a writer, I am as interested in you [my reader] as I am in myself or my subject." Example: Joe Smith writes a brief argument addressed to his neighborhood Advisory Board, a group that acts as a go-between for the citizens of Valley Road subdivision and the City Council. He wants the two-way stop on Valley Road and Race Street to be replaced by a four-way stop. He writes this draft:

> The two-way stop at Valley and Race is at present a real danger to both pedestrians and drivers. Two accidents have occurred there within the last month. Valley feeds into the highway south, and drivers pick up speed two blocks north of the intersection. By the time they arrive at that point they are going quite fast. Race Street drivers or pedestrians (not to mention bike riders) often find it difficult to get across Valley Road safely.
>
> Let's ask the City Council to put a four-way stop at Race and Valley.

This is a decent enough draft, but there is no particular feeling for the readers or their problems. So, after receiving a bit of advice, Joe rewrites his draft, and creates a stronger you-attitude:

Have you, as members of the Advisory Board, thought about making a recommendation to the City Council about the stop at Valley and Race? Most of you are my friends and neighbors, and I've heard you complain about that stop more than once. Rod and Sue Jensen's boy Greg nearly got run over on his bike the other day trying to get across Valley during the rush hour to deliver his papers.

Do you think a four-way stop at Valley and Race might solve our problems? If you believe this might be the best solution, would you mind if I presented a more detailed plan for the stop (including costs) at the August 4th meeting? The City Council would probably be happier with an Advisory proposal if it came with a cost analysis.

Observe that ethical proof and an agreeable you-attitude support each other in evolving an effective *human approach* to an argumentative question. When Joe Smith refers (honestly and accurately enough) to the fact that his friends and neighbors are involved in the traffic problem and that Greg Jensen nearly got run over, he creates interest in the situation. He asks for the Board's judgment concerning the four-way stop instead of bluntly telling them that the stop is necessary. He gives them the impression (again honestly) that he has thought the matter through; he knows what the costs will be, and he will present the figures to the Advisory Board at the next meeting.

A common objection to the idea of using ethical proof and a you-attitude to support a human approach is that "they can be easily faked." Practically speaking, this doesn't seem to be the case. For one thing, the human approach does not ask you to create any aspect of your personality that is not already there; most writers have good sides and certain kinds of genuine interest in other human beings. The approach merely suggests that you make use of all possible avenues of rapport between you and the readers and that you try to show them the proofs of your character that truly exist, along with your genuine interest in them and their welfare.

## GIVE SOLID EVIDENCE

Deep in the seventh tier of our university library, we were hunting for an elusive quotation in a book that didn't seem to exist. After about an hour, we decided to give up and headed for the stairs, which happened to be close to the study carrel of a friend. "Hey," he said, "are you going home? You're going to get wet!"

"But it couldn't be raining—the sun was shining only an hour ago."

Our friend said nothing but merely pointed to a coat rack on which hung his dripping raincoat.

## Factual Evidence

Appropriate cliché: "The evidence [a wet raincoat, for example] speaks for itself." But to allow it to speak for itself in your papers you must put it there in the first place. Always support your arguments with *evidence*—facts, figures, results of experiments, statements from authorities. As you write, check each important statement by asking: "Do I have *evidence* for what I am saying?" Of course, you will seldom, if ever, have perfect evidence, whatever that might be. Argument deals with the *probable,* not with the perfectly true. But to be persuasive, your statements—and your evidence—should be as factual (as "probably true") as you can make them.

A fact is a piece of truth, then, that exists because "somebody" has *verified* it—has read up on it, asked about it, looked at it (even heard, tasted, felt, or smelled it). Here is a list of facts expressed in short sentences:

> Blood is running from a cut on my face.
> The king is on his throne.
> This is a football.
> A leaf fell.
> I am holding a smelly tomato.
> The Common Market was a free-trade idea.
> Babies often get the croup.
> This piece of paper is clean.

Each of these might be considered a statement of "fact" if it has been verified. Genuine facts should be verifiable by more than one reasonable person or authority. If only one person sees a particular flying saucer, the saucer is for all practical purposes not a fact. If no one besides you sees a leaf fall, or sees the leaf on the ground, the leaf and its falling have not been verified. If people around you can't smell the tomato you are holding, never have heard of babies getting the croup, and can't agree that "this piece of paper is *clean,*" then these statements are not to be considered factual.

## General and Particular Facts

A *generalization* (or a *general statement*) is a remark about a class or group of things, actions, or ideas:

> California produces more tennis stars than any other state.
> Most stunt pilots use biplanes.
> Dictators rule by fear.
> Babies often get the croup.

As these statements suggest, the generalization itself can be a *broad* fact concerning a number of *particular,* individual facts. An important relationship between the particular and the general can be illustrated by this inverted pyramid.

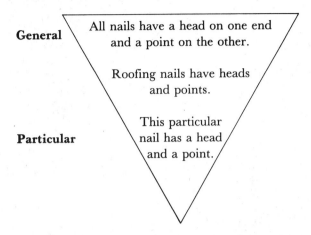

As the diagram shows, the ideas of the general and the particular are relative. "Roofing nails have heads and points" is less general than "All nails have a head on one end and a point on the other," but more general than "This particular nail has a head and a point." Here is another example, working from the particular to the general, that uses single words instead of statements: "John" (referring to an actual young man, age ten) is a particular. "Boys" is more general. "Human males" is more general still.

## General Statements and Value Judgments

General statements based on facts are usually more difficult to verify than particulars are.

"The English have produced great poets" can be considered a decent factual generalization based upon an examination of many particulars: the great English poets, from Chaucer on. Since the statement is also a *value judgment*—a statement of opinion about the worth of something—it is open to simple contradiction by someone using a different standard of judgment: "I don't think the English poets are as great as you say; I don't like Chaucer, for instance. The Italians have produced greater poets than the English have."

The value judgment is necessary in expressing opinions or preferences: "The wine was excellent last night"; "Harding was a poor president"; "I prefer stick shifts." It is often hard, however, to prove that a value judgment has any factual basis unless a standard for judgment has been established.

Even general statements that are relatively free of value judgment can be troublesome when one tries to show that they are factual. The truth of "Babies often get the croup" hinges, according to one physician, on what *often* means. "Many babies do get croup," says he, "but *often* to me implies a majority. *Most* babies don't get the croup." "The Common Market was a free-trade idea" seems to be a clear-cut fact until one realizes that the idea of the Common Market was and is open to various interpretations and that definitions of *free trade* vary according to experts' views of political and economic history.

### Inferences

When we draw a conclusion from one or more facts, we make an inference. General and particular statements of fact are often based upon inferences:

> Yellow fever is transmitted by the mosquito. (*Beginning with the work of Walter Reed in 1900–1901, scientists have repeatedly shown that the mosquito carries yellow fever, a fact that we infer from repeated experiments.*)
>
> Sally is allergic to penicillin. (*Every time she takes the drug, she breaks out in a rash. We infer a factual cause-and-effect relation between the drug and the rash.*)
>
> Mexico is friendly to the United States. (*We infer this general fact after investigating many specific incidents concerning Mexico and the United States. In nearly every incident, either the government or the people of Mexico or both have indicated friendliness to us.*)
>
> The man next door is laughing loudly. (*The voice is that of a man. The noise sounds like laughing. The noise is not soft or moderate, but loud.*)

### Facts: A Summary

The difficulty of obtaining facts can be overdramatized. Don't fall into the trap of believing that factual material on most subjects is impossible to come by, even though it is true that some areas of human investigation—like the nature of political influence or of artistic inspiration—seem to produce very few facts indeed. The main thing to bear in mind is that facts exist because responsible persons (accountable, rational, and ethical persons) *say* they do, which is what we mean by "verifying" and "validating." When, in a certain area of investigation, the methods of verifying and validating change, or when responsible persons change their opinions, the facts may change also.

A generalization may be (or may imply) a decision, a summary, an interpretation, an opinion, or a value judgment. A generalization may also combine two or more of these. For the purposes of essay writing, we will assume that you will make your generalizations *after* you have inspected the facts available on your subject and *that your generalizations are based on the facts*. If you cannot find facts, you cannot generalize accurately.

## Authoritative Evidence

For our purposes, an *authority* is a person who knows what he is talking about. He can be a theoretical expert in his special area of knowledge, someone who has had practical experience in the field, or both. As a former professor of urban studies at a major university and an editor of a scholarly journal, Irving Kristol might reasonably be considered a theoretical authority on the American blue-collar worker. A man (let's call him Jim West) who has worked for a few years in a blue-collar job could be a "practical" expert on his type of job.

Kristol will know more theory and have a broader range of knowledge about the blue-collar worker than West, but West will know more detail concerning his particular job than Kristol. If you were writing a paper on the American worker, you might read Kristol to obtain theoretical knowledge and go to a man like West for practical information on, for example, operating a punch press. Of course, both of these authorities would know something about the other's "area" of knowledge. If you were writing on the alienation of workers, you could certainly take into account West's firsthand knowledge of blue-collar work. Your decisions about which authorities to use depend on the nature of your thesis.

It is wise to remember that all authorities, whether theoretical or practical, are limited to some extent in the type and quality of their knowledge. Furthermore, they may be limited simply by being forgetful, prejudiced, out-of-date on the evidence, or plainly dishonest.

As a writer, you can use authoritative evidence in two ways: (1) you can quote authorities to bolster your own argument; (2) you can act as your own expert or practical authority. From your reading and experience, you should have considerable knowledge that you can use authoritatively. Whether you use your own or others' ideas, consider the following questions as you evaluate the *quality* of authoritative opinion:

1. *Is the person an authority on the subject?* We tend to associate the idea of authority with well-known people in special fields, whether their opinions are authoritative or not. It is wise to accept the artistic evaluations of a good actor on acting, but when that same person gives advice on political matters, we should be wary. The opinions of glamorous or popular persons, like movie stars and sports figures, are seldom authoritative except in their own fields.

2. *Is the authority unprejudiced and sensible?* Just being an authority does not make one free from prejudice or egomania. The pathologist Sydney Smith has written of a world-famous authority on pathology: "Spilsbury, like the rest of us, could make mistakes. He was unique, I think, in that he never admitted a mistake. Once he had committed himself to an opinion he would never change it." An expert can be as prejudiced or obstinate as anyone else.

3. *Is the authority up-to-date in his specialty?* In many fields, last year's knowledge is unreliable. The authority should demonstrate that he knows the latest information in his field.

4. *Does the authority have evidence on the question being discussed?* Unless the expert has seen and examined the evidence for himself, it is

unlikely that his opinion is valuable. A psychiatrist recently diagnosed the mental ailment of a political agitator without ever seeing the man. Under these circumstances, the psychiatrist's opinion was probably not authoritative.

# USE GOOD LOGIC

There is nothing complicated about the basic logic of rhetoric or composition. Such logic simply represents the operation of common sense, which interrelates two activities: (1) finding the *connections* between things; (2) *concluding* what, if anything, these connections mean.

## Avoid Loose Generalizations

You often hear the remark, "Oh, that's just a generalization." This is a misleading comment, for it implies that generalizations are by nature untrustworthy or somehow inferior to other types of statements. As we ordinarily use the term, a fact is "true" by definition; but a generalization is "true" only if the facts have first been found and properly used in making *connections*—in drawing the general conclusion from them. A generalization, therefore, may be *un*true, a *little* true, *partly* true, *mainly* true, or *entirely* true.

In order to make your statements as true as possible, you must avoid making careless or loose generalizations. A loose generalization is a faulty, or partly faulty, statement about a group or class of ideas, occurrences, things, persons, etc. Most loose generalizations are created by thinking carelessly about the subject and the available evidence. Here are some examples:

> City children don't get enough sunshine.

Who says so? What city children? All over the world? What is meant by "city"? How much is "enough"? Who is an authority on *enough sunshine*? How does the writer know this? How many cities has he been in?

> College students are working too hard and have no time for play or private
> thought.

Where? In the United States? In what sort of "college"? Ivy League? Big Ten? Small state college? Large junior college? All colleges in the United States? Could one person be an authority on this subject? What would he have to do to be an authority? What is meant by "working too hard"? By "no time for play or private thought"?

In France, people accept religion for what it is.

Has this writer been in France? When, and for how long? What sample of the population did he see? Did he talk to them about religion? What is meant by "religion"? By "people"? Eighty-year-old men? Young children? The clergy? (Catholic, Jewish, Protestant?) What does "for what it is" mean?

## How to Qualify a Generalization

You do not have to get *all* the facts before you can make connections and draw a reasonably truthful conclusion. Although some subjects require more facts than others for valid generalizing, for many subjects you can draw *tentative* or *qualified* generalizations. To *qualify* means to modify or to limit according to the evidence that is available. Take the three loose generalizations given above. Carefully qualified, they might read:

> Along Parsons Avenue in Chicago, where I lived for ten years, I saw a number of children who didn't get enough sunshine because they usually played indoors.
> The engineering students I know at Collins College have to take so many credit hours that they have only three or four hours a week for relaxation.
> When I was in Paris for three months last summer, I knew several young workingmen who were rather casual about observing the laws of their church.

It is wise to acquire the habit of using qualifying words and phrases where necessary, particularly when you are writing about people and their activities. But be wary of words that state an absolute condition, words like *always, never, continually, every.* Also be wary of implying these words in sentences like ["*All*] people love freedom," or ["*All*] women dislike men who smoke cigars." Here is a list of qualifying words and phrases that you can use with some assurance:

| | | | |
|---|---|---|---|
| usually | often | a lot | customarily |
| nearly | occasionally | many | a little bit |
| some | sometimes | a great deal | ordinarily |
| generally | a few | most | almost all |

To sum up: A generalization is an attempt to find out the truth about something—or a lot of somethings—and to state the truth in shorthand form. Imagine, for example, that we are trying to make a general, true statement about the total assets of the wealthy Mr. Jordan. We discover that he owns stocks and bonds, cash, houses, five automobiles, and two racing horses, with a total value of $300,000. He also keeps in a bank vault a number of gold bars worth about \$285,000. We may generalize roughly that *half of Mr. Jordan's fortune consists of bar-gold.* If Mr. Jordan should be a vigorous buyer and seller of bar-gold, we might from time to time have to change our qualifying statements about his fortune, as follows:*

(100%) Mr. Jordan's fortune consists *wholly* of bar-gold.
(99%) *Practically all* of his fortune consists of bar-gold.
(95%) His fortune consists *almost entirely* of bar-gold.
(90%) *Nearly all* his fortune consists of bar-gold.
(80%) *By far the greater part* of his fortune . . .
(70%) *The greater part* of his fortune . . .
(60%) *More than half* his fortune . . .
(55%) *Rather more than half* his fortune . . .
(50%) *Half* his fortune . . .
(45%) *Nearly half* his fortune . . .
(40%) *A large part* of his fortune . . .
(35%) *Quite a large part* of his fortune . . .
(30%) *A considerable part* of his fortune . . .
(25%) *Part* of his fortune . . .
(15%) *A small part* of his fortune . . .
(10%) *Not much* of his fortune . . .
(5%) *A very small part* of his fortune . . .
(1%) *An inconsiderable part* of his fortune . . .
(0%) *None* of his fortune . . .

## ✦ PRACTICE

### Discussion

The statements below have been represented as satisfactory generalizations in student essays. Which statements make proper "connections"? Upon what kind of authority? Which are loose generalizations? How can these be effectively qualified?

a. In the history of censorship, no book has been banned oftener than the Bible.
b. Sharks do not eat people.
c. The motives of the United States in the Vietnam War were not imperialistic.
d. Football players are good students.
e. A window screen keeps all the flies out.
f. Sonic booms don't hurt you or your property.

---

*This ingenius example involving Mr. Jordan's fortune has been taken from *The Reader Over Your Shoulder* by Robert Graves and Alan Hodge. Try as they might, Graves and Hodge could not make the qualifying phrases very precise. Phrases like *the greater part* and *a large part* are rather ambiguous even when they are presented in a "qualifying scale" like theirs. But the example does show that qualifying can be done with words and that a writer can qualify with a fair degree of accuracy.

g. By the year 2025, the human race will reproduce by cross-pollination.

h. The moon is a military base of great importance.

i. Evolution is true.

j. Humans evolved from apes.

k. Teenage dance steps are immoral.

l. The Wolverine 8s are not selling because people think they are American cars, and American cars are not as popular as they used to be.

m. Freudians have silly theories about sex.

n. If lightning strikes your house, open a window in your basement so that the lightning will find its way out.

o. The cause of juvenile delinquency is parents.

## Induction and Deduction: A Definition

There are two kinds of logic, *inductive* and *deductive*. Whether you are conscious of doing so or not, you use them both a great deal, even when you do something as ordinary as bake bread, replace a defective fuel pump in your car, or put a cut rose in water to preserve it.

Suppose a man says to his wife: "Gee, honey, I hope the Pinkhams' old dog doesn't get loose and bite one of the kids." Hidden in this remark is a fair amount of logic whose *connections* and *conclusions* we can outline by showing you the processes of induction and deduction.

*Induction* moves from facts to a generalization:

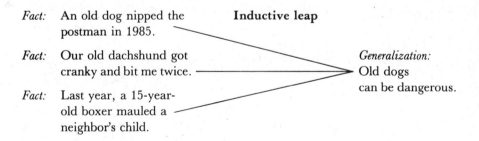

*Fact:* An old dog nipped the postman in 1985.

*Fact:* Our old dachshund got cranky and bit me twice.

*Fact:* Last year, a 15-year-old boxer mauled a neighbor's child.

**Inductive leap**

*Generalization:* Old dogs can be dangerous.

*Deduction* moves from a generalization to a conclusion. (This process can be illustrated by what is known as a *syllogism*.)

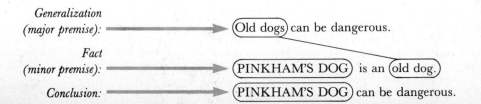

*Generalization (major premise):* Old dogs can be dangerous.

*Fact (minor premise):* PINKHAM'S DOG is an old dog.

*Conclusion:* PINKHAM'S DOG can be dangerous.

"Old dog" is the *middle term*—it connects the major premise to the minor premise. "PINKHAM'S DOG" is the *subject*—it connects the minor premise to the conclusion.

Refer to these examples as we explain inductive and deductive logic more thoroughly.

*Induction* is a logical process in which you make the connections between particulars or facts in order to come to a generalization about them. Practically speaking, every induction has an *inductive leap*—the jump you have to make from a limited number of facts (of varying authoritative quality) to your generalization. If you see three old dogs, and they are all mean and cranky and bite, you can leap to the generalization that "Old dogs can be dangerous," which is not too long a leap—particularly if you don't want to get bitten.

The length of your inductive leap depends on the nature of the subject and how many "facts" you've got. The more old dogs that bite you can find, the smaller the leap to your generalization. If, in a period of twenty years, you hear of only two old dogs that bite, your leap is pretty large, and you may never make a good connection to your generalization. If you step off thirty bridges over streams and fall into the water each time, your inductive leap to "People who step off bridges fall into the water" is pretty small and can be easily made. But the leap, no matter how many "facts" you can muster, always exists. After all, it is always possible that someday you may step off bridge number 1,000,001 and just hang there in space.

*Deduction* is a logical process in which you make connections between a generalization (*major premise*), a fact (*minor premise*), and a conclusion.

Deductive reasoning can be most clearly seen in the *syllogism,* which is a three-sentence chain of reasoning. The classic syllogism in its full form has a broad major premise, a relatively narrow minor premise, and a conclusion drawn from these two premises. The *middle term* and the *subject* connect the parts of the syllogism.

In ordinary writing, deductive reasoning is most often expressed in the *enthymeme,* which is a compressed syllogism. Examples:

> An old dog like Pinkham's can be dangerous.
> Of course, Mike will die eventually; he's human, just like all of us.

Expanded into a full syllogism, the second enthymeme becomes:

| | | |
|---|---|---|
| *Major premise:* | All *persons* die. | *person* = middle term |
| *Minor premise:* | MIKE is a *person.* | MIKE = subject |
| *Conclusion:* | MIKE will die. | |

Here is another example of an enthymeme:

> Since he is an elephant, Herbert can eat peanuts.

And its full syllogistic form:

| | | |
|---|---|---|
| *Major premise:* | All *elephants* eat peanuts. | *elephant* = middle term |
| *Minor premise:* | HERBERT is an *elephant*. | HERBERT = subject |
| *Conclusion:* | HERBERT eats peanuts. | |

## Using Induction and Deduction

Since induction moves from facts to a generalization, and deduction moves from a generalization to a conclusion, these types of logic have often been discussed as if they were two separate things. But actually they are interrelated, as this example shows.

> At a social gathering, a Frenchman remarked to a friend that all the long-haired men he had observed in the United States were political leftists.
>
> "Oh?" said the friend. "What about Jones over there—his hair is so long he's wearing it in a ponytail."
>
> "Of a certainty," said the Frenchman, "Mr. Jones is also a leftist."

The chain of reasoning the Frenchman created looks like this:

Induction

| | |
|---|---|
| *Fact:* | A long-haired man is observed to be a leftist. |
| *Fact:* | Another long-haired man is observed to be a leftist. |
| *Fact:* | Yet another . . . |

[INDUCTIVE LEAP]

| | |
|---|---|
| *Generalization:* | All long-haired men are leftists. |

Deduction (a Syllogism)

| | |
|---|---|
| *Major premise:* | All long-haired men are leftists. |
| *Minor premise:* | Jones is a long-haired man. |
| *Conclusion:* | Jones is a leftist. |

Observe that the major premise of the syllogism is itself a conclusion inductively arrived at. As it turned out, Jones was not a leftist, leaving the Frenchman in a logical error. How can such errors be avoided in your handling of logic? The answer lies mainly in carefully managing logical *connections, generalizations,* and *conclusions:*

1. Make sure your inductive generalization is based on a sufficient number of reliable and authoritative facts. *Keep your inductive leap as small as possible.*

2. Check your deductive reasoning in the following ways: (a) Make sure that each premise is as accurate as you can make it. "All long-haired men are leftists" is a faulty major premise because it states a generalization that simply is untrue. You remember the minor premise in our sample syllogism on p. 357—"Pinkham's dog is an old dog." As it happened (this is a real-life example), Pinkham's dog was not old; he merely looked old because of his gray, mangy fur. (b) Expand each enthymeme into the full three-sentence syllogism to see if the connections and conclusions are properly made. (c) Do not shift your middle term. Examples of illogical shifts:

> All football players are *strong.*
> John weighs 225 *pounds.*
> John is *strong.*

> *Those who commit murder* should be severely punished.
> That police officer just killed a *fleeing bank robber.*
> That police officer *should be severely punished.*

In both examples, the writer has shifted the middle term. Weighing 225 pounds is not the same as being *strong.* A police officer who kills a fleeing bank robber is not ordinarily considered by the law to have committed murder.

## ◆ *PRACTICE*

*Writing*

1. After crash-landing on the planet Vark II, Captain Foubar of the Space Service found that he had plenty of water but no food. Raging with hunger, he explored the area near his ship, finding an abundance of small black flowers about six inches high. After eating two of the petals, he got rather sick and saw strange visions. His sickness passed in a few minutes, but he was still hungry and continued to explore the strange planet. He discovered a yellow weed that resembled a dandelion. He ate a little and found it reasonably good—at least it did not make him sick. He gathered about a pound of the yellow weed and took it back to his ship.

   The next day, he decided to try more of the black flower. After eating about a dozen petals, he became violently ill, and the visions this time were terrifying. In a desperate attempt to counteract the effect of the flower, he ate two yellow weeds. Almost immediately the sickness and the visions left him.

   Captain Foubar wrote down his experiences in the ship's log, using the classic inductive and deductive forms. He expanded each of his enthymemes into a syllogism. What did the captain write in his log?

2. Expand the following enthymemes below into the three-sentence forms of the syllogism. Identify the subject and the middle term. If you can, rewrite the enthymeme to make it more reasonable.

   a. Phil shouldn't have married a girl with a personality so different from his; pluses and minuses cancel each other, you know.
   b. Any businesswoman who makes as much money as Lenora does must be very competent.
   c. Judging from his antisocial behavior last night (talking against the government), Judson must have been either drunk or crazy.
   d. Old Mr. Roberts can't be rich because he's signed up for Medicare.
   e. A typically modern, sexy novelist, Smith has written an evil book.
   f. Paley, make up your mind which side you're going to be on— people have to be either for us or against us. You sound like you don't believe in our position.
   g. As a college student, Joe should enlist because the army needs superior minds.
   h. Holden, you've got to get a job; no patriotic American should live on welfare.
   i. *Alf* is not educational at all; why should it be on television?
   j. Since Barber was definitely at the scene of the crime, he must have committed the murder.
   k. Richard is too ignorant to have gone to college.
   l. Only those who do valuable work for America should be elected to public office. I was in the Air Force for five years.
   m. Yond Cassius has a lean and hungry look; He thinks too much: such men are dangerous.—Shakespeare, *Julius Caesar*
   n. Jorgenson took the Fifth Amendment in a congressional investigation; therefore, he is one of those undermining American democracy.
   o. Since Professor Bunner does not publish, she must be a good teacher.

## AVOID FALLACIES

A fallacy is a weakness or an error in thinking or arguing. Fallacies are ordinarily caused by one or more of six basic human errors:

Oversimplifying
Jumping to a conclusion
Being irrelevant
Being too emotional
Deceiving oneself
Being dishonest

Of course, these human errors can never be totally eradicated from even the best-reasoned argument. However, by being aware of such pitfalls, you can eliminate a great number of them from your thinking, thus making your arguments more persuasive and forceful.

## Recognizing and Correcting Fallacies

Here are descriptions of twelve major fallacies; for each one we suggest a method of improving the thinking or the argument. (The term *question*, when used in connection with fallacies, usually refers either to an argument's thesis or to one of its main points.)

### Begging the Question

This fallacy is the mistake of assuming that some or all of a question or thesis is already proved—before the writer has proved it. To say that "Any person in the neighborhood who refuses to keep up his property should be prosecuted" begs two questions: first, whether refusing to keep up one's property is a bad thing for the neighborhood; second, whether failing to keep up property is covered by statute or is in any way illegal.

The statement that "The mistakes of teachers are buried on the welfare rolls" begs these questions: whether teachers make "mistakes," and whether there is a necessary relationship between teachers' "mistakes" and persons' ending up on welfare. Either of these questions or propositions might profitably be argued, and that is the point—they would have to be argued and *proved*. They cannot merely be assumed. Begging the question is an important fallacy because it often occurs at the starting point of an argument and thus renders the whole argument invalid.

*Correction:* Find the begged question and omit or prove it.

### Rhetorical Question

The rhetorical question is usually a form of indirect attack. The attacker asks a loaded question to which he does not really want an answer. Such questions are inherently argumentative and often question-begging: "Mr. Webb, when are you going to stop being so bad-tempered?" Rhetorical questions are sometimes filled with emotion: "Is our do-nothing police force ever going to stop vicious murderers from roaming our streets at will?"

*Correction:* Customarily, omit the rhetorical question unless you have already proved the question. If you have satisfactorily proved that Webb is bad-tempered, you might inquire if he contemplates controlling his anger—but then the question is perhaps no longer rhetorical. It is worth adding that rhetorical questions are great fun, and it would be a pity to avoid them altogether.

## Ad Hominem ("To the Man")

In this fallacy, instead of attacking the argument, the writer attacks the person who made it. Examples: "You can't trust any statement made by that notorious socialist, Kurt Bleil." Or: "I won't work on the committee's proposal as long as there are psychologists on it. If Professor Ratmaze leaves, I will discuss the proposal."

*Correction:* Drop the attack on the person and consider the question, argument, or proposal at hand. Ask yourself: Are you discrediting the person who made the proposal in the hope that his or her argument will also be discredited? Is your primary aim to evaluate the evidence or to criticize the personalities involved? Evaluating your motives may keep you from committing the *ad hominem* fallacy.

## Stereotyping

In stereotyping, instead of describing persons as they actually are, the writer resorts to a trite description or cliché—every football player is big and stupid, every politician hypocritical and crooked, every movie star frivolous and shallow.

*Correction:* Check your description or generalization for accuracy. Have you, for instance, taken one attribute of a class and applied it to *everyone* in the class? Have you generalized from too few instances and then applied your generalization to the entire class?

## Either-Or Fallacy

Writers commit this fallacy when they oversimplify a complex issue by assuming that there are only two sides to it. Either-or is one of the commonest fallacies, perhaps because all of us naturally think in either-or patterns: "You are either for or against me"; "She loves me, she loves me not"; "We should win the war or get out." Sometimes called the *black-or-white fallacy,* this error in logic is unusually dangerous because it is so easy to fall into and also because it gives no chance for alternatives.

*Correction:* Recognize any other possibilities or alternatives that may exist besides the two stated.

## Faulty Sampling

The flaw in many samples is that they are not representative of the group about which a generalization is made. A classic case of faulty sampling occurred in 1936 when the *Literary Digest* asked people in various parts of the United States whom they were going to vote for (Landon or Roosevelt) in the presidential election. The results of the poll said that Landon would win—but Roosevelt won by a landslide. The flaw in the sampling occurred because the *Digest* polled only persons whose names appeared in telephone directories. Taken in the middle of the Depression, this sampling omitted large numbers of people who did not have a telephone and voted Democratic.

*Correction:* Make sure that your sample is representative of the group under discussion.

### Loose Generalization

A loose generalization is a faulty, or partly faulty, statement about a group or class of ideas, occurrences, things, persons, and so forth. Examples: "Large families make for happy children"; "All small automobiles save gas." In both examples, the writer has made careless and excessively broad statements about a group. Upon examining the evidence, it becomes obvious that some small cars are not "gas savers"—the phrase needs definition too. And one finds unhappy children in some "large families" (again a phrase needs definition).

*Correction:* Reason carefully from the evidence available. Examine broad statements for possible inaccuracy. When necessary, qualify your generalizations. (See pp. 355–356 for further discussion.)

### Causal Fallacy

Three kinds of causal fallacy are important: (a) Mistaking the nature of a cause. Example: A boss believes that an employee does poor work because he is lazy, but the real reason is that he has difficult personal problems. (b) Failing to see that there is more than one cause. Example: "Barbara is a fine violinist because she has great natural talent." Since Barbara's parents required her to practice two or three hours a day for five years, there are probably at least two causes for her fine playing—talent and hard work. (c) Being misled by the order of events. If event B comes after event A, one should not automatically jump to the conclusion that A *caused* B. Example: John started dressing neatly after his mother scolded him for being sloppy. His mother congratulated herself, but the real reason for John's neatness was a new girlfriend who did not like sloppy boys. As you have seen in the discussion of cause and effect in Chapter 12, this common fallacy is called *post hoc* (short for *post hoc, ergo propter hoc*—"after this, therefore because of this").

*Correction:* Identify the true cause or causes in a situation, checking for the nature of the cause, multiple causes, and proper time-sequence.

### Ignoring the Question

Almost any form of irrelevancy can be identified as ignoring the question—the fallacy of failing to stick to the thesis of an argument or of wandering away from an important point of the argument. Accordingly, this fallacy often seems to be the result of other fallacies. For example, if one starts out refuting an argument by Jones but slides into a personal attack on him, the writer falls into both *ad hominem* and ignoring the question. Many cases of ignoring the question are created by carelessly forgetting one's thesis. If a writer begins to argue that all auto mechanics in the United States should be federally licensed, and then breaks into a condemnation of the Pinto as an unsafe car, he is ignoring the question.

*Correction:* Identify the question and rewrite, sticking to the question and omitting irrelevancies.

## ◆ PRACTICE

*Discussion*

In the following examples, identify the fallacy *by name* in two steps. First, determine which of the six basic human errors (pp. 361–362) the writer made. Second, name the specific fallacy. In some examples, you may find more than one fallacy.

*Note:* You may be surprised by the amount of truth in many statements that also include fallacies. Why do truth and fallacy often live happily side by side? One reason is that truths are seldom absolutes but rather mixtures of the true and false. Another reason is that half-truths can, superficially, be more convincing than "whole" truths. As Stephen Leacock ironically remarked, "A half-truth in argument, like a half-brick, carries better."

a. The basic physics courses here at the university are bad. My physics instructor is a weak teacher; he does not know his material and is not interested in his students.

b. Juvenile crime in America is increasing. Over 1,000,000 youths are arrested every year. More than 55,000 youths are in jails. One-fifth of all youth is delinquent. Half the auto thefts, a third of the robberies, and a tenth of homicides and assaults in the United States are committed by youths. What is the cause? Society is to blame.

c. Grades are arbitrary. Students are in college to learn, not to get grades.

d. Making the sale of drugs a crime just makes using drugs more tempting. It is a fact that doctors have the money to satisfy this temptation and it is also a fact that doctors have a higher rate of addiction than people in any other profession.

e. I may or may not concede that some cops honestly try to maintain law and order. I will concede part of this, or all of this partly. If an old lady in respectable clothes falls down on the street, the cop will heroically try to help her, but the sight of an old bum on the same street brings out some atavistic desire in the cop with the cop mentality. The fakery of his charity reveals itself. He loves the old lady? Maybe; but, if so, only because it gives him a justification to beat up the old bum.—Nelson Algren, "Down with Cops"

f. A professor is like a tradesman. Like a plumber or electrician, the professor serves an apprenticeship so that he can learn a skill. Therefore, as the customer judges the worth of a tradesman's skills, we students should be able to judge the worth of a professor's teaching.

g. What are the other candidates afraid of? Mr. Bostwick says we cannot educate *all* of the children "because by definition not all children are educable." What kind of Nazi remark is that? Is he going to tell us which of our children can be educated and which cannot be? Of course all children are educable; they are human, aren't they? Mr. Bostwick should put on his black armband and parade around like the Nazi he is—why (and we demand that he answer this question) is he afraid to educate *all* American children?

h. Our neighbor says about the new divorce law: "Divorce is only a symptom, and you don't cure a disease by treating its symptoms."

# USE A CLEAR ARGUMENTATIVE ORGANIZATION

For your argument to be persuasive, its organization must be clear enough so that your reader will have no doubts about what direction your thoughts are taking. There are basically three major kinds of organization in formal argumentation:

1. The *organization of fact*—in which you argue the truth (or reality) of an idea, opinion, occurrence, and so on;

2. The *organization of action*—in which you argue that something should be done, that an action should be taken;

3. The *organization of refutation*—in which you argue that another person's argument is wrong, invalid, or fallacious.

In practice, these three argumentative organizations often do not appear as distinct and separate forms. You may find yourself combining, for example, fact and refutation organizations in a single essay because you need them both to support your thesis. But the organizations can be most clearly understood if we discuss them separately. An argumentative organization is built around a thesis; accordingly, we will begin our discussion by distinguishing between the thesis of fact and the thesis of action. We will take up refutation later.

## Theses of Fact and of Action

The *thesis of fact* states that something is (or is not) true, or was (or was not) true. Of course the thesis may be qualified by stating that something is or was partly true. Any type of necessary qualification may be made. Examples of fact theses:

> Capital punishment is an uncivilized practice.
> Although it was tried only on a relatively small sample of the population, fluoridation seemed to prevent tooth decay in Sweetbrush, Indiana.

The thesis of fact is ordinarily a statement about the present, the past, or both.

The *thesis of action* states that a change must be made. Examples of action theses:

> We must do away with capital punishment in the United States because it is an uncivilized practice.
> Since fluoridation of drinking water prevents decay in children's teeth, the citizens of Sweetbrush, Indiana, should add fluoride to their drinking water.

The thesis of action is a statement about the future that is based upon a statement of truth, sometimes implied, about the present or past. The thesis of action must be based on a thesis of fact. In other words, you cannot argue for any kind of change in human affairs until after you have proved that there is a *need* for the change. As you will shortly learn, *fact* arguments and *action* arguments differ in both purpose and organization.

## Organization of Fact Arguments

An organization of fact is simply a clear presentation and elaboration of a thesis of fact. You set down your ideas straightforwardly:

| | | |
|---|---|---|
| *Introduction* | { State problem <br> State *thesis* <br> Define terms | Use most reasonable order |
| *Body* | { First point + evidence <br> Second point + evidence <br> Third point + evidence <br> Etc. <br> Evaluate points and evidence (optional) } | Use a graded order; e.g., from the weakest point to the strongest |
| *Conclusion* | Written to fit | |

For a short paper, an introduction of one or two paragraphs is sufficient. In the introduction, be sure to tell your readers all they need to know, especially about the thesis and definition of terms. In the body, separate the main points clearly so that your readers can tell them apart. Use any graded order that seems appropriate; a common one is suggested in the diagram above. It is natural and more convincing to save your strongest point until last. Evaluating the points and evidence may be unnecessary, unless you are trying to prove something important about them. Write the conclusion to fit the whole argument. Don't try to argue a new point in the conclusion—this is usually unconvincing.

## Organization of Action Arguments

As we explained earlier, an action argument must be based on a fact argument. This relationship determines an important part of the action organization. If you have not proved to your reader that there is a *need* for a change (fact argument), then you probably have to provide the argument of fact before going on to the argument of action. This would mean, practically speaking, that you would have to write two separate but related arguments. But we will assume here that the need for a change is evident, so that you have only to explain it briefly before beginning your argument of action. For this type of argument, here is a typical organization:

*Introduction* { State *need* for action (the problem)  State *thesis* (proposed action)  Define *terms* } Use most reasonable order

*Body* { Give as much *fact* argument as necessary  Give details of proposed *action;* expand as necessary  State why action is *practical*  State why action is *beneficial*  State why action is *better* than other proposed or possible actions (optional)

*Conclusion* { Written to fit (Many writers state here why their proposed action will satisfy the need introduced at the beginning)

## Organization of Refutation Arguments

In the argument of refutation, you take someone else's argument and prove that it is, to some degree, wrong, invalid, or fallacious. An argument is like a tower made of rocks. If you pull out one of the rocks near the bottom, the whole tower is likely to fall. If you show that one important part of an opponent's argument is weak, his whole case may topple. Thus before you write a refutation you need to examine your opponent's argument to see if you can find any weak spots in it. Here are some possible weak points to look for:

1. *Faulty premises.* A premise is a basic idea, stated or assumed, on which an arguer builds his argument (or a part of it), or from which he reaches a conclusion. If you can show that your opponent's premises

are faulty, you can probably refute his entire argument. Refuting his major premise is likely to cut him down on the spot. Even refuting one of his minor premises is a victory. Here is a premise from the first student letter:

> Cheating on this scale by a small group of students lowers both the moral and the intellectual tone of the university.

If you can show that cheating by a small group of students does not "lower both the moral and the intellectual tone of the university," you have weakened his argument considerably. Sydney J. Harris wrote: "There is nothing more dangerous than a person with a good mind who begins to reason, logically and coolly, from insufficient premises: for his answers will always be valid, justified, rational— and wrong."

2. *Faulty definitions.* A *definition* is itself a kind of premise, a part of an argument's foundation. If your opponent has been careless in defining, you can answer as follows:

> Mr. Cate says that by *big-time football* he means competition against "state schools with large enrollments and low entrance standards." His definition is meaningless because Ivy does not compete against such schools. B _____ University, it is true, has 30,000 students but it also has high entrance standards—it admits only those from the top quarter of the high-school class. W _____ University has low standards but only 6500 students. We compete against only four state schools, two of which I have mentioned. The other two (J _____ College and M _____ University) do not fit his definition either. Mr. Cate's carelessness in defining throws doubt on his whole argument.

3. *Fallacies in logic or in presenting the argument.* See pp. 362–365 for a complete discussion of fallacies.

4. *Faulty use of evidence and authority.* Mistakes here are usually either those of using insufficient or irrelevant evidence, or using a wrong or doubtful authority. (For further discussion, see pp. 349–354.)

5. *Impractical or undesirable action (applicable only to action arguments).* In many areas of argument, there is general agreement by everyone concerned that something must be done—a definite need for action does exist. But your opponent's suggested action may be impractical, undesirable, or irrelevant. It may bring about greater evils than now exist in the situation. If you believe that your opponent's suggested action is wrong, it is your job to point out *specifically* what is wrong with it. You may also give your own argument of action. But strictly speaking, a refutation states only the flaws in an opponent's argument.

Before writing a refutation, analyze your opponent's argument. Isolate its parts, from the thesis to the premises to the evidence used. If you can show that his thesis is badly worded, vague, or perhaps not stated at all, you can shoot down his argument with a paragraph. You do not have to waste much time on an opponent who does not even know the main point he is supposed to be arguing.

In organization, your refutation might look like this:

| | |
|---|---|
| *Introduction* | State errors in opponent's thesis or main argument |
| | Admit when opponent's argument is strong; this is both sensible and honest |
| *Body* | State flaws in opponent's argument; arrange flaws in graded order, leaving greatest till last |
| | State your own argument of fact or action (optional) |
| *Conclusion* | Written to fit |

# *T*HE TOULMIN *APPROACH TO ARGUMENT*

In recent years, the work of philosopher Stephen Toulmin has become influential in the study and practice of argumentation. This section is based in large part on Toulmin's theory as presented in his book, *The Uses of Argument,* Cambridge, 1964.

*Note:* We have adapted Toulmin's ideas to the special needs of composition students.

The special value of Toulmin's theory is that it suggests both an approach to argumentation *and* a critical mirror held up to your particular argument. To use Toulmin well is to argue a point while watching yourself do it.

The chart below shows the basic elements of the Toulmin approach. In using it, you have two broad choices. First, as you write your argument, you can check yourself against the six major elements in the Toulmin approach. (Note their special *names*—"claim," "warrant," and so on.)

---

### THE TOULMIN APPROACH *(adapted)*

---

*Question: What should I consider when making
(or testing) an argument?*

| | |
|---|---|
| 1. The *CLAIM* | What am I trying to prove? What is my *thesis?* |
| 2. The *SUPPORT* | What is the *evidence* (or *data*) for my **claim**? |

| | |
|---|---|
| 3. The *WARRANT* | What is the *reasoning* involved in my **claim** and its **support**? Are the parts of my argument logically connected? |
| 4. The *QUALIFIERS* | How *certain* is my **claim**? When and where should I use qualifiers like *mainly, mostly, probably, in many cases,* etc.? |
| 5. The *RESERVATIONS* | What are the counter-arguments? Can I be rebutted? How, and in what way(s)? |
| 6. The *MOTIVATIONAL APPEALS* | How do I appeal to the values, needs, or emotions of my readers? |

A second choice in using Toulmin is to write your argument in whatever way you see fit, and afterwards use the chart as a checklist to see if you have done everything you wanted to do. "Everything" refers to more than just the written argument itself; it includes, for example, such matters as your basic reasoning (*warrant*), the probability of your *claim,* the fullness of your attention to the emotions of your audience (*motivational appeals*), and so on. Toulmin intended for his approach to answer the major questions about the overall quality of an argument.

To exemplify the Toulmin approach, we will first present the comments of author Martin Kane Truz on an argument that he is preparing to write on pornography; then the argument itself; and finally, a student rebuttal (pp. 374–376).

### TRUZ'S COMMENTS ON HIS ARGUMENT
#### (made before he wrote it)

I had never heard of Toulmin until you told me about him. I'm a professional writer, and write out of both planning and instinct—and a profound interest in making the reader *react.* That's how I make my living: encouraging readers to think or feel something. It's not surprising that some professor would find a theory for how good arguments work. Clearly, there are only so many ways to affect readers, and when I sit down in a few hours to write this piece on pornography I intend to affect the hell out of them.

Because I am *furious.* Yesterday, I wandered into my den and saw my four-year-old grandson watching a woman being raped in a cable TV movie. That four-year-old boy was clapping his hands in glee. I turned off the TV, went up to my second-floor office, and spent an hour checking and organizing notes in my *pornography* file. I'll write the piece tonight, after a day spent researching a different writing project.

I have been years preparing to write this argument about pornography. My pornography file bulges with clippings and notes, some of them written by me—*to* me. The fact is that I worry as much about *how* I will present an argument as about what's in it. It is useless to have good evidence if you can't present it convincingly. Let me put all this in Toulmin's terms.

I have to make my *claim* right at the beginning. This claim is that when you perform the sexually *unthinkable* in front of an audience, you make that action—no matter how bad it is—*do-able*.

But I also want to start out dramatically, so at the beginning I intend to put the reader into a dramatic situation—into a theatre audience where a pornographic movie is being shown. The reader will see what I saw, feel what I felt. Thus I will also start out with what Toulmin calls *support,* the evidence or data for my claim. And I will keep interweaving *claim, support,* and *warrant* throughout the piece.

This is necessary by the very nature of argument. There is really no such thing as completely disorganized or "untouched" data, not even in a file folder. Almost any file, for example, is organized by the day of the month you put the material in the file. In the argument itself, I will organize my data or evidence by juxtaposition of "pornographic events" with my comments, thus creating a *warrant* by tying the pieces of the argument together. My pattern will be: *evidence-comment, evidence-comment.*

Qualifiers? Everyone who writes for a living knows that you can't say (very often): *Such and such is true.* You have to say: "Such and such is *usually, mainly, sometimes,* or perhaps *once-in-a-blue-moon* true." Using a gimmick in my computer program, I once counted my qualifiers in an article, and I had four or five on every page. I will use many qualifying phrases and remarks.

My big problem is with *reservations*—the question of counter-arguments. In this case, the question of counter-argument is pretty easy to anticipate: I'll be accused of advocating censorship. I am going to respond to that in two ways. The first I won't tell you about; I'll just let it sneak up on you. But the second I'll deal with in a time-honored fashion, by narrowing the argument to one issue implied in my title, thus putting any reservation concerning censorship *outside* the purpose of my argument.

My *motivational appeals* will be very strong and very clear. I will appeal to the decency and commonsense values in my readers. And, yes, I intend to get quite emotional about the whole thing. Believe me, it's an honest emotion!

*Postscript* [after writing the argument (see below)].

The discussion with you has helped me as a writer in one specific way. I am reminded once again how arguments tend to work in a "sandwich fashion." You give some data; you supply a reason for using it; you make a connection between the reason and the claim and the data. The argument works in layers, with *claim, support, reservations,* and *warrant* lying one over the other—but not in random fashion. Try taking particular sentences out of my little argument; if you did, the whole thing would fall apart.

Here is Truz's argument as described above. Note the discussion questions at the end.

## WHEN THE UNTHINKABLE BECOMES DO-ABLE
### BY MARTIN KANE TRUZ

[1] While the lights were up in the pornographic-movie house, I noticed certain people in the audience; a boy and a girl, each about twenty; a middle-aged couple (he was wearing farmer's overalls, she a housedress); and other,

assorted American types, mostly men of various ages and social class. When the lights went down, we saw a movie in which about twenty men "explicitly" sexually attacked, in various ways, one woman. I use the word *attacked* because the verb is accurate. For the record I will add that the woman—who was not merely pretty, but beautiful—enthusiastically joined in the fun and appeared to enjoy every minute of it.

2 Unthinkable, you say? On the contrary, not only thinkable, but *do-able*. Two days after I saw the beautiful woman attacked amid cheers of the movie audience, I read in the paper about a woman who was gang-raped in a tavern in New Bedford, Massachusetts. According to the news story, fifteen men raped her while a dozen patrons of the tavern stood by and cheered.

3 Roderick Anscombe, a psychiatrist who teaches at Harvard Medical School remarks that "increasingly in my practice, I find that what used to be just imagined is now actually being done." Dr. Anscombe adds: "No cruelty is so extreme that it is beyond human perpetration. Incest has lost its capacity to shock. . . . No sexual coupling is unbelievable anymore—fathers, daughters, brothers, babies, sea gulls, nothing is off the map, nothing is so bizarre that it could never really happen."

4 The bizarrely evil occurs when the unthinkable becomes thinkable. There is now more rape (including "date rape"), more child abuse, more incest, more of everything that we used not to think about, much less talk about. Americans once knew, instinctively, that a taboo is not a taboo if it is possible to think calmly about it. Now, in our homes, the unthinkable is calmly pictured at regular intervals on cable television. An arrow sails across the picture on the TV screen and into the eye of a beautiful girl in a scanty bathing suit. This is a "slasher" movie, and watchers immediately make an association: the dreadful sadism of the arrow in the eye and youthful sex. In another movie on cable, a young mother is pounced upon by an invisible monster; she is beaten up and raped. The movie consists of one beating-and-rape after another; in the last scene she is completely naked. More than fifty percent of Americans have cable television. Presumably, about half of all American children can see sexual sadism like the two examples mentioned. Incidentally, the star of the second movie is no pickup from a sex film but an internationally known actress.

5 An argument like mine is very unpopular these days. Many highly educated people will consider it ludicrous.

"What are you calling for, censorship?"

"If you censor cable TV, what next? Bill Cosby? *Cheers?*"

"And books—if you get your way, will we have read the last of *Huck Finn*, Shakespeare, *Catcher in the Rye*, Hemingway?"

6 Instead of responding to such questions, think with me for a minute. Think of the arrow shot into the eye of the sweet-faced half-naked girl; think of the beautiful woman being repeatedly raped in the porno-theatre movie—and enjoying it. Think of these scenes again and again; think of them tomorrow and the day after, next week and the week after that. Watch scenes like them in your own home on your own television set or VCR. As the days and weeks pass, do you find these scenes easier to contemplate? Apparently many people do; how many objections have you heard to cable TV programming lately? And what do you make of the statistic that almost half of the pornographic movies rented for VCR viewing are rented by *women?*

7 No, I am not arguing for censorship. I am arguing one point only: When the unthinkable becomes thinkable, it automatically tends to become do-able.

When the power of a taboo lessens, nothing shocks us any more. And shock (or disgust, or horror—call it what you will) is a primary factor in promoting civilized life. Too many Germans, we might remember, were not shocked by the murder of Jews in Nazi Germany. In part, it was German unshockability that made gassing Jews thinkable, then do-able.

8 I decline to consider the argument that "there is no hard evidence that pornography causes crime." The evidence is all around us, reported in the papers every day. Yet the question of *causation* itself is interesting. One of the strongest arguments for good books, good movies, and good television (public television, for example) is causal. These things, we are told endlessly, "improve us—teach us." No one doubts this. Nor should we doubt that pornographic movies, sadistic television, and sexually obscene books *disimprove* us—teach us, in the final analysis, how not to be human.

## ◆ PRACTICE

### Discussion Questions for Truz's Argument

a. Consider Truz's last comment (in the paragraph just above). Check each paragraph in his argument for *one* sentence that Truz must keep in that paragraph. What sentences did you pick, and why?

b. Do you find any flaws in the *warrant* of the argument?

c. Truz employs a few *qualifiers*. Where are they and what is their purpose?

d. Make some notes on Truz's employment of *motivational appeals*. Do you find them effective?

e. List and explain the parts of Truz's organization. Can you suggest a better organization for his purpose and audience?

f. Finish this statement by writing two or three paragraphs: "I will react to Truz's argument by [_____]." Fill in the blank by describing what you might *do* (what action you might take) in response to Truz. What was there in Truz's argument that encouraged you to take this action?

Your action might include writing a rebuttal to Truz. (See a student rebuttal to Truz below.)

### THE UNTHINKABLE BECAME THINKABLE A LONG TIME AGO

1 What an amazing argument Truz has written. By taking a common psychological phenomenon known as "habituation" and a series of events that happen to occur at the same time, he has—in one clean stroke—explained the cause of: (a) gang-rape, (b) incest, (c) sado-masochism, and (d) the Holocaust of World War II. We Americans shall abolish violent pornography and thereby cure our country of these social ills. The fact that these ills have been with us for all of our recorded history is relatively unimportant to Truz.

2 Truz points to a psychiatrist's lament that there is nothing left that can shock us anymore—no sex act is too bizarre for society. But if a psychiatrist sees

an increase in sexual deviation, it probably means his practice is expanding. He is a psychiatrist. It would be much more worrying if these people were not seeing a psychiatrist.

3 Truz's reasoning is not merely faulty, it is an outright lie. To begin with, his argument is known in the psychological field as "habituation." Habituation is just what its name implies. Through prolonged exposure, people become adjusted or adapted to something. His description of the unthinkable becoming thinkable is a reasonably accurate description of habituation and there is some scientific basis for Truz's assertions about the effect of habituation. We must give the devil his due. However, Truz insults his reader by creating a false cause-and-effect relationship in his examples. For instance, Truz describes the patrons of a pornographic theater as "American types" watching a gang-rape on the screen. He follows this closely with a story about the gang-rape of a woman at a bar. He places the two events next to each other in his essay as though one proves the other. The association is made that watching pornographic violence leads to committing acts of sexual violence. He does not, however, tell us which of the "American types" at the porno theater took part in the New Bedford crime. (Is he merely being cagy? After watching this violent film did he himself go on a rampage of rape and terror? Well, you never know.)

4 I'm still trying to figure out what relevance there is to the fact that half of the pornographic movies on VCR tape are rented to women. What is the point of this trivial, if interesting, statistic? Does Truz mean to suggest that women will be committing sex crimes in large numbers? Are we now a nation at risk from gangs of female rapists roaming our streets? Will women start looking for men who will rape them? If his theory on the effect of habituation is correct, that should be the result. (Even more importantly, have I been making a mistake in choosing comedies and romance movies for my first dates? Truz has given me food for thought here. Unfortunately, it's cotton candy.)

5 Truz has pointed to a variety of social ills and declared pornography their cause. What he fails to mention is that every one of the evils he so righteously denounces is as old as homo sapiens. Truz falls into the logical mistake of assuming that because he is seeing something for the first time, that it is the first time that something has been seen. Pornography has been produced in one form or another with whatever materials were handy. (Ever heard of "French postcards"?) The media have changed and so have the efficiencies of distribution, but this does not make current pornography the cause of our social ills. The writings of the Marquis de Sade, for instance, have been around for some time.

6 The only portion of Truz's essay that begins to merit our respect is his final statement. I respect it, not so much for the logical force of his argument, but the beauty of it. If "good" books and "good" television improve us, then it is very attractive to say that "bad" books and "bad" television "disimprove" us. What could be more sensible? Put pure water on a plant and it will flourish. Put polluted water on a plant and it will wither. Here at last is the simple, undeniable logic that rises above the false cause-and-effect relationships that Truz has attempted to pass off as proof of the need for taboos.

7 Unfortunately, Truz brings us no closer to achieving this goal. Censoring pornography is not a problem. Our history is full of references to censorship. The catch-phrase "banned in Boston" shows that censorship is not a foreign idea to the American people. The problem is that he hasn't told us how to

define "pornography." Is "The Rape of the Sabine Women" "art" while the movie he and the other "American types" were watching was "pornography"? Why? Because one was on film while the other is a painting? The Bible contains explicit sexual passages as well as moral lessons. Is it pornography? So does *Lolita*. Should it be read in church?

[8] A Supreme Court Justice put the problem into a nutshell when he gave us his definition of pornography, "I know it when I see it." Give us more than that, Truz! Show us how to separate the "good" from the "bad." Don't tell us to censor something without telling us how to do it.—Joe Zingher

# ✦ PRACTICE

## *Discussion*

1. On the following theses, which are of fact and which of action? For each action thesis, state the thesis of fact (the *need*, in other words) which would have to be proved before one could argue the action thesis. In each thesis, what terms need definition?
    a. The press should not be allowed to cover in great detail any important murder trials.
    b. Alcohol is a dangerous drug.
    c. The individual states in the Union should be allowed to determine their own educational policies.
    d. Poverty is a cause of crime.
    e. Help abolish poverty.
    f. Scientists should refuse work on any type of nuclear weapon.
    g. Swimming is the best form of general exercise.
    h. Robert E. Lee was a more capable tactician than Ulysses S. Grant.
    i. Undergraduates planning to go to law school should not have to take a foreign language.
    j. I don't care whether you believe me or not; he's got four people on that motorcycle with him!

2. Make a few notes for class discussion of the following argument, taken from a magazine advertisement.

### *FOR EVERY RIGHT THERE IS AN OBLIGATION*

[1] If you kept telling a child about his rights and never about his duties, you'd soon have a spoiled brat on your hands. We're doing the same thing in this country but on a vastly more dangerous scale.

[2] The "right" of unions to strike for more pay but no obligation to earn it.

[3] The "rights" of new nations to independence but no obligation to prove they deserve it, no obligation to use freedom for the good of mankind.

[4] The "right" of young people to education but no obligation to pay their own way to get it.

⁵ The "rights" of criminals and communists to flout the laws of our land, without any obligation to contribute to its worth and its freedom.

⁶ Spoiled children grow into adult criminals, who have to be punished by the decent society they defy. Why wait?

—advertisement by Warner & Swasey in *Newsweek*

## Writing

Write an argument using an organization of fact or action that is based on the ideas in the ad printed above. Sample thesis: *A majority of students at _____ College apparently feel an "obligation" to pay their own way, since over 55 percent of us are working our way through college.* Pick a specific writer's stance for your argument; for example, you might want to address Warner & Swasey directly.

## VIRGINIA WOOLF

# IF SHAKESPEARE HAD HAD A SISTER

*British novelist Virginia Woolf (1882–1941) was born into a Victorian family of respected scholars and artists and, with her sister Vanessa Bell, served as the core of the "Bloomsbury group" of writers and artists. She and her husband Leonard Woolf started the Hogarth Press, which published many then experimental, now famed writers of the early twentieth century. Woolf's own works include essays, reviews, literary criticism, biographies, and sensitive novels of psychology and mood, among them* Mrs. Dalloway *(1925) and* To the Lighthouse *(1927). Her strong advocacy of women's rights is evident in the following essay from the nonfiction work* A Room of One's Own *(1929), in which Woolf argues for respect for and support of creative women. Like Shakespeare's hypothetical sister, Virginia Woolf ended her own life, although not because her talent had been snuffed by society. We may be grateful that Woolf was born into the late nineteenth rather than the sixteenth century.*

¹ It is a perennial puzzle why no woman wrote a word of that extraordinary [Elizabethan] literature when every other man, it seemed was capable of song or sonnet. What were the conditions in which women lived, I asked myself; for fiction, imaginative work that is, is not dropped like a pebble upon the ground, as science may be; fiction is like a spider's web, attached ever so lightly perhaps, but still attached to life at all four corners. Often the attachment is scarcely perceptible; Shakespeare's plays, for instance, seem to hang there complete by themselves. But when the web is pulled askew, hooked up at the edge, torn in the middle, one remembers that these webs are not spun in mid-air by incorporeal creatures, but are the work of suffering human beings, and are attached to grossly material things, like health and money and the house we live in.

² But what I find . . . is that nothing is known about women before the eighteenth century. I have no model in my mind to turn about this way and that. Here am I asking why women did not write poetry in the Elizabethan age, and I am not sure how they were educated; whether they were taught to write; whether they had sitting rooms to themselves; how many women had children before they were twenty-one; what, in short, they did from eight in the morning till eight at night. They had no money evidently; according to Professor Trevelyan they were married whether they liked it or not before they were out of the nursery, at fifteen or sixteen very likely. It would have been extremely odd, even upon this showing, had one of them suddenly written the plays of Shakespeare, I concluded, and I thought of that old gentleman, who is dead now, but was a bishop, I think, who declared that it was impossible for any woman, past, present, or to come, to have the genius of Shakespeare. He wrote to the papers about it.

He also told a lady who applied to him for information that cats do not as a matter of fact, go to heaven, though they have, he added, souls of a sort. How much thinking those old gentlemen used to save one! How the borders of ignorance shrank back at their approach! Cats do not go to heaven. Women cannot write the plays of Shakespeare.

³ Be that as it may, I could not help thinking, as I looked at the works of Shakespeare on the shelf, that the bishop was right in this; it would have been impossible, completely and entirely, for any woman to have written the plays of Shakespeare in the age of Shakespeare. Let me imagine, since facts are so hard to come by, what would have happened had Shakespeare had a wonderfully gifted sister, called Judith, let us say. Shakespeare himself went, very probably—his mother was an heiress—to the grammar school, where he may have learnt Latin—Ovid, Virgil and Horace—and the elements of grammar and logic. He was, it is well known, a wild boy who poached rabbits, perhaps shot a deer, and had, rather sooner than he should have done, to marry a woman in the neighbourhood, who bore him a child quicker than was right. That escapade sent him to seek his fortune in London. He had, it seemed, a taste for the theatre; he began by holding horses at the stage door. Very soon he got to work in the theatre, became a successful actor, and lived at the hub of the universe, meeting everybody, knowing everybody, practising his art on the boards, exercising his wits in the streets, and even getting access to the palace of the queen. Meanwhile his extraordinarily gifted sister, let us suppose, remained at home. She was as adventurous, as imaginative, as agog to see the world as he was. But she was not sent to school. She had no chance of learning grammar and logic, let alone of reading Horace and Virgil. She picked up a book now and then, one of her brother's perhaps, and read a few pages. But then her parents came in and told her to mend the stockings or mind the stew and not moon about with books and papers. They would have spoken sharply but kindly, for they were substantial people who knew the conditions of life for a woman and loved their daughter—indeed, more likely than not she was the apple of her father's eye. Perhaps she scribbled some pages up in an apple loft on the sly, but was careful to hide them or set fire to them. Soon, however, before she was out of her teens, she was to be betrothed to the son of a neighbouring wool-stapler. She cried out that marriage was hateful to her, and for that she was severely beaten by her father. Then he ceased to scold her. He begged her instead not to hurt him, not to shame him in this matter of her marrage. He would give her a chain of beads or a fine petticoat, he said; and there were tears in his eyes. How could she disobey him? How could she break his heart? The force of her own gift alone drove her to it. She made up a small parcel of her belongings, let herself down by a rope one summer's night and took the road to London. She was not seventeen. The birds that sang in the hedge were not more musical than she was. She had the quickest fancy, a gift like her brother's, for the tune of words. Like him, she had a taste for the theatre. She stood at the stage door; she wanted to act, she said. Men laughed in her face. The

manager—a fat, loose-lipped man—guffawed. He bellowed something about poodles dancing and women acting—no women, he said, could possibly be an actress. He hinted—you can imagine what. She could get no training in her craft. Could she even seek her dinner in a tavern or roam the streets at midnight? Yet her genius was for fiction and lusted to feed abundantly upon the lives of men and women and the study of their ways. At last—for she was very young, oddly like Shakespeare the poet in her face, with the same grey eyes and rounded brows—at last Nick Greene the actor-manager took pity on her; she found herself with child by that gentleman and so—who shall measure the heat and violence of the poet's heart when caught and tangled in a woman's body?—killed herself one winter's night and lies buried at some cross-roads where the omnibuses now stop outside the Elephant and Castle.

⁴ That, more or less, is how the story would run, I think, if a woman in Shakespeare's day had had Shakespeare's genius. But for my part, I agree with the deceased bishop, if such he was—it is unthinkable that any woman in Shakespeare's day should have had Shakespeare's genius. For genius like Shakespeare's is not born among labouring, uneducated, servile people. It was not born in England among the Saxons and the Britons. It is not born today among the working classes. How, then, could it have been born among women whose work began, according to Professor Trevelyan, almost before they were out of the nursery, who were forced to it by their parents and held to it by all the power of law and custom?

## ◆ PRACTICE

*Discussion*

1. Why, according to the bishop, could not a woman have written the plays of Shakespeare? Are his reasons stated or implied in the essay? Does Woolf refute his premise or simply proceed from an opposing premise? Explain.

2. Why, according to Woolf, could not a woman have written the plays of Shakespeare? How does she qualify this conclusion in a way that makes it very different from the bishop's conclusion?

3. What prejudices about genius does Woolf betray that may be seen by some as equally objectionable to those of the bishop? What attitudes do you think Woolf would have with regard to the oral literature of the Vikings or the slave narratives of early American blacks?

4. How does Woolf establish authority for her evidence? What particular reference does she specifically name? How does she undermine the authority of the opposing view?

5. To what other strategies of development does Woolf resort in support of her larger argument? In what ways might these strategies be considered a specious strategy to employ in a logical argument? Does Woolf use them fairly? Explain.

6. What is the analogy of a spider's web doing at the start of Woolf's argument? How and why might she have returned to it at the conclusion of the argument? What technique does she use instead in the final paragraph to produce a more dramatic effect?

7. Describe a typical Woolf sentence as you observe it in this essay. Why are the last two sentences in the second paragraph exceptions to her usual style? Can you find any other exceptions elsewhere in the essay? If you can, explain the effect they create.

8. Is Woolf's argument an organization of fact, action, or refutation or is it a combination of two or all three of these? Explain your answer.

### Vocabulary

| | | |
|---|---|---|
| perennial | poached | guffawed |
| perceptible | agog | omnibuses |
| askew | moon | servile |
| incorporeal | | |

### Writing

1. Argue that powers of law and custom still confine women in certain areas. Using Woolf as a model, include a narrative speculating on the potential for success of women in business and industry, the law, medicine, or politics today.

2. Woolf asks, "Who can measure the heat and violence of the poet's heart when caught and tangled in a woman's body?" Argue for or against the idea that her biological make-up restricts a woman's ability to achieve in the world at large.

3. Defend or oppose—with logical arguments—a quota system for hiring and promoting women and minorities.

CHRISTINE DAVIDSON

# WORKING TIME AND A HALF

*Christine Davidson was educated at Ripon College and Boston University and the University of Exeter, Devon, England. She taught English in Boston public schools and was an instructor in nonfiction writing at Antioch–New England and the University of New Hampshire. Now employed as a copyeditor and writer, Davidson concentrates on business, social and women's issues. She lives in New Hampshire with her husband and two children. What Davidson calls "that one little essay"—reprinted below—resulted in a full-length book,* Staying Home Instead, *now in its fourth printing.*

[1] There she is, the working mother of America, self-assured and jaunty with her briefcase swinging at her side. Her smile seems to say she "has it all": husband, children, stimulating job, independence, fulfillment. It doesn't show guilt, frustration, weekend headaches or exhaustion. Well, I have "had it all" since my kids were in diapers, and I have finally had it.

[2] A year ago I decided that being a working wife and mother was not right for me. But I would like to suggest that the image of the working woman that advertisers and the news media portray does not jibe with reality for many American women.

[3] Most of us do not dress in expensive suits; we are waitresses, office workers and teachers. Few of us are executives, and few of us carry briefcases. Even if we felt they looked right with our pink uniforms and polyester pantsuits, we couldn't afford them. We make 59 cents for every dollar a man makes.

[4] Those of us who work to support or help support small children often spend more than 25 percent of our paychecks on child care. We cannot work without day care, and we cannot work happily without quality day care. A businessman who cannot work without a secretary and electricity can be given a 100 percent tax deduction for these as business expenses. Yet for years we have been given only a 20 percent tax credit on $2,000 spent per child for day care, and recent legislation raises this only slightly.

[5] Another factor that is inequitable, though often unavoidable, is that in two-career families most husbands do not split housework 50-50. From everything I have read and observed, I would say it is usually 70-30 at best. In our family, my husband cooked one night a week, washed dishes the nights I cooked, made his lunch and did two loads of laundry a week. With the demanding job he had, we both knew this was all he had the energy for.

[6] But after a while I began to be unhappy that I did the other ten loads of wash, vacuumed and mopped, chauffeured the kids to friends' houses and the doctor and dentist, made their lunches and snacks, ran errands,

paid all our bills, kept our IRS and other business files, did the clothing and food shopping, cooked six nights a week and arranged all day care (including the rearranging when a sitter called at 8 a.m. to say she wouldn't be coming at 8:30).

7 Most of these tasks were simple, but they added up and contributed to my feeling exhausted and frustrated. My jaw would be clenched by 8:45 a.m. as I drove to work.

8 When I got to work I would shut the door to my classroom and force myself to forget everything else. And I did have an interesting job. I taught English at a local college, did free-lance writing and editing and taught a night course to adults. My work was stimulating and fun. But pay for a part-time instructor was low, and I began to take on more free-lance work than was good for me.

9 Yet we continued to think of my work away from home as "just part time," and the work at home as inconsequential. In fact, I did not work "part time,"; I had a teaching job, a damp, dilapidated house to fix up on weekends, two children to care for and usually a short story or article in progress. I worked time and a half.

10 One spring day when my husband came home with a raise, the thought struck me that maybe I didn't have to. Initially I had started working so we could stay solvent and keep up our car payments and home improvement loan. My husband's raise coincided with the last payments on these loans. I could continue working so we could live more comfortably and get household help, or I could stop and we could keep our standard of living low. I quit.

11 Since then our day-to-day living has read like a column of Heloise hints. We wash wool sweaters and air suits on the clothesline instead of taking them to the cleaners. We eat soyburgers and crock-pot soup. We can and freeze our garden vegetables and store cabbages and squash in our drafty front hallway.

12 We sometimes find these and other economies a pain in the neck. And we're broke—all the time. We cannot pay a small bill and buy our children sneakers the same week. But it's OK because I can give my kids something else now. I have stopped saying, "No, not this afternoon, I have to work" or "No, not now, I'm too tired."

13 I will never know whether my working was bad for my kids; I do know it was bad for me. I never knew when one of them would contract the flu or fall from the Jungle Gym when I had a deadline to make. Illnesses and accidents are worries for any mother, but for a working mother they can be real stomach twisters. One thing for sure, none of the swinging-working-mom articles tells you how to make it to the 9 a.m. board meeting—or more correctly, the steno pool—looking fresh and alert when your baby has been vomiting in your arms at 5 a.m.

14 I can understand how working might be good for women who feel confined at home with small children or who have grown children. Women who want to work *should*—and without a 1950s condemnation from any-

one. But I think we should not move from the narrow-mindedness of the '50s to another kind of narrowness in the '80s. Mothers who choose to stay home should not feel they have to justify their decision.

## ✦ PRACTICE

### Discussion

1. An argument like this tends to stand or fall on the convincingness of its *facts*. List five facts you find in the essay. Do you find all five convincing?

2. Is this an argument of *fact* or *action*? How can you be sure?

3. Discuss the sentence that makes up paragraph 6. Is the sentence effective? What major technique of construction does it employ?

4. Davidson doesn't blame her husband, even though he does less work at home than she does. Why might she actually blame her husband, but as a technique of argument not mention it in her essay?

5. Consider the last sentence of paragraph 9, which echoes Davidson's title. Why doesn't she place this sentence earlier?

6. The first sentence of paragraph 13 may seem odd to some readers. Most debates on this subject emphasize the effect on *children,* but Davidson ignores the issue. Is this a mistake?

7. Sample your class. How many students agree with Davidson's thesis? With the way that she narrowed her thesis? (Did she narrow it too much? Should she have employed other issues?)

8. Explain Davidson's use of the phrase *stomach twisters* (paragraph 13).

### Vocabulary

| | | |
|---|---|---|
| jibe | inequitable | dilapidated |
| *quality* day care | inconsequential | soyburgers |

### Writing

1. Write a rebuttal to Davidson.

2. Write a *fact* argument on this subject from a typical husband's point of view.

3. Write an *action* argument based on ideas or issues in the essay.

JOHN RUSSO

# "REEL" VS. REAL VIOLENCE

*John Russo was the producer of* Night of the Living Dead, *the movie that, as critic Dave Kehr remarked, "changed the face of American horror movies. . . ." The idea of the movie was simple: "Let's make a monster movie." It took nine months to make, on practically a non-budget (ten people put up $600 each, and a meatpacker contributed animal intestines). The flesh the ghouls ate was Silly Putty. In 1990, Russo co-produced a new version of the same movie. Russo insists that movies about the living—and the un-living—dead are essentially harmless. What do you think?*

¹ One day I switched on the evening news just in time to see a Pennsylvania politician waving around a .357 magnum, warning reporters to back off so they wouldn't get hurt, then sticking the gun in his mouth and . . .

² Mercifully, the station I was watching didn't show him pulling the trigger, but I learned later that another Pittsburgh station showed the whole suicide unedited. What I saw was enough to make me ill. My stomach was in a knot, and I couldn't get the incident out of my mind. I still can't, even though three years have gone by.

³ I have a special reason for wondering and worrying about blood and violence on TV and movie screens. I write, produce and direct horror movies. I coauthored "Night of the Living Dead," the so-called "grand-daddy of the splatter flicks." And since then I've made a string of movies depicting murder and mayhem.

⁴ I can watch these kinds of movies when they've been made by other people, and I can even help create the bloody effects in my own movies without getting a knot in my stomach. Yet I still retain my capacity to be shocked, horrified and saddened when something like this happens in real life.

⁵ So there must be a difference between real violence and "reel" violence. And if I didn't feel that this is true, I'd stop making the kinds of movies that I make. What are those differences?

⁶ My movies are scary and unsettling, but they are also cautionary tales. They might show witches at work, doing horrible things or carrying out nefarious schemes, but in doing so they convey a warning against superstition and the dementia it can spawn. They might show people under extreme duress, set upon by human or inhuman creatures, but in doing so they teach people how duress can be handled and blind, ignorant fear can be confronted and conquered. My purpose hasn't been to glorify or en-

courage murder and mayhem, but to give horror fans the vicarious chills and thrills they crave.

[7] The most powerful and consequently financially successful horror movies—"Night of the Living Dead," "The Texas Chainsaw Massacre," "Halloween" and "Friday The 13th"—feature a small cast in a confined situation that is made terrifying by the presence of a monster/madman/ murderer. Usually the victims are young, beautiful women. Often the murders are filmed from the point of view of the murderer. For all these reasons, we filmmakers have been accused of hating women and portraying them as objects to be punished for being sexually desirable. Horror fans have been accused of identifying with the psychopathic killers portrayed in these movies and deriving vicarious enjoyment from watching the killers act out the fans' dark fantasies.

[8] But there are two simple, pragmatic reasons why the victims are often filmed from the point of view of the killer. First, it's an effective technique for not revealing who the killer is, thus preserving an aura of suspense. Second, it affords dramatically explicit angles for showing the victim's terror—and the horror of what the killer is doing.

[9] These films *are* horrifying because they reflect—but do not create—a frightful trend in our society. Murders, assaults and rapes are being committed with more frequency and with increasing brutality. Serial killers and mass murderers are constantly making headlines. Most of these killers are men, often sexually warped men, and they most often kill women. So we filmmakers have stuck to the facts in our portrayal of them. That's why our movies are so scary. Too many of our fellow citizens are turning into monsters, and contemporary horror movies have seized upon this fear and personified it. So now we have Jason, Michael and Freddy instead of Dracula and Frankenstein. Our old-time movie monsters used to be creatures of fantasy. But today, unfortunately, they are extensions of reality.

[10] Recently, at a horror convention in Albany, I was autographing videocassettes of a show I had hosted, entitled "Witches, Vampires & Zombies," and a young man asked me if the tape showed actual human sacrifices. He was disappointed when I informed him that the ceremonies on the tape were fictional depictions. He was looking for "snuff movies"— the kind that actually show people dying.

[11] Unfortunately, tapes showing real death are widely available nowadays. A video of the Pennsylvania politician blowing his brains out went on sale just a few weeks after the incident was broadcast. But I don't think that the people who are morbidly fixated on this sort of thing are the same people who are in love with the horror-movie genre.

[12] I'm afraid that the young man I met in Albany has a serious personality disorder. And I don't think he's really a horror fan. He didn't buy my tape, but he would have bought it if the human sacrifices had been real. "Reel" violence didn't interest him. He didn't care about the niceties of theme, plot or character development. He just wanted to see people die.

[13] I haven't seen any snuff movies for sale at the horror conventions I've attended. True horror fans aren't interested. They don't go to the

movies just to see artificial blood and gore, either. The films that gratuitously deliver those kinds of effects usually are box-office flops. The hit horror films have a lot more to offer. While scaring us and entertaining us, they teach us how to deal with our deepest fears, dreads and anxieties.

[14] But modern horror movies aren't to blame for these fears, dreads and anxieties. They didn't create our real-life Jasons, Michaels and Freddys any more than the gangster movies of the 1920s and 1930s created Al Capone and Dutch Schultz. If the movies reflect, with disturbing accuracy, the psychic terrain of the world we live in, then it's up to us to change that world and make it a safer place.

## ◆ PRACTICE

### Discussion

1. Read the brief section on *ethical proof* (pp. 347–348). How does Russo use ethical proof in his argument?

2. What is the thesis of the argument? Did you find it explicitly stated?

3. What is the purpose of paragraphs 10–13?

4. What is the *occasion* for Russo's argument? Why would he—as a producer of what he calls "splatter flicks"—feel compelled to make it?

5. Note the first sentence of paragraph 9. For discussion: *If "splatter flicks" did not help to create a "frightful trend" in our society, then where did the trend come from?*

6. In paragraph 12, sentence 1, Russo uses a jargon term, perhaps the only one in the essay: *serious personality disorder.* Why didn't he employ a less jargonized expression; for example, "The young man was a *vicious psycho*"?

7. Explain the job of paragraph 5.

8. How much are you convinced by Russo's argument? If you wish, take it piece by piece; for instance, do you agree with the last sentence in paragraph 6? With the first sentence in paragraph 9? With the last three sentences in paragraph 12? (Do most of the people who attend splatter movies "care about the niceties of theme, plot or character development"?)

### Vocabulary

| | | |
|---|---|---|
| nefarious | vicarious | fixated |
| dementia | psychopathic | gratuitously |
| duress | aura | |

## Writing

1. Read Discussion question **8** above. Write a paper responding to any one of the "pieces" of Russo's argument. You may agree or disagree with him. Use evidence from your own viewing of "splatter flicks."

2. John Russo appears in his essay as a particular kind of person. Write a detailed description of this person.

3. Write an action argument on the question of "splatter flicks." You might try to answer the question: What—if anything—should be done about them (or an element of them)? You might want to use a fairly limited thesis relating to questions like the following: Should young actors refuse/agree to appear in them? Should parents encourage/ discourage their pre-teen children to see them on cable TV?

MARGARET EDWARDS

# BUT DOES THE NEW WOMAN REALLY WANT THE NEW MAN?

*Margaret Edwards is associate professor of English at the University of Vermont. Her essay on the New Woman/New Man dilemma appeared in the May 1985 issue of* Working Woman *magazine. Her argument may not be a very popular one among New Women, so she needs all the help she can get. A number of the strategies for good writing come to her aid here.*

¹ It used to be that the man would telephone the woman and ask for a date. This was in the days before running shoes (there were only tennis shoes), when "Made in Japan" was a synonym for "shoddy." The man's bad luck was to have to screw up his courage and ask. The woman's bad luck was to have to stifle her hopes and wait.

² But times change.

³ Recently, when a young male colleague in my office mentioned a woman whom he liked, I suggested, "Why don't you two drop by my place for a drink the next time you invite her on a date?"

⁴ "Oh, we don't *date*," he said. "We sort of hang out."

⁵ I have since made further discreet inquiries among the under-30 singles on our staff and have confirmed that dating as I once knew it is indeed dead. Fashion houses may be reviving the 1950s style of ball gowns, but the date, I've been assured, remains moribund.

⁶ Going back to the first source of my information, I asked who had made the crucial phone call to arrange the first meeting. His answer gave no hint of a new protocol. In this particular case, while idly conversing with the young woman—both of them having stopped to stretch their muscles at the same bend in a jogging trail—he mentioned he was going to a reggae concert. She remarked that she had a ticket to the same event.

⁷ It so happened that they bumped into each other afterwards, and in the company of numerous mutual friends, they walked downtown to a favorite bar.

⁸ "But that seems too whimsical and uncertain," I said. "Suppose she hadn't had a ticket to the same concert? Would you have gotten hold of her phone number to call her up and say, 'I've got an extra ticket; do you want to come?'"

⁹ No. Definitely not. He confessed, though, that he might have said, "I've got an extra ticket; do you want to buy it?"

[10] "Can you tell me what's wrong," I asked, "with letting a woman know you're interested?" I began recalling with a certain nostalgia the brave gruff voices on telephones that had wondered if I were free on Saturday night. My friend looked uncomfortable and evasive.

[11] "If I let a woman know I'm interested," he said, "she might expect too much."

[12] His face said it all: She might expect a regular and increasing familiarity. Marriage? Well, not quite that. But all too soon, books and stereos would be packed in cartons, a lease would have been jointly signed, and two sets of parents would begin looking pained but hopeful on Christmas holidays.

[13] "Women make marvelous friends," he affirmed.

[14] And I thought how often that's been said, in the same tone, about dogs.

### New men, wimps and wormboys

[15] Are men getting weaker as women get stronger? This question seems to be preoccupying feminists lately. In the *New York Times,* Barbara Ehrenreich characterized the evolution of Macho Man into New Man as a mutation from tyrant to fop. She praised the new-found domestic independence of the male—he can fix his own quiche—but lamented the "narcissism" that makes him prefer to eat it alone or with a series of pretty companions. She praised his budding sensitivities—he enjoys a shopping spree, he keeps his body trim, he cries—but deplored his self-absorption. There is no commitment in the New Man. He's not out to enslave or dominate a female. In fact, what's wrong with him now is that he feels little urge to create a longstanding or passionate bond with any woman. Bachelorhood, freed of its gay stigma, has become his prime and perpetual state. He accepts that women have joined him on the fast track, yet their paths seem to be parallel, not intersecting.

[16] So, it is not enough, anymore to ask that men become more like women," concluded Ehrenreich. She tried to give a helpful directive: "We should ask that they become more like what both men and women might be"—cultivating in themselves both "masculine" and "feminine" virtues, plus a capacity for commitment and "a broad and generous vision of how we all might live together."

[17] What Ehrenreich advocates is close to a wholesale change in human nature. It would surely call a truce in the war between the sexes. (It might even bring peace among nations as well.) But is it realistic to expect this? Are men going to redouble their efforts to be the best sort of people they can be? Pessimists among us may find the litmus of our predictions turning a shade darker.

[18] Deborah Laake's article "Wormboys"—widely published last year in a number of newspapers—put forth the woman's position bluntly: "As the clock keeps ticking and I'm neither younger nor more firmly settled in love than when I began my research, a primitive inner force wants to wind

things up and have a life with someone. But something stops me. And that something is that I'm surrounded by wimps." She coined another word for wimps—wormboys.

[19] These are men who shrink from marriage, from having children, even from the simplest assertion, such as deciding where to go and what to do on a weekend. They are "lazy," unambitious in their work and unashamed of letting women pay. They do not embrace the roles of provider, arbiter, analyst, manager or leader. They avoid anything the least bit unpleasant. If a confrontation looms, they run and hide.

[20] Laake advised women to assess what it means if they, not the men they spend time with, "comb the entertainment sections of local periodicals" and then choose what to do with leisure time. What does it mean if women allow themselves to be accompanied by men who have offered no suggestions about where to go and are content to "just go along"?

[21] The male ideal in feminist minds is no longer what it was, yet has taken no definite subsequent shape. A superficial make-over of yesterday's he-man won't do. John Wayne with a developed culinary talent will still think it's his woman's role to wash his dishes.

[22] For serious feminists, there is no way back to the style of commitment the he-man was half of—a style requiring the man's providence in exchange for the woman's subservience.

[23] Yet the New Woman, in querulous moments, seems angry with the new possibilities. If a feminist is offered the converse of the old style of commitment—that is, a union in which *she* will provide and *he* will serve—she balks. It is a bond that, by the logic of inverted tradition, ought to have a chance of strength.

[24] Laake's article described her breakup with a so-called wormboy. "I was overwhelmed," she wrote, "by the responsibilities falling on me in our union—those of principal breadwinner, head of the entertainment committee, business manager and mother of souls." Yet think of the years that men were expected to take on the same "overwhelming" role! All as a matter of course. And what was their reward? There was one. It was A Wife of One's Own.

### Does a woman really want a wife?

[25] Laake's pseudonymous boyfriend Henry is a hirsute version of what has been the time-honored, much-idealized Little Woman, with "velvet sheathing the steel demurely." When Laake asked him exactly what he would contribute to their relationship, he replied, "I've observed that I seem to function as an invisible support system."

[26] Invisible support—that's what the more retiring member of a couple offers. This is not the visible cash on the table or paycheck in the mailbox or gold card at the restaurant, but it's support nonetheless. It used to be called "what money can't buy" (although money kept it fed and housed), and still takes amorphous forms; the shoulder to cry on, the home-cooked dinner that's waiting for you (still hot), the calm in the midst of your daily storm.

[27] Laake admitted that she had enjoyed this kind of support from her Henry. To him, she had confided fears and fantasies. From him, she had received encouragement, understanding, sympathy and attention. She acknowledged that often he would talk to her in rambling and irrelevant monologues, but the talk itself provided support. "I'd [be] alternately absorbed in it and comforted by it," she wrote, "the way I sometimes actually watch a TV show and other times just flip on the set and feel glad for the company."

[28] Customarily men have felt "glad for the company" of women offering only invisible support. Why can't women be glad for the same? Perhaps it's bizarre and maybe a little scary to find oneself head of a household that includes an able-bodied man.

[29] *Did we feminists really expect that, as a norm, two equally ambitious careerists could form an amicable partnership under the same roof?*

[30] "Yes!" comes the chorus. "That's what we did expect. Why haven't we gotten it?"

[31] Putting the question of sexual differences aside for the moment, I've asked myself: Are the strong couples I know made of partners who are alike or partners who are complimentary?

[32] My answer: complimentary. A logical mate for a person full of energy and drive and purpose is someone offering that valuable old-fashioned commodity, "invisible support." Tractability (let's not keep calling it passivity) and an amenable disposition, a domestic focus (not necessarily being "lazy" about work) and an enjoyment of being coddled, indulged and led (despite being bright and full of his own opinions)—why aren't these traits considered valuable in a man? For a self-willed, adventurous woman, they might be traits to look for if she wants to form a strong bond with someone who suits her.

[33] Unfortunately, women don't yet admire in men what have been known as the "feminine virtues." It took women so long to get out from under these virtues that one can hardly blame them for still being suspicious of them. Maxims such as " They also serve who only stand and wait" seemed designed to keep women at home. Rather than standing and waiting, and being content to change diapers and fix the dinners for movers and doers, some women have wanted to be the movers and doers themselves.

[34] It is all to the good and only fair that society seems to be moving in the direction of letting temperament and talents, rather than sex and race, determine employment and compensation. But the old maxim still holds true, for those who "also serve" by giving "invisible support" are a vague "they," neither male nor female.

### Little women vs. new women

[35] When will we feminists stop feeling disappointed that the high-salaried males willing to support families often prefer the Little Women types? They seem happier with them in fundamental ways. Those Little

Women, despite Betty Friedan's debunking of their "mystique," are still the ones who willingly pack and move at their husband's decree, who are free to go on business junkets at short notice, who stay home to mind the children and run the errands. We all know by now that each Little Woman is taking a big chance, going at it with that combination of foolhardiness and courage peculiar to the motorbike racer who doesn't wear a helmet. If her marriage crashes, the damage to her will be inevitable and severe, for she's got very little protection. And the statistics are against her.

[36] The New Woman, the mover and doer, is simply carving out new spheres of risk. "We are becoming the men we wanted to marry," *Ms.* editor Gloria Steinem told a large gathering of women. Right now, the "neither younger nor more firmly settled" New Woman may feel that her heaviest liability is a likelihood of winding up alone. The chances of marrying a man like herself seem slim and getting slimmer.

[37] Yet our old dream dies hard. The prince must come and kiss the sleeping beauty. She is still under a dark spell, though this time not a spell of prudery or parents or her own pitiful ineptitude. What currently immobilizes her is loneliness. She feels paralyzed by the work of living up to her own vaunted promise, by the late nights and by the dumb dullness that creeps into any career. She has her independent self and nobody else— nobody else in bed, nobody else across the breakfast table—at least nobody steady enough, ever-present enough, and promised as a part of each day. A prince must arrive who is willing to banish her loneliness permanently, to share half the housework, to become a "participating" father *and* to bring home a full share of income. Is that so much to ask of a man? The answer is that it must be, given how men seem to flee such commitment.

[38] "She might expect too much" echoes beyond the revealing conversation I had with that man at the office. "You won't believe the guy I went out with last week . . ." begins a story I am told by an attractive single woman. "He was so afraid of commitment he checked the fire exits in the restaurant before we sat down!" A contemporary greeting card carries the message "To get a prince, you have to kiss a lot of frogs"—and today's unmarried women can get tired of kissing frogs.

### Fewer frogs, more fish

[39] Fewer frogs, and more fish, appear in the pool of available men if a feminist is willing to consider forming a serious alliance with the sort that the macho tradition taught her to spurn.

[40] What about the man of gentle and unassuming temper? The man of erratic and skimpy income? The man shorter than she? The man less educated? The man from a less privileged background? Or, the man much younger?

[41] A lot of misunderstanding betwen men and women comes from our believing the two sexes are inherently polarized. Actually, they're closer to an androgynous human mean. Men are cursed with the same conflicts we experience—and should not be envied and therefore reviled. The men I

know, like the women I know, find it hard to choose between modern life's contraries: the safe routine and adventurous possibility, the vocation and avocation, the thrill of affairs and the comforts of marriage, the time they spend alone and the time they spend with others, the satisfaction in being free of children and the urge to have kids. If you talk to a man who is worried about his life, he sounds exactly like the worried woman—as if he's being torn along the same seams as she. He even ends a conversation as she does, by saying "There's nobody free in this city. They're all married. I can't meet anyone."

[42] So far, it seems that the work-directed and undomesticated New Woman doesn't like the look of the New Man. But should those of us who have asked to ride the horse turn petulant when we're hoisted astride and handed the reins? There are sincere pleasures in taking command. If a woman calls a new tune because she's earned enough to pay the piper, it doesn't mean she has to dance unpartnered. The New Woman may have to take a chance on living with the type of man who benefits from her energy rather than duplicates it, who admires her clear sense of purpose and doesn't thwart it, who feels inclined not so much to lead her as to enjoy where she leads. She may have to look past the classic knight on the white charger to find the next hero—the one on the dark horse.

## ◆ PRACTICE

*Discussion*

1. Is Edwards a feminist? Why or why not?

2. What arguments, according to Edwards, do Ehrenreich and Laake lodge against the New Man? What do they suggest as an alternative? What faults does Edwards find with their suggestions?

3. What kind of man does Edwards recommend for the strong, successful New Woman? What examples does she give?

4. Why doesn't the essay start with paragraph 15 instead of paragraph 1? What is the relationship between paragraphs 1–14 and paragraph 15? Where is a theme of paragraphs 1–14 picked up again specifically later in the essay?

5. What connection can you see between paragraph 16 and paragraph 41? Does Edwards take advantage of the connection? If so, how? If not, what might she have done?

6. Where does Edwards make reference to her opponents in the argument? How does she treat their arguments? How does this treatment contribute to her argument?

7. Edwards' argument consists of a chain of *inductive* and *deductive* reasoning. Identify the segments of her chain and explain how each is an example of either induction or deduction. How solidly has she grounded her inductive generalizations on facts? Do you detect any flaws in her deductive reasoning?

8. How does Edwards use analogy in the last paragraph of her essay? How does one of her analogies echo others used earlier in the essay? Are her analogies clichéd? How do the analogies contribute to her argument? Could it be made without them? What, if anything, would be lost?

## Vocabulary

| | | |
|---|---|---|
| moribund | providence | tractability |
| fop | subservience | amenable |
| narcissism | querulous | androgynous |
| litmus | hirsute | petulant |

## Writing

1. Do you agree with Edwards' image of the New Woman as career-driven and un- or anti-domestic? If not, write an essay refuting her image and offering what you believe to be the *real* New Woman.

2. How do people date or, if Edwards' colleague is typical, non-date today? How is an evening out arranged? Who pays for what? What is expected of whom? If you agree that dating patterns have changed, write an essay arguing for the superiority of either the old or the new system.

3. Would you rather be a man or a woman today? Write an essay in support of your position.

## MARTIN LUTHER KING, JR.

# *LETTER FROM BIRMINGHAM JAIL**

*Martin Luther King, Jr., was a central figure in the civil rights movement of the 1960s until he was shot and killed in 1968. He was born in 1929 in Atlanta, Georgia, and educated at Morehouse College (B.A.), Crozer Theological Seminary (B.D.), and Boston University (Ph.D.). From his pulpit in Montgomery, Alabama, he preached the politics of peaceful protest and became a national spokesman for the rights of American blacks as founder of the Southern Christian Leadership Conference. In 1964 he was awarded the Nobel Peace Prize. Best known for his keynote speech "I Have a Dream," given during a 1963 protest march on Washington, D.C., King also wrote* Stride Toward Freedom *(1958) and* Why We Can't Wait *(1964), from which "Letter from Birmingham Jail— April 16, 1963" is taken. King's consummate mastery of the great rhetorical style of Southern preaching is as apparent in this letter as it is in the film clips of his famous speeches and sermons.*

April 16, 1963

My Dear Fellow Clergymen:

¹ While confined here in the Birmingham city jail, I came across your recent statement calling my present activities "unwise and untimely." Seldom do I pause to answer criticism of my work and ideas. If I sought to answer all the criticism that cross my desk, my secretaries would have little time for anything other than such correspondence in the course of the day, and I would have no time for constructive work. But since I feel that you are men of genuine good will and that your criticisms are sincerely set forth, I want to try to answer your statement in what I hope will be patient and reasonable terms.

² I think I should indicate why I am here in Birmingham, since you have been influenced by the view which argues against "outsiders coming in." I have the honor of serving as president of the Southern Christian Leadership Conference, an organization operating in every southern state,

---

*Author's Note: This response to a published statement by eight fellow clergymen from Alabama (Bishop C. C. J. Carpenter, Bishop Joseph A. Durick, Rabbi Milton L. Grafman, Bishop Paul Hardin, Bishop Nolan B. Harmon, the Reverend George M. Murray, the Reverend Edward V. Ramage, and the Reverend Earl Stallings) was composed under somewhat constricting circumstances. Begun on the margin of the newspaper in which the statement appeared while I was in jail, the letter was continued on scraps of writing paper supplied by a friendly Negro trusty, and concluded on a pad my attorneys were eventually permitted to leave me. Although the text remains in substance unaltered, I have indulged in the author's prerogative of polishing it for publication.

with headquarters in Atlanta, Georgia. We have some eighty-five affiliated organizations across the South, and one of them is the Alabama Christian Movement for Human Rights. Frequently we share staff, educational and financial resources with our affiliates. Several months ago the affiliate here in Birmingham asked us to be on call to engage in a nonviolent direct-action program if such were deemed necessary. We readily consented, and when the hour came we lived up to our promise. So I, along with several members of my staff, am here because I was invited here. I am here because I have organizational ties here.

<sup>3</sup> But more basically, I am in Birmingham because injustice is here. Just as the prophets of the eighth century B.C. left their villages and carried their "thus saith the Lord" far beyond the boundaries of their home towns, and just as the Apostle Paul left his village of Tarsus and carried the gospel of Jesus Christ to the far corners of the Greco-Roman world, so am I compelled to carry the gospel of freedom beyond my own home town. Like Paul, I must constantly respond to the Macedonian call for aid.

<sup>4</sup> Moreover, I am cognizant of the interrelatedness of all communities and states. I cannot sit idly by in Atlanta and not be concerned about what happens in Birmingham. Injustice anywhere is a threat to justice every-where. We are caught in an inescapable network of mutuality, tied in a single garment of destiny. Whatever affects one directly, affects all indi-rectly. Never again can we afford to live with the narrow, provincial "outside agitator" idea. Anyone who lives inside the United States can never be considered an outsider anywhere within its bounds.

<sup>5</sup> You deplore the demonstrations taking place in Birmingham. But your statement, I am sorry to say, fails to express a similar concern for the conditions that brought about the demonstrations. I am sure that none of you would want to rest content with the superficial kind of social analysis that deals merely with effects and does not grapple with underlying causes. It is unfortunate that demonstrations are taking place in Birmingham, but it is even more unfortunate that the city's white power structure left the Negro community with no alternative.

<sup>6</sup> In any nonviolent campaign there are four basic steps: collection of the facts to determine whether injustices exist; negotiation; self-purifica-tion; and direct action. We have gone through all these steps in Bir-mingham. There can be no gainsaying the fact that racial injustice engulfs this community. Birmingham is probably the most thoroughly segregated city in the United States. Its ugly record of brutality is widely known. Negroes have experienced grossly unjust treatment in the courts. There have been more unsolved bombings of Negro homes and churches in Birmingham than in any other city in the nation. These are the hard, brutal facts of the case. On the basis of these conditions, Negro leaders sought to negotiate with the city fathers. But the latter consistently refused to engage in good-faith negotiation.

<sup>7</sup> Then, last September, came the oppportunity to talk with leaders of Birmingham's economic community. In the course of the negotiations,

certain promises were made by the merchants—for example, to remove the stores' humiliating racial signs. On the basis of these promises, the Reverend Fred Shuttlesworth and the leaders of the Alabama Christian Movement for Human Rights agreed to a moratorium on all demonstrations. As the weeks and months went by, we realized that we were the victims of a broken promise. A few signs, briefly removed, returned; the others remained.

[8] As in so many past experiences, our hopes had been blasted, and the shadow of deep disappointment settled upon us. We had no alternative except to prepare for direct action, whereby we would present our very bodies as a means of laying our case before the conscience of the local and the national community. Mindful of the difficulties involved, we decided to undertake a process of self-purification. We began a series of workshops on nonviolence, and we repeatedly asked ourselves: "Are you able to accept blows without retaliating?" "Are you able to endure the ordeal of jail?" We decided to schedule our direct-action program for the Easter season, realizing that except for Christmas, this is the main shopping period of the year. Knowing that a strong economic-withdrawal program would be the by-product of direct action, we felt that this would be the best time to bring pressure to bear on the merchants for the needed change.

[9] Then it occurred to us that Birmingham's mayoral election was coming up in March, and we speedily decided to postpone action until after election day. When we discovered that the Commissioner of Public Safety, Eugene "Bull" Connor, had piled up enough votes to be in the runoff, we decided again to postpone action until the day after the runoff so that the demonstrations could not be used to cloud the issues. Like many others, we waited to see Mr. Connor defeated, and to this end we endured postponement after postponement. Having aided in this community need, we felt that our direct-action program could be delayed no longer.

[10] You may well ask: "Why direct action? Why sit-ins, marches and so forth? Isn't negotiation a better path?" You are quite right in calling for negotiation. Indeed, this is the very purpose of direct-action. Nonviolent direct action seeks to create such a crisis and foster such a tension that a community which has constantly refused to negotiate is forced to confront the issue. It seeks so to dramatize the issue that it can no longer be ignored. My citing the creation of tension as part of the work of the nonviolent-resister may sound rather shocking. But I must confess that I am not afraid of the word "tension." I have earnestly opposed violent tension, but there is a type of constructive, nonviolent tension which is necessary to create a tension which is necessary for growth. Just as Socrates felt that it was necessary to create a tension in the mind so that individuals could rise from the bondage of myths and half-truths to the unfettered realm of creative analysis and objective appraisal, so must we see the need for nonviolent gadflies to create the kind of tension in society that will help men rise from the dark depths of prejudice and racism to the majestic heights of understanding and brotherhood.

[11] The purpose of our direct-action program is to create a situation so crisis-packed that it will inevitably open the door to negotiation. I therefore concur with you in your call for negotiation. Too long has our beloved Southland been bogged down in a tragic effort to live in monologue rather than dialogue.

[12] One of the basic points in your statement is that the action that I and my associates have taken in Birmingham is untimely. Some have asked: "Why didn't you give the new city administration time to act?" The only answer that I can give to this query is that the new Birmingham administration must be prodded about as much as the outgoing one, before it will act. We are sadly mistaken if we feel that the election of Albert Boutwell as mayor will bring the millennium to Birmingham. While Mr. Boutwell is a much more gentle person that Mr. Connor, they are both segregationists, dedicated to maintenance of the status quo. I have hope that Mr. Boutwell will be reasonable enough to see the futility of massive resistance to desegregation. But he will not see this without pressure from devotees of civil rights. My friends, I must say to you that we have not made a single gain in civil rights without determined legal and nonviolent pressure. Lamentably, it is an historical fact that privileged groups seldom give up their privileges voluntarily. Individuals may see the moral light and voluntarily give up their unjust posture; but, as Reinhold Niebuhr has reminded us, groups tend to be more immoral that individuals.

[13] We know through painful experience that freedom is never voluntarily given by the oppressor; it must be demanded by the oppressed. Frankly, I have yet to engage in a direct-action campaign that was "well timed" in the view of those who have not suffered unduly from the disease of segregation. For years now I have heard the word "Wait!" It rings in the ear of every Negro with piercing familiarity. This "Wait" has almost always meant "Never." We must come to see, with one of our distinguished jurists, that "justice too long delayed is justice denied."

[14] We have waited for more than 340 years for our constitutional and God-given rights. The nations of Asia and Africa are moving with jetlike speed toward gaining political independence, but we still creep at horse-and-buggy pace toward gaining a cup of coffee at a lunch counter. Perhaps it is easy for those who have never felt the stinging darts of segregation to say "Wait." But when you have seen vicious mobs lynch your mothers and fathers at will and drown your sisters and brothers at whim; when you have seen hate-filled policemen curse, kick and even kill your black brothers and sisters; when you see the vast majority of your twenty million Negro brothers smothering in an airtight cage of poverty in the midst of an affluent society; when you suddenly find your tongue twisted and your speech stammering as you seek to explain to your six-year-old daughter why she can't go to the public amusement park that has just been advertised on television, and see tears welling up in her eyes when she is told that Funtown is closed to colored children, and see ominous clouds of inferiority beginning to form in her little mental sky, and see her beginning

to destroy her personality by developing an unconscious bitterness toward white people; when you have to concoct an answer for a five-year-old son who is asking: "Daddy, why do white people treat colored people so mean?"; when you take a cross-country drive and find it necessary to sleep night after night in the uncomfortable corners of your automobile because no motel will accept you; when you are humiliated day in and day out by nagging signs reading "white" and "colored"; when your first name becomes "nigger," your middle name becomes "boy" (however old you are) and your last name becomes "John," and your wife and mother are never given the respected title "Mrs."; when you are harried by day and haunted by night by the fact that you are a Negro, living constantly at tiptoe stance, never quite knowing what to expect next, and are plagued with inner fears and outer resentments; when you are forever fighting a degenerating sense of "nobodiness"—then you will understand why we find it difficult to wait. There comes a time when the cup of endurance runs over, and men are no longer willing to be plunged into the abyss of despair. I hope, sirs, you can understand our legitimate and unavoidable impatience.

[15] You express a great deal of anxiety over our willingness to break laws. This is certainly a legitimate concern. Since we so diligently urge people to obey the Supreme Court's decision of 1954 outlawing segregation in the public schools, at first glance it may seem rather paradoxical for us consciously to break laws. One may well ask: "How can you advocate breaking some laws and obeying others?" The answer lies in the fact that there are two types of laws: just and unjust. I would be the first to advocate obeying just laws. One has not only a legal but a moral responsibility to obey just laws. Conversely, one has a moral responsibility to disobey unjust laws. I would agree with St. Augustine that "an unjust law is no law at all."

[16] Now, what is the difference between the two? How does one determine whether a law is just or unjust? A just law is a man-made code that squares with the moral law or the law of God. An unjust law is a code that is out of harmony with the moral law. To put it in the terms of St. Thomas Aquinas: An unjust law is a human law that is not rooted in eternal law and natural law. Any law that uplifts human personality is just. Any law that degrades human personality is unjust. All segregation statutes are unjust because segregation distorts the soul and damages the personality. It gives the segregator a false sense of superiority and the segregated a false sense of inferiority. Segregation, to use the terminology of the Jewish philosopher Martin Buber, substitutes an "I-it" relationship for an "I-thou" relationship and ends up relegating persons to the status of things. Hence segregation is not only politically, economically and sociologically unsound, it is morally wrong and sinful. Paul Tillich has said that sin is separation. Is not segregation an existential expression of man's tragic separation, his awful estrangement, his terrible sinfulness? Thus it is that I can urge men to obey the 1954 decision of the Supreme Court, for it is morally right; and I can urge them to disobey segregation ordinances, for they are morally wrong.

<sup>17</sup> Let us consider a more concrete example of just and unjust laws. An unjust law is a code that a numerical or power majority group compels a minority group to obey but does not make binding on itself. This is *difference* made legal. By the same token, a just law is a code that a majority compels a minority to follow and that it is willing to follow itself. This is *sameness* made legal.

<sup>18</sup> Let me give another explanation. A law is unjust if it is inflicted on a minority that, as a result of being denied the right to vote, had no part in enacting or devising the law. Who can say that the legislature of Alabama which set up that state's segregation laws was democratically elected? Throughout Alabama all sorts of devious methods are used to prevent Negroes from becoming registered voters, and there are some counties in which, even though Negroes constitute a majority of the population, not a single Negro is registered. Can any law enacted under such circumstances be considered democratically structured?

<sup>19</sup> Sometimes a law is just on its face and unjust in its application. For instance, I have been arrested on a charge of parading without a permit. Now, there is nothing wrong in having an ordinance which requires a permit for a parade. But such an ordinance becomes unjust when it is used to maintain segregation and to deny citizens the First-Amendment privilege of peaceful assembly and protest.

<sup>20</sup> I hope you are able to see the distinction I am trying to point out. In no sense do I advocate evading or defying the law, as would the rabid segregationist. That would lead to anarchy. One who breaks an unjust law must do so openly, lovingly, and with a willingness to accept the penalty. I submit that an individual who breaks a law that conscience tells him is unjust, and who willingly accepts the penalty of imprisonment in order to arouse the conscience of the community over its unjustice, is in reality expressing the highest respect for law.

<sup>21</sup> Of course, there is nothing new about this kind of civil disobedience. It was evidenced sublimely in the refusal of Shadrach, Meshach, and Abednego to obey the laws of Nebuchadnezzar, on the ground that a higher moral law was at stake. It was practiced superbly by the early Christians, who were willing to face hungry lions and the excruciating pain of chopping blocks rather that submit to certain unjust laws of the Roman Empire. To a degree, academic freedom is a reality today because Socrates practiced civil disobedience. In our own nation, the Boston Tea Party represented a massive act of civil disobedience.

<sup>22</sup> We should never forget that everything Adolf Hitler did in Germany was "legal" and everything the Hungarian freedom fighters did in Hungary was "illegal." It was "illegal" to aid and comfort a Jew in Hitler's Germany. Even so, I am sure that, had I lived in Germany at the time, I would have aided and comforted my Jewish brothers. If today I lived in a Communist country where certain principles dear to the Christian faith are supressed, I would openly advocate disobeying that country's antireligious laws.

[23] I must make two honest confessions to you, my Christian and Jewish brothers. First, I must confess that over the past few years I have been gravely disappointed with the white moderate. I have almost reached the regrettable conclusion that the Negro's great stumbling block in his stride toward freedom is not the White Citizen's Counciler or the Ku Klux Klanner, but the white moderate, who is more devoted to "order" than to justice; who prefers a negative peace which is the absence of tension to a positive peace which is the presence of justice; who constantly says: "I agree with you in the goal you seek, but I cannot agree with your methods of direct action"; who paternalistically believes he can set the time table for another man's freedom; who lives by a mythical concept of time and who constantly advises the Negro to wait for a "more convenient season." Shallow understanding from people of good will is more frustrating than absolute misunderstanding from people of ill will. Lukewarm acceptance is much more bewildering than outright rejection.

[24] I had hoped that the white moderate would understand that law and order exist for the purpose of establishing justice and that when they fail in this purpose they become the dangerously structured dams that block the flow of social progress. I had hoped that the white moderate would understand that the present tension in the South is a necessary phase of the transition from an obnoxious negative peace, in which the Negro passively accepted his unjust plight, to a substantive and positive peace, in which all men will respect the dignity and worth of human personality. Actually, we who engage in nonviolent direct action are not the creators of tension. We merely bring to the surface the hidden tension that is already alive. We bring it out in the open, where it can be seen and dealt with. Like a boil that can never be cured so long as it is covered up but must be opened with all its ugliness to the natural medicines of air and light, injustice must be exposed, with all the tension its exposure creates, to the light of human conscience and the air of national opinion before it can be cured.

[25] In your statement you assert that our actions, even though peaceful, must be condemned because they precipitate violence. But is this a logical assertion? Isn't this like condemning a robbed man because his possession of money precipitated the evil act of robbery? Isn't this like condemning Socrates because his unswerving commitment to truth and his philosophical inquiries precipitated the act by the misguided populace in which they made him drink hemlock? Isn't this like condemning Jesus because his unique God-consciousness and never-ceasing devotion to God's will precipitated the evil act of crucifixion? We must come to see that, as the federal courts have consistently affirmed, it is wrong to urge an individual to cease his efforts to gain his constitutional rights because the quest may precipitate violence. Society must protect the robbed and punish the robber.

[26] I had also hoped that the white moderate would reject the myth concerning time in relation to the struggle for freedom. I have just received a letter from a white brother in Texas. He writes: "All Christians know that the colored people will receive equal rights eventually, but it is

possible that you are in too great a religious hurry. It has taken Christianity almost two thousand years to accomplish what it has. The teachings of Christ take time to come to earth." Such an attitude stems from a tragic misconception of time, from the strangely irrational notion that there is something in the very flow of time that will inevitably cure all ills. Actually, time itself is neutral; it can be used either destructively or constructively. More and more I feel that the people of ill will have used time much more effectively than have the people of good will. We will have to repent in this generation not merely for the hateful words and actions of the bad people but for the appalling silence of the good people. Human progress never rolls in on wheels of inevitability; it comes through the tireless efforts of men willing to be co-workers with God, and without this hard work, time itself becomes an ally of the forces of social stagnation. We must use time creatively, in the knowledge that the time is always ripe to do right. Now is the time to make real the promise of democracy and transform our pending national elegy into a creative psalm of brotherhood. Now is the time to lift our national policy from the quicksand of racial injustice to the solid rock of human dignity.

27 You speak of our activity in Birmingham as extreme. At first I was rather disappointed that fellow clergymen would see my nonviolent efforts as those of an extremist. I began thinking about the fact that I stand in the middle of two opposing forces in the Negro community. One is a force of complacency, made up in part of Negroes who, as a result of long years of oppression, are so drained of self-respect and a sense of "somebodiness" that they have adjusted to segregation; and in part of a few middle-class Negroes who, because of a degree of academic and economic security and because in some ways they profit by segregation, have become insensitive to the problems of the masses. The other force is one of bitterness and hatred, and it comes perilously close to advocating violence. It is expressed in the various black nationalist groups that are springing up across the nation, the largest and best-known being Elijah Muhammad's Muslim movement. Nourished by the Negro's frustration over the continued existence of racial discrimination, this movement is made up of people who have lost faith in America, who have absolutely repudiated Christianity, and who have concluded that the white man is an incorrigible "devil."

28 I have tried to stand between these two forces, saying that we need emulate neither the "do-nothingism" of the complacent nor the hatred and despair of the black nationalist. For there is the more excellent way of love and nonviolent protest. I am grateful to God that, through the influence of the Negro church, the way of nonviolence became an integral part of our struggle.

29 If this philosophy had not emerged, by now many streets of the South would, I am convinced, be flowing with blood. And I am further convinced that if our white brothers dismiss as "rabble-rousers" and "outside agitators" those of us who employ nonviolent direct action, and if they refuse to support our nonviolent efforts, millions of Negroes will, out of

frustration and despair, seek solace and security in black-nationalist ide-
ologies—a development that would inevitably lead to a frightening racial
nightmare.

[30] Oppressed people cannot remain oppressed forever. The yearning
for freedom eventually manifests itself, and that is what has happened to
the American Negro. Something within has reminded him of his birthright
of freedom, and something without has reminded him that it can be
gained. Consciously or unconsciously, he has been caught up by the
*Zeitgeist,* and with his black brothers of Africa and his brown and yellow
brothers of Asia, South America, and the Caribbean, the United States
Negro is moving with a sense of great urgency toward the promised land of
racial justice. If one recognizes this vital urge that has engulfed the Negro
community, one should readily understand why public demonstrations are
taking place. The Negro has many pent-up resentments and latent frustra-
tions, and he must release them. So let him march; let him make prayer
pilgrimages to the city hall; let him go on freedom rides—and try to
understand why he must do so. If his repressed emotions are not released
in nonviolent ways, they will seek expression through violence; this is not a
threat but a fact of history. So I have not said to my people: "Get rid of your
discontent." Rather, I have tried to say that this normal and healthy
discontent can be channeled into the creative outlet of nonviolent direct
action. And now this approach is being termed extremist.

[31] But though I was initially disappointed at being categorized as an
extremist, as I continued to think about the matter I gradually gained a
measure of satisfaction from the label. Was not Jesus an extremist for love:
"Love your enemies, bless them that curse you, do good to them that hate
you, and pray for them which despitefully use you, and persecute you."
Was not Amos an extremist for justice: "Let justice roll down like waters
and righteousness like an ever-flowing stream." Was not Paul an extremist
for the Christian gospel: "I bear in my body the marks of the Lord Jesus."
Was not Martin Luther an extremist: "Here I stand, I cannot do otherwise,
so help me God." And John Bunyan: "I will stay in jail to the end of my
days before I make a butchery of my conscience." And Abraham Lincoln:
"This nation cannot survive half slave and half free." And Thomas Jefferson: "We hold these truths to be self-evident, that all men are created
equal. . . ." So the question is not whether we will be extremists, but what
kind of extremists we will be. Will we be extremists for hate or for love?
Will we be extremists for the preservation of injustice or for the extension
of justice? In that dramatic scene on Calvary's hill three men were crucified. We must never forget that all three were crucified for the same
crime—the crime of extremism. Two were extremists for immorality, and
thus fell below their environment. The other, Jesus Christ, was an extremist for love, truth and goodness, and thereby rose above his environment.
Perhaps the South, the nation and the world are in dire need of creative
extremists.

[32] I had hoped that the white moderate would see this need. Perhaps I was too optimistic; perhaps I expected too much. I suppose I should have realized that few members of the oppressor race can understand the deep groans and passionate yearnings of the oppressed race, and still fewer have the vision to see that injustice must be rooted out by strong, persistent and determined action. I am thankful, however, that some of our white brothers in the South have grasped the meaning of this social revolution and committed themselves to it. They are still all too few in quantity, but they are big in quality. Some—such as Ralph McGill, Lillian Smith, Harry Golden, James McBride Dabbs, Ann Braden and Sarah Patton Boyle— have written about our struggle in eloquent and prophetic terms. Others have marched with us down nameless streets of the South. They have languished in filthy, roach-infested jails, suffering the abuse and brutality of policemen who view them as "dirty nigger-lovers." Unlike so many of their moderate brothers and sisters, they have recognized the urgency of the moment and sensed the need for powerful "action" antidotes to combat the disease of segregation.

[33] Let me take note of my other major disappointment. I have been so greatly disappointed with the white church and its leadership. Of course, there are some notable exceptions. I am not unmindful of the fact that each of you has taken some significant stands on this issue. I commend you, Reverend Stallings, for your Christian stand on this past Sunday, in welcoming Negroes to your worship service on a nonsegregated basis. I commend the Catholic leaders of this state for integrating Spring Hill College several years ago.

[34] But despite these notable exceptions, I must honestly reiterate that I have been disappointed with the church. I do not say this as one of those negative critics who can always find something wrong with the church. I say this as a minister of the gospel, who loves the church; who was nurtured in its bosom; who has been sustained by its spiritual blessings and who will remain true to it as long as the cord of life shall lengthen.

[35] When I was suddenly catapulted into the leadership of the bus protest in Montgomery, Alabama, a few years ago, I felt we would be supported by the white church. I felt that the white ministers, priests and rabbis of the South would be among our strongest allies. Instead, some have been outright opponents, refusing to understand the freedom movement and misrepresenting its leaders; all too many others have been more cautious than courageous and have remained silent behind the anesthetizing security of stained-glass windows.

[36] In spite of my shattered dreams, I came to Birmingham with the hope that the white religious leadership of this community would see the justice of our cause and, with deep moral concern, would serve as the channel through which just grievances could reach the power structure. I had hoped that each of you would understand. But again I have been disappointed.

[37] I have heard numerous southern religious leaders admonish their worshippers to comply with a desegregation decision because it is the law, but I have longed to hear white ministers declare: "Follow this decree because integration is morally right and because the Negro is your brother." In the midst of blatant injustices inflicted upon the Negro, I have watched white churchmen stand on the sideline and mouth pious irrelevancies and sanctimonious trivialities. In the midst of a mightly struggle to rid our nation of racial and economical injustice, I have heard many ministers say: "Those are social issues, with which the gospel has no real concern." And I have watched many churches commit themselves to a completely other-worldly religion which makes a strange, un-Biblical distinction between body and soul, between the sacred and the secular.

[38] I have traveled the length and breadth of Alabama, Mississippi and all the southern states. On sweltering summer days and crisp autumn mornings I have looked at the South's most beautiful churches and their lofty spires pointing heavenward. I have beheld the impressive outlines of her massive religious-education buildings. Over and over I have found myself asking: "What kind of people worship here? Who is their God? Where were their voices when the lips of Governor Barnett dripped with words of interposition and nullification? Where were they when Governor Wallace gave a clarion call for defiance and hatred? Where were their voices of support when bruised and weary Negro men and women decided to rise from the dark dungeons of complacency to the bright hills of creative protest?"

[39] Yes, these questions are still in my mind. In deep disappointment I have wept over the laxity of the church. But be assured that my tears have been tears of love. Yes, I love the church. How could I do otherwise? I am in the rather unique position of being the son, the grandson and the great-grandson of preachers. Yes, I see the church as the body of Christ. But, oh! How we have blemished and scarred that body through social neglect and through fear of being nonconformists.

[40] There was a time when the church was very powerful—in the time when the early Christians rejoiced at being deemed worthy to suffer for what they believed. In those days the church was not merely a thermometer that recorded the ideas and principles of popular opinion; it was a thermostat that transformed the mores of society. Whenever the early Christians entered a town, the people in power became disturbed and immediately sought to convict the Christians for being "disturbers of the peace" and "outside agitators." But the Christians pressed on, in the conviction that they were "a colony of heaven," called to obey God rather than man. Small in number, they were big in commitment. They were too God-intoxicated to be "astronomically intimidated." By their effort and example they brought an end to such ancient evils as infanticide and gladiatorial contests.

[41] Things are different now. So often the contemporary church is a weak, ineffectual voice with an uncertain sound. So often it is an arch-

defender of the status quo. Far from being disturbed by the presence of the church, the power structure of the average community is consoled by the church's silent—and even vocal—sanction of things as they are.

[42] But the judgment of God is upon the church as never before. If today's church does not recapture the sacrificial spirit of the early church, it will lose its authenticity, forfeit the loyalty of millions, and be dismissed as an irrelevant social club with no meaning for the twentieth century. Every day I meet young people whose disappointment with the church has turned into outright disgust.

[43] Perhaps I have once again been too optimistic. Is organized religion too inextricably bound to the status quo to save our nation and the world? Perhaps I must turn my faith to the inner spiritual church, the church within the church, as the true *ekklesia* and the hope of the world. But again I am thankful to God that some noble souls from the ranks of organized religion have broken loose from the paralyzing chains of conformity and joined us as active partners in the struggle for freedom. They have left their secure congregations and walked the streets of Albany, Georgia, with us. They have gone down the highways of the South on tortuous rides for freedom. Yes, they have gone to jail with us. Some have been dismissed from their churches, have lost the support of their bishops and fellow ministers. But they have acted in the faith that right defeated is stronger than evil triumphant. Their witness has been the spiritual salt that has preserved the true meaning of the gospel in these troubled times. They have carved a tunnel of hope through the dark mountain of disappointment.

[44] I hope the church as a whole will meet the challenge of this decisive hour. But even if the church does not come to the aid of justice, I have no despair about the future. I have no fear about the outcome of our struggle in Birmingham, even if our motives are at present misunderstood. We will reach the goal of freedom in Birmingham and all over the nation, because the goal of America is freedom. Abused and scorned though we may be, our destiny is tied up with America's destiny. Before the pilgrims landed at Plymouth, we were here. Before the pen of Jefferson etched the majestic words of the Declaration of Independence across the pages of history, we were here. For more than two centuries our forebears labored in this country without wages; they made cotton king; they built the homes of their masters while suffering gross injustice and shameful humiliation— and yet out of a bottomless vitality they continued to thrive and develop. If the inexpressible cruelties of slavery could not stop us, the opposition we now face will surely fail. We will win our freedom because the sacred heritage of our nation and the eternal will of God are embodied in our echoing demands.

[45] Before closing I feel impelled to mention one other point in your statement that has troubled me profoundly. You warmly commended the Birmingham police force for keeping "order" and "preventing violence." I doubt that you would so quickly commend the policemen if you were to

observe their ugly and inhumane treatment of Negroes here in the city jail; if you were to watch them push and curse old Negro women and young Negro girls; if you were to see them slap and kick old Negro men and young boys; if you were to observe them, as they did on two occasions, refuse to give us food because we wanted to sing our grace together. I cannot join you in your praise of the Birmingham police department.

⁴⁶ It is true that the police have exercised a degree of discipline in handling the demonstrators. In this sense they conducted themselves rather "nonviolently" in public. But for what purpose? To preserve the evil system of segregation. Over the past few years I have consistently preached that nonviolence demands that the means we use must be as pure as the ends we seek. I have tried to make clear that it is wrong to use immoral means to attain moral ends. But now I must affirm that it just as wrong or perhaps even more so, to use moral means to preserve immoral ends. Perhaps Mr. Connor and his policemen have been rather nonviolent in public, as was Chief Pritchett in Albany, Georgia, but they have used the moral means of nonviolence to maintain the immoral end of racial injustice. As T. S. Eliot has said: "The last temptation is the greatest treason: To do the right deed for the wrong reason."

⁴⁷ I wish you had commended the Negro sit-inners and demonstrators of Birmingham for their sublime courage, their willingness to suffer and their amazing discipline in the midst of great provocation. One day the South will recognize its real heroes. They will be the James Merediths, with the noble sense of purpose that enables them to face jeering and hostile mobs, and with the agonizing loneliness that characterizes the life of the pioneer. They will be old, oppressed, battered Negro women, symbolized in a seventy-two-year-old woman in Montgomery, Alabama, who rose up with a sense of dignity and with her people decided not to ride segregated buses, and who responded with ungrammatical profundity to one who inquired about her weariness: "My feets is tired, but my soul is at rest." They will be the young high school and college students, the young ministers of the gospel and a host of their elders, courageously and nonviolently sitting in at lunch counters and willingly going to jail for conscience' sake. One day the South will know that when these disinherited children of God sat down at lunch counters, they were in reality standing up for what is best in the American dream and for the most sacred values in our Judaeo-Christian heritage, thereby bringing our nation back to those great wells of democracy which were dug deep by the founding fathers in their formulation of the Constitution and the Declaration of Independence.

⁴⁸ Never before have I written so long a letter. I'm afraid it is much too long to take your precious time. I can assure you that it would have been much shorter if I had been writing from a comfortable desk, but what else can one do when he is alone in a narrow jail cell, other than write long letters, think long thoughts and pray long prayers?

⁴⁹ If I have said anything in this letter that overstates the truth and indicates an unreasonable impatience, I beg you to forgive me. If I have

said anything that understates the truth and indicates my having a patience that allows me to settle for anything less than brotherhood, I beg God to forgive me.

[50] I hope this letter finds you strong in the faith. I also hope that circumstances will soon make it possible for me to meet each of you, not as an integrationist or a civil-rights leader but as a fellow clergyman and a Christian brother. Let us all hope that the dark clouds of racial prejudice will soon pass away and the deep fog of misunderstanding will be lifted from our fear-drenched communities, and in some not too distant tomorrow the radiant stars of love and brotherhood will shine over our great nation with all their scintillating beauty.

Yours for the cause of Peace and Brotherhood,
Martin Luther King, Jr.

## ◆ PRACTICE

### Discussion

1. Why did King place the argument about his disappointment with the white church's leadership in his refutation of *extremism*? Does it fit here?

2. How does King turn the term "extremist" to his own advantage?

3. How does King list the names of white Southerners who have helped his cause? How effective would this list be when read by the white clergy?

4. Why does King begin his criticism of the white church's leadership with compliments? Does this enhance his integrity and trustworthiness?

5. Point out the places where King tells the clergy that he is one of them. Why does he say this? How do you think this affects the readers?

6. Where does King use rhetorical questions? Why? Martin Luther King was also a master of other rhetorical techniques. Note particularly the effect of the long parallel sentence beginning, "I doubt that you would so quickly commend the policemen if you were to observe. . . ." What is the effect of King's beginning the clauses that follow the semicolon with "if"?

7. Is the tone of his letter primarily pessimistic or optimistic? Give specific evidence.

8. Besides the clergy, who is the audience for this letter? How do you know? This letter has had a profound effect on readers since its publication in 1963. Why do you think it has been printed and quoted so often?

## *Vocabulary*

| | | |
|---|---|---|
| affiliated | emulate | pious |
| cognizant | solace | sanctimonious |
| moratorium | manifests | secular |
| status quo | *Zeitgeist* | interposition |
| relegating | latent | mores |
| precipitate | languished | sanction |
| complacency | admonish | inextricably |
| repudiated | | |

## *Writing*

1. Find a letter in your newspaper with which you disagree. Refute two or three of its points.

2. Write an argument refuting a policy position taken by an institution with which you are involved: school, church, political party, civic organization, etc.

3. Choose one of the selections in this reader and refute its main points.

# Acknowledgments

# *I*ndex